Food, Energy and the Creation of Industriousness

Until the widespread harnessing of machine energy, food was the energy which fuelled the economy. In this groundbreaking study of agricultural labourers' diet and material standard of living Craig Muldrew uses new empirical research to present a much fuller account of the interrelationship between consumption, living standards and work in the early modern English economy than has previously existed. The book integrates labourers into a study of the wider economy and engages with the history of food as an energy source and its importance to working life, the social complexity of family earnings and the concept of the 'industrious revolution'. It argues that 'industriousness' was as much the result of ideology and labour markets as labourers' household consumption. Linking this with ideas about the social order of early modern England the author demonstrates that bread, beer and meat were the petrol of this world and a springboard for economic change.

CRAIG MULDREW is Senior Lecturer in the Faculty of History, University of Cambridge.

Cambridge Studies in Economic History

Editorial Board

PAUL JOHNSON   *La Trobe University*
SHEILAGH OGILVIE   *University of Cambridge*
AVNER OFFER   *All Souls College, Oxford*
GIANNI TONIOLO   *Università di Roma 'Tor Vergata'*
GAVIN WRIGHT   *Stanford University*

Cambridge Studies in Economic History comprises stimulating and accessible economic history which actively builds bridges to other disciplines. Books in the series will illuminate why the issues they address are important and interesting, place their findings in a comparative context, and relate their research to wider debates and controversies. The series will combine innovative and exciting new research by younger researchers with new approaches to major issues by senior scholars. It will publish distinguished work regardless of chronological period or geographical location.

A complete list of titles in the series can be found at:
www.cambridge.org/economichistory

Food, Energy and the Creation of Industriousness

Work and Material Culture in Agrarian England, 1550–1780

Craig Muldrew

University of Cambridge

CAMBRIDGE UNIVERSITY PRESS

CAMBRIDGE UNIVERSITY PRESS
Cambridge, New York, Melbourne, Madrid, Cape Town, Singapore,
São Paulo, Delhi, Dubai, Tokyo, Mexico City

Cambridge University Press
The Edinburgh Building, Cambridge CB2 8RU, UK

Published in the United States of America by Cambridge
University Press, New York

www.cambridge.org
Information on this title: www.cambridge.org/9780521881852

First published 2011

Printed in the United Kingdom at the University Press, Cambridge

A catalogue record for this publication is available from the British Library

Library of Congress Cataloguing in Publication data
Muldrew, Craig, 1959–
    Food, energy and the creation of industriousness : work and material
    culture in agrarian England, 1550–1780 / Craig Muldrew.
        p.   cm. – (Cambridge Studies in economic history-second series)
    Includes bibliographical references and index.
    ISBN 978-0-521-88185-2
    1. Diet–England–History.   2. Food consumption–England–
    History.   3. Agricultural laborers–England–History.
    4. Power resources–England–History.   I. Title.   II. Series.
    TX360.G7M85 2010
    641.30942–dc22
    2010035581

ISBN 978-0-521-88185-2 Hardback

To Janine

Contents

Figures

Tables

Preface

The subject of this book occurred almost accidentally. After finishing my first book, *The Economy of Obligation*, I intended to take the themes of that work forward into the eighteenth century, looking at the origin of local banking and networks of trust. While that work has continued, some years ago I became interested in the consumption of the labouring poor through my work into wage payments and research done for the chapter in *The Economy of Obligation* which examined household consumption and market transactions. There I was very surprised at the amount of meat consumed and the high numbers of butchers in early modern towns such as King's Lynn. I presented this information in a quite rudimentary form at a conference in 2000, where the argument for a relatively high level of meat consumption was met with scepticism, if not downright incredulity. Some years later, this spurred me on to do much more research into diets, which in turn led me to consider Robert Fogel's work on human energy. I then attempted to think of human energy in the same way as Tony Wrigley has analysed the input of animal energy into agricultural production.

The study of labourers' inventories also stemmed from work done for *The Economy of Obligation* using probate inventories. When researching in the Hampshire Record Office I noticed that there were much larger numbers of labourers' inventories than I thought existed. Subsequently I found out that Leigh Shaw-Taylor had discovered labourers' inventories in Northampton and Lincolnshire. We then worked together to discover samples of labourers' inventories in other counties and had them made machine readable with two British Academy Small Grants. Here I have analysed this sample and, in doing so, naturally attempted to test aspects of Jan de Vries's theory of what he has termed the 'industrious revolution', which has been one of the most stimulating recent macro-theories of early modern economic development. Doing this led me back to early modern economic pamphlet literature, where, to my surprise, I found that industriousness had already been conceived of as a way to increase England's national wealth. This discovery allowed me to make sense of change over time in a new way. Thus, the whole project grew organically out of what at first seemed to be a series of separate problems which gradually came together. As a result the themes and structure of the book have evolved, often slowly, over the last five or six years, but I think I have learned much more by chance and accident rather than relying on hypothesis.

I have also learned even more from continual interaction with colleagues at Cambridge, the University of Exeter, the University of Bologna and elsewhere. At the beginning of this project it is fair to say my knowledge of agrarian history was limited, as I had previously worked mostly on urban records, but I have learned a great deal from friends and colleagues doing agricultural history. I have benefited most from many conversations with Leigh Shaw-Taylor. I have also learned much from Mark Overton, who kindly provided me with data he already had of labourers' inventories from Kent after 1600, and Bob Allen, who told me how useful Thomas Batchelor was as a source. Naomi Tadmor kindly lent me her photocopy of Turner's original diary to investigate his dinners. James Bates also shared his great knowledge of brewing as well as his excellent beer. I would also like to thank Ian Archer, Matthew Clark, John Chartres, Martin Daunton, Diccon Cooper, Mark Dawson, Amy Erickson, Laurence Fontaine, Peter King, Peter Kitson, Alysa Levene, John Money, Carlo Poni, Emma Rothschild, Thomas Sokoll, Richard Smith, Sarah Pennell, Roberto Scazzieri, Alexandra Shepard, Helen Speechley, John Styles, Phil Withington and John Walter. Joe Barker, Sarah Brown, Alec Corio, Nicola Henshall, Ian Keefe, Matt Ward, Ali Warren and Matthew Westlake all worked as researchers transcribing probate inventories and account books for me, and the book would have been impossible without their excellent work. I would also like to thank Tony Wrigley, Keith Wrightson, Paul Warde and Ken Sneath for reading parts of the book, and finally Janine Maegraith for not only reading the entire manuscript and making many helpful comments but attempting to correct my dyslexic word-processing in heroic fashion. Finally it remains to thank the various funding bodies which have helped make this research possible. Since, as I said, it is a work which evolved in pieces, it required a number of small grants, which in this way are just as useful and necessary to the research community as large grants. Over the gestation of the book the Ellen Macarthur Fund, the Centre for History and Economics and Queens' College Fellows Research Fund have all helped. The British Academy awarded Small Research Grant no. SG-40825, 'The Material Wealth and Work of the Labouring Poor in England as Reflected in Probate Inventories, 1570–1790', to transcribe the labourers' inventories. The Bologna Institute for Advanced

Studies provided me with a three-month fellowship from February to April 2005 which allowed me to start writing and to present my findings there. I would like especially to thank Carlo Poni and Roberto Scazzieri for showing such hospitality during my visit. Finally I would like to thank the Arts and Humanities Research Council, whose award of a term of leave in 2008 under their Research Leave Scheme allowed me to finish the first draft of the book.

Note on measurements and inflation

The weights and measurements used in this book are British Imperial and avoirdupois measurements, which are the closest to those used by contemporaries. In many cases, however, historical measurements of certain things were different, and such instances are discussed specifically in the text. When comparing monetary values before 1650 inflation has been taken into account, where it has been appropriate to do so, using the price data collected by Phelps Brown and Hopkins, as summarised by Christopher Clay. After this date there was a slow overall deflation of grain prices to around 1765. Unfortunately there are no similarly ample price data for manufactured goods, but there is evidence that prices here also went down after 1650. I have chosen not to deflate values, but rather to discuss how lower prices could have affected the amount of food and household goods purchased.

In many of the calculations which follow I have often expressed values in exact numbers. This has been done for consistency, so that the method of calculation can be traced. But it needs to be mentioned that with any historical figures there will almost always be some degree of approximation, which I have tried to stress in the text.

The standard unit for grain was the bushel (equal to 8 gallons), and 8 bushels made a quarter. The weight of a bushel of grain could vary, but a bushel of wheat weighed about 56 lb or roughly 25 kg, a bushel of barley 48 lb, and a bushel of oats 38 lb. The unit of measurement for area was the acre, equivalent to about 0.4 hectares. Before 1971 the English pound (£) consisted of 20 shillings (s); each shilling comprised 12 pence (d); and a penny comprised 4 farthings. In some tables monetary amounts are given in pounds with decimal places for ease of calculation and comparison. Dates given are modern, with the year beginning on 1 January.

Abbreviations

AHEW, IV	Joan Thirsk (ed.), *The Agrarian History of England and Wales*, IV, *1500–1640* (Cambridge, 1967)
AHEW, V	Joan Thirsk (ed.), *The Agrarian History of England and Wales*, V, *1640–1750* (Cambridge, 1984)
AHEW, VI	G. E. Mingay (ed.), *The Agrarian History of England and Wales*, VI, *1750–1850* (Cambridge, 1981)
CKS	Centre for Kentish Studies
CRO	Cambridgeshire Record Office
ERO	Essex Record Office
HRO	Hampshire Record Office
NCS	Northumberland Collections Service
NRO	Norfolk Record Office
SRO	Somerset Record Office
WRO	Wiltshire Record Office
WYASB	West Yorkshire Archive Service, Bradford
WYASL	West Yorkshire Archive Service, Leeds

1 Introduction

'Tis Labour then which puts the greatest part of Value upon Land, without which it would scarcely be worth any thing ... For 'tis not barely the Plough-man's Pains, the Reaper's and Thresher's Toil, and the Baker's Sweat, is to be counted into the Bread we eat; the Labour of those who broke the Oxen, who digged and wrought the Iron and Stones, who felled and framed the Timber imployed about the Plough, Mill, Oven, or any other Utensils, which are a vast Number, requisite to this Corn, from its being seed to be sown to its being made Bread, must all be charged on the account of Labour ... 'Twould be a strange Catalogue of things, that Industry provided and made use of, about every Loaf of Bread, before it came to our use, if we could trace them; Iron, Wood, Leather, Bark, Timber, Stone, Bricks, Coals, Lime, Cloth, Dying-Drugs, Pitch, Tar, Masts, Ropes, and all the Materials made use of in the Ship, that brought any of the Commodities made use of by any of the Workmen.

John Locke, Two Treatises of Government[1]

[O]ur *People* are strong and able for Work at Home ... and naturally as ingenious, industrious, and willing to labour as any part of Mankind, so long as they can have a reasonable fruit of their Labours.

William Petyt, Britannia Languens or a Discourse on Trade[2]

Two shillings and sixpence a day, will undoubtedly tempt some to work, who would not touch a tool for one shilling. A fellow that has been used to lounge at home, in an idle cottage, may be tempted out by high wages, though not by low ones: Another that in cheap times used to bask himself all day in the sun, holding a cow by a line to feed on a balk in dear ones, betakes himself to the pick-ax and the spade. In a word, idle people are converted by degrees into industrious hands; youths are brought forward to work; even boys perform their share, and women at the prospect of great wages clap their hands with cheerfulness, and fly to the sickle. Thus a new race of the

---

[1] John Locke, *Two Treatises of Government*, ed. Peter Laslett (New York, 1963), Second Treatise, §43, p. 298.
[2] William Petyt, *Britannia Languens or a Discourse on Trade* (London, 1680), in J. P. McCulloch, *A Select Collection of Early English Tracts on Commerce* (Cambridge, 1954), p. 313.

industrious is by degrees created, and its increase is proportioned to its creation; an effect so undoubted, that any village in this country might by an increasing employment be presently raised to a *Sheffield*, or a *Birmingham*.

Arthur Young, *A Six Month Tour through the North of England*[3]

This book begins with food and ends with work. Its aim is to examine the living standards of agricultural labourers in much greater detail than has been attempted until now. In doing so it will advance two central theses about the early modern period. One is that the culture of eating needs to be given more importance, because the calories contained in the food consumed by labourers were the petrol of the early modern economy. The other concerns the changing demand for labour in the economy over time. By the early seventeenth century a growing population meant that the supply of labour started to outgrow demand. This is a situation well known to historians who have drawn on the evidence of rapidly rising food prices compared to more slowly rising wages. Lack of rural employment led to increased labour mobility as the young took to the road in search of work, and the poor laws were established to deal with the growing problem of relieving the sick and elderly without family or community support.[4] However, after the mid-seventeenth century this situation was reversed and demand for labour outstripped supply. There were a number of reasons for this, including the emigration of a considerable number of young men to the New World and much slower population growth after 1650. At the same time, however, by the early seventeenth century rising food prices began to motivate farmers to engage in 'improving' their farms to profit by selling more food. This had the effect of increasing the demand for agricultural labour to increase crop production. Agricultural historians have debated when crop yields went up, but certainly by 1700 England was producing enough grain to start exporting a surplus to the continent in most years once population stabilised. The increased availability of food energy produced by agriculture also led to an increased number of people being able to work in non-primary sectors of the economy, such as shop keeping or cloth production. E. A. Wrigley has estimated that the percentage of the population engaged in primary agricultural production fell from 76 per cent in 1520 to only 36 per cent by 1801.[5]

[3] Arthur Young, *A Six Month Tour through the North of England* (London, 1771), I, pp. 175–6.
[4] See the excellent summary in Keith Wrightson, *Earthly Necessities: Economic Lives in Early Modern Britain* (New Haven, 2000), pp. 115–31, 145–9, 194–201.
[5] E. A. Wrigley, 'Urban Growth and Agricultural Change: England and the Continent in the Early Modern Period', in E. A. Wrigley, *People, Cities and Wealth* (Oxford, 1987), pp. 170.

In absolute terms this meant that the population engaged in agriculture in 1800 was about 3,140,000, compared to 2,870,000 in 1600, even though the amount of land under cultivation had increased considerably and crop yields were much higher. This certainly suggests that agricultural labour had become more productive over this period. Authors who advocated 'improvement' also promoted the 'industriousness' of labour as necessary for improvement. More employment would eventually lead to more production and more wealth for all, including those who laboured. This is indicated by the quotations given above, even if they were expressed with the buoyant optimism of proselytisers.

Trends in standards of living have hitherto been dominated by the measurement of real wages; that is the purchasing power of money wages over time. But, here, I intend to look at the relationship of standards of living to the nature of work in much more detail. The nature of the alleged improvement in the industry of labour will be examined using material drawn from a wide range of sources, including pamphlets, published budgets, many account books and probate inventories taken of the goods of labourers when they died. The examination of food in this context is especially important, because it not only represents a vital aspect of labourers' material standard of living, but was equally the essential source of energy for the early modern economy. Although coal was increasingly being used in certain industrial applications after 1580 and water and wind power were also harnessed by mills and ships, most of the economy relied on human and animal power. E. A. Wrigley has termed this an organic economy, implying that the main form of energy came from food production.[6] He has also persuasively shown how the increasing energy available from crops grown to feed horses led to more animal energy being available in the eighteenth century.[7] But horses did not replace human labour; rather they allowed, for instance, more things to be carried from place to place, or ground to be ploughed more often. Both these activities would have also required more human labour to load and unload carts, to drive the horses and to look after them. This labour required calories supplied by food.

The chronology of this study will range from the mid-sixteenth century to about 1780. Inevitably there will be more discussion of the later part of the period because more records exist. I will also draw on

---

[6] E. A. Wrigley, *Continuity, Chance and Change: The Character of the Industrial Revolution in England* (Cambridge, 1988), pp. 27, 34ff.; Paul Warde, *Energy Consumption in England and Wales, 1560–2000* (Istituto di Studi sulle Società del Mediterraneo, 2007), ch. 2.

[7] E. A. Wrigley, 'The Transition to an Advanced Organic Economy: Half a Millennium of English Agriculture', *Economic History Review*, 59 (2006), pp. 435–80.

sources from all over England, discussing regional differences wherever appropriate. It needs to be kept in mind that different regional patterns of manorial custom concerning levels of rent or entitlements to common land could affect standards of living in a way which is impossible to measure nationally. Gathering data on labourers is difficult because they left few of their own records. However, I hope I have unearthed a sufficient amount of information to do the subject justice.

I have chosen to stop in 1780 to avoid the question of living standards during the industrial revolution, which has been debated at length.[8] This is a quite conscious decision, as the rapidly expanding growth of population after about 1775, together with the rapid wartime inflation which lasted well into the nineteenth century, created a situation which was significantly different for labour from that in the early part of the eighteenth century. By 1820 the very nature of living for many was being changed by the growth of industrial cities, and this has a different historiography. However, since current work focuses more on long-term gradual industrialisation which began in the early modern period, the results of this study will certainly be able to shed light on this question.[9]

Even though I have chosen to stop before the end of the eighteenth century, no study of labouring households can afford not to use the work of the Rev. Mr David Davies and Sir Frederick Eden. Both of these individuals were motivated to investigate the living standards and earnings of labouring households in the 1790s because of the hardships brought about by the very rapid rise in food prices. By the end of the eighteenth century enlightened reformers had gathered data on a wide variety of subjects, including farming techniques, prison conditions and the condition of slaves, in order to provide empirical arguments for reform. This is what Eden and Davies set out to do for labourers, in order to show how their poverty might be alleviated. Davies had been a manager of a sugar plantation in Barbados in his early life, who returned to England in 1771 at the age of twenty-seven to become a tutor. He subsequently took holy orders and became deacon of Barkham, Berkshire in 1782, where he remained until his death in 1819.[10] He undertook his work,

[8] The debate is discussed in Martin Daunton, *Progress and Poverty: An Economic and Social History of Britain 1700–1850* (Oxford, 1995), ch. 16; Gregory Clark, Michael Huberman and Peter H. Lindert, 'A British Food Puzzle, 1770–1850', *Economic History Review*, 48 (1995), pp. 215–37; Charles Feinstein, 'Pessimism Perpetuated: Real Wages and the Standard of Living in Britain During the Industrial Revolution', *Economic History Review*, 58 (1998), pp. 625–58.

[9] E. A. Wrigley, 'The Quest for the Industrial Revolution', in E. A. Wrigley, *Poverty, Progress and Population* (Cambridge, 2004), pp. 17–43.

[10] Pamela Horn, 'Davies, David (1742–1819)', *Oxford Dictionary of National Biography* (Oxford, 2004), www.oxforddnb.com/view/article/7229, accessed 19 May 2009.

entitled *The Case of the Labourers in Husbandry Stated and Considered*, out of concern for the increasing poverty of agricultural labourers in his parish, which he expanded to include reports on the condition of rural workers elsewhere.[11] Eden also had colonial connections, being the son of the governor of Maryland. He lived in London and was chairman of the Globe Insurance Company, but became interested in the active debates over the question of how best to manage poor relief and to encourage the poor to save more as insurance for sickness and old age.[12] His three-volume investigation was entitled *The State of the Poor, or a History of the Labouring Classes in England*. In his preface he stated:

The difficulties, which the labouring classes experienced, from the high price of grain, and of provisions in general, as well as of clothing and fuel, during the years 1794 and 1795, induced me, from motives both of benevolence and personal curiosity, to investigate their condition in various parts of the kingdom. As I advanced in my enquiries, the subject became so interesting, that I persuaded myself the result would be acceptable to the Public, if I might be able to lay before them accurate details respecting the present state of the Labouring part of the community, as well as the actual Poor.[13]

As befitting someone who worked in the expanding insurance industry he set out to discover information through a parish-based questionnaire asking such questions as:

> The extent and population of the parish?
> Occupations of parishioners, whether in agriculture,
>   commerce, or manufactures?
> What manufactures?
> Price of provisions?
> Wages of labour?
> Rent of land, and land-tax on the net rental?
> Number of inns or ale-houses?
> Farms large or small? Principal articles of cultivation?
> Commons and waste-lands?
> How are the Poor maintained?
> Houses of industry (if any,) their state; numbers therein,
>   and the annual mortality; diet; expenses, and profit, since
>   their establishment?
> Number of Friendly Societies?
> Usual diet of labourers?

---

[11] David Davies, *The Case of the Labourers in Husbandry Stated and Considered* (London, 1795; reprinted 1977).

[12] Donald Winch, 'Eden, Sir Frederick Morton, second baronet (1766–1809)', *Oxford Dictionary of National Biography* (Oxford, 2004), www.oxforddnb.com/view/article/8450, accessed 19 May 2009.

[13] Sir Frederick Morton Eden, *The State of the Poor, or a History of the Labouring Classes in England*, 3 vols. (London, 1797), I, pp. i–vi.

> Earnings and expenses of a labourers' family for a
> year: distinguishing the number and ages of the family members?

Some parishes he visited himself, but he also used information collected by agents. As a result of the systematic nature of his investigation, his book is hugely valuable.[14]

I will also focus almost exclusively on agricultural labourers and servants in husbandry for the same reason given by David Davies at the beginning of his work:

> For the bulk of every nation consists of such as must earn their daily bread by daily labour ... It is chiefly on these that every nation depends for its population, strength, and security. All reasonable persons will therefore acknowledge the equity of ensuring to them at least the necessary means of subsistence.
>
> ... But of all the denominations of people in a state, *the labourers in* husbandry are by far the most valuable. For these are the men, who, being constantly employed in the cultivation of the earth, provide the staff of life for the whole nation. And it is the wives of these men, who rear those hardy broods of children, which, besides supplying the country with the hands it wants, fill up the voids which death is continually making in camps and cities. And since they have thus a peculiar title to public regard, one might expect to see them every where comfortably accommodated. Yet even in this kingdom, distinguished as it is for humanity and political wisdom, they have been for some time past suffering peculiar hardships. To make their case known, and to claim for them the just recompense of their labour, is the chief purpose of this publication.[15]

Agricultural labourers had a different set of skills from other workers, though equally developed, and it will be part of my argument that we need to consider labourers, or what is often termed the 'labouring poor', as a more diffuse group of people, with different skills and work habits. Thus the term used here will be 'labourers' rather than the 'labouring poor', although of course many were poor. But, as indicated in the quotation from Eden given above, the poor in need of relief were considered a different, more destitute group than the labouring poor. It has been estimated that rarely did those on relief form more than 5–6 per cent of parish populations at any one time. Of course, many labouring families found themselves in need of relief at some point in their lives course, and Steve Hindle has described how many labouring families also survived through 'shift', that is combining numerous odd jobs. But since there is a much larger historiography of the poor on relief, I will focus on those labourers in employment, and the nature of the demand for their labour.[16]

---

[14] Idem.   [15] Davies, *Case of Labourers*, pp. 1–3.
[16] Steve Hindle, *On the Parish: The Micro-Politics of Poor Relief in Rural England c. 1550–1750* (Oxford, 2004), pp. 271ff.

Another reason for examining agricultural labourers separately from other workers such as miners, weavers, combers, building workers or porters is that although agricultural labourers were paid wages, they were less vulnerable to the problems created by the shortage of small coins in the economy. Agricultural workers could be paid their wages in food, pasture and rent because they were usually working for larger farmers in their neighbourhood. In contrast, industrial workers had to rely more on credit because the lack of coins made paying regular wages difficult.[17] Industrial workers were also much more vulnerable to long periods of unemployment caused by rapidly changing market demand for the products manufactured, whereas food was always in demand somewhere.

Excellent work has also been done on the living standards of building labourers in the north of England in this period by Donald Woodward, and on coal miners in the parish of Wickham by David Levine and Keith Wrightson.[18] But although many historians have discussed living standards, no one has focused specifically on agricultural labourers since Alan Everitt's essay on the subject published over forty years ago in volume IV of the *Agrarian History of England and Wales*.[19] I will also focus on England, because living standards for Scotland have been examined by Alex Gibson and Christopher Smout in their *Prices, Food and Wages in Scotland 1550–1780*, which looks at food consumption and nutrition of the poor through various diets, as well as providing a history of wages and prices.[20] Clarkson and Crawford's *Feast and Famine* also deals with the diet of the poor in Ireland over the long term from 1500 to 1920, although it does not examine housing, work or wages.[21]

As already suggested, most work on the question of standards of living has focused on the best way to construct real wage series to track change over time. This is typically done by looking at evidence of daily

[17] Craig Muldrew, 'Wages and the Problem of Monetary Scarcity in Early Modern England', in Jan Lucassen (ed.), *Wages and Currency: Global Comparisons from Antiquity to the Twentieth Century* (Berne, 2007), pp. 391–410.

[18] Donald Woodward, *Men at Work: Labourers and Building Craftsmen in the Towns of Northern England, 1450–1750* (Cambridge, 1995); David Levine and Keith Wrightson, *The Making of an Industrial Society: Wickham 1560–1765* (Oxford, 1991).

[19] Alan Everitt, 'Farm Labourers', in *AHEW*, IV, pp. 396–465. Leigh Shaw-Taylor, however, has dealt with the effect of enclosure on the labouring poor after 1750. Leigh Shaw-Taylor, 'Proletarianisation, Parliamentary Enclosure and the Household Economy of the Labouring Poor, 1750–1850', University of Cambridge Ph.D. thesis, 1999.

[20] A. J. S. Gibson and T. C. Smout, *Prices, Food and Wages in Scotland 1550–1780* (Cambridge, 1995).

[21] L. A. Clarkson and E. Margaret Crawford, *Feast and Famine: Food and Nutrition in Ireland 1500–1920* (Oxford, 2001).

food consumption, together with the cost of clothes, fuel, rent and other household costs, to create a 'typical' 'basket of consumables' bought over the course of a year, for a family of a certain size. Prices of these goods are examined to work out their changing cost for different years. Evidence of monetary wage payments is then collated to form a time series, and the real wage is calculated to be the percentage of the basket of consumables which could be bought by a single family in a year. The first, and until recently the only, long-term attempt to do this was the work of Henry Phelps Brown and Sheila V. Hopkins in their two articles, 'Seven Centuries of Building Wages' and 'Seven Centuries of the Prices of Consumables, Compared with Builders' Wage-Rates', published in the journal *Economica* in 1955 and 1956.[22] In these articles they used builders' wages collected largely from southern England, together with a large dataset of prices collected previously in the nineteenth and early twentieth centuries by historians such as James Thorold Rogers and William Beveridge.[23]

In order to measure a historical standard of living all the way from 1260 to 1954 Phelps Brown and Hopkins attempted to construct four baskets of consumables for 1275, 1500, 1725 and 1950, to introduce a rough measure of change over time. But the evidence they had of both diet and the consumption of household goods before the nineteenth century was very limited – consisting of only one medieval account book of two priests and David Davies's and Frederick Eden's budgets for poor families during the hard years of the late eighteenth century. Since they were not interested in actual consumption, they did not investigate the accuracy of what building workers might actually have been consuming. They were more interested in having a reasonable standard measure which could track the changing prices of comparable units. However, their real wage series became a seminal tool in explaining socio-economic change in the early modern period. Figure 3 in their second article famously showed that real wages, owing to the price inflation of the sixteenth century, fell to a nadir during the run of bad harvests in the late 1590s. Prices of food were shown to have risen by over six times between 1550 and 1650, while nominal money wages only rose by 2.5 times in the same period. In contrast real wages were at their highest when food prices and population were low in the

---

[22] Henry Phelps Brown and Sheila V. Hopkins, 'Seven Centuries of Building Wages', in Henry Phelps Brown and Sheila V. Hopkins, *A Perspective of Wages and Prices* (London, 1981), pp. 1–12; Henry Phelps Brown and Sheila V. Hopkins, 'Seven Centuries of the Prices of Consumables, Compared with Builders' Wage-Rates', in ibid., pp. 13–59.

[23] J. B. Thorold Rogers, *A History of Agriculture and Prices in England from 1259 to 1793*, 8 vols. (Oxford, 1866–1902); William Beveridge, *Prices and Wages in England* (London, 1939).

fifteenth century. After 1650, gradually rising money wages, together with falling food prices, led to slowly rising real wages.[24] These figures were puzzling because their work showed that building workers would have been better off in the fifteenth century, which experienced a long trade depression and market contraction. In addition they showed that it would have been impossible for a family to survive on just the husband's wages which were paid at this time.

Following from this work, a pioneering attempt was made by Keith Wrightson and David Levine to reconstruct a poor family's actual minimum survival budget based on poor law payments in the Essex village of Terling in the late seventeenth century, and by Ian Archer, who constructed some budgets for poor widows supported by poor relief in London in the 1580s and 1590s.[25] The most detailed attempt to reconstruct early modern family budgets so far, however, has been Donald Woodward's work on building workers in the north, where he looked at how many days male wage earners would have had to work to support families of various sizes in Hull and Lincoln from 1540 to 1699. To do this he used a diet outlined for famine years which left out drink, but there were still many years when it appears that a family with three or four children would have found it impossible to survive on just the husband's wage earnings, even on a diet advocated for years of severe shortage.[26]

However, apart from Wrightson and Levine, none of this work was done for agricultural labourers. Recently, though, a new long-term series of farm labourers' wages from 1209 to 1869 has been constructed by Gregory Clark. Clark looked at a much larger sample of farm labourers' wages from all over England, in contrast to Phelps Brown and Hopkins, who based their series on building labourers' wages from the south.[27] For his price series, Clark relied on those collected by William Beveridge with additions from his own new research. However, he

---

[24] Christopher Clay, *Economic Expansion and Social Change: England 1500–1700*, 2 vols. (Cambridge, 1984), I, ch. 2.

[25] Keith Wrightson and David Levine, *Poverty and Piety in an English Village, Terling 1525–1700* (New York, 1979), pp. 39–41; Ian Archer, *The Pursuit of Stability: Social Relations in Elizabethan London* (Cambridge,1991), pp. 190–1.

[26] Woodward, *Men at Work*, pp. 276–84. Steve Rappaport has also shown that the rise in the price of bread in London was not as great as Phelps Brown and Hopkins thought for the sixteenth century. Steve Rappaport, *Worlds within Worlds: Structures of Life within Sixteenth-Century London* (Cambridge, 1989), ch. 5.

[27] Phelps Brown and Hopkins, 'Prices of Consumables', pp. 13–57; Gregory Clark, 'The Long March of History: Farm Wages, Population, and Economic Growth, England 1209–1869', *Economic History Review*, 60 (2007), pp. 97–135; Gregory Clark, 'Farm Wages and Living Standards in the Industrial Revolution: England, 1670–1869', *Economic History Review*, 54 (2001), pp. 477–505.

based his basket of consumables on a single example, that constructed by Sarah Horrell based on budgetary evidence from 1787 to 1796. In order to trace change over time he expressed the composition of different components as a geometric index based on changing prices of different goods.[28] In comparison to Phelps Brown and Hopkins, Clark's data show that the fall in real wages from the mid-fifteenth century to 1600 was only of the order of about 50 per cent, rather than 60 per cent, and, much more surprisingly, that real wages rose much less over the course of the early eighteenth century.[29]

Such real wage series are valuable in that they provide a rough index of very long-term change over time, and they also provide a way of comparing living standards in different countries or areas of the world.[30] But the numerical abstraction of such series often masks the difficulties in collecting evidence robust enough to be used in comparative terms, given the sweeping changes which have occurred in England since 1209 or those which existed in comparison to other areas in Europe, early modern China, the Ottoman Empire or India. The adult male wage was only one aspect of the way in which a family earned wealth, as has been pointed out in much recent work.[31] In the most comprehensive set of contemporary budgets from the period, those made by David Davies and Sir Frederick Eden in the late eighteenth century, the earnings of a household head, in the majority of cases, constituted less than two-thirds of household income, and this was after the introduction of spinning machinery radically diminished the most significant employment for women.[32] Furthermore, basing consumption on a sample of small diets can obscure the tremendous geographical and temporal changes in the consumption of food and other goods, even within England. This

[28] Clark, 'Long March', pp. 105–8; Gregory Clark, 'The Price History of English Agriculture, 1209–1914', *Research in Economic History*, 22 (2004), pp. 41–124; Sara Horrell, 'Home Demand and British Industrialization', *Journal of Economic History*, 56 (1996), pp. 565–71.

[29] Clark, 'Long March', pp. 131–4; Phelps Brown and Hopkins, 'Prices of Consumables', pp. 28–31.

[30] Robert Allen, 'Progress and Poverty in Early Modern Europe', *Economic History Review*, 56 (2003), pp. 403–43; Süleyman Özmucur and Sevket Pamuk, 'Real Wages and Standards of Living in the Ottoman Empire, 1498–1914', *Journal of Economic History*, 62 (2002), pp. 293–321; Stephen Broadberry and Bishnupriya Gupta, 'The Early Modern Great Divergence: Wages, Prices and Economic Development in Europe and Asia, 1500–1800', *Economic History Review*, 59 (2006), pp. 2–31.

[31] Lucassen (ed.), *Wages and Currency*; Peter Scholliers and Leonard Schwarz (eds.), *Experiencing Wages: Social and Cultural Aspects of Wage Forms in Europe since 1500* (New York and Oxford, 2003); Michael Sonenscher, 'Work and Wages in Paris in the Eighteenth Century', in Maxine Berg, Pat Hudson and Michael Sonenscher (eds.), *Manufacture in Town and Country before the Industrial Factory* (Cambridge, 1983), pp. 147–72.

[32] Carole Shammas, 'Food Expenditure and Economic Well-Being in Early Modern England', *Journal of Economic History*, 43 (1983), p. 95.

was recognised by Gibson and Smout as well as Woodward, who chose not to construct single real wage series because of the differences in diet which they discovered by examining a wide variety of sources.[33]

Thus, my guiding principle here will be not to reduce standards of living to statistical series, but rather to look at the meaning of differences in diet, household goods and earnings discovered in my research. The book is organised around this principle, and first, in chapter 1, I will examine the nature of food eaten by labourers, describing what sort of food was recommended for work, how it was prepared and how this differed geographically. A great deal can be learned about how labourers ate and how they lived, and not surprisingly their experiences were much more varied than constant malnutrition. There was much hardship, but it was far from constant and incapacitating. The types of food eaten were based on a very complex system of knowledge about what was healthy, which often had little to do with what we now know scientifically to be nutritious. Beer and meat, for instance, seem to have constituted a much larger portion of some diets than is generally assumed, being considered good for work. A pound of beef was generally a penny cheaper than a pound of cheese. Cheese, however, was easier to preserve, and could be carried into the field without much preparation. A large amount of meat had to be consumed because the slaughter of livestock was necessary to provide enough leather for the economy. Diets also changed over time and, more importantly, fluctuated yearly according to changes in price.

After examining what sort of food was eaten, I will look at a wide variety of diets covering the whole period from 1550 to the end of the eighteenth century to determine how much food farm labourers were eating. This will be done in order to discover how many calories they were consuming, which can then be compared to the calorific energy required for the agricultural work which needed to be done. The energy provided by food is an important concept in what is termed biometric history. A fairly substantial amount of work has been done by econometricians on height and nutrition from the eighteenth century to the present, in which measurement of calorific intake has played a large role.[34] This work has been more concerned with energy inputs and outputs,

---

[33] Gibson and Smout, *Prices, Food and Wages*, pp. 337–64; Woodward, *Men at Work*, pp. 212–49, 276–84.

[34] Robert Fogel, 'New Sources and Techniques for the Study of Secular Trends in Nutritional Status, Health, Mortality, and the Process of Aging', *Historical Methods*, 26 (1993), pp. 5–43; Robert Fogel, *The Escape from Hunger and Premature Death, 1700–2100: Europe, America, and the Third World* (Cambridge, 2004); Roderick Floud, Kenneth Wachter and Annabel Gregory, *Height, Health and History: Nutritional Status in the United Kingdom, 1750–1980* (Cambridge, 1990).

but since diet accounted for the greatest part of household expenditure for poor families, this is obviously related to standards of living. The best-known work on this subject has been that of Robert Fogel, who has published in book form views which have been taking shape in various articles and unpublished papers of his for about twenty-five years. Fogel concluded that the national average daily calorific consumption in 1790 was only 2,826 kcal, based on the evidence of various sources, but most prominently the Davies–Eden budgets for England, as well as the much shorter height of labourers who became soldiers in comparison to their wealthy officers. Based on a log normal distribution among various income classes, he concluded that the bottom 20 per cent of the population could not have done more than six hours of light work or sixty-five minutes of heavy work a day.[35] Carole Shammas has reworked the Davies–Eden data and also looked at a number of earlier workhouse diets in a much more detailed study of food consumption, but has come to largely similar conclusions about calorific intake, although she is more cautious about the representativeness of her sources.[36] Many historians have shown understandable incredulity towards Fogel's conclusion, because if it is true, what were farm labourers doing for the other nine hours a day they were supposed to be working? Scepticism has also been voiced by Joachim Voth, who has argued that hours worked were actually increasing during the late eighteenth century by looking at a completely different set of evidence, descriptions of work in Old Bailey trial depositions.[37]

Most work on diet and food consumption to date has focused on the budgets made and collected by David Davies and Sir Frederick Eden.[38] But Fogel's results point to an obvious problem with using the Davies–Eden budgets. Both Eden and Davies were motivated to investigate the standards of living of the labouring poor because of the poverty created by huge increases in food prices in the late 1780s and 1790s. According to Phelps Brown and Hopkins's index, prices doubled between 1770 and 1800. The price of wheat rose from an average of 37s a quarter in the 1760s to 77s in the 1790s.[39] Thus the budgets were made at a

[35] Fogel, 'New Sources', p. 12
[36] Carole Shammas, *The Pre-Industrial Consumer in England and America* (Oxford, 1990), pp. 135–6.
[37] Hans-Joachim Voth, *Time and Work in England 1750–1830* (Oxford, 2000), pp. 161–75; Jan de Vries, *The Industrious Revolution: Consumer Behaviour and the Household Economy, 1650 to the Present* (Cambridge, 2008), pp. 116–21.
[38] See ns. 11 and 13 above.
[39] John Rule, *Albion's People: English Society 1714–1815* (London, 1992), pp. 176–86; Phelps Brown and Hopkins, 'Prices of Consumables', pp. 55–6; Thorold Rogers, *Agriculture and Prices*, VII, pp. 143–76.

time when consumption had to be cut back significantly. In addition, both Davies and Eden probably underestimated the amount of beer consumed since there is an obvious reason why families in debt would be reluctant to tell how much they had spent on drinking, especially to a clergyman, however well intentioned. Here I will argue that more extensive research into earlier sources, which detail food consumption, shows that concentrating primarily on the Davis and Eden budgets significantly underestimates food consumption. Beer, for instance, formed a large part of the diet. Working labourers had to consume upwards of 4,000 kcal a day (the modern norm for a middle-class man would be about 2,900) in order to work 8–10 hours a day. To test this assumption, in chapter 3 I will also look at national estimates of food production in England. Here I will use agricultural historians' estimates of land under cultivation, crop yields and stocking densities to see if the country was capable of producing enough food to support such work for six days a week, for most of the year. This will be done for different dates from 1600 to 1800. Unfortunately, similar height data to that used by Floud, Wachter and Gregory does not exist for individuals born before 1750, but the present study will hopefully show that it is important to consider the nutrition of infants and young children's food separately from that of adults who were engaged in hard labour, as the latter might have had to consume a disproportionate amount of the pool of calories available to a family.[40]

In chapter 4, attention will shift from food to the nature of labourers' household possessions. Here almost 1,000 probate inventories for labourers from the counties of Cambridgeshire, Norfolk, Hampshire, Lincolnshire, Cheshire and Kent will be examined. Probate inventories are lists of deceased people's material possessions and working stock, drawn up upon death in order to facilitate the payment of debts and the division of the remaining property among the benefactors of the will or of inheritance custom. In other studies on material culture which have used probate inventories, it is commonly noted that they have survived for much greater numbers of wealthier members of society than for labourers. While this is true in aggregate terms, given the sheer number of inventories which have survived from the sixteenth to the eighteenth century, the absolute number of labourers' inventories is still large enough to provide a statistically significant sample. Here the goods possessed by labourers will be examined to see if they changed over time. Goods in the inventories, such as linen, beds and furniture, as well as luxury items such as clocks, looking-glasses and eating utensils, will be

---

[40] There is not space to do this here, but see the comments on p. 160 below.

examined. In addition, the number of rooms in houses will be examined, as will hearths and cooking equipment to see how food production could have changed over time and place.[41]

Then, in the remaining three chapters of the book, I will consider the question of the industrious revolution. The industrious revolution is a concept which has been developed by Jan de Vries through a number of articles and a recently published book.[42] The theory originates in de Vries's work on Dutch rural inventories from the provinces of Friesland, Groningen and Holland in the early modern period. His book argues that households need to be considered as a unit, whose members make decisions about both participation in labour markets and about consumption, in relation to what they think about themselves as a household and family. De Vries argues that, in the early modern period, households increased their labour market participation in order to buy new consumer goods with the money they earned from their labour. This increase in work could be achieved in a number of different ways: by individuals working more hours, or more intensely over the course of a day, or it could involve more members of the family participating in work, such as the wife and children working in the cloth industry. He termed this the 'industrious revolution' to account for this increased work. In the remainder of his book he goes on to examine why middle-class households reduced their labourer market participation in the nineteenth and first three-quarters of the twentieth century, and why such participation has again been increasing in the last forty years or so. One of the key features of his theory is that poorer labourers were just as likely to be motivated to work harder by the desire to purchase new consumer items as the middling sort:

The evidence for growth in consumer demand is, I believe, compelling, and it cannot be explained away as a phenomenon restricted to a small social group, a few goods or a brief period of propitious price and wage movements.

Consumer demand grew, even in the face of contrary real wage trends, because of reallocations of the productive resources of households. A series of household-level decisions altered both the supply of marketed goods and labour and the demand for market-bought products. This complex of changes in household behaviour constitutes an 'industrious revolution', driven by

---

[41] Clothing will be touched on, but it has recently been dealt with extensively by John Styles in his *The Dress of the People: Everyday Fashion in Eighteenth-Century England* (New Haven, 2007).

[42] Jan de Vries, 'The Industrial Revolution and the Industrious Revolution', *Journal of Economic History*, 54 (1994), pp. 249–69; Jan de Vries, 'Between Purchasing Power and the World of Goods: Understanding the Household Economy in Early Modern Europe', in Roy Porter and John Brewer (eds.), *Consumption and the World of Goods* (London, 1993), pp. 107–8; de Vries, *Industrious Revolution*.

Smithian, or commercial, incentives, that preceded and prepared the way for the Industrial Revolution.[43]

In his earlier work, de Vries specifically focused on household goods as the key items of new consumption. However, in his recent book he has retreated from this claim somewhat by noting that not enough inventory evidence exists to argue that the consumption of household goods by labourers increased. Instead, he has focused on the growth in the popular consumption of new food items such as tobacco, sugar and tea.[44]

With this sample of labourers' inventories I have enough evidence to look at the accumulation of household goods for this part of the population over the course of most of the early modern period for the first time. What this evidence shows is that while there was little rise in the value of labourers' household goods before 1650, there was a sustained and quite rapid rise afterwards. But rather than buying more novel consumer items, labouring households bought better quality bedding, furniture and kitchenware. However, the approach I wish to take here differs from de Vries. He adopted the term 'industrious revolution' from the Japanese historian Akira Hayami.[45] When looking at contemporary discourse in Holland, France and Britain, de Vries focuses on how ideas about consumption, desire and luxury were reconceptualised.[46] He notes that some writers like Defoe and Berkley advocated the role of consumption 'as the agent of arousal that would motivate a greater work effort', but does not discuss this in depth.[47]

In fact, the concept of industriousness was one created in early seventeenth-century England, when the population was growing faster than the food supply. There were a great number of authors in England who discussed the problem of labour in relation to the production of goods. For them the promotion of 'industriousness' was just as important, if not more important, than the promotion of consumption. The concept was actually one developed by puritan polemicists in England during the first half of the seventeenth century, and then most intensely during the Commonwealth period. As Christopher Hill pointed out as early as 1964, in a short essay entitled 'The Industrious Sort of People', it derived from Protestant theology's focus on application to one's calling, or occupation, as a sign of grace. But puritan writers took it a step further in focusing on labour as a means of social improvement involving the increased production of both food and manufactured

---

[43] De Vries, 'Purchasing Power and the World of Goods', pp. 107–8.
[44] De Vries, *Industrious Revolution*, pp. 149ff.
[45] Ibid., p. 9.   [46] Ibid., pp. 58–72.   [47] Ibid., pp. 67–8.

goods.[48] They saw such social improvement as a manifestation of spiritual well-being. Here the key term was 'improvement', and new agricultural techniques were advocated to improve grain yields and animal husbandry.

The education of the poor in schools of industry was also advocated to teach skills which could be used to make them better able to participate in the labour market – to make them more industrious.[49] Samuel Hartlib, the German émigré who helped promote the discussion and publication of works in science, improvement and industry, wrote a tract where he proposed setting up reformed workhouses as schools for 'civilising' children that 'lie all day in the streets in playing, cursing and swearing'.[50] Hartlib specifically noted that his workhouse was not to be considered a house of correction, such as those which already existed to punish vagrants, but a place of education, a 'Nursery' or 'Magazin of Charity'.[51] Here the concept of industriousness was first developed. For Hartlib, the 'godly and laborious poore [were to] be countenanced and cherished', and those who could not find work were to be helped by providing them with employment, while workhouses would make 'such industrious as are not'.[52] Proposals were also made to develop a banking system whereby the money supply would be increased in order that more day labourers and industrial workers could be paid wages.[53]

The idea of industriousness here is not simply one involving harder work, or working more hours, motivated by the desire for more goods. It is rather a response to falling real wages and labour market competition in the first half of the seventeenth century, which eventually resulted in greater earnings. Many labourers migrated in search of more lucrative work, like Edward Barlow, the son of a poor husbandman from Prestwich, Lancashire, who in 1657

decided I had as good to go seek my fortune abroad as live at home, always in want and working hard for very small gains. Likewise I had never any great mind to country work, as ploughing and sowing and making of hay and reaping, nor also of winter work, as hedging and ditching and thrashing and

---

[48] Christopher Hill, *Society and Puritanism in Pre-Revolutionary England* (Harmondsworth, 1964), pp. 121–40.

[49] Andrew McRae, *God Speed the Plough: The Representation of Agrarian England, 1500–1660* (Cambridge, 1996), ch. 5; Paul Slack, *From Reformation to Improvement: Public Welfare in Early Modern England* (Oxford, 1998), ch. 4.

[50] Slack, *Reformation to Improvement*, p. 79.

[51] Ibid., p. 82.

[52] Joyce Oldham Appleby, *Economic Thought and Ideology in Seventeenth-Century England* (Princeton, 1978), pp. 139–40.

[53] This last aspect is being investigated by Carl Wennerlind.

dunging amongst cattle, and suchlike drudgery. And I thought I had as good go see what I could, knowing that it could not be much worse.[54]

Industriousness, in this case, suggests an entire attitude towards the improvement of both goods and effort, aimed at superior production and the increase of profit and wealth for both individuals and the nation.

In chapter 5 I will begin my investigation into work in England by looking first at the composition of the male day wage in different places and at different times of the year. The nature of hiring and possible perquisites will also be taken into consideration. Then the possible contribution of wives and children to household earnings will be described. Such information on earnings will be compared to estimated expenditure in family budgets for a number of sample years from 1570 to 1770. This will be done to see what possibilities there were for families to earn enough to be able to spend more. Throughout, the family will be the unit of production discussed, as most single people working in agriculture did so as servants within wealthier families rather than as day labourers.[55] Then in chapter 6 I will move on to look at the amount of human labour needed for agricultural work and attempt to make some estimates of how much demand there was for such work and how this changed over time. This empirical investigation will show that the contemporary writers on industriousness were describing a process that actually happened. Increases in agricultural production, although notoriously hard to pin down to any one part of the early modern period, did occur and occurred as a result of the increasing application of both human and horse-powered work to implement new farming techniques. The diets examined in chapter 3, which provided such a large number of calories, were required by those doing a lot of work. Before 1650, when food prices were rising, for most labouring families this meant working harder to merely maintain their living standards to avoid a fall towards poverty.[56] It was only from the late seventeenth century, until the 1770s, that increasing food production and falling food prices, together with the slowing of population growth (and the increasing migration of employment to industry), made it possible for labourers to earn more and then increase spending on their households.

---

[54] Basil Lubbock (ed.), *Barlow's Journal of His Life at Sea in King's Ships, East and West Indiamen and Other Merchantmen from 1659–1703* (London, 1934), p. 21.

[55] Single women might have supported themselves in the cloth industry, while working in agriculture in the summer, however.

[56] De Vries allows for this, but does not stress it as a cause in the rise of early modern popular consumption. De Vries, *Industrious Revolution*, pp. 115–16.

The book concludes with a consideration of the development of the concept of industriousness and a consideration of how we should think of the place of labour in the early modern social order. Much has been written about the degree to which the early modern labourer possessed a *mentalité* of what economists term 'labour preference'. This concept postulates that workers used the money earned from higher day wages to work fewer days, rather than increasing their material wealth or financial savings.[57] This, of course, contradicts the concept of industriousness, but there is certainly plenty of contemporary comment that it did occur. Labourers also certainly enjoyed holidays and worked less on some days of the year.[58] Evidence shows that it is impossible to talk of a 'common' labourer's attitude towards work in this sense. Some were industrious, or what their employers termed 'honest labourers', while others, for whatever reason, had to search for enough work among many employers or took to the road in search of work. Moreover, the degree of work involved in being industrious could vary geographically, depending on how much emphasis there was on agricultural improvement in an area or how much local demand there was compared to the supply of labourers.

To begin we need first to consider how many agricultural labourers there were and what the term meant. There is no straightforward contemporary description of what the occupational term 'labourer' meant, just as there was no precise demarcation between the farming activities of husbandmen or yeomen. The closest we can come to a definition is someone who worked using physical strength for wages, as when in *As You Like It* (III.2.69) the shepherd Corin states to Touchstone 'I am a true labourer, I earn that I eat, get that I ware.' The majority of labourers were farm labourers, and before the mid-seventeenth century 65 per cent of labourers' inventories studied here possessed agricultural tools of their own. Building labourers, who have been described by Donald Woodward, were designated as 'carpenters' in probate documents.[59] Those who lifted and carried the countless barrels and packs of merchandise traded were most usually termed 'porters' or 'carriers'. However, some were termed 'labourers' in towns, such as those labourers who worked in the naval dockyards in Portsmouth, and left inventories, or those who worked on roads, walls and ditches.

---

[57] John Hatcher, 'Labour, Leisure and Economic Thought', *Past and Present*, 160 (1998), pp. 65–115.

[58] Robert W. Malcolmson, *Popular Recreations in English Society 1700–1850* (Cambridge, 1973), ch. 2; Voth, *Time and Work*, pp. 100–6.

[59] Woodward, *Men at Work*, pp. 244–7.

Farm labourers were also not unskilled, as the modern sense of 'labour' often implies. Various schedules of published legal wage rates, drawn up by JPs in accordance with the provisions set out in the Elizabethan 'Statute of Artificers, Labourers and Servants in Husbandry' of 1563, define different levels of wages for skills. In the sessions of the peace held in Chester in 1596, for instance, servants in husbandry were divided into the best sort, as well as the second and third sort, with yearly wages ranging from 20 down to 8s a year with board. This was also the case in Oakham in 1610, where a 'man servant, for husbandrie of the best sort, which can eire, sow, mow, thresh, make a ricke, thacke, and hedge the same; and can kill a hog, sheepe, and calfe' was to be paid £2, in contrast to 'A meane servant, which can drive plow, pitch cart, and thresh, but cannot expertly sow and mow', who was to be paid only £1.[60]

The relationship between the occupational designation of 'labourer' and poverty also needs to be considered. It is often assumed that working as a labourer was a *de facto* indication of poverty, and the term 'labouring poor' is often employed to refer to labourers. However, contemporaries generally referred to agricultural labourers as 'day labourers' or simply 'labourers'. In William Harrison's often-quoted division of society he stated:

The fourth and last sort of people in England are day-labourers, poor husbandmen, and some retailers (which have no free land) copyholders, and all artificers, as tailors, shoemakers, carpenters, brickmakers, masons, etc.[61]

For most writers in the seventeenth and early eighteenth century, the terms 'poor' and 'labourer' were not yoked together as a single group. As Paul Slack has shown, though, there were instances where similar phrases were used to refer to the working poor as a *category* of the poor in times of high prices or low demand for labour. This was the case in a volume of officially approved homilies, published during the dearth of 1596, which pointed out that the needy included those who

labour and take pains in their vocation and trade, yet by reason of the extremity of the world ... they cannot live by their labour, nor maintain their charge, but suffer want and are poor.

The same people were categorised in parish surveys of the poor undertaken in 1597 and 1598 as 'poor able labouring folk', or 'labouring persons not able to live off their labour'.[62] The first incidence I have

---

[60] Eden, *State of the Poor*, III, pp. xciv–xcvi.
[61] William Harrison, *The Description of England*, ed. George Edelen (New York, 1994), p. 118.
[62] Slack, *Poverty and Policy*, pp. 27–9.

been able to find of the phrase 'the labouring poor' used to refer to labourers in general is in Daniel Defoe's pamphlet *The Great Law of Subordination Considered or, The Insolence and Insuffrable Behaviour of Servants in England Duly Enquired Into*, from 1724, in which he complained of the lack of obsequiousness towards masters and employers on the part of household and agricultural servants, as well as day labourers.[63] This was also the pamphlet in which he termed the poor the 'plebs', another uncommon term which, however, has been made famous by E. P. Thompson:

> The miserable Circumstance of this Country is now such, that, in short, if it goes on, the Poor will be Rulers over the Rich, and the Servants be Governours of their Masters, the *Plebeij* have almost mobb'd the *Patricij* … in a Word, Order is inverted, Subordination ceases, and the World seems to stand with the Bottom upward.[64]

After this, 'labouring poor' does not seem to have been a term which came into common usage before the late eighteenth century, when high food prices and the introduction of spinning machinery impoverished many previously sufficient working families. James Steuart, for instance, did not use it at all in his *Inquiry into the Principles of Political Economy* of 1767, although Adam Smith employed it quite often in the *Wealth of Nations* (1776), as did Frederick Eden.

Gregory King did not use the term in his famous table, published in 1699 by Charles Davenant, entitled the 'Scheme of the Income and Expense of the Several Families of England'. Instead he divided what he called those who were 'decreasing the wealth of the kingdom' into soldiers, sailors, 'labouring people and out servants', and 'cottagers and paupers'. In his earlier notes for these estimations he divided 'Poor People usually exempt from Taxes in all Polls [the poll tax]' into five more distinct categories:

(1) 'the Men and Women in the Kingdom who receive Alms [700,000] and their children under 16 are [300,000]'
(2) 'poor Housekeeping Men and Women not paying to Church and Poor [740,000] and their children under 16 [460,000]'
(3) 'the Day Labourers and their Wives are about 400,000 and their children under 16 [250,000 plus 150,000 servants in husbandry]'
(4) 'Servants in Husbandry and their wives are about 300,000 and their children under 16'

---

[63] Daniel Defoe, *The Great Law of Subordination Consider'd* (London 1724), ed. J. A. Downie in W. R. Owens and P. N. Furbank (eds.), *Religious and Didactic Writings of Daniel Defoe* (London, 2007), VI, p. 47.
[64] Ibid., p. 51; E. P. Thompson, *Customs in Common* (London, 1991), pp. 16–96.

(5) 'the Parents who have 4 Children or more and are not worth 50*li* are about 150,000 [200,000] and their children under 16'.[65]

Here King simply took the definitions from the Acts for collecting the poll taxes. King's numbers have rightly been criticised as very rough guesswork, but the distinctions set down by the Act are very interesting and show that there were distinct ways of categorising people at the bottom of society.[66] Both adults and children in categories 1, 2 and 5 were fully exempt from paying taxation, but only the children under sixteen of day labourers and servants in husbandry were exempt. The adults had to pay the tax of 1–4s per person per year. Clearly the framers of the various Poll Tax Acts from 1678 to 1698 thought that day labourers with fewer than four young children were different from those in other categories.[67]

Another tax which is often used to define the poor is the hearth tax, which was collected numerous times between 1662 and 1689. Under the terms of the hearth tax, exemption was based on a person being also exempted 'from the usual Taxes Payments and Contributions towards the Church and Poor' or having a dwelling house, or any Messuage, Lands or Tenements, not worth 20s in full improved rent, or having 'Lands Tenements Goods or Chattels' which were worth less than £10.[68] Rates of exemption from the hearth tax could be very high,

---

[65] Joan Thirsk and J. P. Cooper (eds.), *Seventeenth-Century Economic Documents* (Oxford, 1972), pp. 769, 780–1.

[66] Geoffrey Holmes, 'Gregory King and the Social Structure of Pre-Industrial England', *Transactions of the Royal Historical Society*, 5th ser., 27 (1977), pp. 41–68; Paul Slack, 'Measuring the National Wealth in Seventeenth-Century England', *Economic History Review*, 57 (2004), pp. 607–35.

[67] The Act exempted 'such persons as shall receive Alms of the Parish where they dwell and their children being under the age of sixteen years att the time of the execucōon of this Act And ... all poor Housekeepers or Housholders who by reason of their poverty onely are exempted from contributing to the Church and Poor and their children being under the age of sixteen years And alsoe ... all children being under the age of sixteen years of all Day Labourers and of all Servants in Husbandry And alsoe ... all Children being under the age of sixteen yeares of such who have four or more children and are not worth in Lands Goods and Chattells the sum[m] of fifty pounds. *William and Mary, 1691: An Act for raiseing money by a Poll payable quarterly for One year for the carrying on a vigorous War against France* [Chapter VI. Rot. Parl. pt. 2. no. 4.]', *Statutes of the Realm*, VI, 1685–94 (1819), pp. 302–10, www.british-history.ac.uk/report.aspx?compid=46360&strquery=poverty, accessed 4 May 2009. Tom Arkell, 'An Examination of the Poll Taxes of the Later Seventeenth Century, the Marriage Duty Act and Gregory King', in Kevin Schurer and Tom Arkell (eds.), *Surveying the People: The Interpretation and use of Document Sources for the Study of Population in the Later Seventeenth Century* (Oxford, 1992), pp. 142–77.

[68] From 'Charles II, 1662, *An Act for establishing an additional Revenue upon His Majestie His Heires & Successors for the better support of His and theire Crown and Dignity*', *Statutes of the Realm*, V, 1628–80 (1819), pp. 390–3, www.british-history.ac.uk/report.aspx

anywhere from 20 per cent to over 60 per cent.[69] However, the definition of exemption here says nothing about day labourers. In his examination of the relationship between occupation and exemption in the
Warwickshire communities of Knowle and Chilvers Coton, Tom Arkell
found that, indeed, 70 per cent of labourers were exempt compared
to only 3 per cent of husbandmen. However, many in other occupations, including butchers, weavers, shoemakers, turners and sawyers,
had similar levels of exemption.[70] Also, the exemption list for the town
of King's Lynn shows that there were many poor tradesmen in the town
also poor enough to merit exemption under the provisions of the statute.[71] I will return to a discussion of labourers and the hearth tax in
chapter 4, but the point of mentioning it here is to show that it does not
equate poverty with being a day labourer.

One source where poverty is equated with labour are witnesses' statements from cases brought before the church courts. In order to test the
creditworthiness (or trustworthiness) of the witnesses, the courts asked
them for a statement of what they believed they were worth in goods
after their debts were paid. Recent work by Alex Shepard has shown
that many witnesses who described themselves as poor or of 'little
worth' defined this as the condition of being a wage labourer. This was
the case in an example of a servant in husbandry appearing in Salisbury
in 1590, who claimed that he was a 'poore hired servant and liveth
onely by his hard labour not being otherwise any thing worth'.[72] Those
in other occupations, such as blacksmiths, also described themselves as
poor owing to their labour. The point of the questioning was to estab-
lish the degree to which a poor person was dependent on others and
could potentially be persuaded to be dishonest because of this dependency. Thus the possession of some material goods, and especially land,
was seen as increasing worth, and there were labourers who cited their
worth as the value of their household goods, not just their labour.[73] This
equation with dishonesty was also an assumption which coloured what

---

?compid=47313&strquery=poor, accessed 4 May 2009. Schurer and Arkell (eds.),
Surveying the People, pp. 31–64.

[69] Margaret Spufford and James Went, *Poverty Portrayed: Gregory King and the Parish of
Eccleshall* (Keele, 1995), p. 16; David Levine and Keith Wrightson, *The Making of an
Industrial Society: Wickham 1560–1765* (Oxford, 1991), p. 157.

[70] Tom Arkell, 'The Incidence of Poverty in England in the Later Seventeenth Century',
Social History, 12 (1987), pp. 36–7.

[71] Craig Muldrew, 'Credit, Market Relations, and Debt Litigation in Late Seventeenth
Century England, with Particular Reference to King's Lynn', University of Cambridge
Ph.D. thesis, 1991, pp. 313–39.

[72] Alexandra Shepard, 'Poverty, Labour and the Language of Social Description in
Early Modern England', *Past and Present*, 201 (2008), pp. 51–3, 58–61, 86.

[73] Ibid., pp. 66–9, 81–6.

has been termed the language of sorts, with the 'poorer sort' being seen as untrustworthy because of their lack of independent means.[74] Certainly, here, wages and service were relations of dependency which would have placed labourers among the poorer sort, although certainly not uniquely so. But as the analysis of their inventories in chapter 4 will show, some had more means in goods, which they largely achieved through harder work, and these families became known as the 'honest' or 'laborious' poor, to whom we will return in the last chapter. Also, as Andy Wood has shown, 'poorer sort' could be used in a more positive way to denote those who had suffered at the hands of unfair enclosure or rack-renting.[75]

Another term which was sometimes used to describe farm labourers and poor families was 'cottager'. The best-known usage of this term is Gregory King's in the 'Scheme of the Income and Expense of the Several Families of England' cited above. This division implies that King believed cottagers were poorer than day labourers. But, as I have argued elsewhere, it is quite clear from the context of his discussion that he was concerned only with that portion of income and expenditure which could reasonably be *taxed*, or what was earned only in coin, or possibly bills which could be transferred to London. This is why King divided his scheme of the income and expense of the different qualities of families in England into those who increased the wealth of the kingdom by earning profits which could be taxed, and those poorer households who could not earn enough profits to live above a very basic level, and who thus decreased the wealth of the kingdom because their wages had to be paid in small coins. This was also because the very poor required cash doles and other forms of income redistribution in the form of small coins. For cottagers, this meant that any home production was not needed in his calculations, as it did not require payment in coins, which implies that cottagers were not necessarily as 'poor' as paupers.

Elsewhere, 'cottager' was not usually a term used to describe either individual labourers or labourers as a group. It was most typically used in a geographical sense in terms of manorial surveys, referring to dwellings with very low rental values and little land attached, usually only a garden or close. Richard Gough, when describing Myddle Wood

---

[74] Craig Muldrew, *The Economy of Obligation: The Culture of Credit and Social Relations in Early Modern England* (London, 1998), pp. 303–12. Keith Wrightson, '"Sorts of People" in Tudor and Stuart England', in Jonathan Barry and Christopher Brooks (eds.), *The Middling Sort of People: Culture, Society and Politics in England, 1550–1800* (London, 1994), pp. 28–51.

[75] Andy Wood, 'Fear, Hatred and the Hidden Injuries of Class in Early Modern England', *Journal of Social History*, 39:3 (2006), pp. 803–26.

Common in his history of the parish of Myddle, noted that in the early eighteenth century, 'several persons have cottages on this common, and one or two peices incloased to every cottage'.[76] Perhaps the best-known description of a cottage comes from the Elizabethan legislation on the erection of cottages, which stipulated that each cottage built and rented by a landlord on agricultural land should be possessed of a minimum of four acres.[77]

The size of labourers' land holdings raises what has been one of the most important themes in the historiography of early modern England – the decline of the smallholder and the rise of the landless labourer. Smallholders were small, self-supporting farmers generally termed, as Harrison called them, 'poor husbandmen'. But they could also be labourers who farmed for themselves and did some work for others, but were not dependent on it. Most of this work has been based on estate surveys which show that the number of smaller farms declined between the sixteenth and eighteenth centuries.[78] However, as Wrightson and Levine have cautioned, and as Hipkin's work on Romney Marsh has demonstrated, without records of subtenancy within holdings it is impossible to know exactly how many very small farms there were.[79]

Another important aspect of this debate has been about the effects of enclosure on the living standards of the poor, as pasture needed less work per acre than tillage. As early as the late fifteenth century, contemporary moralists were claiming that the engrossing of common fields and the conversion of fields to sheep pasture was reducing employment for labourers. One contemporary went so far as to claim that tillage maintained 100 people to every 20 employed in pasture.[80] Cardinal Wolsey's investigation into enclosure in the late fifteenth and early sixteenth century was the theme of Tawney's famous book *The Agrarian Problem in the Sixteenth Century*.[81] Wolsey's investigation did not show that there had been as much conversion as the moralists had claimed, and there is no way of measuring the amount of pasture compared to tillage until Gregory King's estimates of the late seventeenth century.

[76] Richard Gough, *History of Myddle*, ed. D. Hey (Harmondsworth, 1981), pp. 63, 92, 97, 108, 109, 126, 127, 145, 183, 192, 236; Spufford, *Poverty Portrayed*, 74–5.

[77] See below pp. 109–11. 31 Elizabeth ch.7. *Statutes of the Realm*, IV, Part I.i, pp. 804–5.

[78] Margaret Spufford, *Contrasting Communities: English Villagers in the Sixteenth and Seventeenth Centuries* (Cambridge, 1974), pp. 46–57, 65–72, 144–59.

[79] Wrightson and Levine, *Poverty and Piety*, p. 28; Stephen Hipkin, 'Tenant Farming and Short-Term Leasing on Romney Marsh, 1585–1705', *Economic History Review*, 53 (2000), pp. 646–76.

[80] Joan Thirsk, *Economic Policy and Projects: The Development of a Consumer Society in Early Modern England* (Oxford, 1978), p. 104.

[81] R. H. Tawney, *The Agrarian Problem in the Sixteenth Century* (London, 1912; reissued London and New York, 1967).

The evidence of diets in the mid-sixteenth century, however, indicates that, with plentiful land in the fifteenth century, grazing animals for meat was common, and a preference for meat certainly seems to have survived into the seventeenth century.[82] Thus as population grew in the sixteenth and early seventeenth centuries, and the price of grain rose sixfold, it seems unlikely that the proportion of land devoted to cattle rearing would have increased. In addition, after the mid-sixteenth century until 1650 wool exports and cloth production stagnated. To feed this growing population, tillage had to increase, which required more labour. However, it does seem to have been the case that more of this took the form of wage labour rather than small-scale farming.

By the seventeenth century a much more important grievance than the conversion of pasture was the rationalisation of common fields, which saw smallholdings being engrossed into larger fields for cash settlements. Equally complained of was the effect of enclosure on the common rights of the poor to pasture animals on the commons, and the attempts by landlords to diminish common rights of tenants to forage for firewood in the woods of a manor and to glean.[83] In many enclosure agreements of the period between 1600 and 1760, when, as J. R. Wordie has argued, 28 per cent of enclosures took place, commons were reduced and rationalised into separate fields which were apportioned according to wealth at the same time as the strips of common arable fields were distributed and parcelled together.[84] In many of these agreements the smallest tenants who had the right to pasture only a very small number of animals on the common were commonly awarded only cash settlements instead of pasturage or given the poorest quality land. This sometimes resulted in so-called enclosure rioting, which involved the destruction of hedgerows at night by those opposed to the enclosure. Unfortunately, in terms of examining standards of living, unless legal documents survive in estate archives or in legal disputes over enclosure, it is impossible to know what sort of common rights labouring tenants might have enjoyed. It is often assumed that before enclosure common rights were widespread, but Leigh Shaw-Taylor has argued that many of these rights were limited before enclosure took place, and that few remained by the end of the eighteenth century. However, the cottage

---

[82] See below, pp. 83ff.
[83] B. Sharp, *In Contempt of All Authority: Rural Artisans and Riot in the West of England, 1586–1660* (Berkeley and Los Angeles, 1980), chs. 4–5; Steve Hindle, 'Persuasion and Protest in the Caddington Common Enclosure Dispute 1635–1639', *Past and Present*, 158 (1998), pp. 35–78; Andy Wood, *Riot, Rebellion and Popular Politics in Early Modern England* (2002), pp. 82–95.
[84] J.R. Wordie, 'The Chronology of English Enclosure, 1500–1914', *Economic History Review*, 36:4 (1983), pp. 483–505.

economy of the poor remained important until the end of our period. Possession of a cow or other animals could be important. Many labourers who worked for wages also had their own small farms and possessed animals and crops.[85] Sixty-eight per cent of the inventoried labourers, for instance, possessed farm animals, while there is evidence that 51 per cent were growing crops, although on a very small scale. But unfortunately there is no way of knowing if they paid rent for pasture or had customary right to a commons.

Other sources have also been used to look at the increase of the number of wage earners in England in addition to those documenting the decline of the smallholder. Christopher Dyer has estimated, from poll tax evidence, that already in 1377–81 the proportion of people who earned most of their living from wage work must have exceeded a third of the population of England.[86] This proportion had risen somewhat by the time of subsidy of 1524–5 and, in Alan Everitt's estimates, seems to have been roughly the same a century later, although there could be large regional differences.[87] By 1688, Gregory King estimated that the proportion of households who had to be paid wages or poor relief (labouring people, out-servants, cottagers and paupers) had reached 47 per cent of the population.[88] According to Lindert and Williamson's revisions of Joseph Massie's social table of 1759 and Patrick Colquhoun's occupational headcount of 1801–3, the number of labouring families and cottagers, as well as those who earned wages through textile work, building and mining, was about the same at mid-century, but had risen to 60 per cent or more by the beginning of the nineteenth century.[89]

But, as E. A. Wrigley has argued, the proportion of the population involved in non-agricultural occupations rose from 25 per cent in 1520 to over 60 per cent by 1800, and many of these occupations employed labour. A better way to look at changes in the proportion of agricultural labourers in rural populations is to use parish baptism registers, where occupation of the father is recorded, as David Hey did for Myddle parish. Currently all available parish registers containing occupational data

[85] Leigh Shaw-Taylor, 'Parliamentary Enclosure and the Emergence of an English Agricultural Proletariat', *Journal of Economic History*, 61:3 (2001), pp. 640–62; Leigh Shaw-Taylor, 'Labourers, Cows, Common Rights and Parliamentary Enclosure: the Evidence of Contemporary Comment *c.* 1760–1810', *Past and Present*, 171 (2001), pp. 95–126.

[86] Christopher Dyer, *Standards of Living in the Later Middle Ages: Social Change in England c. 1200–1520* (Cambridge, 1989), pp. 213–14.

[87] Everitt, 'Farm Labourers', pp. 163–4; J. A. Sharpe, *Early Modern England: A Social History 1550–1760* (London, 1987), pp. 211–12.

[88] Peter Laslett, *The World We Have Lost Further Explored*, 3rd edn (London, 1983), pp. 36–7.

[89] Peter H. Lindert and Jeffrey G. Williamson, 'Revising England's Social Tables 1688–1812', *Explorations in Economic History*, 19 (1982), pp. 385–407.

Table 1.1 *Labourers as a percentage of agricultural occupations over time*

Gloucestershire 1608		%
Gentry	430	6
Yeomen	927	13
Husbandmen	3,774	53
Labourers	1,939	28[a]
Myddle parish, Shropshire, 1571–1630		
Gentry		9
Yeomen		25
Husbandmen		39
Labourers		27
Myddle parish, Shropshire, 1631–60		
Gentry		8
Yeomen		22
Husbandmen		30
Labourers		39
Eccleshall parish, Staffordshire, 1690s		
Gentry		16
Farming		25
Labourers		39
Cottagers		30
Sample of c. 600 southern and Midland parishes, c. 1710		
Farmers		10
Yeomen		17
Husbandmen		18
Labourers		54
Northamptonshire parishes, 1777		
Labourers		75

Note: [a] This figure includes shepherds, but not servants in husbandry, who will be discussed below in chapter 5.

for the late seventeenth and eighteenth centuries are being collected and analysed by the Cambridge Occupational Structure project run by Leigh Shaw-Taylor and E. A. Wrigley. These show that the percentage of labourers in rural parish populations could differ greatly according to geography, although to date only relatively few of these studies have been published. The results of some of this work, together with an analysis of a muster list which listed occupations for Gloucestershire from 1608 and work done on Eccleshall parish, are presented in Table 1.1.[90]

[90] A. J. Tawney and R. H. Tawney, 'An Occupational Census of the Seventeenth Century', *Economic History Review*, 5 (1934–5), pp. 25–64; Spufford, *Poverty*

Although these samples in no way present a systematic analysis, they do seem to show that the numbers of labourers were increasing in proportion to other farming occupations. In addition, when the values of labourers' inventories are compared to those of husbandmen, the latter have considerably more valuable household goods and much more valuable farming stock.[91] This, then, suggests that more farm work was being done by labourers on other people's land by the eighteenth century, thus contributing to social polarisation.

Both the increase in the percentage of labourers as part of the rural population and the declining percentage of that population as a proportion of England's occupational structure further emphasise the importance of understanding the lives and work of agricultural labourers over the course of the whole early modern period. In the eighteenth century wages rose for both agricultural and industrial workers, but this would have been impossible without the increasing work of the former to produce more food. Since Phelps Brown and Hopkins published their series of long-term changes in real wage rates in southern England in the 1950s, the question of labourers' standards of living has been one of the most puzzling aspects of early modern economic and social history. Putting more pieces into this puzzle is crucial because it is fundamental to understanding any economic growth in the period.

Portrayed, p. 47; David Hey, *An English Rural Community: Myddle under the Tudors and Stuarts* (Leicester, 1974), pp. 52–7; Leigh Shaw-Taylor and Amanda Jones, 'The Male Occupational Structure of Northamptonshire 1777–1881: A Case of Partial De-Industrialization?', p. 5, www.geog.cam.ac.uk/research/projects/occupations/abstracts/. The figures for *c.* 1710 were kindly supplied by Leigh Shaw-Taylor and Peter Kitson and come from part of the research being undertaken as part of the 'Occupational Structure of England and Wales *c.* 1379 to *c.* 1729' project funded by the Leverhulme Trust.

[91] Mark Overton, Jane Whittle, Darron Dean and Andrew Hann, *Production and Consumption in English Households, 1600–1750* (Abingdon, 2004), p. 188.

2 What did labourers eat?

Beef the best of which is *English* bred and fed ... is hard of conction [digestion], thick, flesh, it doth not easily pass through the Veins ... the frequent use thereof causeth dry and melancholly humours, without exercise and labour of body, especially if it be old Cow Beef or Oxe Beef, that with labour and much working hath contracted drynes and hardness of Flesh ... above all meats it is most profitable for laborious people ... and gives much strength where it is concocted by labour.'

John Archer, *Every Man His Own Doctor*, 1671[1]

Though never so much a good huswife doth care,
That such as doe labour have husbandlie fare.
Yet feed them and cram them til purse doe lack chinke,
No spoone meat, no bellifull, labourers thinke.

Thomas Tusser, *Five Hundred Points of Good Husbandry*, 1573[2]

It makes sense to begin any discussion of labouring families' standard of living with food, since it formed the greatest part of their expenditure. Food generally comprised up to 70–75 per cent of a pauper or labouring family's yearly expenditure. In the mid-eighteenth century, for instance, food for a very poor family of five from Berkshire would have cost between £9 and £13 a year, and between £24 and £43 for a well-employed family of nine people.[3] In contrast the median value of the household goods listed in labourers' probate inventories from the eighteenth century was only £9 12s, and the value of their farm equipment and stock only £3.[4] Furthermore, these were goods collected over their lifetimes, together with what they had inherited. But regardless of such considerations, food is an important topic in its own right. Its production and consumption at this time was central to the economy, as well as to the social life and health of all members of society. Oddly, though, the history of food is somewhat of a Cinderella in the historiography of early

---

[1] John Archer, *Every Man His Own Doctor* (London 1671), pp. 27–8.
[2] Thomas Tusser, *Five Hundred Points of Good Husbandry* (Oxford, 1984), p. 95.
[3] See Table 5.3 below. Shammas, *Pre-Industrial Consumer*, pp. 124–5; Wrightson and Levine, *Poverty and Piety*, p. 40.
[4] See Tables 3.11, 3.13 and 4.6 below.

modern English social and economic history. Although the productivity of arable farming and the breeding of livestock has been a hotly debated and much written about topic in recent years, how it was consumed had received little attention, apart from the work of Sarah Pennell, until the publication of Joan Thirsk's *Food in Early Modern England* in 2007.[5] Before this the standard general book was Drummond and Wilbraham's *The Englishman's Food* originally published in 1939 and still in print.[6] In contrast, there is a lively literature on food in England for the Middle Ages and for the nineteenth and twentieth centuries.[7] In addition, two excellent books have been written on diet in Ireland and Scotland. Clarkson and Crawford's *Feast and Famine* deals with food in Ireland over the long term from 1500 to 1920 and examines such things as the diets of different classes, the types of food cultivated and the nutritional value of such food; while Gibson and Smout's *Prices, Food and Wages in Scotland 1550–1780* looks at food consumption and nutrition of the poor through various diets, as well as providing a history of wage and price information for Scotland to match English price series. The history of food in England has generally also been left out of the literature on consumption, unlike in France, where it forms an integral part of the work of Fernand Braudel and more recently that of Daniel Roche.[8]

Drummond and Wilbraham's book examined examples of the amount of different sorts of food consumed by different classes and how it was prepared, together with an analysis of nutrition and disease. Indeed, nutrition can be said to be the main focus of the book. Before his mysterious murder in France in 1952 Drummond was a professor of biochemistry at University College London and a scientific adviser to the Ministry of Food in World War II. The book is representative of the tremendous scientific interest in the measurement of nutrition in the 1930s and 1940s. It is still in many ways the most valuable book to read

---

[5] Joan Thirsk, *Food in Early Modern England: Phases, Fads, Fashions 1500–1760* (London, 2007); J. C. Drummond and Anne Wilbraham, *The Englishman's Food: Five Centuries of English Diet* (Oxford, 2001). Sarah Pennell 'The Material Culture of Food in Early Modern England, circa 1650–1750', University of Oxford D.Phil. thesis, 1997. On the debate over agrarian production see Mark Overton, *Agricultural Revolution in England: The Transformation of the Agrarian Economy 1500–1850* (Cambridge, 1996), chs.3 and 4.

[6] Gibson and Smout, *Food and Wages in Scotland*; Clarkson and Crawford, *Feast and Famine*.

[7] See, for instance, Dyer, *Standards of Living*; John Burnett, *Plenty and Want: A Social History of Diet in England from 1815 to the Present Day* (London, 1979); Derek Oddy, *From Plain Fare to Fusion food: British Diet From the 1890s to the 1990s* (Woodbridge, 2003).

[8] Fernand Braudel, *Civilization and Capitalism*, I, *The Structures of Everyday Life* (New York, 1981), chs. 2–3. Daniel Roche, *A History of Everyday Things: The Birth of Consumption in France, 1600–1800* (Cambridge, 2000), ch. 9. A notable exception is Peter Clark's *The English Alehouse: A Social History 1200–1830* (London, 1983).

on food, and its style is a model of concision. However, since it covered five centuries from 1500 to the First World War there are inevitably limitations. Joan Thirsk's more recent book is a much more comprehensive study of the early modern literature on food, as well as being a compendium of examples of cooking and eating. Her main theme is the change in the types of food eaten over time, as well as changes in its preparation, and the book is especially valuable in charting the introduction and diffusion of foreign foods. However, unlike Drummond and Wilbraham (or more recently Clarkson and Crawford or Gibson and Smout), Thirsk is not interested in nutrition, but rather in contemporary attitudes to what was eaten. She also has some examples of poor people's diet but inevitably most examples come from the tables of the well-to-do. Pennell's doctoral thesis is also very valuable in examining changes in food preparation by looking at equipment found in kitchens and how this was related to the dissemination of recipes in manuscript and increasingly print by the second half of the seventeenth century.[9]

Apart from the sections in Drummond and Wilbraham and Thirsk, almost all other work dealing with the diet of the poor looks at it only in terms of cost in order to compose a so-called 'basket of consumables' to construct a real wage series. In this chapter I will go much further than this to examine the place of food in the working lives of labourers. In the first section of this chapter contemporary books and pamphlets will be examined to see what their authors had to say about what the poor ate. Then I will examine individual foodstuffs – bread, beer, meat, dairy products, fruit, vegetables and spices – looking at how they were prepared as well as regional differences in their consumption. Finally, I will also look at the nutritional and calorific content of some of this prepared food. This will be done to prepare for the next chapter, where account books and institutional diets will be used to measure the calorific intake and nutritional value of actual food eaten.[10]

Work and health

Like today, contemporary writing on food was preoccupied with the question of what was healthy to eat. But unlike today, where the properties

---

[9] Pennell 'The Material Culture of Food'. There have also been a number of very useful books on recipes and cooking by historians such as Peter Brears who are interested in recreating actual historical methods of preparation.

[10] See, for instance, Woodward, *Men at Work*, pp. 2, 15–18, and Shammas, *Pre-Industrial Consumer*, ch. 5. Both Shammas and Robert Fogel look specifically at calorific consumption and concentrate on what they see as the nutritional shortfall of the diets of the very poor in the late eighteenth century, which will be discussed in more detail in the next chapter.

which make a food healthy are very distinct from those which provide taste and pleasure, in the early modern period the taste and texture of the food were what was considered to give it its healthy or unhealthy qualities. Today, for instance, it is understood that the fat and cholesterol in a Stilton cheese can cause cardio-vascular and heart disease if consumed in too great quantities, but at the same time give the cheese its texture and much of its taste. Similarly we know the vitamin content of foods and what we need to eat to optimise our health. Modern nutrition is based on the accumulation of scientific research and observation of cause and effect in eating and disease, much of which is ongoing and has a great influence on the culture of eating, as for instance claims about how too much salt may be unhealthy, or whether vegetable-fat margarine is more healthy than butter. With such knowledge historians of food have looked at the possible nutritional effects of past diets to see whether there were vitamin deficiencies leading to such diseases as rickets or scurvy.[11]

If anything, early modern people were even more concerned with the link between health and diet than we are, but their frame of understanding was based on the completely different classical Galenic model of humoral physiology. In this system, health consisted of a balance between four humours in the body: blood, which was hot and moist; choler, which was hot and dry; phlegm, which was cold and moist; and bile or melancholy, which was cold and dry. Different people might have different 'complexions' of humours and tend towards one or the other, but health was considered to be an ideal balance of all in a right proportion, in keeping with classical ideas of avoiding extremes. These humours were considered to have fluid properties within the body which affected people's emotional well-being and motivations, as well as general health, and they could be affected by many external stimuli, including air, exercise, work, food and supernatural forces such as the position of the planets.[12] For instance, scholars and students were considered especially prone to melancholy if they spent too much time reading and did not get enough exercise.[13]

Both astrology and medicinal cures were thought to work through such principles, but by far the most important consideration when considering physical health was food, as eating could be undertaken with

---

[11] Drummond and Wilbraham, *Englishman's Food*, pp. 121–68; Clarkson and Crawford, *Feast and Famine*, ch. 8; Shammas, *Pre-Industrial Consumer*, pp. 136–48.

[12] Drummond and Wilbraham, *Englishman's Food*, ch. 4; Andrew Wear, *Knowledge and Practice in English Medicine 1550–1680* (Cambridge, 2000), pp. 37ff.

[13] Richard Burton, *Anatomy of Melancholy*, ed. Thomas C. Faulkner, Nicolas K. Kiessling and Rhonda L. Blair (Oxford, 1989), I, pp. 211–28, 242–5.

preventive medicine in mind, just as it is today. Food was thought of in terms of hot and cold or wet and dry, but also in terms of texture, such as heaviness, lightness, toughness or sliminess, which would have an effect on one's health. From the 1470s to the late seventeenth century there was an outpouring of dietary literature all over Europe which formed part of the general literature on health, the number of publications on which was also prodigious.[14] This literature has been analysed by Ken Albala in his book *Eating Right in the Renaissance*, which charts it through three periods. He begins with the first publications, which were written for Italian Renaissance princely patrons and were heavily dependent on medieval Arab and Jewish texts. He then moves to the early sixteenth century revival of Galen and a whole corpus of Greek medical thought, and ends by demonstrating how strict Galenic ideas were modified and adapted to local customs in the late sixteenth and seventeenth centuries.[15] Looking further ahead in time to the eighteenth century, such notions began to decline as increased anatomical knowledge cast doubt on the humours. The humeral system was increasingly supplanted by more emphasis on pills and doses of medicine based on what would now be considered an equally spurious theory of the chemical basis of meals and their effect on digestion.[16]

What is most striking about the Galenic literature is how it dealt with flavour almost entirely in terms of health rather than palatability or olfactory pleasure. Albala deals with the full complexity of this system and there is no need to repeat it in detail here, but some examples will suffice to provide, as it were, a flavour of the system. Thus, sweetness indicated heat and moisture and had a powerful attractiveness to our bodies, especially to newborns. In contrast, bitter foods were the opposite of sweet foods and were not naturally nutritious, being cold and dry. Hot flavours were also considered to be very dry. Foods were effective in 'degrees' from the first (mildest) to third (strongest), and this survives in our expression to experience the 'third degree' of something. Thus parsley and cloves were considered to be both hot and dry in the third degree, indicating that they were foods which had to be modified by combining them with other food.[17] For instance, hot and dry pepper could be used to render cold and moist fish more temperate

---

[14] Mary Fissell has estimated that 2,500 editions of popular medical texts were published between 1641 and 1800, many of which also mixed cookery with medical advice and recipes for medicine. Mary Fissell, 'The Marketplace of Print', in Mark Jenner and Patrick Wallis (eds.), *Medicine and the Market in England and Its Colonies, c. 1450–c. 1850* (London, 2007), pp. 108–32.

[15] Ken Albala, *Eating Right in the Renaissance* (Berkeley, 2002).

[16] Wear, *English Medicine*, chs. 8–9.   [17] Albala, *Eating Right*, pp. 82ff.

for a phlegmatic person.[18] One author gave this typical sort of advice on cucumbers:

Cucumbers growing in hot grounds and well ripened with the Sun are neither moist nor cold in the second degree. They agree well with hot stomachs being eaten with vinegar, salt, oil, and pepper: but if you boil them (whilst they are still young) with white-wine, vervin, dill, and salt liquor, they are not a bad nourishment (as *Galen* took them) but engender good humors, and settle a very cold weak stomach.

Likewise of butter he claimed:

Butter is hot and moist, of gros nourishment, softning rather then corroborating the stomack, hastening meat into the belly before it be concocted … it is best at breakfast, tollerable in the beginning of dinner; but at supper no way good, because it hinderesth sleep, and sendeth up unpleasant vapours to anoy the brain … Weak stomacks are to eschue all fat, oily, and buttered meats, especially when they swim in butter; for naturally butter swimeth aloft, and consequently hindereth the stomacks closing, wherby concoction [digestion] is foreslowed.[19]

The diaries of people such as Ralph Josselin or Samuel Pepys bear witness to the same thinking. For instance Samuel Pepys worried that some pain he suffered had been caused by drinking cold small beer in a cold room in a tavern.[20] Josselin noted once that 'Such and aboundance of cherries, brought by carts … a sickly fruite, and great sickness feared.'[21]

Much of this advice was common to books published in different countries, but local authors were always willing to find a way to alter strict Galenic principals to accommodate regional difference. William Harrison, in his *Description of England* of 1577, for instance, thought that the situation of England 'lying near unto the north, doth cause the heat of our stomachs to be of somewhat greater force; therefore our bodies do crave a little more ample nourishment than the inhabitants in the hotter regions are accustomed withal'.[22] From the 1530s important English authors participated in the intellectual revival of Galenic ideas as part of the general humanist movement of the late Henrician

---

[18] Ibid., pp. 88–9.
[19] Thomas Moffet, *Health's Improvement: or, Rules Comprizing and Discovering the Nature, Method, and Manner of Preparing All Sorts of Food Used in This Nation* (London, 1655) pp. 129–30, 218.
[20] Robert Latham and William Mathews (eds.), *The Diary of Samuel Pepys* (London, 1970–1983), VI, p. 386.
[21] Alan Macfarlane (ed.), *The Diary of Ralph Josselin, 1616–1683* (Oxford, 1976), p. 510.
[22] Harrison, *Description*, p. 123; Albala, *Eating Right*, ch. 7.

period. Thomas Elyot, for instance, who wrote the very influential humanist text *The Boke of the Governor*, also wrote the *Castle of Helthe* around 1539.[23] Other popular pamphlets of this period on diet and health were the travelling physician Andrew Boorde's *A compendyous Regymnet or a Dyetary of Helth* (1542) and *Breviary of Health*, a self-help book of remedies and preventives. Notable works from Albala's second period which stressed local customs were William Bulleyn's *A Newe Booke Entitled the Government of Healthe* (1558), Thomas Cogan's *The Haven of Health* (1589) and, most comprehensively, Thomas Moffet's *Health's Improvement: or Rules Comprizing and Discovering the Nature, and Manner of Preparing All Sorts of Food* (1655). The seventeenth century also saw the publication of smaller pamphlets for the use of poorer families such as Thomas Cock's *Kitchen Physick: or Advice to the Poor ... with Rules and Directions, How to Prevent Sickness, and Cure Diseases by Diet* (1676) and the new genre of books of 'receipts' and food preparation aimed to help housewives prepare meals rather than advising on health, such as *A Proper New Booke of Cookery* (1575), Thomas Dawson's *A Book of Cookery, and the Order of Meats to Be Served to the Table, Both for Flesh and Fish Dayes* (1650). By the eighteenth century, although the genre of Galenic diet advice manuals was declining, books on diets and health such as Francis de Valangin's *A Treatise on Diet, or the Management of Human Life; by Physicians* (1768) show that Galenic ideas were still a part of popular consciousness, but most writing on food was now done through the genre of cookery books, the number of which increased considerably after the Restoration, such as William Rabisha's *The Whole Body of Cookery Dissected* (1673), *The Compleat Cook: Or the Whole Art of Cookery* (1694) and the work of Hannah Wooley.[24]

Much of this literature was aimed at wealthy readers, with advice on the nature of venison or imported exotic fruit such as pineapples and recipes which called for much sugar and imported spices like nutmeg and ginger. But even the most sophisticated recipe books had preparations for pottage and contained recipes and advice on fruit and herbs which grew commonly in England. In addition books on health also mentioned what was healthy for labourers, not so much because this was an intended audience for these authors, but because farm servants would have been fed by many yeoman and gentry families. One of the

---

[23] Muldrew, *Economy of Obligation*, pp. 133–4.
[24] Wear, *Knowledge and Practice*, chs. 8–9. Roy Porter, *The Greatest Benefit to Mankind: A Medical History of Humanity from Antiquity to the Present* (London, 1997), ch. 10. On the diffusion of recipes see Pennell, 'Material Culture of Food', ch. 3.

earliest, Andrew Boorde's *Dyetary of Health*, introduced the importance of meat in the English diet in this way:

> Beefe is a good meate for an Englysshe man, so be it the beest be yonge ... yf it be moderatly powdered that the groose blode by salt may be exhaustyd, it doth make an Englysshe man stronge ... Veal is nutrytyue meate: and doth nowrysshe moche a man, for it is soone dygstyd ... Bacon is good for carters and plowmen, the whiche be ever labouringe in the earth or dung ... Potage is not so moch used in al Crystendom as it is used in Englande. Potage is made of the lyquor in which fleshe is soden in, with puttyng-to chopped herbs and otemel and salt ... there is not so muche pleasure for harte and hynde, bucke and doo ... as in England, and although the flesshe be disparaysed in physycke I pray god to send me part of the flesshe to eate physcke notwithstanding ... it is a meate for great men. And great men do not set so moch by ye meate as they do by the pastyme of kyllying of it.[25]

The emphasis here on meat is typical of sixteenth-century writing, but this passage is more notable in that diet for both lords and labourers is described in the same paragraph, and fortunately from this literature we can extract much advice on what was considered healthy for the poor to eat.

Since much of this advice is very similar, I will concentrate on describing what the most comprehensive of these tracts, Thomas Moffet's *Health's Improvement*, had to say, with reference to some other works. Moffet (or Muffett) was an Elizabethan physician and naturalist who studied under John Caius at Cambridge in the 1570s. Like Boorde and other sixteenth-century physicians he spent much time travelling on the continent learning from other physicians before returning to England in 1580, working as a physician first in Ipswich and then in London. By the early 1590s he had been persuaded by one of his patients, Mary Herbert, the Earl of Pembroke's wife, to leave London and move to their estate in Wiltshire, where he was given the manor house of Bulbridge and where he spent his remaining days until 1604. It was here that he wrote *Health's Improvement*, combining his medical knowledge with his new concerns as a landlord farmer. This circulated in manuscript during his lifetime, but was not formally published until 1655, 'corrected and enlarged' by Christopher Bennett, a member of the College of Physicians. Bennett also wrote medical treatises and pamphlets on silkworms, insects and fish.[26] Moffet had a daughter named Patience, and it is sometimes claimed that the nursery rhyme 'Little Miss Muffett'

---

[25] Andrew Boorde, *A Compendyous Regymnet or a Dyetary of Health* (London, 1542), ch. 16.

[26] Victor Houliston, 'Moffet, Thomas (1553–1604)', *Oxford Dictionary of National Biography* (Oxford, 2004), www.oxforddnb.com/view/article/18877, accessed 19 March 2009.

refers to her, as he both wrote about insects and advocated the health of curd cheese over harder cheese, the eating of which by non-labouring people 'stoppeth the Liver, engendereth choler, melancholy, and the stone, lieth long in the stomack undigested, procureth thirst, maketh a stinking breath and a scurvy skin'.[27]

Moffet began his instructions by defining diet as 'an exact order in Labour, Meat, Drink Sleep and Venery ... Labor was appointed formost to invite meat and drink: they to draw on sleep, for the ease of our labours.'[28] 'Meat' here is being used in its broader contemporary sense of food as opposed to drink, rather than just flesh. Contemporaries also referred to 'white meat' meaning dairy products and sometimes veal and poultry; however, I will use 'meat' in its modern sense. It is noteworthy that labour is accorded a central place in the conception of diet as exercise was considered necessary for good health. In 1671 John Archer wrote a pamphlet on health entitled *Every Man His Own Doctor* based on Galenic principles showing how everyone could know his own 'complecion' and be his own doctor 'in a Dietical way'. Here he argued:

Exercise is of it self, sufficient to keep the body from Diseases, because it brings a solidity and hardness to the parts of the body, that they that use exercise moderately, need little other Physick, this makes the labouring mans sleep sweet, and pleasant, this shews the Justice of divine providence distributing the happiness ... of all Ranks of men, for they that are poor and forced to labour, are recompensed with the rich Jewel of health.[29]

Diet also had to be organised economically within a household by giving each member proper amounts, as Moffet pointed out: 'giving (like a wise Steward) every part his allowance by geometrical proportion, that the whole household and family may be kept in health'.[30]

We should take those kinds of meats which are best for our own particular bodies, for our own particular age, temperature, distemperature and complexion ... so labourers and idle persons, children and striplings, old men and young men, cold and hot bodies, phlegmatick and cholerick complexions must have divrs Diets.

Young, hot, strong and labouring men's stomachs may feed of meats, giving both an hard and a gros juice (as beife, bacon, poudred-fleash and fish, hard cheese, rye-bread and hard egs, etc.) which may nourish slowly, and be concocted by degrees; for if they should eat things of light nourishment (as veal, lamb, capons, chickens, poacht-egs, partridges, pheasants, plovers, etc.) either their meat would be too soon digested, or else wholy converted into choler.[31]

[27] Moffet, *Health's Improvement*, p. 131.   [28] Ibid., p. 1.
[29] Archer, *Every Man His Own Doctor*, pp. 97–8; Moffet, *Health's Improvement*, p. 255.
[30] Moffet, *Health's Improvement*, p. 7.
[31] Ibid., pp. 285–6. 'Concoction' means digestion.

A full diet was recommended for those who were young and 'strong, lusty, and able through their good constitution to endure much exercise', whereas a moderate diet was for those of middle health and not too strong or weak.[32] In addition, occupation and wealth also created conditions which required different diets. When describing the difference between 'meats' (foodstuffs) he recommended those of 'thin and light' substance for 'idle citizens' and 'tender persons', which consisted of things such as young pheasants and little fishes, whereas food that was more 'gross, tough, and hard' was suited

chiefly to country persons and hard labourers: but secondarily to all that be strong of nature, given by trade or use to much exercise, and accustomed to feed upon them; as poudered beife, bacon, goose, swan, saltfish, ling, tunnis, salt samon, cucumbers, turneps, beans, hard peaze, hard cheese, brown and rye bread.[33]

Finally, like Boorde, Moffet described the national preference for beef, not as something marking the wealth of the gentry or aristocracy, but as something needed for labour. Moffet pointed to beef as 'of all meats [food] most nourishing unto English bodies'. By this he meant 'the youngest, fattest, and best grown Ox, having awhile first been exercised in wain or plough to dispel his foggie moisture'. He claimed that 'for sound men, and those that labour or use exercise, there is not a better meat under the Sun for an English man; so that it be also corned with salt before it be roasted'.[34] John Archer advanced a similar argument in the extract quoted at the head of this chapter.

Moffet recommended mutton to all people, but sow's flesh, 'sweetly dieted with roots, corn and whey', was specifically stated to be 'good and tolerable meat for strong stomacks'. Rabbits were also good 'for the poors maintenance' but pheasants 'to strong stomacks it is inconvenient, especially to Ploughmen and labourers'. Fresh fish was not highly recommended by Moffet as a nourishing dish, especially fish that was caught in ponds or slow-running rivers as they were thought to be of a nature akin to what they ate, which was slimy and dirty like the water and mud they lived in. In contrast, salted seafish such as cod and ling was thought to be good for labourers as the salt dried the moist flesh for their strong stomachs.[35]

These sorts of recommendations of coarser food for digestions toughened by hard work continued when Moffet came to discuss bread and other foods. He recognised that bread was necessary for energy from experience, even knowing nothing about carbohydrates: 'Bread doth

[32] Ibid., p. 8.   [33] Ibid., p. 32.   [34] Ibid., p. 59.
[35] Ibid., pp. 68, 76–7, 94, 141–2, 170.

of all things best nourish and strengthen … insomuch that with a little Bread they are enabled for a whole dayes journey, when with twice as much meat they would have fainted.'[36] Bread was the 'meat of meats' and '*Wheaten-bread* … generally the best for all stomachs.'[37] Rye he called a 'wild kind of wheate, meet for Labourers, Servants and Workmen, but heavy of digestion to indifferent stomachs'.[38] It was of a 'cold hard concoction' which bred 'wind and grippings in the belly' whereas wheaten bread was the 'best for all stomachs'. Barley bread was also 'tough and heavy of digestion, choking the small veins, engendering crudities'. However, he acknowledged the healthiness of oats, contradicting Galen, who claimed they were fit only for assess and horses, pointing out that if Galen had seen the oat cakes and oatmeal of the north of England he would have been convinced they were also meat for 'tall, fair and strong men and women of all callings'. Although Moffet did not discuss drink, as he intended to write a separate tract on the subject, which, if it was written, has not survived, he mentioned barley, which when made into malt, 'proveth meat, drink and cloth to the poorer sort'.[39]

Moffet also went through a long list of vegetables ('fruits of the garden') and orchard fruits which were consumed in England, noting that the poor ate apples, pears and other orchard fruit, but especially blackberries. Leeks, he noted, were 'esteemed so wholesome and nourishing in our Country, that few thinke any good Pottage can be made without them', although as they were hot he advised soaking them first in milk and to cook them with other meat.[40] Carrots, parsnips and turnips were all mentioned as root vegetables suitable for boiling with meat, although, surprisingly at such an early date, roast turnips were also mentioned. Lettuce was popular, as Galen had especially recommended it as a vegetable he himself had eaten to delay the heat of his stomach. Moffet recommended cooking it unless one had a strong stomach, but since salads were popular, he said it could be eaten raw mixed with a little tarragon and fennel as long as one didn't wash it, which would remove the most nourishing part near the skin. Additionally labourers' stomachs were able to tolerate such hot vegetables as raw onions and garlic, which were not recommended for medium diets unless well cooked. 'Rustics' were also noted as being able to safely eat radishes raw.[41]

For the most part it might seem that the system of dietary health outlined here conveniently justified the recommendation of cheaper food for the poorer sort such as oats, rye bread, leeks and onions, by equating coarseness with working or 'strong' stomachs, reflecting an essential

---

[36] Ibid., p. 235.   [37] Ibid., pp. 236, 239.   [38] Ibid., p. 231.
[39] Ibid., pp. 231–3, 239. Albala, *Eating Right*, ch. 7.
[40] Moffet, *Health's Improvement*, p. 222.   [41] Ibid., pp. 225–6.

social division that went back to classical times. But as Albala argues, Galenic essentials could always be modified to suit local or national preferences. Thus, beef as central to the labourer's diet was justified as a national characteristic, contrary to what modern stereotypes might lead us to believe.

Regional variation and change over time will be examined more closely below in the sections on individual food types, but before going on to this it is worth examining the author William Ellis in some detail, as he had much to say about labourers' diet from a practical point of view, and from a later period. From his work we can get a better sense of how food was eaten than from the more theoretical medical literature. Ellis began his career as a customs officer and then worked in the brewing industry before buying a farm near Hemel Hempstead in Hertfordshire with money from his second wife. Ellis became one of the first of the popular advocates of agricultural improvement in the eighteenth century and published eight volumes of *The Modern Husbandman* in instalments during 1730s and 1740s. This made him famous, and as a result he was invited to view farming methods in different parts of the country. He also wrote on brewing and cider making.[42]

Ellis's rather longwinded tract *The Country Housewife's Family Companion*, published in 1750, took a less modern form, that of the household advice manual. In intent it is similar to Gervase Markham's *The English Housewife*, published in 1625 and also written by someone who took up farming later in life, which provided advice on cooking, gardening, brewing and cloth production.[43] Ellis, though, organised his tract around advice aiming to make the running of a farm household by the wife more economically efficient. He did this by supplying information on the best ways of preparing food he had gleaned from his travels, and by analysing the way his wife ran their own farm household. He addressed it to 'the Country Gentleman's, the yeoman's, the Farmer's, the Labourers' wives, and Others', and it does indeed contain much advice for poor housewives, as well as advice for wealthier farmers on how to feed servants.[44] It is also a compendium of what sorts of food were grown and eaten in England by the mid-eighteenth century. But rather than discussing such foods in terms of health, he focused on their popularity and especially on local methods of preparation, primarily on

[42] Anne Pimlott Baker, 'Ellis, William (*c.* 1700–1758)', *Oxford Dictionary of National Biography* (Oxford, 2004), www.oxforddnb.com/view/article/8718, accessed 19 March 2009; R. C. Richardson, 'Metropolitan Counties: Bedfordshire, Hertfordshire, and Middlesex', in *AHEW*, V.I, pp. 263–5; Thirsk, *Food*, pp. 167–9.

[43] Thirsk, *Food*, pp. 91–3.

[44] William Ellis, *The Country Housewife's Family Companion* (London, 1750), p. 1.

small farms in Hertfordshire, but also elsewhere in England. What he had to say about individual foods, such as the salting of pork, making oatmeal puddings or using vegetables in the boiling of beef, I will discuss in the specific sections on these foods. Here I will focus on some of the general comments he made on how servants in husbandry should be fed, and what sort of foods day labourers' wives were able to afford and prepare.

In numerous incidental comments about the feeding of servants, Ellis makes clear the importance of feeding and treating servants well if a farmer wanted to attract the best workers to employ on a yearly live-in basis. He cited the case of a neighbouring farmer who 'disgraced himself' by trying to save money when he went into debt by making his servants' apple pasties – which locally it was common to take into the field to eat – with the stalks and cores of the apples included and using water and suet instead of skimmed milk and yeast to make the crust. As a result 'he could hardly get a good Servant to live with him, and those that did, grumbled much, and worked the worser for it'.[45] Of food for his own servants Ellis noted that they should normally live on a 'piece of Bacon or pickled Pork, and a Pudding or Apple Dumplins for Dinners and Suppers'.[46]

He was a great advocate of serving pork to servants rather than beef, except at harvest time. He advocated pork as an element of economy, as he thought a farmer's wife could feed a pig more cheaply and then slaughter it, rather than buying fresh beef at the butcher each week. He also wrote that pork kept better when it was salted than beef, and of course could also be preserved as bacon or dried ham.[47] He quoted an unnamed 'eminent Physician' who claimed that swine's flesh was most nourishing to those 'in their flourishing Age, sound and strong, who are excised with much Labour'.[48] As we have seen, he could have taken this from Moffet or a similar tract, but he rather conveniently neglected to mention that beef was cited as being just as 'nourishing' for labourers. But whatever the possible advantages of pork over beef, he took it as given that servants needed to eat meat, and he did not mention fish or fast days. He also noted that the common means of preparing meat was boiling it with vegetables such as broad beans, peas, carrots, turnips, celery, potatoes, cabbages, onions or using bacon to make boiled puddings. He especially noted what he called 'Welch Onions', or leeks, which 'so relishes fat bacon or salt Pork, that the Men often eat it with a good Stomach to the saving of much Expence in the Consumption

[45] Ibid., p. 45.   [46] Ibid., p. vi.   [47] See below, p. 88.
[48] Ellis, *Country Housewife*, p. 51.

of beef and other Meat'. Herbs such as parsley, thyme and savory were also recommended.[49]

In addition to meat, Ellis also noted how common boiled puddings were as food for labourers:

PUDDING is so necessary a Part of an *Englishman's* Food, that it and Beef are accounted the victuals they most love. Pudding is so natural to our Harvest-men, that without it they think they cannot make an agreeable Dinner.[50]

His maidservant made a plain pudding from a pint of new milk, flour, egg, salt and ginger boiled for one and a half to two hours to be ready when the ploughman and boy came in from work and served it with a sauce of sugar and milk together. For a better pudding she used grated bread and suet with sugar, ginger, nutmeg and flour. He claimed that with 'such a Pudding and a Piece of Pickled [salted] Pork boiled, my Family makes a Dinner to their Satisfaction; for where they eat one Pound of Bacon, they eat more than fifty of pickled Pork'. The puddings here were evidently seen as a replacement for bread, as they are always said to be eaten with meat. He also provided a number of recipes for different puddings, including apple pudding, hasty pudding and rice pudding. For harvest he made plum pudding, which was the most expensive as it used half to three-quarters of a pound of raisins as well as spices.[51]

However, not all farmers were as generous as Ellis claimed to be. Another neighbouring farmer fed his servants and labourers on cheaper fare. He rented a farm at £160 a year and kept two taskers (general servants in husbandry), two ploughmen, a shepherd and a horse keeper, besides hiring several day labourers. He fed them most days with just two boiled puddings made with wheat flour, ginger and skimmed milk, together with a piece of bacon or a calf's pluck (a piece of offal).[52] If a family wanted to save money by serving less meat, Ellis recommended pancakes, which could also save time and fuel in preparation. Servants could be served with plain pancakes as 'a light and pleasant Diet, for either Breakfast, Dinner, or Supper. And ... a proper Sort may be made for both Masters and Servants Uses.' These were not intended as food for hard work, and the plainest sort were made much like modern pancakes flavoured with powdered ginger and eaten with sugar. They could also be made with apples or with pieces of bacon to 'fill our plowmens and others bellies instead of intire flesh'. In comparison, the recipes for pancakes for rich people included more eggs and spices such

---

[49] Ibid., pp. 49–51.   [50] Ibid., p. 33.   [51] Ibid., pp. 33–6.   [52] Ibid., pp. 35–7.

as cinnamon, nutmeg and mace, or other ingredients such as rosewater or sack.[53]

For harvest, however, a much more substantial diet was required. In part this was because the men were working much harder (as we shall see in chapter 5 women were also hired in harvest, but Ellis only discusses men), but also because the demand for labour in areas of corn husbandry was very intense. In Hertfordshire, he claimed that men were hired long before harvest 'by Way of Security' and they were given 30 to 36s for a month (although they could be kept up to two months if the harvest required) besides victualling and lodging. He noted that those housewives who could provide harvest food most cheaply and satisfactorily were accounted the best, and

[t]hat gentleman, Yeoman, or Farmer, manages best, who victuals his Harvestmen with Beef, Bacon, or pickled Pork, Beans, Pease, Puddings, Pyes, Pasties, Cheese, Milk, with other culinary Preparations, and with well brew'd strong and small Beer and Ale; for such a one stands the best Chance of hiring the best Hands, that will go on briskly with their Work, and do a good deal of it in Day.[54]

These harvest workers would have been day labourers for the rest of the year, and although it was possible that they would have been fed at work, their continuous employment was not guaranteed, and their wives would still have had to feed themselves and their children from family earnings. Unfortunately Ellis never discussed the regular family diet prepared by a day labourer's wife, but mentions how often they were forced to save money in hard times when the price of wheat was high or employment irregular. He described one labourer's, or 'Daysman's', wife who normally baked wheaten bread for her husband and five children. She baked a bushel of flour every 10 days for her family, which works out to about 1.2 lb for the husband per day (see below p. 119), but as her money was short and yeast expensive she had to save her own from one baking to the next.[55] During the great frost of 1740 which began at Christmas and held for three months, ruining that year's wheat crop in Hertfordshire, wheat sold for 7 to 8s a bushel (a more normal price in the 1730s would have been 2 to 4s). At this time Ellis reported that many of the poor were forced to grind barley into meal and bake bread from it as a replacement for wheat or rye.[56] Even in years of lower prices, other poor day labourers' families often used barley to save money in piecrusts or pancakes. One wife of a labourer who worked for Ellis threshing and hedging, who had four children, mixed barley and wheat meal together to make bread, but added skimmed milk

---

[53] Ibid., pp. 27–30.   [54] Ibid., pp. 47–8.   [55] Ibid., pp. 16–17.   [56] Ibid., pp. 24, 26.

and more yeast to make the bread 'whiter and eat sweeter'. Another told him that 'most of the poor Men's families in her Neighbourhood made use of Barley-Meal for the greatest part of their Subsistence', but that her husband had grown fat on grilled barleymeal cakes and on barleymeal puddings.[57] Ellis never mentioned oats as a replacement food for wheaten bread, although in the diets of some southern workhouses porridge was listed as being served regularly.[58]

He also noted that poor housewives without cows often had to save fat from swine, or lard from a butcher, to use when they could not afford to buy butter, and were often also forced to use skimmed milk, which implies that they were forced to go without meat for some period of time.[59] His assumption that the poor did not always have access to milk implies that many poor families in the county did not have cows to make butter and cheese, even though the area to the north and west of Little Gaddesden where Ellis had his farm was dairy pasture. However, it was reported by a Swedish visitor in 1748 that the parish was all enclosed, and given the town's proximity to London (it was about 30 miles distant) the cost of pasture must have been too high for the poor. It was also an area where much barley was grown and malted for London brewers and most of the oats grown would have been for animals, either those being fattened for London markets or for the large number of horses in the metropolis which had to be fed, which is probably why Ellis does not record the poor eating much oatmeal in harder years.[60]

Finally, Ellis provided a very detailed description of when a labourer ate his meals. On normal days labourers ate four times. Moffet also noted that 'labourers and workmen [need] to feed often (yea four or five times a day if their work be ground-work or very toilsome) because continual spending of humours and spirits, challenge an often restoring of the like by meat and drink'.[61] Ellis, though, did not mention time allotted for sleep after the midday meal, which was common and recommended by Moffet. Meals could be taken in the field as well as in the farmer's house. Ellis's description is for the harvest and warrants quoting in full; however, he also noted that such a diet was advisable for other sorts of hard work that men might do in the summer. In addition the poor would have been treated to seasonal feasts by their employers at New Year and after the harvest. He stated:

In Wheat Harvest Time ... our Men set out for the Field by four of the Clock in the Morning, and return Home about eight at Night. In *Lent* Grain Harvest

[57] Ibid., pp. 23–4, 26–7.   [58] See below, pp. 61.
[59] Ellis, *Country Housewife*, pp. 25–6.
[60] Richardson, 'Metropolitan Counties', pp. 263–5.
[61] Moffet, *Health's Improvement*, p. 292.

Time later in a Morning, and sooner at Night as the Days are shorter. In either, the Men generally eat five times a Day: At their first setting out, they eat a little Bread and Cheese or Apple-pye, with a Draught of small Beer, or half a Pint of strong each Man, in Part of his Quart for one Day: At eight o'Clock some send, for Breakfast, boiled Milk crumbled with Bread; others, Milk-porridge with Bread; others, Posset with Bread, Bread and Cheese besides, or instead of Bread and Cheese, Apple-pasty; others send into the Field for Breakfast, hashed or minced Meat left the Day before; others send it cold (as left) but hashing or mincing is best because if it is a little tainted, it is thus taken off by a Mixture of shred Onions and Parsley, or with Butter and Vinegar, which relishes it, and makes it well suffice for a Breakfast, and now they drink only small Beer. At Dinner Time, which should be always at one O'Clock, the Victuals should be in the Field; for it was the Saying of a notable Housewife, that as the Men expected it at that Hour, if it was not brought accordingly, they would lag in their Work, and lose Time in expecting it. Broad Beans and Bacon or Pork one day, and Beef with Carrots, or Turnips or Cabbage, or Cucumbers, or Potatoes, another Day, is, with Plumb-pudding in Wheat-Harvest-Time, and Plain-pudding in *Lent* Harvest, good Dinner Victuals. But this Method of victualling Harvest-men is not a general Rule; for I know a Farmer that rents above a hundred a Year in *Hertfordshire* … who kept his Men almost a Week together on only fat Bacon and Pudding, and when at other Times his Wife only dressed Beef for Dinner, she seldom boiled it enough, on purpose to prevent the Men's eating too much … At four o'Clock in the Afternoon, is what we call Cheesing-time, that is to say, a Time when the Men sit on the Ground for half an Hour to eat Bread and Cheese with some Apple-pasty, and drink some strong Beer; then to work again, and hold it till near Eight of the Clock at Night, when all leave off and come Home to Supper, where is prepared for them, Messes of new Milk crum'd with Bread or Posset sugar'd and crumb'd with Bread, or fat Bacon or pickled [salted] Pork boiled hot with broad Beans; but although fat Bacon at Night is in common Use with some Farmers, with Roots or with Beans, yet others refuse to make this Supper Victuals, because it is apt to make Men sick. No Matter say some we must give them that which cloys their Stomachs soonest.[62]

Meals and household purchases

All in all, Ellis provides us with the best single account of how labouring families ate and how their food was prepared, and he certainly shows that labourers ate a more varied diet than common stereotypes about cheese and pottage would have us believe. But before going on to look at the preparation and consumption of individual foods for labourers, it will be useful to examine the dinners and consumption of the wealthy and middling sort to provide a context within which we can place labouring families.

[62] Ellis, *Country Housewife*, pp. 71–2.

Extracts from the household book for Lord Howard, Earl of Surrey provide a very detailed account of what was served to whom in a great household in 1523. For breakfast the earl, together with the Duke and Duchess of Norfolk and some others, ate boiled capon, beef, a breast of mutton and a chicken. Then, for the same group, dinner consisted of two boiled capons, a breast of mutton, beef, seven chevets, a swan, a pig, a breast of veal, two roast capons and a custard for the first course. The second course consisted of four messes of morts (salmon), six chickens, eight pigeons, three rabbits, two shovelers, four sepyes, twelve quails, two venison pasties, a tart with nuts and pears. Supper consisted of a rack of mutton boiled, four slices of beef, a calf side, a shoulder and breast of mutton, a capon, three chickens, three rabbits, six quails and a venison pasty. For the rest of the household eating in the hall and kitchen, including twelve gentlemen, twelve yeomen and twelve grooms, the meals consisted of similar preparations, but with the grooms listed as eating only boiled and roast beef and veal. In addition to this 130 eggs and 43 loaves of finest white bread (manchet), 27 loaves of household bread and 15 loaves of trencher bread were consumed that day, indicating that there were more servants eating than the twelve visiting grooms.[63] Although this might seem indulgent, at a banquet such consumption became spectacular. At the marriage of his daughter in 1582, Lord Burghley served, among other things, the following over the course of three days of feasting: 1,000 gallons of wine, 6 veal calves, 26 deer, 15 pigs, 14 sheep, 16 lambs, 4 kids, 6 hares, 36 swans, 2 storks, 41 turkeys, over 370 poultry, 49 curlews, 135 mallards, 354 teals, 1,049 plovers, 124 knotts, 280 stints, 109 pheasants, 277 partridges, 615 cocks, 485 snipe, 840 larks, 21 gulls, 71 rabbits, 23 pigeons and 2 sturgeon.[64]

The accounts kept by Sir Edward Coke's wife Bridget for his London household for the week beginning 21 November 1596 show her buying 176 lb of beef (25 lb per day), two quarters of veal and a side of pork for the week. She also bought 6 lb of sugar, which was very expensive at 1s a pound, a bunch of onions, a peck of salt, a peck of oatmeal, 2 pecks of wheat flour and paid the baker 34s for bread. Over the course of the week, she bought such things as capers and olives, vinegar, milk, eggs, butter every day, sack (wine), various sorts of fish such as sprats, pickerel and whiting, as well as pieces of mutton, larks, chickens, rabbits and an apple pie. The household also consumed about 500 gallons of

---

[63] These accounts were printed by Frederick Eden in an appendix to his *State of the Poor* and consist of extracts rather than the full accounts. Eden, *State of the Poor*, III, pp. cxvii–cxix.

[64] Lawrence Stone, *The Crisis of the Aristocracy, 1558–1641* (Oxford, 1965), p. 560.

ale in October, which works out to 126 gallons a week.[65] Such accounts were typical for great houses throughout our period, and although we do not know how many people were dining, these two examples give an impression of the huge amounts of meat and beer consumed, and the scale and variety of preparation required in their kitchens.

On a relatively smaller scale the meals recorded in the diary of Parson Woodforde from the mid to late eighteenth century give an indication of what wealthy yeomen would have been eating. Woodforde, who resided in Norfolk for much of his adult life, has become famous (or infamous) as a sort of eighteenth-century caricature of the fat, gluttonous parson, as he filled his diary with descriptions of food such as the following descriptions of dinner from 1782 and 1783:

We had for dinner some fresh Water Fish, Perch and trout, a Saddle of Mutton roasted, Beans and Bacon, a Couple of Fowls boiled, Patties and some white soup – 2nd Course –pigeons roasted, a Duck roasted, Piggs Petty-toes, Sweetbreads – Rasberry Cream, Tarts and Pudding and Pippins.[66]

We had for Dinner a roasted Pike, Rump of Beef boiled, a Beef Stake Pye, Mutton Stakes & rosted Bullocks Heart – 2nd Course – Fill'd Oysters, a rost Fowl, Pudding, Rammikins. After tea we played at Loo, at which I lost.[67]

We had for Dinner boiled Turkey and Oyster Sauce, a very fine Ham, Piggs Fry, and Peas Soup – 2nd Course Rabbit Fricasse'd, a fine Hare rosted, Rice Pudding, Patties of Lobster, Tartlets & rasberry-Jam Tarts.[68]

It seems a relief, when suffering from numbness in his hand and tongue in May 1783, that while taking physic he had to eat 'very hearty for dinner to day. No Malt Liquor, Cheese, or Salt Meats or Beef or anything seasoned am forbid making use of for some time.'[69]

However, as the editor of the most recent edition of the complete diary has pointed out, just taking the detailed descriptions of dinners can give the wrong impression, as Woodforde rarely described the dinners he had at home with his niece Nancy and his servants. When he ate only with his niece his dinners were simpler: 'We had for Dinner a Piece of boiled Neck of Pork & Greens and a Shoulder of Mutton rosted.'[70] The meals he recorded in great detail were always those he ate with others and are a sort of recorded history of hospitable reciprocity between Woodforde and others. The first dinner listed above,

[65] Eden, *State of the Poor*, III, pp. cxx–cxxii.
[66] R. L. Winstanley (ed.), *The Diary of James Woodforde*, X, *1782–1784* (Parson Woodforde Society, 1998), p. 158.
[67] Ibid., p. 116.   [68] Ibid., p. 80.   [69] Ibid., pp. 95, 134.
[70] Ibid., p. 109; Roy Winstanley, *Parson Woodforde: The Life and Times of a Country Diarist* (Bungay, 1996), pp. 127–8.

for instance, was for eight people at the house of a gentry family. The food was recorded because of its social importance.

We can get a better sense of the course of everyday dining from the dairy of the Sussex shopkeeper Thomas Turner. Although his accounts do not survive, the financial information in the diary indicates that Turner's retail trade was small and local, and his profit limited. His wife had to work picking hops to make extra money, and he continually worried about his financial stability. In August 1756 he fretted about the precariousness of trade in his small country town of East Hoathley and estimated that while previously his trade had been worth £15 to £30 a week, this had dropped to £5 to £10 in 1756. If this weekly estimate was roughly the same over the whole course of the year this represents average sales of £1,170 in a good year, which at a rate of profit of 10 per cent would have yielded Turner an annual income of about £117. However, in 1756 his sales would only have been £390, providing a profit of £39, earnings only slightly more than those of a well-off labouring family.[71] In January 1758, after two years of high grain prices, Turner recorded how this affected his diet. He dined on a soup made of meat, peas, turnips, potatoes, onions and leeks, the recipe for which he had found in the *Universal Magazine*, where it was recommended 'to all poor families as a cheap and nourishing food'.[72] Later that year he recorded that it was:

A very melancholy time occasioned by the dearness of corn, though not proceeding from a real scarcity, but from the iniquitous practice of engrossers, forstalling, etc. My trade is but very small, and what I shall do for an honest livelihood I cannot but think. I am and hope ever shall be content to put up with two meals a day, and both of them I am also willing should be of a pudding; that is I am not desirous of eating meat above once or at the most twice a week.[73]

Like Woodforde, Turner also recorded his meals in greatest detail when he ate out, as when he and his wife dined at Mr French's, the largest tenant farmer in his parish, on 26 January 1758 with another family:

on three boiled ducks, two rabbits, roasted, part of a cold loin of roasted pork, sausages, hogs [puddings] and pear pie … We came home between twelve and one o'clock, and I may say quite sober, considering the house we was at, though

---

[71] David Vaisey (ed.), *The Diary of Thomas Turner* (Oxford, 1985), pp. 31, 61, 137, 169; Richard Grassby, *The Business Community of Seventeenth Century England* (Cambridge, 1995), pp. 162, 258. See below, pp. 136.

[72] Vaisey (ed.), *Diary of Thomas Turner*, p. 132.

[73] Ibid., p. 143.

undoubtedly the worst for drinking ... having I believe contracted a slight impediment in my speech, occasioned by the fumes of the liquor operating too furiously on my brain.[74]

Turner took great pleasure describing the foibles of his neighbours, as in this humorous example:

We dined at my uncle's in company with my mother and brother ... on a leg of very ordinary ewe mutton half boiled, very good turnips, but spoiled by almost swimming in butter, a fine large pig roasted, and the rind as tough as any cowhide (and seemed as if it had been basted with a mixture of flour, butter and ashes), and sauce which looked like what is vomited up by suckling children, a butter pond pudding, and that justly called for there was almost enough in it to have drowned the pig had it been alive ...[75]

However, Turner ate with others much more than he entertained at home, which is another indicator of his limited financial capability, and might also indicate that such hospitality was a sort of interest or partial payment for the work he did in the community.[76] When he ate at home with just his family his meals were much simpler. A large meal was normally cooked on Sundays and then the meals for the rest of the week were based on the remains, as in the examples summarised below from a week in October 1757:

> 2 October
> Turner and his family dined on piece of beef roasted in the oven yesterday, boiled plum suet pudding and a hard pudding, turnips and onion sauce.
> 3 October
> He gathered apples and dined with one other on the remains of yesterday's dinner with the addition of an apple pudding and some turnips.
> 4 October
> He bought a loaf of bread, and one large plaice. At 3.00 p.m. he dined on a cold beef pie and some apple pudding while his family dined on the remains of yesterday's dinner
> 5 October
> The family dined on what they had left, and some boiled plaice.

---

[74] Ibid., p. 131. [75] Ibid., p. 66.

[76] Turner, who was also an overseer of the poor and local accountant, took 15–30 per cent of his meals away from home at various neighbours'. Pennell, 'Material Culture of Food', p. 232.

6 October

He bought 4½ stone of beef and the family dined on the remains of yesterday's dinner, a piece of boiled beef, apple pudding and turnips.

7 October

The family dined on a piece of the scrag-end of mutton, boiled, and the remains of yesterday's dinner.

8 October

The family dined on the remains of yesterday's dinner with the addition of some boiled tripe.

9 October

The family dined on beef pudding, carrots and some cold raisin suet pudding.

10 October

Turner dined on the remains of yesterday's dinner with the addition of beef pudding, small pike and eels given by Roger Vallon.

Turner commonly ate tripe, but the amounts of meat cooked on Sundays must have been very large, as he recorded the weight of meat he bought from the butcher. On 29 September 1757 he bought 15 lb of beef for seven days, and on 6 October he purchased 36 lb for 20 days, while on December 22 of the same year he purchased 42 lb for 14 days over Christmas and New Year. In 1757 he was living with his first wife Peggy, their maid Mary and two young nephews under the age of ten.[77] On a daily basis this works out to much less than the wealthier households listed above, but would still have been about 6 to 8 oz a day for the adults.[78] However, from March 1758, when he vowed to eat meat only twice weekly, he indeed did start to buy less. Whereas in February he had been purchasing the equivalent of 2 lb of beef per day from the butcher, from this point he began eating more offal and making smaller purchases of veal rather than beef.[79]

Finally, it is very fortunate that the account book of Richard Latham of Lancashire has survived, from which we can get an idea of what a smallholding labourer might have been able to afford to purchase. His accounts list many small purchases from which not only his diet but

[77] Naomi Tadmor, *Family and Friends in Eighteenth-Century England: Household, Kinship, and Patronage* (Cambridge, 2001), pp. 29–33.

[78] This assumes that the children ate less; see below, p. 135.

[79] Since the published version of the diary does not contain the full text, the references to Turner's purchases and meals cited here are from the original manuscript of the diary by date. Thomas Turner Papers, Manuscripts and Archives: The Diary of Thomas Turner, 1754–65, Yale University Library.

also household consumption patterns can be examined.[80] They begin in 1724, the year after he married when he was twenty-five years of age, and continue to his death in 1767. They start with the setting up of his household and purchase of a feather bed and many kitchen utensils. His first daughter was born in 1726, followed by a son in 1727. Six more daughters followed in 1729, 1731, 1733, 1736, 1737 and 1741. The son Richard (called Dicy) died at twenty-one and one daughter died in infancy. His relatives were local yeomen, and he was obviously educated enough to keep the accounts as well as purchase small books such as *Pilgrim's Progress* and the Psalms.[81]

He is usually described as a small farmer, but, as Charles Foster has recently suggested, it is equally likely that he can be described as a carter or labourer. His farm was too small to occupy the labour of one man all year round, yet he continually hired labour to do work, implying that he was working elsewhere.[82] He also bought more things than the profit from his farm suggests would be possible unless he had a further source of income. Thus, these accounts can be used to provide an idea of what a well-off labouring family would purchase in a year. In many ways Latham was similar to many of the labourers whose surviving inventories will be analysed in chapter 4.

Latham's father, Thomas, seems to have been wealthier than Richard, with an interest in a water corn mill, windmill and malt kiln at Ormskirk. When he died his main asset seems to have been the lease of the farm which Richard inherited. This was 19 acres in size and had a capital value of about £140. The farm was just to the north of Liverpool in the parish of Scarisbrick, roughly where present-day Southport is, and was just behind the coastal sand dunes. However, it was an advantageous customary lease for three lives, and cost Latham only about £1 a year as he made a payment of £40 at the beginning of the diary in 1728 and a further payment of £42 13s in 1760. This compares to the annual market rent of 16s he paid for only a meadow.[83] But he still had to borrow £34 from his relations and neighbours without security to pay for this lease, which he was able to pay off at £2 a year. During the first seven years of Richard's ownership, from 1717 to 1723, it is likely that he rented the property out, which would have been worth about £10 a year on the market, to pay off the portions due to his four

[80] Lorna Weatherill (ed.), *The Account Book of Richard Latham 1724–1767* (Oxford, 1990).

[81] Ibid., pp. xii–xiv.

[82] Charles F. Foster, *Seven Households: Life in Cheshire and Lancashire 1582–1774* (Northwich, 2002), pp. 142–50.

[83] Ibid., p. xvii.

siblings while working himself. Once this was done he married in 1724 and set up house in the main building on the farm, described as a house with three bays. Foster has surmised that it is likely that he rented at least two parts of it to his siblings in exchange for any remaining parts of their portions and for payment of tithes and any land tax due on the land.[84]

The part he farmed was certainly very small, probably only about 3–5 acres per year. He also possessed, on average, three cows and a pig or two. Unfortunately the accounts are only for his expenditure, so there is no record of what he earned or how he earned it, but certainly the produce of his farm was small. He hauled things with his mare and cart for others, as a brief account with Peter Modsley from 1756 in the back of the book demonstrates.[85] In addition, as John Styles has discussed, his daughters and wife earned money from spinning which they used to buy quite a wide range of clothing. But however the total family income was earned, there was never much of a surplus. After paying interest and repayments on his borrowing and farm costs, his family generally spent between £7 and £11 on food and other consumption goods in the first fifteen years of the diary, and between £15 and £22 thereafter, once the girls were older.[86]

Latham's farm was composed of lowland moss, moor and marsh, some of which had been recently reclaimed. Latham lists fields and grounds which he referred to as 'moss field', 'near moss field', 'middle moss field', 'far moss field', 'moss ground' 'near field meadow', 'little field'', 'old moss mere' and his yard. Some of these may have been different terms all used to refer to the moss field which was his main arable land. No size is ever given for the fields but information is given on ploughing, sowing and harvest. The amount of time recorded which was spent ploughing is the best indication of a field's size. Although Latham owned a mare, a plough needed two horses so he normally hired someone to plough the land. It took 3.5 days to plough the middle moss field, 2 days for the moss ground and 4 days to plough the moss field. Since it took just over a day to plough an acre, these were very small fields. Since they were not all sown each year, his crop would have been small.[87] On many occasions Latham also recorded how much seed he sowed. On 15 April 1730, for instance, about four bushels of oats were sown in the near field, and in 1741 the same amount of barley seed was sown in the moss

[84] Ibid., pp. 146, 149.   [85] Ibid., p. 122.   [86] Ibid., pp. 149–69.
[87] Weatherill (ed.), *Account Book of Richard Latham*, 3–4, 6–7, 9–10, 11–12, 43, 46–7, 50, 52–4, 70–2, 78–9.

ground.[88] Since the seeding rate for oats was 4–6 bushels an acre this indicates these fields were only about an acre each, implying that the moss ground was ploughed over twice.[89] In fallow years Latham also sowed his fields with clover seed and generally not more than 12 lb were used. Although harvest yields are not given, Latham did pay to have the oats he harvested dried and here the amount varied from 20 to just over 40 bushels, which given that oat yields varied between 24 and 34 bushels per acre in these years indicates his crops were small.[90] Thus it is unlikely that with a farm of such size he was selling his crops for a profit. He would have sold them to his neighbours in times when they needed them, just as he continually bought corn meal, oats and other grain from them, but there would have been little surplus for a profit.

Undoubtedly more important in this regard were his cows, which he was able to pasture on the manor's mere land – a large area of marsh reclaimed from the sea – at little charge.[91] In the first year of the accounts he bought three cows and a calf, which cost £12 9s. Judging from the entries of the costs of bulling his cows, he seems to have kept between one and three cows, and to have grown all of his own hay, although again his crops were not large. In 1749, when he did not record harvesting hay, he had to purchase 10 stone.[92] Throughout the period of the accounts he continued to buy cows and calves. After a few years of milking Latham appears to have sold the cows to a butcher in exchange for meat, and then bought younger ones (see Table 2.1). In 1747 he sold a cow to the butcher Jonathan Rodgers for £3 10s, and over the course of the next 16 months purchased about 114 lb of meat.[93] As we will see in chapter 5 the butter, milk and cheese produced by these cows in the mid-eighteenth century might have been worth £3–4 each if sold on the market, depending on the quality of the pasture. However, Latham bought very little cheese or milk and only about 4 lb of butter a year, implying that the cows produced most of what the family consumed, so less would have been available to sell on the market. In addition, he always kept a swine with his cows, which he presumably fed with whey

[88] The measurement Latham used was what he termed a 'measure' but a comparison of the price of a measure of wheat with the price of a peck sold to the mill at the same time shows the measure to have been about the same as a bushel. Ibid., pp. 38–9, 56–8, 91.

[89] Overton, *Agricultural Revolution*, p. 73; M. E. Turner, J. V. Beckett and B. Afton, *Farm Production in England 1700–1914* (Oxford, 2001), pp. 166–72.

[90] Weatherill (ed.), *Account Book of Richard Latham*, p. 158.

[91] Some payments for pasture are listed called 'scores' and 'removing', but not continuously. Ibid., p. xxxviii

[92] Ibid., p. 74.   [93] Ibid., p. 123.

Table 2.1 Richard Latham's expenses (£)[a]

Year	Household size	Gross expenditure	Cows, pigs	Financial	Marling	Funeral	Tithe	Household expenses	Percentage spent on animals
1724	2	37.75	17.65	0.8	—	—	—	13.7	47
1725	2	16.95	—	1	—	—	—	8.9	0
1726	3	16.95	3.2	7	—	—	—	6.75	19
1727	4	14.3	3.3	0	—	—	—	11.28	23
1728	4	55.15	5.75	41	—	—	—	7.2	10
1729	5	12.1	3.2	0	—	—	—	8.85	26
1730	5	12.45	3.05	2	—	—	—	7.35	24
1731	6	9.65	1.35	0	—	—	—	8.25	14
1732	6	24.15	—	16.5	—	—	—	8.15	0
1733	7	19.6	1.7	10.3	—	—	—	7.85	9
1734	7	19.75	2.95	6.3	—	—	—	10	15
1735	7	24.4	3.2	9.5	—	—	—	10.35	13
1736	7	15.15	—	0	—	1.6	—	11.3	0
1737	8	9.9	—	2.4	—	—	—	7.25	0
1738	8	16.9	1.45	1	—	—	3.9	10.5	9
1739	8	23.95	4.25	10	—	—	—	10.45	18
1740	8	31.2	—	8.85	5.3	—	—	16.8	0
1741	9	30.45	—	13.75	—	—	—	17.2	0
1742	9	30.8	—	14	—	—	—	16.75	0
1743	9	33.65	4.45	15	—	—	—	14.15	13
1744	9	17.55	1.35	0	—	—	—	16.4	8
1745	9	21.65	3.15	1	4.25	—	—	17.95	15
1746	9	31.3	2.9	6	—	—	—	18.2	9
1747	8	24.95	—	2.1	—	1.85	—	22.9	0

1748	5	31.2	3.2	1.15	—	—	—	16.8	10
1749	5	28	0.7	0	—	—	—	27	3
1750	5	19.95	1.45	0	—	—	—	18.45	7
1751	5	21.15	6.5	0	—	—	—	14.95	31
1752	5	24.35	4.2	0	—	—	—	20.2	17
1753	5	25.15	4.1	3.3	2.25	—	—	18.1	16
1754	5	29.85	—	8	—	—	—	21.8	0
1755	5	19.1	4.1	0	—	—	—	14.95	21
1756	4	20.3	—	0	—	—	—	20.25	0
1757	4	17.9	—	0	—	—	—	17.85	15
1758	4	26.75	4.1	0	—	—	—	22.25	0
1759	4	15.15	—	42.65	—	—	—	15.15	0
1760	4	54.7	—	15	—	—	—	11.05	0
1761	4	30.15	—	5.15	—	—	—	15.1	0
1762	4	17.75	—	0	—	—	—	12.7	0
1763	4	16.15	—	0	—	—	—	16.15	15
1764	4	21.05	3.2	3	—	—	—	18.3	0
1765	4	18.15	—	—	—	—	—	18.15	0
1766	4	24.25	—	3	—	—	—	16.1	0
Average	—	23.53	3.78	5.74	3.93	—	—	14.51	9

Note: [a] Adapted from Foster, *Seven Households*, pp. 168–9.

left over after butter- and cheese-making. He slaughtered a pig in thirteen of the first eighteen years of the accounts and almost every year thereafter, and two in some years.

But Latham was in no way a self-sufficient farmer. He bought a great deal of food on the market, and his accounts list such purchases in great detail as well as many other household expenditures every year. In 1736, for instance, when he spent £15 3s in total, he bought about 12½ bushels of corn and barley costing just over £1 on the market.[94] Given that his family was composed of two adults and four children under ten (one child died during 1736) if they ate only wheaten bread and Richard ate 1.5 lb of bread a day the whole family would have needed approximately 27 bushels.[95] However, Latham dried 39 bushels of oats he had grown, so the family probably consumed some of these and sold what was not required. In addition to his purchases of grain he also bought 58 lb of beef, mutton and various other poorer-quality animal parts, such as cow cheeks, calf's heads and sheep's plucks, and killed one of his own swine. He also made 24 purchases of salt, 27 purchases of sugar amounting to about 24 lb, as well as buying pepper, starch, nutmeg, gingerbread and many items of clothing. From 1714 to 1733 he spent on average only £18 a year, but with this he made about 250 small purchases of different things worth 1s to 2s each. Even in 1731, when he spent as little as £9 13s, which would certainly be the minimum a family might survive on, he still made 229 purchases of numerous items including sugar, soap, salt, treacle, eggs, currants, biscuits, pepper, white wine, mutton, nails, candles, pudding, skins, French wheat, coal, medicine and a midwife's fee.[96]

What strikes one about the accounts is just how many times Latham was able to purchase sugar and imported food such as spices given his low level of expenditure. Over the course of the diary he made over 1,000 purchases of sugar. It is true that he had an advantage living near Liverpool, where much sugar was imported and refined and therefore cheaper then further inland, but the quantities are still significant. In the 1740s, for instance, he bought on average 50 lb of sugar and 20 lb of treacle. In 1742 he bought 9 oz of pepper and 1 lb in 1750. He also bought small amounts of ginger, caraway seeds and nutmeg as well as turmeric, and a pound of currants per year. Other things he bought every so often included brandy, his 'little books', and onion, carrot,

---

[94] During the same year he also paid for 57 measures of oats and meal of his own production to be dried. Ibid., pp. 32–5.

[95] This is based on the amount of wheat meal needed to make bread and the assumption that Latham's wife ate 0.8 of what he did and his small children ate 0.5. See below, p. 135.

[96] Weatherill (ed.), *Account Book of Richard Latham*, pp. xix–xxiv.

lettuce and other garden seeds. In addition, many clothes were purchased, which has been discussed by John Styles. Before 1743 about 50s a year was spent on clothes, but once Latham's daughters were old enough to begin earning wages from spinning a much wider variety and better quality of clothing was purchased, including blue flowered damask. Money was now also spent on tailoring bills to make gowns as well as silk hats and handkerchiefs.[97]

It is unclear from the accounts just how Latham made enough money to purchase these goods. His crop of oats would not have been worth more than £1 to £2 at a price of 1s 1d a bushel, and it is possible that the profit from his cows was worth £2 to £6 a year. Thus he must have made money working for others. The accounts clearly show that the local labour market worked as a system of exchange just as much as did the market for local produce. Latham bought small amounts of meat and grain from others, and might well have been working for them to pay for his purchases, just as others, such as his brother, John, or John Prescot, often worked for him. One Henry Bell received many payments for ploughing, carting and other work, and Latham in turn bought seed, oatmeal and pigs from him. John Worthington, who called himself a yeoman in his will, regularly did ploughing, harrowing and sowing for Latham.[98] Latham made many large purchases from one William Parker, and borrowed money from him, so he might well have been a farm labourer working for him. This was a common way of organising the manorial economy to overcome the lack of small change, but also to create a web of obligations on which local social systems were based. So far was Latham's small farm from being autarkic that it makes little sense to even consider it as a possibility. Production and labour were in a constant state of exchange, of which unfortunately Latham's accounts only present half a picture, but which will be discussed further in the section of the book on work and labourers' earnings. However, his purchases show that a labourer with a small piece of land and some cows could afford to buy meat and sugar as well as luxury items on the market.

Types of food eaten

Bread

Bread is a food so necessary to the life of man, that whereas many meats be loathed naturally, of some persons, yet we never saw, read, nor heard of any man that naturally hated bread. The reasons whereof I take to be these. First

---

[97] Styles, *Dress of the People*, pp. 141.
[98] Weatherill (ed.), *Account Book of Richard Latham*, p. xvii.

because it is the staff of life, without which all other meats would either quickly putrifie in our stomachs, or sooner pass through them then they should ... Bread is never out of season, disagreeing with no sickness, age, or complexion, and therefore truly called the companion of life.[99]

While bread was the most important source of carbohydrates for early modern labouring families, the diets examined in the next chapter show that its predominance was not nearly so great as many modern assumptions suggest. But still, in Moffet's words, it was 'the meat of meats' and formed the basis of most meals; most working adults ate about a pound per day, generally washed down with beer or cider.[100] There were many different types of bread available, but wheaten bread was the most common and was the bread made by bakers, generally cooked in a specialised bread oven. Bread made from barley or oats could be cooked more cheaply near an open fire in closed pots. In addition, griddle cakes or pancakes made from all types of grain could be cooked over fires, as could pottage or porridge, which will be discussed below. The general types of bread available were described in publications concerning the Assize of Bread, a set of laws governing the quality and the size of the loaves which bakers sold. There were four main types of wheaten bread listed in the Assize published in 1636: the white loaf drawn from the fine cocket, the white loaf drawn from the course cocket, the wheaten loaf drawn from the course cocket and the household loaf drawn from the course cocket. The cocket was a measure of the quality of grain sold in the market, and the household loaf contained the most bran. The size of a household loaf was double that of a white loaf, so a very high premium was placed on the quality of the grain used, and very little on fibre.[101] In his *Description of England* Harrison made a similar distinction, although he used different names, which were common earlier:

Of bread made of wheat we have sundry sorts daily brought to the table, whereof the first and most excellent is the manchet, which we commonly call white bread ... The second is the cheat, or wheaten bread, so named because the color thereof resembleth the gray or yellowish wheat, being clean and well dressed, and out of this is the coarsest of the bran (usually called gurgeons or pollard) taken. The raveled is a kind of cheat bread also, but it retaineth more of the gross and less of the pure substance of the wheat; and this [manchet], being more slightly wrought up, is used in the halls of the nobility and gentry only, whereas the other [cheat bread] either is or should be baked, in cities and good towns, of an appointed size ... The next sort is named brown bread, of the color, of which we have two sorts, one baked up as it cometh from the mill, so that neither the bran nor the flour are any whit diminished ... The other hath

[99] Moffet, *Health's Improvement*, p. 235.   [100] Ibid., p. 236.
[101] 5+6 Edward VI, ch.14; John Powel, *The Assize of Bread* (London, 1636).

little or no flour left therein at all and it is not only the worst and weakest of all the other sorts but also appointed in old time for servants, slaves, and the inferior kind of people to feed upon. Hereunto likewise, because it is dry and brickle in the working (for it will hardly be made up handsomely into loaves) some add a portion of rye meal in our time, whereby the rough dryness or dry roughness thereof is somewhat qualified, and then it is named miscelin [maslin], that is, bread made of mingled corn, albeit that divers do sow or mingle wheat and rye of set purpose at the mill, or before it come there, and sell the same at the markets under the aforesaid name.[102]

Gervase Markham also provided a recipe for brown bread fit for what he termed 'hinde-servants' which he described as the 'coursest bread for man's use' which also included barley and peas.[103] In 1523 the kitchen in the household of Lord Howard, the Earl of Surrey served forty-three loaves of finest white bread (manchet), twenty-seven loaves of household bread and fifteen loaves of trencher bread, which was possibly such coarse bread. It is impossible to know how common such very coarse bread was as part of the diet of poor families in the sixteenth century, but given the scattered evidence we have it seems more likely that household bread, perhaps made, or mixed, with rye rather than peas or barley, was most common.[104] However, by the early seventeenth century, the yeoman farmer Robert Loder only mentioned baking wheaten bread for his servants, and by the eighteenth century it was generally assumed that household wheaten bread was normally eaten by labourers except in regions where oats were more common.[105] Charles Smith, the author of *Three Tracts on the Corn-Trade and Corn Laws*, reported that, after the poor harvests of 1756 and 1757, he could not obtain any account of barley bread being eaten except for that 'of an old careful man, who hath occasionally fed a large family with barley-bread in dear times, and saith that he always found it as cheap to feed his family with Wheat as with Barley'.[106] William Ellis similarly noted that wheaten bread was the normal food for day labourers at Little Gaddesten, but noted that barley was eaten there in times of high wheat prices, or when family income was stretched.[107]

---

[102] Harrison, *Description*, pp. 133–5.

[103] Gervase Markham, *The English Housewife, Containing the Inward and Outward Vertues which Ought to be in a Compleat Woman* (London, 1664), p. 187.

[104] Soldiers at Boulogne used wheat, rye and barley corn to make bread flour, and in the Bury St Edmunds house of correction the bread was stated to be made from rye. See below, p. 124–6.

[105] G. E. Fussell (ed.), *Robert Loder's Farm Accounts 1610–1620*, Camden Society, 3rd ser., 53 (1936), pp. 44–5, 67–8, 86–8, 106–7, 122, 136, 151, 172.

[106] Charles Smith, *Three Tracts on the Corn-Trade and Corn Laws*, 2nd edn (London, 1766), p. 199.

[107] Ellis, *Country Housewife*, pp. 16–17, 23–4, 26–7.

It was estimated that in 1758, in England as a whole, 63 per cent of the population consumed wheaten bread, 15 per cent rye bread, 12 per cent barley bread and 10 per cent oats in some form.[108] But there were significant regional differences. As Harrison had noted, 'The bread throughout the land is made of such grain as the soil yeildeth … In champaign [champion] countries much rye and barley bread is eaten.'[109] By far the largest percentage of wheat was eaten in the southeast, where the figure was 89 per cent. In the southwest it was 75 per cent and in the Midlands it was 67 per cent. In the north, however, the amount of wheat eaten was only 30 per cent. There, more oats and rye were eaten than wheat, accounting for 35 per cent and 25 per cent of grain consumption respectively. Barley bread was most popular in the southwest, where it comprised 24 per cent, and in the northwest, where it comprised 17 per cent of grain consumed. In contrast it comprised less than 2 per cent of consumption in the southeast and East Anglia.[110]

Eden noted that labourers in the south considered white bread to be healthier than rye, and even when farmers consumed bread made partly of rye, as in Nottinghamshire, their labourers refused to eat the same as they did not consider it good for work, stating they had 'lost their rye teeth'. Even Eden considered rye to be too laxative, not good for work and to have an unpleasant taste, despite its cheap price.[111] Both Ellis and Eden noted that oats were the staple grain in northern counties rather than wheat. Ellis noted that in the north:

They make vast Consumption of Oatmeal, having little Wheat growing in these Parts, and with this they make Cakes that supply Bread mixing Oatmeal with Water and a little Salt, which they let stand together twenty or more hours, and then knead into a Dough or batter, and bake it like Pancakes on a Stone that has a fire under it … At the great and popular Town of *Manchester*, their sacks of Oatmeal stand for Sale in their Markets as our Sacks of Wheat do at *Hempstead*.[112]

Oatmeal was cheap to prepare as it could be done in a pot over an open fire, and was often eaten with the addition of butter, sugar, beer or milk. Eden also described the various types of leavened and unleavened barley bread and oat cakes, or hearth cakes, which could be cooked at home and were baked by most families in the north, from substantial farmers to day labourers. In Cumbria, though, he noted that it was

---

[108] David Davies also stated that wheat was more common than rye. Davies, *Case of Labourers*, p. 32

[109] Harrison, *Description*, p. 135.   [110] Smith, *Three Tracts*, pp. 182–5.

[111] Eden, *State of the Poor*, I, p. 526.

[112] Ellis, *Country Housewife*, pp. 11, 18, 23–4, 26. Eden, *State of the Poor*, II, pp. 88, 94, 97–8, 105–6.

more common to make leavened loaves of barley bread of 12 lb each. These were baked in common ovens fired by cheap furze which could bake eighteen loaves at a time. Such a loaf would last four to five weeks in the winter.[113] Eden also pointed out the healthiness of oats, which indeed are more nutritious than other grains in that they contain more vitamins.[114] As we shall see below in the discussion of pottage and porridge in the section on vegetables, Eden was always very keen to emphasise the northern preference for oats as a cereal grain because he wanted to encourage their use in the south as a way for labouring families to save money during the rise in food prices when he was writing. However, as the eighteenth century statistics cited above show, almost the same amount of wheat as oats was consumed in the north. Wheat could grow well in the lower areas of Lancashire, Cheshire and Yorkshire, and much was also imported by coast into Newcastle, where it was consumed by labourers in the coal industry.[115]

Oats were more common in the north because they have a lower summer heat requirement and greater tolerance of rain than other cereals like wheat, rye or barley, and in the colder climate of Scotland they formed the great majority of carbohydrates eaten.[116] Rye also produces a better crop in poor environments than wheat. It does better in acidic, drought-prone thin soils and at higher altitudes. Barley, too, is more tolerant of soil acidity and dry and cool conditions than wheat. It also has a shorter growing season than wheat.[117] Increasingly over time the English preferred to plant barley over oats for human consumption because it could be malted for beer in most years, and could be consumed as bread if the price of wheat went very high because of a bad harvest. In addition more beans and pulses were grown where soil conditions were better, generally in the southeast. They were used to make pease pudding for labourers and the poor inmates of workhouses, but most were used to feed animals.

In all areas there was an incentive to plant some balance between wheat, oats and barley because of their different reactions to drought or excess rainfall.[118] Oats and barley were also much cheaper than wheat in terms of the number of calories provided per penny. The former was on average 60 per cent cheaper and the latter an astounding 165 per cent

[113] Eden, *State of the Poor*, I, pp. 510–11.
[114] Ibid., I, pp. 497–99; Gibson and Smout, *Prices, Food and Wages*, p. 236
[115] Smith, *Three Tracts*, p. 194.
[116] Gibson and Smout, *Prices, Food and Wages*, pp. 226–8, 256–60. Peter Bowden, 'Agricultural Prices, Farm Profits, and Rents', in *AHEW*, IV, pp. 619ff.
[117] www.farm-direct.co.uk/farming/stockcrop/barley/crop.html.
[118] Peter Bowden, 'Agricultural Prices, Farm Profits, and Rents', in *AHEW*, V.I, pp. 41–62.

cheaper than wheat.[119] This was due to a combination of greater demand for wheat, the higher rent of better land to grow it on and the greater cost needed to harvest it by reaping with a sickle rather than mowing with a scythe.

There are no earlier estimates of the relative amounts of different grains people ate, but these figures can be compared to percentages of crops listed in probate inventories for certain counties measured by Mark Overton. Percentages of crops grown cannot be compared to grain consumed as bread, of course, since the majority of barley went to brew beer and some also went to feed pigs. Much of the oat crop also went to feed horses, and a percentage of all grown crops would have to be used for seed corn.[120] However, a rough comparison can be made. Although the most northerly county studied by Overton is Lincolnshire, his figures show that the proportion of wheat grown in the southeast and Cornwall was always higher than in the north, but that the percentage of wheat grown rose in the north over time. More strikingly they show that the percentage of rye grown was never over 19 per cent, even in the sixteenth century, and declined everywhere over time until by 1801 it only formed at most 2 per cent of crops. The proportion of barley grown was generally higher than that of wheat because of the amount of beer brewed. The percentage of oats was also high and rose or remained steady in most places. The amount of oats under cultivation was highest in Cornwall, Kent and Hertfordshire, but much of the production of the latter two counties must have gone to supply food for horses in London. Overton's figures clearly show that there was already an overwhelming preference for wheaten bread over rye in England from the mid-sixteenth century.[121]

Bread-making

Baking leavened wheaten bread as opposed to bread baked by the fire was more expensive, as it needed a purpose-built oven in which the bricks or stones had to be heated to a high and constant temperature. In towns most people bought leavened bread from bakers, but in the countryside distances were often too great to rely on the baker. In a militia list from Gloucestershire from 1608 which lists the occupations of a large percentage of the adult men in the county, there was only one baker for every 205 families listed outside of the county's three

---

[119] This was worked out using Greg Clark's price series for the three grains, divided by the calories per bushel taken from Table 3.14 below. Clark's database can be found at: www.econ.ucdavis.edu/faculty/gclark/English%20Data/farm2002.xls.

[120] See below, pp. 146–8.

[121] Overton, *Agricultural Revolution*, pp. 94–5.

principal towns of Gloucester, Tewkesbury and Cirencester, compared to one for every 30 families in Gloucester. In comparison there were over twice as many butchers in the countryside.[122] Most larger houses with numerous servants or guests had ovens, as it was more economical to bake for large numbers. Home baking in smaller households before the introduction of iron ranges and ovens in the eighteenth century is more difficult to estimate because bread ovens are not mentioned in probate inventories as they were not movable, although separate bake houses were mentioned, as was baking equipment such as kneading boards and troughs and peels. Overton *et al.* in their study of probate inventories from Kent and Cornwall in the seventeenth and eighteenth centuries found that 34 per cent of inventoried households in Kent had baking equipment at the beginning of the seventeenth century, rising to 46 per cent by 1719. In Cornwall, however, less than 6 per cent had baking equipment, perhaps because barley bread was more popular. In the sample of labourers' inventories examined in chapter 4 below only 14 per cent of households had such equipment before 1600, rising to 17.5 per cent after 1650 and 25 per cent in the first half of the eighteenth century. In contrast, over 70 per cent of inventories had pots and equipment for boiling food over an open fire, and barley, oats, peas and beans could all be added to mixtures of meat and stock together with garden vegetables and spices to make pottage, which will be discussed below in the section on vegetables.

Most of the baking equipment consisted of variously named kneading tubs. Out of 970 households only 27 possessed bread peels (the instrument used to put loaves into and to take them out of ovens). This is because it was quite common to take risen bread to a local baker, or in some cases a communal oven, for baking at a small price. This was the case in the area around Lutterworth, and it was a practice also noted by the eighteenth-century diarist John Cannon, who claimed that in Lyford, Somerset:

A custom there was in the neighbourhood to get up before the light to Bake and it was often my fortune to arise and heat ye oven whilst ye women prepared the Batch and they would make bread Cakes which were soon got ready for breakfast which we eat with butter or sopped in beer, ale or cyder before our other employment came.[123]

---

[122] *Men and Armour for Gloucestershire in 1608 compiled by John Smith* (Gloucester, 1980; reprint of 1902 edition); Tawney and Tawney, 'Occupational Census', pp. 36, 59–63. This census is described in more detail below on p. 221.

[123] For a description of the diary, see John Money, 'Teaching in the Market-Place, or "Caesar adsum jam forte: Pompey aderat": the Retailing of Knowledge in Provincial England During the Eighteenth Century', in Brewer and Porter (eds.), *Consumption and*

In addition poor people could buy bread from bakers and sell it door to door in the countryside, as in the case of Cannon's wife. When they were very poor, he reported that she 'took up the Trade of selling Bread for the bakers and butter for the dairy folks, in which she continued about two years, but the profit was so small and the trust so large that it only served to increase our poverty'.[124] Nor does the use of sourdough seem to have been common in England, and most bread relied on brewer's yeast, which was termed 'ale barm', to make bread rise.[125] This means that most home baking would have also relied on a steady supply of yeast from a local brewer, or access to a neighbour's yeast from a recent brewing, which would have been another disincentive to small-scale home use of an oven. It is perhaps also indicative that, in Gervase Markham's *English Housewife*, the instructions for baking were very peremptory and short compared to the detail for brewing or cooking, implying that it was seen as a less important skill.[126]

Further evidence of the purchase of bread from bakers by the poor comes from the laws of the Assize of Bread. Bread was sold by the penny and half penny loaves, or upwards in multiples of pennies, where the size of a loaf changed according to the changing market price of grain. This was done for two very practical reasons. The first was that there were very few small coins in circulation, the smallest being the farthing, and it was easier to make adjustments in the size of the loaf rather than the cash price to reflect small changes in the market price of a quarter of wheat (512 troy lb). This was especially true as the average price of a quarter of grain rose with inflation in the sixteenth and seventeenth centuries. The lack of small change also meant that most bread was sold on credit, and since it was always worth a penny or multiples thereof it was easier for bakers to keep track of what poor families owed for their bread.[127] There were many publications of the Assize of Bread in the seventeenth century, and although there were many fewer published in the eighteenth century the types of bread and their weights in relation to the price of grain remained the same.[128]

---

the World of Goods, pp. 347ff.; SRO, DD/SAS/1193/4, John Cannon's Memoirs, p. 34; Thirsk, *Food*, pp. 234–5.

[124] John Cannon's Memoirs, p. 181.

[125] Thirsk, *Food*, pp. 232–4; Eden, *State of the Poor*, I, p. 533.

[126] Markham, *English Housewife*, pp. 185–8.

[127] 5+6 Edward VI, ch.14; Powel, *Assize of Bread*.

[128] A much more detailed analysis of milling and baking after 1770 can be found in Christian Peterson, *Bread and the British Economy c. 1770–1870* (Aldershot, 1995), chs. 2–4.

Beer and other drink

Before brandy, which is now become common and sold in every little ale-house had come into England in such quantities as it now doth, we drank good strong beer and ale, and all laborious people (which are for the greater part of the Kingdom) their bodies requiring after hard labour, some strong drink to refresh them, did therefore every morning and evening used to drink a pot of ale or a flagon of strong beer, which greatly helped the promotion of our own grain, and did them no great prejudice; it hindereth not their work, neither did it take away their senses nor cost them much money.[129]

> One bushell well brewed, outlasteth some twaine,
> And saveth both mault, and expences in vaine.
> Too new is no profite, too stale is as bad,
> Drinke dead or else sower makes laborer sad.[130]

The importance of beer in early modern English culture hardly needs to be stressed.[131] Since the publication in the early 1980s of Peter Clark's comprehensive *The English Alehouse: A Social History 1200–1830* and Keith Wrightson's seminal article 'Alehouses, Order, and Reformation in Rural England, 1590–1660' on the politics of sociability and the ale-house, the importance of the institution as a place of leisure activity as well as potential disorder and drunkenness has been central to any study of popular culture.[132] It is a commonplace that beer was the uni-versal drink of all members of society, and was drunk because water was potentially harmful. Keith Thomas estimated that perhaps almost two pints were consumed daily per capita in the late seventeenth century. Another estimate puts the production of cider, which was generally drunk instead of beer in the West Country, at 10 million gallons annu-ally in Devon alone by the mid-eighteenth century.[133] In addition to

---

[129] A petition presented to Parliament in 1673, asking that brandy, rum, coffee and tea be prohibited, as quoted in H. A. Monckton, *A History of English Ale and Beer* (London, 1966), p. 134.

[130] Tusser, *Five Hundred Points*, p. 167.

[131] Hopped beer had become the normal drink by the beginning of the seventeenth cen-tury rather than the older drink of unhopped ale. By this time 'ale' had come to refer to a stronger version of beer, and this is how the word ale will be used in the following discussion. Pamela Sambrook, *Country House Brewing in England, 1500–1900* (London, 1996), pp. 17–18. See also Peter Mathias, *The Brewing Industry in England 1700–1830* (Cambridge, 1959).

[132] Clark, *English Alehouse*; Keith Wrightson, 'Alehouses, Order, and Reformation in Rural England, 1590–1660', in E. and S. Yeo (eds.), *Popular Culture and Class Conflict 1590–1914* (Brighton, 1981), pp. 167–87.

[133] Keith Thomas, *Religion and the Decline of Magic* (Harmondsworth, 1971), pp. 21–2. It has been estimated that an acre of apple trees could produce 200 gallons of cider annu-ally. Robin Stanes, *The Old Farm: A History of Farming Life in the West Country* (Exeter, 1990), pp. 61, 66.

beer and cider, in some years as much as 3,528,000 gallons of wine were imported into England – equivalent to 17,791,120 modern bottles of 750 ml, although little of this would have been drunk by labourers.[134]

It is generally assumed that most beer consumed was small or weak beer. As a result, the importance of beer as a source of energy and nutrition has not been properly acknowledged. Beer was used to supply a necessary amount of water to the body, but it is often overlooked as a source of calories (as well as vitamin B and protein from the barley).[135] Beer, like bread or porridge, is made from grain, and was a major source of calories from both carbohydrates and alcohol in the early modern period. As we shall see, the malting of barley converted the starch in the kernel of the grain into soluble sugar, and then the fermentation of the wort (malt and boiling water) converted some or all of this sugar into alcohol. The body needs calories to supply its energy, and sugar is the fastest way food energy can be digested. Alcohol also provides much more concentrated energy for the body, but it must be chemically broken down by the liver before it can be used as energy, and this normally occurs at a very much slower rate than the digestion of sugar in the gut.

In the Galenic works discussed above, beer was considered a healthy drink, while cold water was considered potentially very unhealthy.[136] James Hart in *The Diet of the Diseased* of 1633 spent a great deal of space discussing the qualities of water and its effects on digestion. Although nothing was known at the time about water-borne contagion, theories of health did stress that stagnant water was unhealthy, because it was brackish and muddy.[137] Rain water was considered best, followed by spring water and then fast-running river or stream water. Many doctors noted that they, or others, had become very ill after drinking water from rivers, but under Galenic theory this was usually attributed to the water being too cold and thus having a debilitating effect on the heat of digestion in the stomach. It is possible that some water could have been boiled before drinking. Hart discussed whether boiling water was good or bad for the stomach, and suggested that the poor preferred beer to water for its intoxicating effect, rather than its healthiness.[138] Certainly water was drunk, and most tracts on brewing recommended the use of fresh spring water to make the best beer, and if it was available for

[134] Rod Phillips, *A Short History of Wine* (New York, 2000), pp. 130, 189–90.

[135] Andrew Campbell, *The Book of Beer* (London, 1956), pp. 103–4.

[136] Thomas Cock, *Kitchin-Physick or, Advice to the Poor by Way of a Dialogue* (London, 1676), p. 46; Archer, *Every Man His Own Doctor*, pp. 85, 90.

[137] Moffet, *Health's Improvement*, pp. 68, 76–7, 94, 141–2, 170.

[138] James Hart, *The Diet of the Diseased* (London, 1633), pp. 109–29. Thirsk, *Food*, pp. 14, 304–5.

brewing it would have been available for drinking.[139] Where the problem of contamination was greatest, in larger towns, fresh water was brought in through aqueducts and then piped to individual houses for a fee, and to public conduits paid for by the town.[140] But in the countryside there must have been good water from wells and fresh running streams. Regardless, though, drinking beer was considered healthier, and it is always possible where animal and human waste were used for fertiliser that streams and wells could have become polluted with bacteria or parasites.

Beer was also considered good for work, as a liquid nourishment which produced perspiration, which was considered healthy.[141] Hart asked, 'where can you find stronger, healthfuller, and lustier people, than in those countries where this drinke is most ordinarily used?'.[142] One pamphlet on beer advocated that good strong beer was 'most cherishing to poor labouring people, without which they cannot well subsist, their food being for the most part of such things as afford little nourishment, nay and sometimes dangerous, and would infest them with many Sicknesses and Diseases'.[143] Hopped beer was also superior to ale as the hops were said to open 'obstructions of the liver, spleen, and kidneys, cleereth the blood, and cleaneth choler'.[144] The hops were also considered to have an active effect on infections, which is actually a rare case of early modern medical knowledge being accurate. Both the humulon and lupulin constituents of hops, together with the antiseptic quality of the alcohol, killed many bacteria and bacilli. In addition, being unfiltered early modern beer contained significant amounts of riboflavin and protein.[145]

Hart claimed that beer needed to be aged a while, and should be of medium strength to provide substance. William Ellis in his *The London*

[139] See, for instance, Edward Whitaker, *Directions for Brewing Malt Liquors* (London, 1700), pp. 3–5; George Watkins, *Compleat English Brewer or, the Whole Art and Mystery of Brewing, in All Its Various Branches* (London, 1767), p. 22. Clark, *English Alehouse*, pp. 112–13; Stanes, *The Old Farm*, p. 71; N. A. M. Rodger, *The Wooden World: An Anatomy of the Georgian Navy* (London, 1986), p. 91; Davies, *Case of Labourers*, p. 39.

[140] Mark Jenner, 'From Conduit Community to Commercial Network? Water in London, 1500–1725', in Paul Griffiths and Mark Jenner (eds.), *Londinopolis: Essays in the Cultural and Social History of Early Modern London* (Manchester, 2000), pp. 250–71.

[141] Hart, *Diet of Diseased*, p. 109; Whitaker, *Directions for Brewing Malt Liquors*, pp. 16–17; William Cockburn, *An Account of the Nature, Causes, Symptoms and Cure of the Distempers That Are Incident to Seafaring People with Observations on the Diet of the Sea-men in His Majesty's Navy* (London, 1696), p. 6.

[142] Hart, *Diet of the Diseased*, p. 127.

[143] *A Vindication of Strong Beer and Ale* (London, 1647), p. 3.

[144] Hart, *Diet of the Diseased*, p. 127.

[145] Davies, *Case of Labourers*, p. 38. Campbell, *Book of Beer*, pp. 106–7; Drummond and Wilbraham, *Englishman's Food*, p. 114.

and Country Brewer claimed that for those occupied in a sedentary life, table (or middle beer) was allowed by physicians to be the most agreeable, but for the laborious man strong beer made from 10 bushels of malt to the hogshead (56 gallons) and aged for at least 9 months was considered to promote perspiration and provide a better supply of energy which could easily be digested into nourishment. The same pamphlet warned against the dangers of trying to work consuming small beer;

for small beer, especially in a Farmer's Family where it is not of a Body enough, the drinkers will be feeble in hot Weather and not be able to perform their work and will also bring on distempers besides a loss of time, and a great waste of such Beer that is generally much thrown away; because drink is certainly a Nourishment of the Body, as well as Meats, and the more substantial they both are, the better will the Labourer go through his work, especially at Harvest.[146]

Indeed most yeomen brewed an extra strong beer, which they called harvest ale, at the end of one harvest which they stored for the next.

The amount of barley grown is perhaps the chief indication that a great deal of beer was drunk in England. In chapter 3 below we will see that the total calories provided by barley for the population were similar to those provided by wheat. Some of this was baked into bread, as we saw above, but this was only a small percentage of the total crop, as barley bread was only eaten in certain areas.[147] Beer consumption, however, has been underestimated when historians have constructed their baskets of consumables for households, largely because it did not figure prominently in the Eden–Davies budgets. But since both Eden and Davies were motivated to investigate the standards of living of the labouring poor because of the poverty created by huge increases in food prices in the late 1780s and 1790s, these budgets were done in a time when consumption had to be cut back significantly, and as a result beer is absent from many of the household budgets they printed.[148] Both Eden and Davies specifically noted that the poor were drinking less beer brewed at home than in the past, and Eden famously decried the replacement of beer with tea and sugar, which he thought was unhealthy.[149] In addition, both Eden and Davies probably underestimated the amount of beer consumed at the alehouse, since there is an obvious reason why very poor families, many of whom were in debt, would be reluctant

---

[146] William Ellis, *The London and Country Brewer ... By a Person Formerly Concerned in a Common Brewhouse at London* (London, 1736), pp. 114–16.

[147] Eden, *State of the Poor*, I, p. 521.

[148] Davies, *Case of Labourers*, pp. 131–91; Eden, *State of the Poor*, II, pp. 15, 74–5, 88–9, 170–1, 174, 204, 228–9, 358–9, 380–1, 433–4, 448–9, 585–6, 622, 645–6, 660–1; III, cccxxxix–cccl, 767–70, 796, 890.

[149] Davies, *Case of Labourers*, p. 40; Eden, *State of the Poor*, II, p. 644.

to tell how much they had spent on drinking. This would have been especially true in the case of Davies, who was a vicar in Berkshire and wrote in *The Case of Labourers in Husbandry* that alehouses tempted the poor to waste their money, corrupted their morals and led to theft and the loss of sleep. He advocated suppressing all alehouses that were not absolutely necessary.[150]

As a result, it is likely that beer drinking had not decreased to the extent that Eden's and certainly Davies's budgets would suggest. Eden, in fact, often gives the numbers of alehouses in parishes.[151] In the parish Frome in Somerset, for instance, which had 1684 houses in 1785, and where there were over 700 labourers and cloth workers, he stated there were 36 alehouses selling 6,700 hogsheads (375,200) gallons of strong beer annually. But in the budget Eden provides for a poor cooper in the parish, he has him only brewing 8 bushels of malt himself into beer, which would produce only about 82 gallons of table beer for his family of 7 per year.[152] Kendal and Kirkland in Cumbria were said to contain 48 alehouses in which 6,620 barrels of ale (225,080 gallons) were drunk annually, which works out to 116 gallons a family per year (1,938 families).[153] Also in Cumbria, miners in Kirkoswald were described as being much given to drinking, but no beer is listed in the budget Eden gives for a miner's family.[154] Eden also gave examples of 2–3 pints of beer being supplied daily in some workhouses.[155]

Although nothing as extensive as the Eden–Davies budgets exist for earlier times, there are examples which show that families were indeed consuming large amounts of beer. It has been calculated that in 1636, guests, servants and casual labourers at the Cecil household consumed 3–5½ pints of beer each per day (depending on its strength).[156] The accounts kept by Sir Edward Coke's wife Bridget for his London household for the week beginning 21 November 1596 show that the household also consumed about 500 gallons of ale in October, which works out to 126 gallons a week.[157] Lower down the social scale, William Harrison's description of the amount of beer his wife brewed every month would have provided 5 pints a day for every member of a family of 10 people.[158] In Salisbury in the 1630s it was reported that the town brewed 1,072 gallons of beer a week for the poor, some of which was strong beer.[159]

---

[150] Davies, *Case of Labourers*, pp. 59–60.
[151] Clark, *English Alehouse*, p. 46.   [152] Eden, *State of the Poor*, II, pp. 643–6
[153] Eden, *State of the Poor*, III, p. 753.   [154] Eden, *State of the Poor*, II, pp. 87–9.
[155] Ibid., II, pp. 147, 230.   [156] Sambrook, *Country House Brewing*, pp. 190–2.
[157] Eden, *State of the Poor*, III, pp. cxx–cxxii.   [158] Stanes, *The Old Farm*, p. 61.
[159] Paul Slack (ed.), *Poverty in Early-Stuart Salisbury*, Wiltshire Record Society, 31 (1975), pp. 113, 118.

The diets outlined in Tables 3.2–3.7 in the next chapter also demonstrate the importance of beer as part of the diets of soldiers and sailors, a yeoman's family including servants and the inmates of early houses of correction. All show the importance of beer both as an important component of meals and as a source of calories for work.[160]

In most institutional diets the amount of beer for men doing moderate work was 4 pints and for working women it was 2 pints a day.[161] But for men doing heavy agricultural work the allowance was generally 6 pints a day to over a gallon. For even heavier work, the herbalist Thomas Culpeper wrote that 'common porters, coal heavers, chairmen, chiefly exist on them [ale and porter] drinking some four gallons a day and indeed such whose labour is very fierce require it'.[162] Beer was considered so important as a means of nourishment for work that it was often an integral part of labourers' wages. Eden noted that in the parish of Halifax in Yorkshire it was the custom to allow drink both in the forenoon and afternoon to labourers of every description.[163] In his *Tour of the Southern Counties* from 1768 Arthur Young noted that beer was often reckoned at 2d in the shilling or one sixth of wages. During the years of very high food prices in the 1790s, William Marshall complained about the traditional amount of beer consumed:

In this country the waste of malt is beyond measure. Beer and ale are not only brewed unreasonably strong; but the quantity allowed to workmen is unnecessarily great. That which is termed 'beer' or 'small beer' is nearly equal in strength, to the harvest mild ale of many counties ... In hay and corn harvest the customary allowance is a gallon of beer a man (in hot weather they drink more), and, besides this, mowers expect two quarts of ale, and never have less than one ... With some difficulty I got turnep hoers to accept of two quarts of beer and one of ale: they demand two of beer and two of ale! enough to stupify any man, and to make a sober man drunk from morning to night.

During the winter months, the quantity of small beer drank is not much less than in the harvest. Mr William Moor of Thorp, a leading man in this neighbourhood, allows his laborers a gallon a day the year round! ... Each man has his gallon bottle filled, in the morning, and what he does not drink, he takes home to his family. His motive for establishing this custom, I understand, was that of his men, when they had the beer cask to go to, or had it given them, whenever they asked for it, by careless wasteful servants, getting drunk, or becoming so muddled and stupid, as to be unfit for their work; and, upon other farms, this seems is no uncommon case. Hence, it is wise to allowance them; for, under this regulation, they drink no more, probably, than is serviceable to

---

[160] Drummond and Wilbraham, *Englishman's Food*, pp. 465–7; Rodger, *Wooden World* p. 92.

[161] Eden, *State of the Poor*, II, pp. 247, 230. In one workhouse it was reported that those who worked received beer at 10.00 a.m. and 4.00 p.m. Ibid., III, p. 822.

[162] Campbell, *Book of Beer*, p. 111.   [163] Eden, *State of the Poor*, III, p. 821.

them; carrying home to their wives and children, that which, if drank, would probably have done them harm.[164]

Many farms brewed their own malt for this purpose, which is discussed in Pamela Sambrook's excellent *Country House Brewing in England*. The accounts of the Newdigate household at Arbury, Warwickshire, from the 1670s shows daily consumption was a gallon for men and half a gallon for women. Other large household accounts show consumption at over 1,000 gallons a month, most of which went to servants. The records of the Middletons at Wollaton in 1781 show this clearly. During the period from June 1781 to January 1782 the butler issued a total of 2,484 gallons of ale and 4,178 gallons of small beer for the servants' consumption, over half of which was consumed in the two months of July and August.[165]

Eden reported that in Gloucestershire drinking a gallon bottle of cider at one time was not uncommon, and he complained about certain farmers, who offered their workers too much strong drink at work, and who drank even more themselves. A Severn man's stomach was said to hold exactly 2 gallons and 3 pints![166] In the Midlands, in harvest time, the common allowance as part of wages was a gallon of strong beer per man and more small beer on hot days, but the mowers always negotiated for at least one more quart of middle beer and often two. Turnip hoers negotiated for 2 quarts of small, and 1 of middle beer per day. Like Marshall, Eden noted that some farmers allowed their labourers a gallon a day all year round in a bottle to prevent them from drawing more from a cask.[167] The late eighteenth-century Norfolk farmer Randall Burroughes offered anywhere from 2 to 7 pints a day, or 2 pints per acre to mowers, of what must have been very strong beer as he valued it at 2d a pint home-brewed.[168] However, Eden did claim that there was a difference in the consumption of beer at work between the north and the south. Southern labourers considered it a necessity to indulge themselves in a certain quantity of malt liquor every day, while those

[164] Arthur Young, *A Six Weeks Tour, Through the Southern Counties of England and Wales* (London, 1768); William Marshall, *The Rural Economy of the Midland Counties* (London, 1796), II, pp. 44–6, as quoted in Sambrook, *Country House Brewing*, pp. 223–4
[165] Sambrook, *Country House Brewing*, pp. 190–240, esp. pp. 194, 201, 207, 211, 229.
[166] Eden, *State of the Poor*, I, pp. 246–7.
[167] Ibid., I, pp. 546–7; III, p. 821. Thomas Batchelor noted that two quarts of ale a day was worth 15s towards harvest wages for a labourer in 1808. Thomas Batchelor, *General View of the Agriculture of the County of Bedford* (London, 1808), p. 80. Building labourers were also often provided with drink at work. Woodward, *Men at Work*, pp. 151–7.
[168] Susanna Martins and Tom Williamson (eds.), *The Farming Journal of Randall Burroughes (1794–1799)*, Norfolk Record Society, 58 (1995), pp. 55, 59, 61, 65, 123, 124, 84–7. The alehouse price in London in the early eighteenth century was 6d a gallon. Ellis, *London and Country Brewer*, p. 121.

in the north drank mostly at festivities and in the alehouse, although a northerner was 'no less prone to brutalize himself by drunkenness' as Eden put it.[169]

Ale consumed in the alehouse would also have added considerably to this consumption as there were certainly a lot of alehouses in England. The number of alehouses in Shrewsbury rose more than threefold from 70 in the 1560s to 220 in the 1620s, while the population went up by less than a half, from 4,700 to 6,300, meaning that there were 28 inhabitants per alehouse, or one for every 6 families by the 1630s.[170] Peter Clark has estimated that there were about 55–60,000 retailers of beer and cider at the end of the seventeenth century, although the number had dropped to about 49,000 by 1810.[171] In the parish of Frome in Somerset, noted above, the 36 alehouses sold 6,700 hogsheads of strong beer annually. There were 1,684 households in the parish, and if we subtract 20 per cent for the wealthy and for widows and the elderly, this works out to 254 gallons per household per year. One calculation made for Coventry in 1520 shows that there was enough malt brewed by the town's 60 brewers to produce 17 pints of strong beer per head of population in the town per week, which is certainly a considerable amount.[172]

Leisure drinking generally took place in the evenings, or on Sunday and holidays, but despite the concerns of governors many town workers, especially in London, used alehouses for drink and food while working, and field labourers could have walked to one in their village if they had a two-hour midday break.[173] In addition, as Wrightson noted, many poor day labouring families relied on alehouses for their supply of beer for their family meals.[174] Although beer might have been purchased at the alehouse by farmers to feed their servants and workers, most evidence shows that for the wealthy brewing continued to be practised at home. Most large country estates possessed large-scale breweries to supply drink for the household, servants and workers.[175] Also Overton et al. have shown that the number of farmers' inventories with brewing or cider-making equipment in Kent actually increased quite dramatically from 33 per cent to 79 per cent between 1650 and 1750.[176] Gregory King also argued that private brewing increased in the four years between 1688 and 1695, and Frederick

[169] Eden, *State of the Poor*, I, p. 542.   [170] Clark, *English Alehouse*, pp. 42–4.
[171] Ibid., p. 46.   [172] Monckton, *English Ale*, p. 95.
[173] Woodward, *Men at Work*, p. 216; John Collins, *Considerations on the Expediency of Raising at this Time of General Dearth, the Wages of Servants That Are Not Domestic* (London, 1767), pp. 5–9.
[174] Wrightson, 'Alehouses', pp. 1–2.
[175] Sambrook, *Country House Brewing*, pp. 1–19.
[176] Overton et al., *Production and Consumption*, pp. 57–60.

Eden claimed the same was true for the eighteenth century as a result of the excise tax. [177]

Beer was brewed in different ways at home and for alehouses, and in order to determine both the calorific content of beer and its potency as a drug, we need to look at the way it was brewed. Traditionally, before the end of the sixteenth century, the English drank unhopped 'ale' rather than 'beer', a name adopted from the Dutch. But since hops act as a preservative, beer lasted much longer than ale.[178] By the seventeenth century most beer was brewed with hops, even if some of it was still called ale (see below) and alehouses retained their traditional name. There were three strengths of beer, small beer, middle beer and strong beer, depending on how much malt was used in proportion to water during the brewing. The process of commercial brewing was described in great detail in William Ellis's *London and Country Brewer* (1736), which he wrote before moving to Hertfordshire, and in Edward Whitaker *Directions for Brewing Malt Liquors* (1700). To prepare for the brewing water was boiled; which was called the liquor. This was then poured hot over the malt, which was called the mash. The liquor was then drawn off the mash and put into a copper kettle or tub (a common household kettle was the size of a barrel or 36 gallons). Hops would then be added before it was boiled for about two to three hours. The hops would be removed and yeast would be added to the fermentation, for which the temperature had to be controlled at between 60–70° F. If the temperature rose above this the beer would be too sour, and since fermentation created its own heat brewing was not done in the summer, except in very cool places.[179]

Most home brewing, though, was more complicated than this as it involved making three worts from the same mash – that is pouring liquor over the same malt three times to make three different strengths of brew, with the first being the strongest and the last the weakest. The amounts of water added for each wort were usually the same, but amounts could vary to make more of one strength of beer, as could the time before the liquor was run off the mash. Records which survive from country house brewers show that in most of the brewing done there, twice as much stronger ale was brewed as small beer. If more small beer was desired, then the second and third worts were run

[177] Gregory King, 'The Burns Journal' (*c.* 1695–1700), in Peter Laslett (ed.), *The Earliest Classics: John Graunt and Gregory King* (London, 1973), p. 59; Eden, *State of the Poor*, I, pp. 540–1.

[178] Clark, *English Alehouse*, pp. 31–2, 96–8.

[179] Ellis, *London and Country Brewer*, pp. 43ff.; Whitaker, *Directions for Brewing Malt Liquors*, pp. 1–20; Sambrook, *Country House Brewing*, pp. 89–104.

together. But without actually replicating such a recipe it is impossible to tell how strong the final wort would have been.[180] This method of brewing gave rise to the names of the three basic strengths of English beer in the period. Strong beer went by various names, and could also be called October or harvest beer. Table beer was also called common or middle beer, which was still very strong by modern standards, while small beer was the weakest. Table beer could also be called 'ale' by this period even though it was hopped, and during the eighteenth century 'ale' came to refer to a light-coloured drink, while 'beer' was darker and thicker. In the eighteenth century a newer dark strong beer called porter was developed.[181]

The small beer produced by such means was undoubtedly very weak, as most of the sugar in the malt would have been used up in the first two mashings and it would have provided little energy. This is why authors such as Thomas Tyron considered it injurious to health. It was thin, and some referred to it as 'trough beer' or 'penny-prick'. Such beer was of little value and was used primarily for children and for immediate hydration. It did not last long, especially in the summer, when it was most needed.[182] It would have been preserved by hops to an extent, and usually had other additives such as pepper, wormwood or berries of various sorts, but all recipes advocated drinking it right away, and since almost all stronger beer had to be brewed in the autumn or winter when it was cooler and the temperature could be controlled, inevitably separate single brewings of small beer had to be done in the summer for rapid drinking. It was not advised to make such separate brewings too weak, as without enough alcohol bacteria could grow, not just 'foxing' the beer, as it was called, but infecting the wooden brewing vessels and potentially damaging future brewings.[183]

Fortunately quite a few recipes for beer survive so it is possible to get an idea of how much malt, hops and water were used, but there is a difficulty in that a bushel of ground malt could vary in weight. The measurement of a bushel of barley was generally 48 lb, but ground malt weighed less depending on the heat applied in drying. In the eighteenth century darker malts for porter became common, which weighed less per bushel because they were dryer, but most home-brewed beer would not have used this malt.[184] Brewers in the early twentieth century took the quarter of malt to be 336 lb, or 42 lb per bushel, which is the

---

[180] Sambrook, *Country House Brewing*, p. 108ff.   [181] Ibid., pp. 17–18.

[182] Watkins, *Compleat English Brewer*, pp. 28, 58–9.

[183] Sambrook, *Country House Brewing*, pp. 119–21, 142.

[184] Overton, *Agricultural Revolution*, p. xiv; Mathias, *Brewing Industry*, pp. 405–16; Sambrook, *Country House Brewing*, p. 130.

measurement used here.[185] One source which gives proportional ingredients for all three strengths of beer is the *London and Country Brewer*. Ellis provided separate recipes for strong, middle and small beer, claiming that separate brewing was the common practice of larger-scale brewers because the small beer produced by the three-wort method was too weak to last very long. For this reason he also advocated making different strengths of beer in different brewings at home as well as in large-scale breweries. Thus although we have a recipe for small beer it is probably stronger than much that was brewed at home using the remains of the malt sugar left in the wort after the first two mashings. The proportions given by Ellis are as follows:

Strong beer	10 bushels (42 lb each) malt produces	1 hogshead beer (54 gal.)
Middle beer	6 bushels malt produces	1 hogshead beer
Small beer	8 bushels malt produces	5 barrels beer (180 gal.)[186]

This results in ratios of 7.8, 4.7 and 1.9 lb of malt used per gallon of beer produced. If this much malt was used in the production of modern beer, using a conversion rate of malt being 80 per cent sugar, these recipes would result in small beer of about 5 per cent alcohol, middle beer of 8–10 per cent and strong beer of about 15 per cent alcohol. However, as I shall discuss below, such high levels of fermentation were unlikely, and most of this malt would have remained in the beer as sugar for energy.

Ellis also included another recipe for country brewing of middle and small ale in which 5 bushels of malt would produce 1 hogshead of middle beer and 1 of small beer. Assuming the middle beer was twice as strong as the small beer this would result in the middle beer using 2.6 lb of malt per gallon, and the small beer 1.3 lb of malt per gallon. The author claimed that when the malt was good enough this would produce a middling ale strong enough for friends, but if it was not strong enough for one's taste he recommended brewing only 36 gallons first for the strong beer, leaving the rest for the second wort.[187] Another almost contemporary pamphlet, *The Theory and Practice of Brewing* by Michael Combrune (1762), gave amounts of malt per barrel which would have resulted in 1.9 lb of malt per gallon of common small beer, 5.3 lb for pale ale and 8.75 lb for Burton strong ale.[188]

---

[185] Campbell, *Book of Beer*, pp. 62–3; Sambrook, *Country House Brewing*, pp. 130.
[186] Ellis, *London and Country Brewer*, pp. 114–17.   [187] Ibid., pp. 43ff.
[188] Sambrook, *Country House Brewing*, p. 112.

In *Directions for Brewing Malt Liquors* Edward Whitaker recommended adding enough water for the first wort so that 11 bushels of malt would produce 1 hogshead of beer, which is even stronger than Ellis's recipe! For the second and third worts he recommended only adding as much water as one wanted to drink, allowing a loss of a sixth for boiling and some for waste. He claimed that this would produce 1 hogshead of middle beer, which was stronger than the common alehouse drink, and one of small beer. For a not very strong drink he claimed 6 or 7 bushels would make 1 hogshead of strong and 1 of small beer, or 3.4 lb of malt per gallon for the strong, and 1.7 lb per gallon for the small beer. He also claimed that unless a man was indigent it was not worth making smaller beer, which he described as being 'like the washing of Graines, it will prove poor Stuff. and if not drank presently, it will apt to stink'.[189] George Watkins in *The Complete English Brewer* of 1667 provided recipes with strengths of 12 lb of malt per gallon for October ale, 6 lb per gallon for what he called family ale, 4 lb per gallon for household beer for common drinking and 2 lb per gallon for small beer.[190] Gregory King estimated that each barrel of strong beer was made with 3 bushels of malt and each barrel of small beer with 1 bushel. This would produce relative strengths of 4.7 lb malt per gallon of strong beer and 1.6 lb per gallon of small beer. Of course, as with all King's figures, these are estimations, and we can see in his rough notes how he made calculations with 2.5 and 3.5 bushels of malt per barrel of strong beer before reaching his final figures, but his strength roughly agrees with the published recipes listed above.

In addition there are examples of accounts which list the amounts of ingredients used in actual brewing. In 1795 Parson Woodforde recorded having brewing a barrel of beer which he made with 1 coomb of malt (168 lb) and 1½ lb of hops, or a ratio of 4.7 lb of malt to the gallon of a heavily hopped beer.[191] Two hundred years earlier, in 1577, William Harrison described his wife's method of making beer which involved making 3 worts with 8 bushels of malt and 80 gallons of liquor. She boiled this with 1½ lb of hops each for 2 hours in the winter and 1½ hours in the summer. Rather than keeping the worts separate Mrs Harrison mixed them together, producing 3 hogsheads of what Harrison described as good beer for poor men, which he provided to his servants and workers. This would produce beer of 2.8 lb malt per gallon. In 1639,

[189] Whitaker, *Directions for Brewing Malt Liquors*, pp. 7–9.
[190] Watkins, *Compleat English Brewer*, pp. 66, 110, 111, 117. For more strengths see Campbell, *Book of Beer*, pp. 63–70.
[191] John Beresford (ed.), *The Diary of a Country Parson: The Reverend James Woodforde* (Oxford, 1968), IV, p. 255.

in *The English Housewife*, Gervase Markham recommended using a quarter of malt with a peck of peas, wheat and oats each to produce a hogshead of strong March beer which would take a year to mature and last for 3 years, as well as a hogshead of ale and one of small beer, or an average of 3 lb of malt per gallon. It has been estimated that following this recipe would produce an initial strong beer of about 12 per cent alcohol.[192] For ordinary beer, which he described as that which noblemen, yeomen and husbandmen would brew to maintain their families for a year, he recommended using 2.8 lb of malt per gallon so that it would last the year and be strong enough for anyone to drink.[193] In 1674 on the Trentham estate of the Dukes of Sutherland in Staffordshire, small beer was brewed with 1.6 lb of malt per gallon, strong beer with 2.7 lb and ale with 7.7 lb. Pamela Sambrook has looked at other examples, and the amount of malt used per gallon ranged from 4.7 to 8 lb. She also examined the brewing of small beer separately, and the strengths of these beers ranged from 1.75 to 2 lb of malt per gallon.[194] Thomas Batchelor noted that most farmers in Bedfordshire in the early nineteenth century brewed ale for their labourers at a strength of 4–4.5 lb per gallon.[195] On the estate of Morval Barton in Cornwall the household accounts record that in 1744, 76 hogsheads of small beer, 53 of ale and 5 of strong beer were brewed from 300 bushels of malt, which produces an average of 1.7 lb of malt per gallon. This is the lowest ratio of malt used per gallon that I have found, but cider was also made on the farm, which might have been consumed in addition to the beer.[196]

Estimating what proportions of strong, middle and small beer were consumed is very difficult. Amounts of different sorts of beer consumed could vary from place to place. In the account books of country houses examined by Pamela Sambrook, some brewed mostly strong beer, while others brewed only ale and small beer.[197] Gregory King estimated that 42 per cent of the beer consumed was strong beer, but he did not distinguish between household and small beer.[198] John Haynes, an Exeter grocer, recorded in his accounts that his family of himself, his wife and two servants drank 1.75 gallons of beer a day in 14 months between July 1639 and September 1640. They drank 77 per cent middle beer priced

[192] Campbell, *Book of Beer*, p. 69.   [193] Markham, *English Housewife*, pp. 181–4.

[194] Sambrook, *Country House Brewing*, pp. 116–23, 207.

[195] Batchelor, *General View*, pp. 74–5.

[196] N. J. G. Pounds, 'Barton Farming in Eighteenth Century Cornwall', *Journal of the Royal Institution of Cornwall*, n. s., 7 (1973), p. 69.

[197] Sambrook, *Country House Brewing*, pp. 159, 161–2. See also the example of Morval Barton on p. 77 above.

[198] King, 'Burn's Journal', pp. 55–6.

at 6s 8d a barrel, 18 per cent best beer and ale priced at 10s a barrel and 5 per cent small beer at 4s a barrel.[199] Most beer consumed was probably stronger middle beer, with small beer being drunk for thirst, especially in the summer, and very strong beer in the alehouse. The fact that alehouses served the strongest brews was complained about in Parliament. Such brews were given special names such as huff-cup or nipitatum. In polite company they were drunk in small glasses of 3–4½ oz each, more like a modern liqueur. We do not know how they were served in an alehouse, but it was claimed that nipitatum could 'make a man look like he had seen the devil'.[200] However, in some documents strong beer is specifically referred to as being drunk at work, as in the case of harvest work. More surprisingly, John Ivie, one of the aldermen of Salisbury, noted in 1661 that the town had brewed both strong beer and ale for the poor.[201]

Weaker beer was generally served at workhouses to the aged and young poor. Information of the amount of malt used in brewing at such institutions shows its strength was generally between 1.5 and 2 lb of malt per gallon. In general, diets show that women usually drank less beer than men, and that much small beer went to supply children with drink. In the Northampton workhouse, children were allowed beer in proportion to their age.[202] At Christ's Hospital 3 pints of beer were served per day, and at a girls' school in Northampton 2 bushels of malt were brewed into a hogshead of beer per week for 20 poor girls.[203] The records of the Foundling Hospital show that after a number of years experimenting with feeding children cow's milk and water, the hospital went back to the more common practice of serving small beer to the children.[204] Children, together with women, must have accounted for much of the consumption of small beer.

---

[199] T. N. Brushfield, 'The Financial Diary of a Citizen of Exeter 1631–43, *Transactions of the Devonshire Association for the Advancement of Science, Literature, and Art*, 33 (1901), pp. 36–7.

[200] Campbell, *Book of Beer*, pp. 69–70.

[201] Slack, *Poverty in Salisbury*, p. 112. For the price of strong beer see Clark, *English Alehouse*, p. 103.

[202] Eden, *State of the Poor*, II, p. 537. At the Great Yarmouth workhouse mutton and veal were allowed to the sick on Sundays. Ibid. II, p. 526.

[203] Ibid., III, p. 808; *An Account of Several Workhouses for Employing and Maintaining the Poor* (London, 1725), pp. 62, 96–7, 114; Timothy V. Hitchcock (ed.), *Richard Hutton's Complaint Book: The Notebook of the Steward of the Quaker Workhouse at Clerkenwell 1711–1737*, London Record Society, 24 (1987), p. 66.

[204] London Metropolitan Archives, Foundling Hospital General Court Minutes, A/FH/K/01/1, 17th Dec., 1745, Steward's Account Book, Household Expenses, A/FH/B8/7/1 (1758); Ruth K. McClure, *Coram's Children: The London Foundling Hospital in the Eighteenth Century* (New Haven, 1981), pp. 197–8.

I have gone through so many examples here to show that most beer contained a lot of malt, and that the assumption that most of the beer drunk was small beer is erroneous. In anticipation of the next chapter, I will now attempt to estimate how many calories might have been provided by each strength of beer by measuring the original calories in the malt used per gallon. Malt contains about the same number of calories as raw barley (1,652 kcal per pound) but the barley husks are all lost in the brewing so they have to be eliminated from the weight of the barley crop, which amounts to about 20 per cent.[205] In addition, brewing that involves only one wort will never be able to use up all the sugar in the barley corns. Most modern industrial brewing can extract 90 per cent of the sugars, while modern home brewers normally obtain 80 per cent extraction (or 65 per cent of the total weight of the original barley). But in the early modern period, as we saw, almost every home-brewing involved two to three worts to extract as much sugar as possible from the barley so none would go to waste. Only large town brewers would have made beer with only two worts, and they would have sold the spent grains to feed cattle and pigs.[206] Some of the calorific value of the malt would thus have been lost in this way, but it is unlikely to have been a large percentage. Also, as all of the authors cited above noted, some of the small beer would have undoubtedly spoiled if it could not be drunk in time. In addition, there would have been losses to vermin and in transport, so I have used a 27 per cent reduction in calories to account for all of these factors, which results in malt providing 1,206 kcal per pound.[207] Using this calculation, Ellis's recipes in the *London and Country Brewer* would have produced a pint of strong beer with an astounding 1,300 kcal per pint, and even 286 kcal for a pint of small beer. In comparison a pint of modern bitter

---

[205] John Palmer, *How to Brew* (Boulder, CO, 2006), ch. 12.

[206] Peter Mathias, 'Agriculture and the Brewing and Distilling Industries in the Eighteenth Century', *Economic History Review*, n.s., 5 (1952), pp. 249–57. Much more food value was contained in distillers' waste.

[207] This is much less than the very large figure for waste of 70 per cent used by Overton and Campbell in their calculations. This was based on a calculation originally done in a volume on medieval London's grain supply which involved using evidence of the number of pints of ale derived from a bushel of malt in wealthy medieval households and then comparing the number of calories in the raw barley with average calorific values for modern strong and weak beer, taken from the 1960 edition of *The Composition of Foods*. This showed a difference of about 70 per cent, which was interpreted as a loss. But since the ratio of malt to water in early modern beer was much higher, using calorie counts for modern ale is inappropriate. There were more calories per pint in this beer, and weaker beer would also have been obtained from subsequent worts. Mark Overton and Bruce M. S. Campbell, 'Production et productivité dans l'agriculture anglaise, 1086–1871', *Histoire & Mesure*, 11 (1996), p. 296, Table 13; B. M. S. Campbell, J. A. Galloway, D. Keene and M. Murphy, *A Medieval Capital: Agrarian Production and Distribution in the London Region c. 1300*, Historical Geography Research Series, 30 (1991), p. 34 n.59.

contains about 180–200 kcal and a pint of extra-strong beer about 400 kcal. Most of the other recipes indicate that such strong beer was for special drinking and most of the 'strong' or middle beer intended to be drunk by workers was made with between 2.7 and 4 lb of malt per gallon, which would have provided 350–500 kcal per pint. Small beer made from the third wort would have varied even more in strength, but the above examples indicate that a pint would have contained between 200 and 250 kcal. When doing the calculation for diets in the next chapter I have adopted a strength of 600 kcal for strong beer, assuming that very strong beer was not drunk that often at work. For table or middle beer I have used a value of 400 kcal per pint, and 200 for small beer.

Having considered calories in beer, it remains to consider alcohol content and intoxication. As noted previously, using modern yeast, a beer made with a ratio of 1.5–2 lb of malt per gallon would produce a beer of 5–7 per cent alcohol, while 4 lb of malt to a gallon would produce a beer with about 10–12 per cent alcohol and a small beer of 0.5–1 lb malt per gallon would result in a beer of about 2 per cent alcohol. The very strongest ales with 8 or more lb of malt per gallon would have produced beer of such a strength that the alcohol produced would have eaten the yeast and stopped fermentation, providing an extremely strong and extremely sweet brew. If this was the strength advocated to be drunk by labourers for work, a gallon would have been the equivalent of about four bottles of strong modern wine, which some labourers might have drunk every day of the week. Even small beer drunk by children would have been intoxicating. If this was the case it is not surprising that Francis Bacon claimed that not one person in a thousand in England died a natural death.[208]

However, from modern nutritional knowledge we know that if the strong beer indeed had as much alcohol as most strains of modern yeast would permit (between 11 and 13 per cent) it is difficult to see how it could have been a good provider of energy, as the calories in alcohol are not carbohydrates, but have to be broken down by the liver into acetaldehyde. This process can only be done at a limited rate of, on average, around a third of an ounce of alcohol per hour, which is why the alcohol stays in the blood, producing intoxicating effects and hangovers.[209] At such a rate, the body can only deal with about four pints of very strong beer in a day. But modern yeasts are standardised to ferment the malt sugar to a certain degree, while in contrast early modern yeasts were variable and there is much evidence that the alcoholic content of different brews varied considerably.[210] It also seems probable that the

[208] Ellis, *London and Country Brewer*, p. 97.   [209] Campbell, *Book of Beer*, pp. 96ff.
[210] Sambrook, *Country House Brewing*, pp. 93, 132–4; Mathias, *Brewing Industry*, pp. 48–9, 73–6.

yeast strains used must have stopped fermenting at a lower concentration of alcohol, as with some wine yeast, and that smaller quantities of yeast were used. Thomas Batchelor noted that the mode of country brewing produced a less intoxicating beer than that made by public brewers.[211] William Ellis, both in his *London and Country Brewer* and *Country Housewife*, cautioned against adding too much yeast to a wort, because he considered it to be unhealthy in itself, describing it as a poisonous acid, arguing that too much 'will make the Liquor so heady that five Bushels of Malt may be equal in strength to six, and that by the stupifying Narcotick Qualities of the Yeast'. He went on to blame the symptoms of hangovers on yeast rather than alcohol.[212] Many of the pamphlets on brewing also contain instructions to the brewer to intervene in the fermentation process when a more potent beer was desired by beating the wort, or alternatively slowing the process of fermentation by adding cold water.[213]

In terms of providing energy for hard labour, a sweet brew would make more sense to our understanding of nutrition, and the English taste for sweet Spanish wine from Madeira and the Canaries in the seventeenth century perhaps reflects such a preference for sweetness. It would also make sense when we think that before the mid-eighteenth century refined sugar from cane had to be imported and was extremely expensive, while the only natural sweeteners were honey and ripe fruit. If this was so, then a desire for sweetness could have been met from the malt in beer. The fact that beer was commonly taken as part of medicinal treatments in the form of a posset – that is, heated and mixed with milk, eggs and spices, or mixed with porridge in the morning for breakfast – indicates that it was probably sweet. One author, however, did describe beer of middle strength as being possibly too bitter, although this might have been relative.[214]

Given such uncertainties it is probable that we will never know exactly how strong beer was in this period. But it is very likely that a great deal of it was much stronger than most modern beer, and it was consumed in large amounts. The amount of alcohol present in a pint of beer is crucial to understanding how people worked in early modern society, but the effect on their state of mind and abilities is difficult to determine because very few workers would now be encouraged to drink a gallon of very strong beer or wine during a day's work. But beer, in more

---

[211] Batchelor, *General View*, pp. 74–5.
[212] Ellis, *London and Country Brewer*, pp. 80–1; Ellis, *Country Housewife*, pp. 12, 14.
[213] Ellis, *London and Country Brewer*, pp. 83–4; Watkins, *Compleat English Brewer*, pp. 44–6, 60ff.; Whitaker, *Directions for Brewing Malt Liquors*, pp. 16–17.
[214] Hart, *Diet of the Diseased*, pp. 125–7.

moderate quantities, was still considered very good for work well into the twentieth century in many jobs requiring hard labour.[215] It was both the alcoholic content of the beer and its taste which made it so attractive. Furthermore, in areas of the south where porridge was less common it must have made eating bread easier. Beer was drunk both with meals and at breaks in the morning and afternoon at work, and must have played an important part in making the very long working days pass, by lubricating sociability.[216] On the other hand, given its strength, it must also have played a role in the many accidents and disputes which happened at work in this period. As James Sharpe has noted for homicide cases in Essex between 1620 and 1680, killings involving sticks, staffs, tools and other blunt instruments such as pots or pieces of hard earth, which were the result of fights, outweighed killings with guns or knives.[217] It is difficult to determine from pamphlets on diet and health where the cut-off line between drunkenness and 'normal' intoxication was. For moralists, as Keith Wrightson has shown, disorder was the key behavioural feature, but descriptions of people staggering down the street and vomiting or collapsing on the street were common features in descriptions of drunkenness. When discussing drink, writers in the Galenic tradition inevitably fell back on the classical golden mean, with too little drink not providing enough sustenance for work, and too much leading to drunkenness. Hart, in *Diet of the Diseased*, described the condition of drunkenness almost exclusively in moralistic terms, a form of criticism he thought more appropriate to be undertaken by the clergy. Only as an afterthought did he claim that he thought most people who drank heavily died before old age from 'dropsies, consumptions, and palsies'.[218]

In years of dearth puritan moralists argued that barley should be made into flour rather than malt. In fact the saving in calories would not have been that great, since with three worts little was wasted, except what went bad.[219] However, bread was cheaper to make as the expense of both malting and brewing was greater than baking, and bread was more important as a provider of calories for the sick and young, who suffered most in dearths. Moralists were much more concerned with drinking in alehouses for pleasure, rather than for sustenance, which they saw as the real immoral result of brewing beer in times of dearth. This was

---

[215] Monckton, *History of English Ale*.

[216] Eden, *State of the Poor*, III, p. 822. Sambrook, *Country House Brewing*, pp. 221–3.

[217] J. A. Sharpe, *Crime in Seventeenth-Century England: A County Study* (Cambridge, 1983), pp. 128–30. See also John Bettie, *Crime and the Courts in England 1660–1800* (Oxford, 1986), pp. 94–5.

[218] Hart, *Diet of the Diseased*, pp. 128–37.   [219] Campbell, *Book of Beer*, p. 50.

especially true of Sundays, St Monday or other days when labourers might take the whole day off in the alehouse, where the motivation had much more to do with alcohol, tobacco and good fellowship rather than calories for work. In sixteenth-century Coventry, for instance, there were concerns on the part of its governors that labourers would spend all day in the alehouse playing cards, so they enacted an order that 'noo labourer, journeyman, or prentyse upon any worke daye' should resort to any inn, tavern or alehouse upon pain of a day's imprisonment.[220] The vestrymen of eighteenth-century Terling in Essex, while accepting the need of 'the Industrious and Honest labourer [to] proper Refreshment', were unhappy with labourers and other working persons frequenting the parish's sole remaining alehouse, and so disallowed the sale of drink during working hours and limited the sale of beer to one quart per person per day.[221]

Frederick Eden, interestingly, was much more sympathetic to alehouses than earlier moralists, or his contemporary David Davies. He was well-disposed to beer drinking compared to tea, but also thought that the practice of drinking stream water or milk, as well as watery soup at work, was better than relying on beer in hard times. However, in a lengthy footnote he actually praised alehouses as an institution which provided welfare on credit to labourers during necessary periods of unemployment between jobs, in return for all the money spent normally on drink. In this way they helped the labour market function. Disorder, he claimed, was only the abuse of a beneficial institution.[222]

Meat

As we saw in the section on health, meat was one of the foods advocated for labourers as necessary for work, and there is convincing evidence to back this up. Andrew Boord's claim about the English being especially great meat-eaters in the sixteenth century is echoed elsewhere. Foreign visitors noted the fact, with one saying the English were 'flesh eaters and insatiable of animal food'.[223] William Harrison noted that:

In number of dishes and change of meat, the nobility of England (whose cooks are for the most part musical-headed Frenchmen and strangers) do most

[220] Monckton, *History of English Ale*, pp. 99–100.
[221] Wrightson, 'Alehouses', p. 21.
[222] Eden, *State of the Poor*, I, pp. 545–6. See also Leonard Schwartz, *London in the Age of Industrialisation: Entrepreneurs, Labour Force and Living Conditions, 1700–1850* (Cambridge, 1993), pp. 119–23.
[223] Drummond and Wilbraham, *Englishman's Food*, p. 53.

exceed ... they have not only beef, mutton, veal, lamb, kid, pork, cony, capon, pig ... deer ... beside great variety of fish and wild fowl.[224]

We have already seen just how much meat the Earl of Surrey and Lord Burghley served, and this was not unusual. Lawrence Stone noted how other noble households ate huge numbers of animals, such as that of the Earl of Shrewsbury, which in one week in September 1602 consumed twenty-three sheep and lambs, two bullocks, one veal calf, fifty-nine chickens, capons and pullets, five pigs, twenty-four pigeons and fifty-four rabbits.[225] For the aristocracy the consumption of a great quantity and variety of meat was symbolic of their status. Although most of the meat eaten was domestic, game still featured large in aristocratic diets, and the consumption of meat reflected the privilege of hunting for wild animals, when society required land for fuel, pasture and crops.[226] Even members of the gentry like Nicolas Blundell who had little woodland exercised themselves coursing hares on a regular basis.[227]

But there is plenty of evidence of others consuming much meat as well. William Harrison noted that husbandmen's and artificers' food included

beef, such meat as the butcher selleth, that is to say, mutton, veal, lamb, pork, etc. ... beside souse, brawn [boar] eggs ... In feasting also [the husbandmen] do exceed after their manner, especially at bride-ales, purifications of women [churchings] ... where it is incredible to tell what meat is consumed and spent, each one bringing such a dish or so many with him as his wife and he do con-sult upon, but always with this consideration, that the liefer [dearer] friend shall have the better provision.[228]

The scholars at King's College, Cambridge ate between 1 and 2 lb of meat a day outside of Lent.[229] The accounts of William Cecil, the second Earl of Salisbury from Salisbury House on the Strand in London from the week ending 24 January 1635 provide evidence that many servants were being fed in aristocratic houses as well. There the accounts show that an incredible 1,176 lb of beef were consumed that week in addi-tion to a likely 190 lb of veal, lamb and suckling pig, which works out to about 200 lb day. We know from other records that in addition to the earl's family and guests, which varied between five and ten people per

[224] Harrison, *Description*, p. 126.
[225] Stone, *Crisis of the Aristocracy*, p. 557.
[226] Daniel C. Beaver, *Hunting and the Politics of Violence before the English Civil War* (Cambridge, 2008), ch. 1.
[227] Frank Tyrer and J. J. Bagley (eds.), *The Great Diurnal of Nicholas Blundell*, 3 vols., Record Society of Lancashire and Cheshire, 110, 112, 114 (1968–72), II, pp. 1–51 *passim*, 76–150 *passim*, 211–75 *passim*; III, pp. 1, 3, 25, 61, 96, 127, 150, 192, 194, 197.
[228] Harrison, *Description*, p. 131.   [229] See below, Table 3.2.

meal, ninety-four meals were given to the guests' servants per week, and there were probably about sixty servants of Salisbury's to feed. This works out to about 75 people to serve a day, or 2.6 lb of meat per person. To this would have to be added many fish, chickens, a turkey and over a hundred songbirds. However, there is evidence that many other casual employees, perhaps as many as another sixty-five, were also fed in the household.[230] The Duke of Chandos's servants were also eating 8.5 lb of meat each per week in the eighteenth century.[231] Mutton and veal were considered good food to feed the sick, and veal was fed to young children in the Foundling Hospital.[232]

But not only the wealthy and their servants ate meat. There is much evidence to suggest that labourers ate as much as the literature on diets suggested they should. What seems to have distinguished upper-class meals from those eaten by labourers was the wider variety of meats in different courses, and above all the availability of a wide variety of expensive fish or sea-food, including, in one case, a porpoise. In contrast, it has been noted by Fernand Braudel and other historians that Europe in general was very carnivorous in the fifteenth century and earlier, but that meat-eating declined precipitously with the general rise in population in the sixteenth and seventeenth centuries. This put pressure on agrarian resources, which required more pasture to be turned into arable land. Agricultural labourers in the country around Narbonne ate about 40 kg (88 lb) a year on average between 1480 and 1534, which had dropped to 20 kg of meat a year by 1583. In Rome the average was 38 kg between 1600 and 1605, which had dropped to about 23.5 kg in the 1780s. In Germany by the early nineteenth century the average was less than 20 kg per head.[233] England, however, seems to have been an exception to this rule, where in the eighteenth century a foreign visitor could still note that the English ate nothing but meat.[234]

Two of the most famous images of the eighteenth century marked the new identity of Britishness with the eating of beef, in contrast to French society. William Hogarth's famous painting *O the Roast Beef*

---

[230] Lionel M. Munby (ed.), *Early Stuart Household Accounts*, Hertfordshire Record Society, 2 (1986), pp. xvii–xviii, 40–2. The servants of Thomas Barrington were recorded in John Petre's accounts as eating a lot of meat when travelling, including chickens, rabbits and mutton. ERO: D/DBa: John Petre's Account Book, 1576–7, f.39v, 40r–v. I would like to thank Dr Matthew Clark for this reference.

[231] Stone, *Crisis of the Aristocracy*, p. 558.

[232] McClure, *Coram's Children*, p. 197; London Metropolitan Archives, Steward's Account Book, Household Expenses, A/FH/B8/6/2, i.e. 28 Nov. and 5 Dec., 1746; Eden, *State of the Poor*, II, p. 526.

[233] Raffaella Sarti, *Europe at Home: Family and Material Culture, 1500–1800* (New Haven, 1999), p. 177: Braudel, *Civilization and Capitalism*, I, p. 196.

[234] Braudel, *Civilisation and Capitalism*, I, pp. 198–9.

of Old England or Calais Gate from 1748 shows an innkeeper carrying a huge joint of beef imported from France to an English inn, while French soldiers eat a watery broth. A fat Catholic monk tests the meat and a group of poor French women look at a few paltry small fish with vegetables in the background. The second image, from the period of the French Revolution, James Gillray's *French Liberty: British Slavery*, shows an emaciated sansculotte sitting on a stool beside a meagre fire in rags, but with a badge of liberty in his cap, eating leeks, with a chamber-pot full of snails on the table. By way of contrast, in the facing panel, an enormously fat John Bull uses a knife and fork to cut into a piece of roast or boiled beef while complaining of taxes.[235] Both these images contributed to the formation of national stereotypes, but were based on what measurement indicates were real differences in the consumption of meat.

The most common types of meat eaten by the poor were beef and mutton, and then bacon. The evidence analysed in the next chapter on diets certainly shows that meat was provided for those engaged in hard physical labour, with 1.2–2 lb of salt beef per day being provided to soldiers and sailors in the mid-sixteenth century. Robert Loder's farm servants also consumed between 1 and 2 lb of meat a day. Perhaps the most striking example is the amount of meat advocated for the London Bridewell in 1600 of 1.5 lb of meat per day, apart from fast days, when a smaller amount of cheese replaced the meat, and the amounts provided in the Westminster and Bury St Edmunds houses of correction were not dissimilar.[236]

Other evidence for the seventeenth and eighteenth centuries from farm accounts supports the high level of meat consumption for farm servants. The servants of the Blowfield family of Suffolk must have been consuming a large amount of in meat the 1660s and 1670s. With an annual average expenditure of around £150, the family purchased almost 1,600 lb of beef alone in 48 transactions in 1674, and this was in addition to hundreds of pounds of mutton and veal. This works out to about 5½ lb of meat per day, each day of the year. The accounts do not give an indication of how big Blowfield's immediate nuclear family was, but he seems to have employed 5 or 6 servants on average, so they were probably eating between ½ and 1 lb of meat a day.[237] In 1656 Giles Moore bought 210 lb of meat for 8 weeks, which works out

[235] Mark Hallett and Christine Riding, *Hogarth* (London, 2006), pp. 216–17; Linda Colley, *Britons: Forging the Nation 1707–1837* (London, 1992), pp. 33–5.

[236] See below, p. 126.

[237] Suffolk Record Office, HA 30: 369/249; Harrison, *Description*, p. 131; Norman Jones, *The Birth of the Elizabethan Age: England in the 1560s* (Oxford, 1993), p. 253.

to 3.75 lb per day when he employed 2 servants.[238] Somewhat later, during the harvest of 1705, the Rev. Mr John Crakanthorp purchased 982 lb of beef, mutton and lamb for the harvest. At this time he would probably have had only one son at home, together with his wife and their maidservant. For the harvest he hired 8 extra workers. In 1706 he bought 692 lb of meat and slaughtered a hog for 26 days of harvest work, for which he employed 7 harvest workers at wages of £1 10s each. If we conservatively assume the hog provided 100 lb of meat this works out to the enormous figure of 3 lb of meat a day per person for 10 people in 1705.[239] This was in addition to 80 lb of cheese, 18 lb of sugar and 70 lb of currants and raisins, most of which would have been for the harvesters. Similarly, in 1715, the Cotton family of Madingley in Cambridgeshire made purchases of meat over the course of the year which are listed in Figure 2.1 below. When odd purchases of pieces of veal and mutton are added to these totals this works out to about 4,570 lb of meat per year or 12.5 lb per day. The accounts of the hiring of labour do not survive, but the farm was a large one with 1,026 acres, of which 533 were pasture. But, as we can see, this average went up dramatically to around 20 lb per day during the three harvest

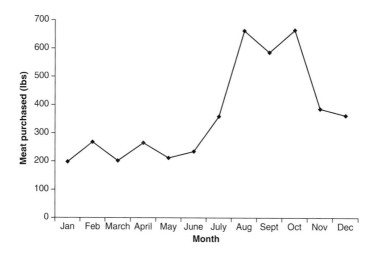

Figure 2.1 Cotton family meat purchases, 1715

[238] Ruth Bird (ed.), *The Journal of Giles Moore*, Sussex Record Society, 68 (1971), p. 62.
[239] Paul Lambert Brassley and Philip Anthony Saunders (eds.), *Accounts of the Reverend John Crakanthorp of Fowlmere 1682–1710*, Cambridgeshire Records Society, 8 (1988), pp. 142–3, 186, 224. In 1707 the amount consumed during 30 days of harvest work was about 2.6 lb per person.

months of August, September and November as well as during July and December, when weeding and threshing respectively would have been taking place. This implies that meat was being served to servants and/ or labourers, as William Ellis recommended doing during the harvest in order to attract the best workers.[240]

Parson Woodforde's butcher's bills ranged from £33 to £46 a year in the 1780s. He did not specify what sort of meat he was purchasing, but at individual occasions during the year he also recorded buying fine cuts such as loins of veal or neck of pork as well as much poultry, and on occasion he also killed a pig. His veal generally cost him 3–4d a pound, which would imply that beef might have been 3d a pound. During his life at Weston in Norfolk, Woodforde lived unmarried with his niece Nancy and always had 5 live-in servants to help with the household and to farm the rectory glebe land of 46 acres. There was one servant in husbandry, a footman who also did odd jobs, a yard boy of under ten years of age who helped on the farm and two female domestics – a cook and a maidservant. The amount Woodforde spent on meat was enough to have provided about 7–10 lb a day from the butcher alone. Even given the prodigious amounts he served when he entertained guests there must still have been much which was also fed to the servants.[241]

The widow Frances Hamilton ran a small farm at Bishops Lydeard, Somerset, at the end of the eighteenth century. Most of the produce of the farm was sold in small amounts to local people. She employed 2 female servants and one male servant, and she also hired parish apprentices as well as other farm labour. She kept meticulous accounts, and in 1800 estimated that between January and March she bought 365 lb of butcher's meat when there were 7 people in her family, which worked out to 4.25 lb per person per week.[242] At the Crowcombe Barton farm, also in Somerset, 18 lb of meat was consumed per day in 1736. Here there were 7 family members, and on average 10 labourers were hired to do farm work.[243]

There are also examples from northern account books which show that meat consumption was equally high there. Although Ellis argued that more bacon was eaten in the north than beef, the account books of larger farms show that, at least there, this was an exaggeration.[244] A set of very detailed calculations of meat consumption exists for

[240] CRO, Cotton 588A2, E9; Ellis, *Country Housewife*, p. 47.
[241] Woodforde, *Diary*, ed. Winstanley, III, pp. 94, 186; X, pp. 10, 24, 84, 89, 107, 17, 180, 181, 196, 302, 287, 300; XI, pp. 26, 17, 22, 91, 194, 296. Winstanley, *Parson Woodforde*, pp. 187–9.
[242] SRO, DD/FS/5/9, DD/FS/7/4, DD/FS/7/5. Steedman, *Master and Servant*, p. 17.
[243] SRO, DD/TB/14/8, DD/TB/14/11.   [244] Ellis, *Country Housewife*, p. 95.

Harewood House, Yorkshire, the home of the Lascelles family, for the years 1799 and 1802. In the former year, it was recorded that fully 31,640.75 lb of butcher's meat and slaughtered stock was consumed in the six months previous to 28 February, which works out to 174 lb per day. During the same period they had an average of nine guests per day dining with the family, and they probably employed about fifty servants and twenty-five day labourers and boys.[245] The Tempest family of Tong Hall, northeast of Leeds, consumed an average of 4.5 lb of butcher's meat a day between November 1762 and November 1763, and in 1772 £53 3s was spent on meat from the butcher, and £87 9s the following year. At a price of 4d a pound this works out to 8.7 lb per day and 14.4 lb per day respectively. Here the estate demesne farm was small and seems to have been largely pastoral. Although no wage books exist for these years, in 1787 only one servant in husbandry was hired year round, but in July and August about eighteen different men and women were hired from periods of a day to three weeks for weeding and harvest work.[246]

The Allgood family of Nunwick Hall near Hexham in Northumberland also ate a considerable amount of meat. In 1746, besides slaughtering a pig they purchased £77 worth of meat, which at 3d a pound works out to 16.8 lb per day. In 1760 the farm produced about 1,624 bushels of oats and 160 bushels of malt and a little bit of wheat.[247] The farm employed about eight household and farm servants, and four day labourers were hired who worked regularly, as well as various other irregular workers. The size of the household is unknown, but given such large consumption, even if the family was entertaining constantly, much of this meat must have been fed to the labourers.[248] In fact, a separate ledger broke down the year's expenses for 1746 in money spent on the cellar (£58 18s 10d), kitchen (£168 9s 6d), furniture (£29 7s 1d) and servants (£271 15s 6d). The ledger does not specify what the servants' expenses were, but presumably they consisted of wages, food and lodging. The fact that this figure is considerably larger than the kitchen

---

[245] WYASL, WYL/250/3/214, 222, 263, 266.

[246] WYASB, Tong/5a/5, Tong/5a/7, Tong/4b/7, Tong/4b/23. On the Spencer Standhope farm at Cannon Hall, Cawthorne, between Huddersfield and Sheffield, 2.68 lb of meat was eaten per day in 1787, with much more being eaten during August. The farm accounts do not list any fields or pasture, only dog kennels and a garden. There was one servant until 16 March and two thereafter. A little bit of work was done by the first servant's wife. WYASB, Sp St/6/2/1/2, Sp St/5/4/1/7.

[247] The harvest of oats is given as 812 bolls worth £104. The Northumberland boll could vary from 2 to 6 bushels, and here the price suggests it was 2 bushels, which would amount to 1.3s a bushel. NCS, ZBL/274/1.

[248] NCS, ZAL/44/1, ZAL/45/6, ZAL/46/8, ZAL/57/26.

expenses indicates that much of the expenditure must have been on the servants.[249]

This evidence certainly shows that farm servants were eating a lot of meat, but it is more difficult to know how much meat self-employed day labourers ate while working. Day labourers on the Tabor farm in late seventeenth-century Essex were paid with quite large quantities of meat in exchange for their work, so they were certainly eating it.[250] In 1736 the poor Lancashire farmer Richard Latham (see above, p. 56) spent £15 3s when his family was composed of 2 adults and 4 children under 10 years of age (one child died during the year). In that year he bought 58 lb of beef, mutton and various other poorer-quality animal parts such as cow cheeks, calves' heads, sheep's plucks worth about 10s, and killed 2 of his own swine. In 1747 he sold a cow to the butcher, Jonathan Rodgers, for £3 10s and over the course of the next 16 months purchased about 114 lb of meat and killed a swine.[251] There is no way of knowing how heavy the pigs he killed were, but this might have provided him with about a pound of meat a day during this period divided between his whole family, which would have been less than a servant was fed, but again it is also likely that Latham himself received some food while he was working as a carter.

Some examples exist of skilled labourers' consumption of meat in the eighteenth century. Pitmen and keelmen in Newcastle who could earn between 16 and 20s a week were said to consume 'a great deal of butchers meat during the first three or four first days of the week' until their earnings became exhausted.[252] In the prosperous cloth towns of Halifax and Leeds butcher's meat was said to be very generally used by labourers.[253] A calico weaver's family in the parish of Wetheral in Cumberland was said to spend £8 10s a year on butcher's meat, which at 3d a pound works out to 680 lb, which for the family of eight would work out to 4 oz per person per day, or 5.5 oz for the man and eldest boy, assuming they ate more. In addition 50 lb of butter was also purchased.[254] Some farm labourers were boarded by the farmer employing them (see below, p. 226) and presumably ate the same diet as the farm servants, but, in addition, their families would still have had to have been fed. When we examine some budgets in the next chapter it will become evident that it

---

[249] NCS, ZAL/46/7.
[250] Other labourers were paid with similar amounts of beef and pork. ERO, D/DTa/A1, 12 Nov. 1690–22 Sept. 1690; July, 1784; 1 and 22 Oct, 5 Nov. 1785.
[251] Weatherill (ed.), *Account Book of Richard Latham*, p. 123.
[252] Eden, *State of the Poor*, II, p. 551.   [253] Ibid., II, pp. 820, 847.
[254] Ibid., II, pp. 98–9. A dyer in Manchester spent 2s 3d a week on butcher's meat, which at 3½d a pound works out to 7 lb 12oz a week. He was 65 and lived with his wife only, but often fed his children and grandchildren. Ibid., II, p. 358.

would have been difficult for labourers working for day wages to be able to afford to feed their entire families with as much meat as servants ate. Eden also included a great deal of information on workhouses throughout the country, which included both diets and the amount of food provided, and from these it is possible to show that meat consumption was often quite high, even as food prices rose in the 1780s and 1790s. He usually included the numbers and types of inmates in the workhouses, so it is possible to get an idea of what the poor were eating in institutions in the latter half of the eighteenth century, including meat. For instance, in the Nottingham workhouse weekly consumption of meat was 4 lb a week per person on average, with three hot-meat days and three cold-meat days. There were forty-two boys aged between six months and fourteen years, thirty-five girls under twenty, thirty men aged between twenty and sixty, and sixty-one women aged between twenty and eighty, although some of the children worked in the cotton mills.[255] Here Eden worked out the meat consumption from the actual account book for the workhouse, and for the adults the consumption must have been close to a pound a day. When describing the workhouse in Halifax, Eden noted that the rules there were specific about the need for meat at work: 'those who work out of doors, in the kitchen or in other house business, are allowed butcher's meat for every dinner in the week, others have meat dinners on Sundays and Thursdays: children have pudding instead of boiled meat. Working people receive a pint of beer each at 10 a.m. and 4 p.m. Those who have been used to tobacco have ½ lb a month.'[256] The workhouse in Buckingham also served meat every day, as did the Hampton workhouse in Middlesex, which served meat every day with vegetables from its garden, which the men cultivated. It was always boiled beef, alternating with cold leftovers the next day.[257]

At workhouses where inmates were less robust, meat consumption was less. At the workhouse in St Alkmund parish, Derby, of the thirty-six inmates, six were under the age of seven, and eight were between the ages of seven and twelve who only did 'a little work', while the rest were chiefly middle-aged women who were employed in silk and cotton mills. They all received 8 oz of meat each on three meat days a week. In All Saints parish in the same town, the master of the workhouse allowed 3 lb of meat a week to each inmate on six meat days. Here there were fifty-three inmates, most of whom were described as old and infirm, who worked twelve hours a day exclusive of meals.[258] At the Oxford

---

[255] Ibid., II, pp. 576–7.   [256] Ibid., III, p. 822.
[257] Ibid., II, pp. 26, 435–6.   [258] Ibid., II, pp. 115–21.

workhouse men received 6 oz of meat, women 5 oz and boys 4 oz without the bone, although the yearly accounts printed by Eden indicate that enough for 8.6 oz per person was bought.[259] In the Northampton workhouse the poor had as much bread and meat as they could eat three days a week, and the victuals were not weighed. Children were allowed beer in proportion to their age.[260]

Clearly these accounts show that the amount of meat on offer could vary according to the way the workhouses were set up, financed and managed, but in none of the examples does the amount offered seem mean or tight-fisted. It is interesting that Eden commented of Hampton in Middlesex that 'the food seems wholesome and good and it is certainly much better than a labouring man could afford his family'.[261] This is not the only time Eden made such a comment, but again we need to remember that the price of food had risen greatly in the 1780s and 1790s, and that day labourers would have not been able to afford to keep up their previous standard of living. It is possible that workhouse diets might have been better to entice people in, thus saving money on rent and outdoor relief. However, earlier in the century when a workhouse was set up in St John's parish, Glastonbury, the diarist John Cannon commented that it was only intended to house about a third of the town's poor, presumably the old and young, although he also commented that the 'noise of a workhouse so terrified most of them that they compared the same no less than a house of correction'.[262]

Workhouses were set up to save money on rent and food by cooking in bulk, and there is little evidence that diets were designed by their managers to be better than what the working poor ate. The diets were meant to be healthy. Because workhouses were managed by boards or people hired especially for that purpose, ratepayers seem less likely to have interfered to reduce payments as they did with individual cases in vestries controlling outdoor relief.[263] Some diets were very generous indeed. Eden quoted at length from a pamphlet published detailing reforms made at the two Norwich workhouses in the 1780s by a member of the court of guardians which ran the institutions. The older workhouse was housed in a former palace of the Duke of Norfolk, and was one of the largest and oldest in the country. Together they housed 1,200–500 paupers. The workhouses were run by a court of sixty

---

[259] Ibid., II, pp. 592–3.
[260] Ibid., II, pp. 537. At the Great Yarmouth workhouse, mutton and veal were allowed to the sick on Sundays. Ibid., II, p. 526.
[261] Ibid., II, pp. 435–6.
[262] John Cannon's Memoirs, 10 Dec. 1734, p. 201.
[263] Hindle, *On the Parish*, pp. 187–90.

guardians elected from among the aldermen and common councillors of the city and were thus under the control of those who paid the rates. However, the report detailed, much to Eden's incredulity, an extremely generous diet:

[T]he total quantity of meat distributed in shares much exceeded what was usually eaten by persons in perfect health. The following statements by which they exemplified the truth of their assertions, in the instance of *beef* are extremely curious ...

> Account of Beef, Sunday, April 11, 1784.
> 77 persons had each 10 ounces
> 26 persons had each 11 ounces
> 42 persons had each 12 ounces
> 26 persons had each 8 ounces
> 171 persons had 1768 ounces

This sum of 1,768 oz. divided by 16 gives 110 lb 8 oz. and which is of beef cooked, and without the bone; and which, according to the butcher's and master's account, being to beef uncooked, and with the bone, only as 8 lb to 14 lb amounts to 193 lb of meat, as bought from the butcher ... [which] gives the average share of uncooked meat for each person which is 18 oz.

In the old work-house, no account has yet been taken ... but it appeared to this court, from actual shares produced and weighed in court that the weavers' allowance ... consisted of 17 ounces of boiled beef, with a large bone and some fragments upon it, for each person; and which ... must be, uncooked, at least 1¾ lb.

From the above account, the truth of which cannot be controverted, it is evident, that the dinners of the above number of persons, three times a week, cost more than if the Poor were to dine at a cook's shop, or a public house; as it is well known, that many respectable artificers dine at such places for less money; and that the quantity, for each person, exceeds, considerably, the proportion of what is usually eaten at the tables of most private families.[264]

The review was instigated because of the rising cost of provisions in the 1780s, and it resulted in the diet being reformed. In 1794 the amount of meat was vastly reduced to only 11 oz a week per person together with 12 oz of cheese and 4 oz of butter and beer.[265] The report is valuable for the amount of detail it supplies on what must have been considered an acceptable diet for the poor by the guardians for a long period of time.

There also exists a fascinating discussion of the importance of meat from the complaint book of Richard Hutton, the steward of the charitable Quaker workhouse in Clerkenwell from 1711 to 1737. This resulted from the complaints of one of the more cantankerous members of the

---

house named William Townsend. He had entered voluntarily, agreeing to pay a small fee for his board, and so thought he deserved better treatment. But according to the ideals of Quakerism all members of what was seen as a family living under the same roof had to be treated equally, and all were to have the same meals including Hutton and his wife. Townsend objected that the beef served was salt beef and that the pork and mutton were too tough and bought too cheaply. In March 1717 he also complained that Hutton's wife, who oversaw the cooking in the house, added 'nasty sour pickle to spoil' the beef, implying that she had used vinegar to preserve the meat.[266] On another occasion he looked at the meat of other members and asked if it was tender, and on yet another occasion cut open a calf's foot Hutton's wife had bought and smelled it claiming it was not sweet (i.e. fresh), whereupon she showed it to other women in the family, who contradicted Townsend. Townsend also complained that he was getting short measure in the allowance of meat that was served to him, causing Hutton to bring down his scales to show that the weight was accurate (Townsend apparently bought a set of scales for the purpose of testing Hutton's!).

This was a special workhouse funded by private donations from people who were concerned to do well by the poor, so perhaps it was not typical, but Townsend claimed that it was actually worse than other charity houses in that the bills of fare prevented the inmates from giving away or selling their provision if they could not eat it, implying this was a right the poor in other institutions had. Also Townsend was especially cantankerous and presumably needed to be humoured as he was paying something. But Hutton had to go to great lengths to counter Townsend's claims. He consulted other poor members in the house to prove to the Quaker benefactors that he was not being stingy in order to earn more profit on the house.[267]

Most of the meat listed in the examples above was purchased from butchers. Butchers were important in this society because of the need for specialist slaughtering, and also because meat would soon go bad if it was not sold quickly to a fairly large number of people. Pigs, however, were generally slaughtered by a butcher hired to come to a farm or household, as was the case with Richard Latham, and then the meat would be salted and most usually smoked in a chimney as bacon. Beef, as we shall see, could also be salted, but this was a much larger operation owing to the quantity of meat involved. It was generally sold by

[266] This was a new method of preservation introduced in the seventeenth century, and was faster than salting meat. Thirsk, *Food*, p. 133.

[267] Hitchcock (ed.), *Hutton's Complaints Book*, pp. xvii–xviii, 41–9.

the pound or stone of 14 lb, except in London and some other places where the stone was one of 8 lb.[268] The meat sold generally consisted of meat and bone, but, of course, some cuts of meat have more bone than others, and this was reflected in slight variations in prices per stone or pound. Meat was generally bought every week or over longer periods in the winter and in larger amounts than we are used to today (c. 5–15 lb), so there would be less variation in the amount of bone.[269] In workhouse and other institutional diets it is much more difficult to determine if the meat was served with or without bone, as in most cases this is not specified. When it is specified, however, it is said to be meat without bone, as in Eden's description of the Oxford and Norwich workhouses.[270] The most striking case of this is the London Bridewell diet, where the rules specified that the offenders were to have the 'fineth' part of a pound of beef.[271] The 1713 diet of the Quaker workhouse in Clerkenwell also specified '8 ounces boiled meat without the bone'.[272]

In addition, very little of a slaughtered animal was wasted. Most of the edible internal organs were eaten or put in meat pies. Thomas Turner, Richard Latham and Frances Hamilton, for instance, often recorded buying or eating calves' or sheep's hearts as a dish of meat. The heads would also be boiled (without the brain) to produce a stew. Feet were eaten, too. It is even possible that a high level of meat consumption was necessary to supply the leather needed for clothing, harnesses and other uses, as well as the internal organs which were rendered down to produce tallow for candles and soap. At least one contemporary noted that the value of leather was second only to the value of woollen cloth.[273] There was a constant demand for leather for shoes, boots, gloves, saddles, horse collars, harnesses, workmen's aprons, leather doublets, parchment and other things. In King's Lynn there were forty-eight people working in the leather trades compared to eighty-two working with woollen and linen fabric. There were also eleven tallow chandlers and two soap makers.[274] Gregory King made some estimations of the consumption of cattle hides for shoes, boots, spatterdashes and coach harnesses, as well as tallow needed to make candles and soap. He estimated

---

[268] This measurement originated at a time when whole live animals were sold, with the remaining 6 lb of the stone left off to account for the skin and offal, which were not as expensive. But by our period, the London stone was simply a smaller form of measurement which was generally proportionally cheaper than other stones.

[269] See, for instance, WYASB, Sp St/6/2/1/2; WRO, WRO/314/1/1.

[270] See above, p. 93.   [271] Archer, *Pursuit of Stability*, pp. 189–90.

[272] Hitchcock (ed.), *Hutton's Complaints Book*, p. 97.

[273] L. A. Clarkson, 'The Organization of the English Leather Industry in the Late Sixteenth and Seventeenth Centuries', *Economic History Review*, 2nd ser., 14 (1960–1), p. 245.

[274] Muldrew, 'Credit, Market Relations', pp. 282–5.

that, on average, everyone went through two pairs of shoes per year resulting in a demand for 10,600,000 pairs (given his population estimate of 5,400,000 with 100,000 people going barefoot).[275] Although the actual size of the population was closer to 5 million, there were wealthier individuals like the Oxford undergraduate William Freake, who, in his three years as a student from 1619 to 1622, expended £108 in total. This included the purchase of twenty-two pairs of shoes and boots which also had to be repaired nine times.[276] King then estimated that cattle and calf's hides, at an average area of 25 and 6 feet respectively, would have provided 20,000,000 lb of leather. He then calculated that 16,500,000 lb would have been needed just to make shoes. This would have left only 3,500,000 lb for boots and the other items mentioned above.[277] In addition, he did not make any estimation of the amount of sheepskin used for gloves, but given the huge numbers given away at funerals, they must have been consumed in even greater numbers than shoes.[278]

He worked out the average consumption of candles and soap based on his own family's yearly consumption of 36 lb of candles and 20 lb of soap per person. At first he estimated that, since poor families used less, for the population as a whole the consumption would have been half of his consumption of soap, or 10 lb per person per annum, and 15 lb of candles. This would have required 132,500,000 lb of tallow. Since this was much higher than his estimate of 40,000,000 lb of tallow which could be produced from his estimation of the number of cattle, sheep and pigs slaughtered each year, he proceeded to halve his estimates of consumption. In the next chapter we will see that his estimates of meat consumption were almost certainly too low. My estimate of meat consumption in c. 1695 presented in Table 3.15 would have produced 73,000,000 lb of tallow for soap and candles, using King's estimate that 1 lb of tallow could be extracted for every 1 lb of meat taken from a carcass.[279] Despite King's guesstimates of popular consumption, his figures do show how important animal products other than meat were to the economy.

Few sources exist to measure occupations in the countryside before the data collected from militia lists and other sources from the late

---

[275] King's Figures are reproduced in N. B. Harte, 'The Economics of Clothing in the Late Seventeenth Century', *Textile History*, 22 (1991), p. 284.

[276] H. V. F. Somerset, 'An Account Book of an Oxford Undergraduate in the Years 1619–1622', *Oxoniensia*, 22 (1957), pp. 85–6.

[277] King, 'Burn's Journal', pp. 243, 257.

[278] Ralph Houlbrooke, *Death, Religion and the Family in England 1480–1750* (Oxford, 1998), pp. 252, 274, 276–7, 280–3, 285–6, 288.

[279] Modern calculations estimate that the internal fat in a slaughtered animal is 8–15 per cent of its weight.

eighteenth century. However, occupational listings do exist for towns which can certainly demonstrate the importance of the consumption of meat through its retailing. Towns required more butchers because fewer households would have owned animals that could have been slaughtered at home and then salted. Towns also served as hubs for their surrounding rural areas.[280] In the militia list from Gloucestershire from 1608 there was one butcher for every seventy-three families listed outside of the main towns of Gloucester, Tewkesbury and Cirencester, but one butcher for every twenty-seven households within those towns.[281] In late seventeenth-century King's Lynn there was one butcher for every forty-one households in the town, compared to one baker for every sixty-seven households.[282] One contemporary inventory has survived for a Lynn butcher, that of Thomas Thaker, who died in 1686 worth £99 14s. He had stalls and a shop listed in his inventory, so was clearly selling meat. He also possessed twelve bullocks and sixty-one sheep, but these were probably intended to be slaughtered for his own sale.[283] There is evidence from probate inventories that many butchers in towns were also engaged in the selling of fast food to the population. In late sixteenth-century Ipswich, for instance, one butcher was clearly using his front chamber as an ordinary or victualling house as he possessed fifty-seven plates, as well as tables and benches. The fact that he also possessed £40 cash on hand, and was still owed £110 in debts, suggests that he was serving meals.[284] Similarly, a butcher from mid-sixteenth-century Chesterfield was doing the same, as he possessed many cooking implements, 26 saucers and other plate weighing 548 lb.[285]

Most other research where numbers can be compared has been done for the Elizabethan period, but it shows that the number of butchers was already high by the mid to late sixteenth century. In midsummer 1599, twenty-three native butchers paid rent for thirty-three stalls, and sixteen foreign butchers for seventeen stalls in Manchester's shambles.

[280] D. M. Woodward, 'Cattle Droving in the Seventeenth Century: A Yorkshire Example', in W. H. Chaloner and Barrie M. Radcliffe (eds.), *Trade and Transport* (Manchester, 1977), pp. 35–58.

[281] *Men and Armour*; Tawney and Tawney, 'Occupational Census', pp. 36, 59–63. This census is described in more detail below on p. 221.

[282] Muldrew, *Economy of Obligation*, pp. 69–75.   [283] NRO, INV 64/10.

[284] Michael Reed, *The Ipswich Probate Inventories, 1583–1631*, Suffolk Records Society, 22 (1981), p. 35.

[285] J. M Bestall and D. V. Fowkes (eds.), *Chesterfield Wills and Inventories 1521–1603*, Derbyshire Record Society, 1 (1977), pp. 91–3. On the provision of victualling in London, see Sara Pennell, '"Great Quantities of Gooseberry Pye and Baked Clod of Beef": Victualling and Eating Out in Early Modern London', in Griffiths and Jenner (eds.), *Londinopolis*, pp. 228–9.

This means that a town which might have had a population of about 2,000 people, at most, possessed fifty stalls used by thirty-nine butchers, or one butcher for every eleven households. T. S. Willan has suggested some customers must have been coming from the rural hinterland of Manchester to support these sellers.[286] Also, if the situation was similar to King's Lynn eighty years later, then there might have been other butchers who were quite well off selling from shops *only*, and not renting stalls in the shambles. There, in 1681, there were twenty-nine stalls in the Tuesday market shambles and another eighteen in the Saturday market. However, eight stalls were empty, and there were nineteen butchers from Lynn who sued in the town court but did not rent a stall.[287]

Alan Dyer has calculated from probate records that there were at least thirty butchers in Elizabethan Worcester. Given that this figure is not taken from a contemporary list of some sort, it is probably a minimum estimate, but it still means that for a population of about 4,250 in 1563 there would have been about one butcher for every thirty-one households.[288] The inventories for these butchers show they were worth between £3 and £489, and that they were not acting as butcher-graziers, but, like Thomas Thaker, kept small numbers of animals as a source of meat supply.[289] In Tudor York 128 butchers were admitted to the freedom between 1550 and 1600, or 2.6 a year, in a town of 8–10,000 people.[290] If we assume they had careers of about twenty years, there would have about fifty butchers in the town. Some of these men undoubtedly moved away or died young, but there would also have been butchers who were not freemen.

In Worcester, like King's Lynn, there were more butchers than bakers, while in Norwich in 1569 there were thirty-two free butchers compared to thirty-two bakers. However, many more butchers were admitted to the freedom of the city between 1550 and 1600. More bakers were admitted to the freedom than butchers after 1600, but there were still more freemen butchers listed in the 1671 hearth tax.[291] This indicates that there were commonly as many if not more butchers than bakers in early modern towns. It is possible that some households were baking their own bread, but in Worcester, by the end of the sixteenth century, ovens were valued at about £3, and the cost of firing them for

---

[286] T. S. Willan, *Elizabethan Manchester* (Manchester, 1980), pp. 38–9, 68–70.
[287] NRO, KL/C39/105, 107.
[288] Alan Dyer, *The City of Worcester in the Sixteenth Century* (Leicester, 1973), pp. 26, 136.
[289] Ibid., pp. 136–7.
[290] D. M. Palliser, *Tudor York* (Oxford, 1979), pp. 112–13.
[291] Dyer, *Worcester*, p. 137; John Pound, *Tudor and Stuart Norwich* (Chichester, 1988), pp. 36, 61–4. In York, there were more bakers made freemen than butchers between 1550 and 1600, but the number is not hugely different. Palliser, *Tudor York*, p. 152.

a single family would have been uneconomical. It is also possible that there might have been more large-scale bakers than butchers, but again in Worcester the butchers were on average wealthier than the bakers, and in King's Lynn the figure for the average wealth of both groups was almost identical.[292] Thus occupational data support the story told by account books that meat processing and consumption was as important a part of people's diet as bread.

On farms, where butchers were further away, it remained common to salt both beef and pork, and salting tubs were a common feature in both farm and labourers' inventories. In the wealthy agricultural economy of Kent the number of inventories recording food preservation equipment rose from 65 per cent at the beginning of the seventeenth century to 83 per cent by the beginning of the eighteenth century.[293] Of the sample of labourers, inventories analysed in chapter 4, 49 per cent listed salting tubs or troughs before 1650, 41 per cent between 1650 and 1700 and 36 per cent thereafter. This certainly demonstrates that salting meat was common, although most of it was subsequently smoked as bacon. Salted meat was only mentioned 24 times in the sample of 972 inventories, in contrast to bacon, which was listed 104 times. By comparison, in the 240 inventories collected by Margaret Cash for seventeenth-century Devon, powdered beef was found just over 20 times while flitches of bacon were listed 40 times.[294] Ellis, as well as Eden and Davies, all commented on the economy of keeping a pig for fattening instead of buying butcher's meat, and by the hard years of the late eighteenth century bacon or salted pork seems to have been the only meat used in pottage by the poorest families.[295]

Salting beef would have had the advantage of avoiding higher prices in the winter, and would have ensured a reliable supply if one lived some distance from a butcher. Salting meat involved cutting it into large pieces. One pamphlet advised cutting an ox into 4-lb-pieces, and then rubbing these with a mixture of salt, a little saltpetre and perhaps sugar. They were then put into salting tubs, or a cask, for up to a fortnight, during which time what was termed 'the bloody pickle' or 'bloody gravy' was run off and the meat sufficiently desiccated. Once this was done it was then packed in sealed barrels between layers of salt. Another method was to fill the barrel with a brine

[292] Dyer, *Worcester*, p. 138; Muldrew, 'Credit, Market Relations', pp. 315–16.
[293] Overton *et al.*, *Production and Consumption*, p. 62.
[294] Margaret Cash (ed.), *Devon Inventories of the Sixteenth and Seventeenth Centuries*, Devon and Cornwall Record Society, n.s., 11 (1966), p. xix.
[295] Ellis noted that it could also be cooked in pancakes. Ellis, *Country Housewife*, pp. 33, 95–6, 98, 100.

Table 2.2 *Presence of cooking equipment over time in labourers' probate inventories*

Period	Boiling (percentage)	Frying (percentage)	Roasting (percentage)	Items per inventory with roasting equipment	Number divided by all inventories
1550–99	70	20	49	2.7	2.5
1600–49	78	25	46	2.2	2.2
1650–99	64	18	33	2.2	1.2
1700–99	69	22	21	2.5	1.6
All	71	19	37	2.5	1.9

solution. William Ellis noted that a peck (14 lb) of salt was needed for a 25-stone hog.[296] Ellis noted that 'in the County of Kent, where pickled Pork is in such general esteem ... a Dish of pickled Pork, with Apple Dumplins, etc. is there deemed an agreeable Repast, from the Peer to the Peasant'.[297]

Meat preparation

Meat in institutions was generally boiled, and only roasted on occasion, usually for Sunday dinner. Table 2.2 compares the number of times pots, kettles, and so on were listed in the sample of labourers' probate inventories (see chapter 4) with the number of times equipment which could be used for roasting such as spits, jacks or roasting pans was listed. This shows that boiling seems to have been the most common way for the poor to prepare meat. However, roasting equipment was found in almost half of the inventories in the late sixteenth century, but had dropped significantly by the eighteenth century. This was most likely the result of wood becoming more expensive and scarcer, as boiling could be done with the least amount of fuel. In addition boiling was safer for older cuts of meat and necessary for salted meat.[298] Although boiling reduces the food value of raw meat by about 30 per cent, since the meat was often boiled with vegetables what was lost could have been consumed in the broth.[299] In the late eighteenth century, however,

[296] Ibid., p. 54; John Collins, *Salt and Fishery* (London, 1682), pp. 121–3.
[297] Ellis, *Country Housewife*, p. 51.
[298] Hitchcock (ed.), *Hutton's Complaints Book*, pp. 60–1, 96–7.
[299] This was shown in the example of the Norwich workhouse cited by Eden where boiled meat, minus bone, was considered to be 60 per cent the weight of raw meat with the bone. Eden, *State of the Poor*, II, pp. 483–6. See above, p. 93.

Fredrick Eden complained of labourers in the south wasting the stock from their boiled meats which he thought could have been mixed with oatmeal or barley to form soups, which they termed 'washy stuff', claiming it did not supply enough nourishment for labour.[300] Roasting reduces the food value less depending on how rare the meat is cooked, and although some fat would be lost, dripping pans were commonly used, and Ellis noted that poor women would use saved fat for baking or inclusion in porridge rather than more expensive butter when money was tight.[301] In addition, it can be seen in Table 2.2 that a constant number of households possessed frying pans which could be used for cooking meat and also pancakes and other things.

The price of fuel is certainly something which needs to be considered when thinking about food preparation. The late eighteenth-century writer on the question of poverty Count Rumford complained about the poor design of most labourers' fireplaces, which were large and open to facilitate cooking, but which sucked most heat up the chimney.[302] In the winter, when fire was needed to heat a dwelling, food could be prepared using a larger fire for both cooking and warmth, but in the summer boiling for long periods of time over a smaller fire would have been much more efficient. In fact, Eden noted that the higher price of fuel in the south, especially in areas where coal was more expensive to transport, led labourers to eat much more cheese than beef, despite its higher price. However, such a diet meant that much beer had to be consumed to make swallowing dry bread and cheese easier.[303] Meat was only roasted once or twice a week (which, as we saw, was the case with Thomas Turner, who lived in Sussex) or was taken to the baker's to be made into a pie. Eden even complained that labourers in Banbury wasted much of their income cooking at the baker's rather than at home, owing to the dearness of fuel.

In contrast, owing to the cheapness of coal as a fuel in much of the north, the boiling of stews, pottage, furmenty and oatmeal porridge was very common.[304] Eden also claimed that soup was something common in the north, made with meat, herbs and barley or oatmeal, with a pound of beef or mutton being used in 3 quarts of finished soup. He spent a lot of time praising the cheapness of what he termed the northern diet of various forms of oatmeal porridge, pottage and soup, as well as oaten bread, over the southern diet, which he found wasteful and

---

[300] Eden, *State of the Poor*, I, pp. 525–6.   [301] Ellis, *Country Housewife*, pp. 25–6.
[302] Eden, *State of the Poor*, I, p. 548.
[303] Ibid., I, pp. 496–7, 535, 547–8; II, pp. 137, 587.
[304] This is borne out by the samples of labouring family diets collected by Eden. See n. 50 above for reference.

overly reliant on meat, white bread and beer.[305] But, as John Styles has cautioned, we should take Eden's north–south contrasts with a pinch of salt, as he had a morally rhetorical purpose in trying to get labourers to save money and be more thrifty in years when their real wages were being rapidly reduced.[306] In addition, he was influenced by Count Rumford's advocacy of soup as a solution to the high price of food, although he did not consider how it would provide enough energy for work.[307] In fact he lists many instances of high-wage workers in the northern cloth trades eating meat every day. He also listed workhouses which served meat as commonly as in the south. Richard Latham ate beef, and many farm servants and labourers were served as much beef as in the south. In addition, many of the cattle which were slaughtered in the south were raised in the north and then driven south, so meat was available there at cheaper prices.

Dairy products

Cow keeping was an essential part of the economy of many labouring households.[308] As we shall see in chapter 5 almost half of labouring households had cows, and for those who did not, milk could be purchased from neighbouring farmers with cows.[309] But it is difficult to determine how much fresh milk was consumed because those labourers with a cow might have sold most in the form of butter or cheese. In a sample of inventories of all occupations from Huntingdonshire 70 per cent of those engaged in agriculture owned cattle, and in Yorkshire the figure was 74 per cent.[310] Milk was thought to be healthy, and according to Moffet was a sort of blood whitened in the breast which gave nourishment to the young. Moffet claimed that women's milk was best for the young and also for the very old who had difficulty with other food. He even told the story of Dr Caius of Cambridge who became 'peevish and full of frets' in his last sickness because he sucked the milk of

---

[305] Eden, *State of the Poor*, I, pp. 522–6, 533.

[306] John Styles, 'Clothing in the North: The Supply of Non-Elite Clothing in the Eighteenth Century North of England', *Textile History*, 25 (1994), pp. 139, 160–2.

[307] Count Rumsford wrote much advocating cheap soups for the poor. See Sandra Sherman, *Imagining Poverty: Quantification and the Decline of Paternalism* (Columbus, OH, 2001), pp. 165–215.

[308] Shaw-Taylor, 'Labourers, Cows, Common Rights', pp. 95–126.

[309] See below, p. 250.

[310] Not all of these would have been cows, though. Ken Sneath, 'Consumption, Wealth, Indebtedness and Social Structure in Early Modern England', University of Cambridge Ph.D. thesis, 2009, p. 204. See also, Barrie Trinder and Jeff Cox (eds.), *Yeomen and Colliers in Telford: Probate Inventories for Dawley, Lilleshall, Wellington and Wrockwardine, 1660–1750* (Chichester, 1980), pp. 72ff.

both a forward woman with a bad diet and a quiet and well-mannered woman at the same time! Cow's milk was also considered to be good for all humours. It was said that it 'nourisheth plentifully, encreaseth the brain, fatneth the body, restoreth flesh, asswageth sharpness of urine, giveth the face a lively and good colour', though ewe's or goat's milk was not considered very good.[311] Milk is an excellent source of calcium and vitamins, and its lack can cause rickets, so it would have been advantageous to those who drank more of it or ate more cheese. It was also, probably, a great advantage to the health and size of growing children who were able to drink it or eat it in porridge.

William Harrison thought that milk, butter and cheese were an important part of labourers' diets in the sixteenth century, and some indication of the place of milk in eighteenth-century diets can be gained from looking at the information provided in Eden's budgets and workhouse diets. What is most striking about the workhouse diets is the difference between workhouses in the northern counties and those in the south. In the north milk was commonly served almost every day in milk pottage and porridge. The Liverpool workhouse, for instance, bought enough milk to provide its inmates with between ½ and 1 pint a day. Almost every breakfast consisted of milk pottage or gruel, and most workhouses served milk again at the evening supper, while cheese was mainly served for dinner on non-meat days. In the south, by contrast, only four workhouses mentioned by Eden served milk pottage, and then only at breakfast. In the south, cheese was almost universally eaten instead, with bread for breakfast and supper, as well as on non-meat days for dinner.[312] Since fresh milk was generally 1d a quart and cheese at least 4d a pound the latter was more expensive.

A similar pattern emerges when we look at the actual labourers' diets provided by Eden. Most of the diets he provided were for labourers who did not own cows, and thus listed amounts spent on milk. But they were also for a period when the ability to purchase milk would have been much reduced owing to the rise in the price of grain. However, for the purposes of geographical comparison they show labourers in the north purchasing much more milk. One labourer from Cumberland bought 1,040 quarts in a year, and others commonly purchased a quart a day, while in the south it is usually absent from the labourers' budgets

---

[311] Moffet, *Health's Improvement*, pp. 119–25; Harrison, *Description*, p. 311.
[312] Eden, *State of the Poor, passim*. In Shrewsbury, the workhouse had twenty cows, and Eden says it did not use any of the butter these cows produced. Nor does he mention milk being sold. However, the profit he lists indicates a sale of only 70 lb of butter per cow a year, which is very low, so perhaps some milk was being used in the workhouse. Eden, *State of the Poor*, II, p. 634. See below, pp. 253–6.

except for children. Most milk was eaten in gruel, furmenty and porridge, which were mostly made from oats, whereas the southern preference for wheaten bread made the demand for cheese or butter to eat with it more pronounced. This is something both Eden and Davies certainly noticed, and was one of the reasons for their advocacy of land for the poor to keep cows (see below, p. 254). The diarist John Cannon also noted that milk was less common in the south when relating how he helped out in a bakery some mornings where cakes and bread 'were soon got ready for breakfast which we eat with butter or sopped in beer, ale or cyder ... and sometime we sopped it in milk. This, when it happened, was reputed a most noble feast and came round about once a month.'[313]

Cheese and butter were also commonly consumed, and could be preserved for much longer periods of time than milk or cream. But still the consumption of cheese, as noted earlier, was much less than that of beef, although it was eaten regularly. Cheese was certainly no cheaper than beef, and often more expensive because of the extra labour involved in making it. But because hard cheese kept for a long time, there was already a national market for regional cheeses. Ellis noted that a market was held in Baldock, Hertfordshire, where he could buy Leicester or Warwickshire cheese, and he also purchased Cheshire cheese locally.[314] His harvest workers ate cheese with bread for breakfast and supper before bed, as well as for snacks when they were in the field, and many workhouse diets provided cheese for the same meals.[315] However, the amount eaten was small in comparison to meat, bread or beer, with usually only about 1–4 oz being eaten in a day, although more cheese might be eaten in certain regions. Eden noted that in the south of England labourers were more accustomed to eating dry cheese and bread.[316] Much more cheese was also needed for the harvest. During the harvest of 1706, John Crakanthorp purchased 80 lb.[317]

Moffet, like Harrison, noted that butter was one of the chief foods of the poorer sort, but the amount eaten does not seem very large, varying from less than an ounce to 4 oz a day, although the Liverpool workhouse purchased enough for over ½ lb a day for each inmate in 1792.[318] It could be eaten in various ways, including being put in porridge and furmenty or in a posset. Most was probably used in baking pies, but it could also be

---

[313] John Cannon's Memoirs, p. 41.   [314] Ellis, *Country Housewife*, p. 74.
[315] See the quotation on p. 45, above.
[316] Eden, *State of the Poor*, I, p. 479; II, p. 137.
[317] Ellis, *Country Housewife*, p. 73; Brassley and Saunders (eds.), *Accounts of the Reverend John Crakanthorp*, p. 179.
[318] Moffet, *Health's Improvement*, p. 129; Eden, *State of the Poor*, II, pp. 333–6.

used to prepare vegetables, and Thomas Turner recorded eating a 'butter pond pudding', but this was undoubtedly too expensive for the poor.

Fish

Fish is mostly absent from any diets or sources mentioning labourers' food. Eden noted this in the late eighteenth century, with some surprise in the case of labourers in London. But moving fresh fish any distance from the coast was expensive, and thus the price of ocean fish was high.[319] Two fresh salmon cost 9s 6d in Oxford in 1601, and even in London in 1594 two turbot cost 7s 6d. At the Bacons' Gorhambury residence during Lent in 1638 a trout cost 6d and a salted eel was a shilling. Even salted fish were 9d each. For such a price a labourer could buy 3 lb of beef at the time, and 15 lb for the price of a turbot![320] Thus even though Thomas Moffet had recommended salted fish as suitable for 'sailors and ploughmen', it is unsurprising that it was largely the wealthy who ate fish.[321] In addition, since fish contain fewer calories, they would have been an even more expensive way of obtaining energy. Accounts of great houses always contain the purchase of some fish, as do Cambridge and Oxford colleges, and most of this was salted fish such as ling, green fish, herrings and stockfish.[322]

It is perhaps more surprising that workhouses and hospitals in London do not record very much fish being served. The London Bridewell served cheese instead of fish on fast days, and none of the diets for the Liverpool workhouse cited by Eden included fish.[323] The Foundling Hospital in London, though, always purchased a small amount of fish, and during Lent it stopped purchasing veal, mutton and beef and bought mackerel instead. On 27 May 1650 the hospital bought 30 mackerel at a cost of 6s 3d. For the same price they could have bought 25 lb of meat.[324] Thomas Turner, who lived only 9–10 miles from the coast, often bought herring and whiting to boil at much cheaper prices, but they were small fish and not meant to be an entire dinner.[325] Turner was also given trout as a present on many occasions, which had presumably

---

[319] Eden, *State of the Poor*, I, p. 532; Mumby (ed.), *Stuart Household Accounts*, pp. 148–50.
[320] Thorold Rogers, *History of Agriculture and Prices*, VI, pp. 392–401.
[321] Moffet, *Health's Improvement*, pp. 141–2; Archer, *Pursuit of Stability*, p. 46.
[322] Robert Willis Blencowe (ed.), 'The Journal and Accounts of Timothy Burrell Esq., Barrister-at-Law, 1683–1714', *Sussex Archaeological Collections*, 3 (1850), p. 152.
[323] Eden, *State of the Poor*, II, pp. 334–6.
[324] London Metropolitan Archives, Steward's Account Book, Household Expenses, A/FH/B8/6/3, 1747–1754.
[325] Turner, 'Diary' (Yale MS). See, for example, entries for 24 Sept. 1757, 12 Oct. 1757, 26 Oct. 1757, 15 May 1758.

been caught by the giver, and it is possible that labourers would have been able to fish in some places depending on manorial customs.[326] In contrast to fish, oysters were eaten very cheaply by everyone, especially in London, although as snacks rather than meals. One hundred oysters cost about a shilling.

Vegetables

[Fruit and vegetables were] the first and onely [meat] Whilst mens hands were neither polluted with the blood of Beasts, not smelt of the most unwholesome sent of fish.[327]

One of the most prevalent myths about early modern diet, which has been recently, and thankfully, exploded by Joan Thirsk, is that people ate few vegetables.[328] This claim is as false for the poor as it is for the wealthy. Such an assumption has most probably arisen because vegetables do not show up in account books very often, but this is simply a result of the fact that almost all houses which kept accounts had their own private gardens where vegetables were grown.[329] Outside of large conurbations such as London, where space was at a premium, population was relatively low and this allowed houses to have large plots, which inevitably included a garden. Moreover, for London we know that market gardening was a huge industry after 1600, needed to supply enough fruit and vegetables to the metropolis. Garden ground around London was estimated to have expanded from around 10,000 acres in 1660 to 110,000 by 1721 and other towns with market gardens in their vicinity included Oxford, Banbury, York, Nottingham, Norwich, Colchester, Bristol and Ipswich.[330] Visitors to London in the eighteenth century recorded eating roots, cucumbers, lettuce, salad, spinach and green beans and peas with their meat.[331]

Although we are not dealing with London here, its lack of gardens makes it possible to measure the amount of vegetables being imported into the city. Gregory King estimated how much market garden produce was brought into London by water and from the surrounding countryside by cart in the 1680s. Although King's calculations have to be treated

---

[326] Thirsk, *Food*, pp. 265–6.
[327] Moffet, *Health's Improvement*, p. 194. He also included grain as a 'fruit of the field'.
[328] Stone, *Crisis of the Aristocracy*, p. 559. Thirsk, *Food*, pp. 5, 7, 24, 73–4, 284–94.
[329] Thorold Rogers recorded numerous prices for vegetable seeds purchased by the pound to be planted in the gardens of the institutions which he used as sources. Thorold Rogers, *History of Agriculture and Prices*, VII, pp. 556ff.
[330] Malcolm Thick, 'Market Gardening in England and Wales', in *AHEW*, V, pp. 503, 506–7.
[331] Ibid., pp. 508–9.

with caution, he was able to measure what was landed at St Paul's wharf to be carted to Newgate market himself, as it was next to the College of Heralds where he worked. He would also have been able to investigate the numbers of carts arriving at other markets for himself. He worked out that St Paul's wharf porters (both male and female) carried an average of 112 lb per load and could move on average 12 loads each a morning.[332] From this he calculated the total weight of fruit and vegetables for the whole of London by multiplying this figure by ten for other markets, and adding an extra third for goods brought in by cart. According to Defoe, Newgate was only one of fourteen markets which sold vegetables (or herbs as he termed them), including Covent Garden, which was the largest vegetable market in the metropolis, so King's multiplier does not seem unreasonable.[333] He worked out that for 500,000 people this worked out to 6 oz of vegetables a day per person. By the mid-nineteenth century, when London's population stood at about 2 million, Henry Mayhew calculated that every year there were over 89,000,000 cabbages and over 14,000,000 heads of broccoli and cauliflower, as well as 16,817,000 carrots and about 800,000 bushels of peas and beans, as well as many onions, cucumbers, marrows and other vegetables sold in four London markets, including Covent Garden. Over a million bushels of apples, pears, plums and cherries were also sold.[334]

Further, Malcolm Thick has argued that much of the expansion for market gardening was to meet demand from the London poor, citing contemporary sources which suggest that the poor substituted vegetables for meat and even bread.[335] Prices for vegetables sold on the market in London are difficult to come by, but onions seem to have been cheaper by the bushel than grain, although they would have been no substitute for the working poor who needed calories. But whatever the cost of vegetables, the poor must have been a major force driving demand in London because they were the majority of the population.

As for rural society, where access to gardens was normal, the consumption of vegetables was most likely higher. King noted this in his attempt to estimate the value of their consumption of vegetables when he stated:

But in regard Country People and poorer sort spend double in proportion to what they do in London, many of them Living in a manner wholly upon [*crossed*

---

[332] Laslett (ed.), *Earliest Classics*, p. 213.

[333] Daniel Defoe, *A Tour Thro' the Whole Island of Great Britain* (London, 1968), I, p. 343; Peter Earle, *The Making of the English Middle Class* (London, 1989), p. 47. Ian Archer, Caroline Burrow and Vanessa Harding (eds.), *Hugh Alley's Caveat: The Markets of London in 1598*, London Topographical Society, 137 (1988), pp. 2–3, 9–10. Thick lists seventeen markets for all of London, 'Market Gardening', p. 503.

[334] Henry Mayhew, *London Labour and the London Poor* (London, 1861), I, pp. 80–1.

[335] Thick, 'Market Gardening', p. 508.

out Pudding water porridge and] Roots and Plants with the help of Oatmeal and Rye or Barley Bread. And even in Farmers houses scarce a day passes without Apple pyes or Pear Pyes (and Damson Pyes in season). It follows that y whole Consumption may well be a million [£] per anum.[336]

The rural Sussex shopkeeper Thomas Turner recorded eating, in the mid-eighteenth century, turnips (most commonly), carrots, onions, cabbage, cauliflower, savoy and turnip greens and cucumbers, as well as apple pudding and pear pie in the winter, while in the summer he most often ate green salad and gooseberry pie as well as spinach, garden beans and peas.[337] William Harrison, rather curiously, argued that roots and vegetables had been common in the Middle Ages but wholly went out of fashion between the reign of Henry VI and beginning of the reign of Henry VIII. However, he claimed that by his time they were commonly consumed by all, although the rich consumed, 'new seeds out of strange countries' including 'such as are very dangerous and hurtful, as the verangenes [eggplant], mushrooms, etc.'. The vegetables listed as being consumed by the 'poor commons' were 'melons, pompions [pumpkins], gourds, cucumbers, radishes, skirrets, parsnips, carrots, cabbages, navews, turnips, and all kinds of salad herbs'.[338] Thomas Tusser also provided an incredibly long list of plants which could be grown for the kitchen in a farmer's garden which is much more varied than one would find today. He listed over eighty vegetables and herbs including a group entitled 'herbs and roots for salads and sauces'. These included such plants still common today as fennel, parsley, cabbage, lettuce, mint, beets, sorrel, spinach, thyme, artichokes, cucumbers, cress, endive, mustard seed, radishes, rocket, tarragon, violets for salad, beans, carrots, parsnips, gourds, peas, basil, camomile, lavender, marjoram, tansy and dill. Others no longer common included bloodwort, runcivall, French mallows, lungwort, langdebrief and marigolds for cooking.[339]

As we saw in the section on health, vegetables were considered an integral part of healthy eating for all including labourers, albeit mostly when cooked. Carrots, leeks, parsnips and turnips were all mentioned as root vegetables suitable for boiling with meat.[340] Most vegetables, especially in the winter, would have been cooked in pottage, stews and soups. Ellis also recommended that a prudent housewife needed to have 'broad Beans, Pease, Carrots, Turnips, Potatoes, Cabbage, Onions, Parsley, and other Kitchen ware' to feed labourers, and he

---

[336] Laslett (ed.), *Earliest Classics*, p. 213.
[337] Turner, 'Diary' (Yale MS), entries for 24 Sept. 1757 to 22 July 1758.
[338] Harrison, *Description*, pp. 264.   [339] Tusser, *Five Hundred Points*, pp. 88–91.
[340] See above, pp. 106–11.

advised stocking up on such vegetables before harvest so enough would be available to 'prove a sauce, but also to help meat go further'. More surprisingly, Moffet noted that by his time even the very poorest were great eaters of artichokes, boiled in beef broth and eaten with vinegar, pepper and butter.[341] Both potatoes and turnips also became much more common features of the diet in stews and pottage during the late eighteenth century as a source of carbohydrates. Potatoes eventually became cheaper than grain, and Eden mentions them often growing in labourers' gardens.[342] In the summer, labourers also ate vegetables raw, either with salt or in a salad.[343]

Pottage and labourers' food is often described as being very bland, but Moffet made a list of spices grown in England which is similar to that published by Tusser somewhat earlier, many of which could have been gown in a labourer's garden. They were: 'Aniseed, Dill, Fennel-seed, Alcost, Commen, Carawayes, Clary, Corianders, dried Mints, dried Nep, dried Origanum, Parsley-seed, dried Gilly-flowers, roots of Galinga and Orris, dried Primroses, Pennirial, Rosemary, Saffron, Sage, Oke of Jerusalem, Bay-berries, Juniper-berries, Sothernwood, Tansie, Tamarisk, Time, dried Wal-flowers, Violets, Varvein, Wintersavory, Wormwood, and such like'.[344] Many of these could have been used for spicing stew and pottage, as well as for salads and sauces.

The minutes of the general committee of the Foundling Hospital in London also show that vegetables were thought to be healthy for the children. The diets advocated listed both the vegetables provided for the children and how they were cooked. That for 11 March 1730 listed the following meals: 'Mon: stewed beef with turnips and carrots; Tues; roast mutton; Wed; boiled beef with greens or roots ... Thurs; stewed beef with turnips and carrots'. On 13 March of 1740 it was resolved by the governors to offer 'beans, pease, greens/roots in their proper seasons' to replace meat at certain times.[345] The hospital, because of its location, was also able to grow its own vegetables in its 4½-acre garden. In 1791 the gardener planted peas, five varieties of beans, red and white radishes, spinach, potatoes, cabbage, kale, cauliflower, broccoli, carrots, several varieties of lettuce, mustard, cress, celery, cucumbers, onions, leeks, parsnips, turnips, parsley, marjoram, savory and thyme.[346] Eden

---

[341] Moffet, *Health's Improvement*, p. 215.
[342] Eden, *State of the Poor*, I, pp. 504–7. Thirsk, *Food*, pp. 179–81.
[343] Ellis, *Country Housewife*, pp. 51–2, 67. Salad was eaten at the Foundling Hospital: McClure, *Coram's Children*, p. 20.
[344] Moffet, *Health's Improvement*, p. 252.
[345] London Metropolitan Archives, Foundling Hospital General Court Minutes, A/FH/K/01/1.
[346] McClure, *Coram's Children*, pp. 198–9.

also noted that many eighteenth-century workhouses had their own gardens. One which did not was the workhouse in Shropshire, which instead had a grazing farm of 50 acres on which 20 cows were kept for the production of butter for sale. There, the accounts list the purchase of garden stuff, and the amount was significant: £125 was spent on 'garden stuff' per year compared to £525 on butcher's meat, £798 on flour and £253 for brewing.[347]

It is difficult to find direct information on the size of poor people's own gardens but there is much evidence that most possessed a garden of some size for fruit and vegetables. John Woridge in 1700 noted that 'The meanest Cottager may well afford that little ground (if he hath any) that is contiguous to his tenement, for the propagating of some or other of these Escuents.' 'Rusticks', he claimed, had been encouraged to grow vegetables not only because they could earn money by selling them to those with 'curious Pallats' but also for 'frugal Meats for their own Families'.[348] Eden noted that 'every cottager in South-Wales has a little garden in which he grows his own leeks for pottage, and his potatoes, cabbages, cole-worts, pease, etc.', and in the neighbourhood of Mount Sorrel in Leicestershire that, 'most of the Poor have little gardens, in which they chiefly cultivate potatoes'. He also made a point of noting when a labourer did not have a garden.[349] Davies also termed it a 'hard circumstance' that a parish had not allowed a poor woman a garden with her house rent. In Newent in Gloucestershire, he related that rent could vary between 20 and 50s depending on the size of the garden, with larger gardens permitting the cultivation of potatoes to be used as a replacement for bread.[350] Perhaps the best-known piece of evidence is the Elizabethan legislation on the erection of cottages which stipulated that each cottage built and rented by a landlord on agricultural land should be possessed of a minimum of four acres.[351] This was intended to prevent landlords increasing their rent by crowding poor tenants onto their land, but without providing them with enough land to support themselves.[352] Of course this was not always obeyed by landlords, but even half an acre would have provided enough space to plant a sizeable garden and fruit trees.

It is difficult to know, though, what happened to the size of labourers' gardens over the subsequent 200 years. Some estate surveys contain detailed maps of messuages in townships, and can be used to

[347] Eden, *State of the Poor*, II, pp. 239, 368, 458, 636–67.
[348] John Worlidge, *Systema Horticultra; or The Art of Gardening* (London, 1700), pp. 145–6.
[349] Eden, *State of the Poor*, I, pp. 503, 553, 569.
[350] Davies, *Case of Labourers*, pp. 23, 150, 161.
[351] 31 Elizabeth ch. 7. *Statutes of the Realm*, IV, Part I.i, pp. 804–5.
[352] Hindle, *On the Parish*, pp. 314–16.

examine the size of yards. A good example, which has been analysed by Moto Takahashi, is that of early seventeenth-century Willingham in Cambridgeshire, where landless occupiers can be identified as living on plots of about an acre in size in the southeast of the village or smaller plots of about 1,700–800 square yards in the northwest corner.[353] Similarly, an estate survey of Orwell from the 1670s indicates that most messuages in the town ranged from 2,000 square yards to a few acres.[354] David Davies, however, argued that the gardens of many poor families in Berkshire were too small to grow enough potatoes because 'engrossing farmers' had converted former farms into dwellings to rent to the poor. Here, old gardens were divided into small plots of one quarter of a rood each with one or two apple trees. This would be an eighth of an acre, or 605 square yards (approximately 25 × 25 yards). The poor used this to grow 'beans, pease, cabbages, onions as well as a few potatoes', but not enough to replace bread in any quantity. Davies referred to this as a 'scanty bit of ground', but it still certainly would have been enough to grow a significant amount of vegetables for a single family, as well as providing apples for their use.[355] Finally we need to consider that the larger the garden, the more work it would have required to weed and control birds and insect pests, although the latter could have been done by children. Given this constraint it seems unlikely that, unless a labouring family lived close to a town where there was a valuable outlet to sell extra vegetable produce, gardens would have been bigger than needed to provide vegetables for home consumption.

Fruit

The quotation from William Ellis cited earlier (p. 41) shows that the consumption of fruit was as common as that of vegetables. He provided a variety of recipes for plum pudding which he recommended for the harvest, requiring, besides plums, milk and eggs, a pound of raisins, suet and nutmeg or cloves.[356] Both Ellis and Moffet recommended cooking fruit for easier digestion, although Ellis noted that it gave harvest men pleasure to eat ripe pears and sweet apples raw. As we have seen, fruit trees were considered to be a natural part of a garden, and labourers with gardens would have had access to apples.[357]

[353] Motoyasu Takahashi, *Village Inheritance in Early Modern England: Kinship Structure, Inheritance Customs and Generation Continuity* (Matsuyama, Japan, 2003), pp. 236–7.
[354] Spufford, *Contrasting Communities*, p. 93.
[355] Davies, *Case of Labourers*, pp. 34–5; Eden, *State of the Poor*, I, p. 569.
[356] Ellis, *Country Housewife*, pp.39–40. See also Tusser, *Five Hundred Points*, pp. 35–6.
[357] Ellis, *Country Housewife*, p. 41

Richard Latham, for instance, had apple trees in Lancashire. Cottages were listed as possessing orchards in an estate survey of the manor of Elmswell in Yorkshire from 1624, and in the West Country it was said, in an enquiry from 1750, that every tenement had an orchard and every cottage some apples.[358] Pears, as well as plums and cherries, when in season, would have been available throughout most of the south, with the largest harvests occurring in the southwest. Ellis claimed to obtain a harvest of 20 bushels per tree of both apples and pears near Hemel Hempstead. In 1618, Robert Loder obtained a crop of 226 bushels of apples or 9,482 lb (a bushel of apples weighs 42 lb) and 1,735 lb of cherries (although in 1619 his cherry crop was 6,402 lb) from four orchards he harvested. He paid a tithe of 12s 4d on this land, and it seems that the orchards were also attached to cottages which he rented out for 10s, although he does not mention if the families renting them had access to any part of the orchards. He also never gave the size of the land involved, but the size of his crops implies that he had about ten to fifteen trees. He did calculate that the cost of gathering his fruit was 14s, which implies that more than two weeks' work was involved. He provided more information on the cost of gathering his cherries, where he claimed that he hired women, and paid 4d for every 20 lb gathered. Interestingly, he thought he should hire men instead as they 'would do twice soe much I think; and ther might be perhaps half those eaten by our gatherers saved', which implies that children being looked after by the female workers were eating the cherries. At home his family consumed 18 bushels or 756 lb of apples – just over 2 lb a day – and probably about 100 lb of cherries in total when in season.[359]

Ellis claimed that apples, which could be stored for long periods of time, were ready at all times to be made into pies and pastries. He provided recipes for poor labourers' wives to make pastry, and he also noted that round apple pies were made for ploughmen to take into the field to satisfy their hunger until they came home for dinner. Most interestingly, though, he noted that apples were a protection against scurvy.[360] Most of the recipes Ellis provided required sugar, but a century earlier it probably would have been too expensive for labourers to put in pies so they would have had to rely on the sweetness of the fruit itself. Ellis did note, however, that with his best ripe apples no sugar was required.

---

[358] Donald Woodward (ed.), *The Farming and Account Books of Henry Best of Elmswell, 1642* (Oxford, 1984), pp. 218–19; Stanes, *The Old Farm*, p. 64.
[359] Fussell (ed.), *Robert Loder's Farm Accounts*, pp. 83, 147–8, 185.
[360] Ellis, *Country Housewife*, p. 39. See also Rodger, *Wooden World*, p. 102.

Sugar and spices

In the sixteenth and early seventeenth century, sugar would have been much too expensive to have been used by labourers as it cost 1s 6d to 2s a pound depending on the quality. Honey might have been used as a substitute, but it was also expensive at about 5s a gallon, so unlikely to have been used as a sweetener unless one possessed hives. Only 4 per cent of the labourers' inventories examined in chapter 4 mentioned bees. However, sugar was bought by farmers such as Robert Loder to include in harvest cakes and pudding.[361] In 1618 he bought 28s worth of raisins, currants and prunes, 12s worth of cinnamon, cloves, mace, ginger and pepper, and 6 lb of sugar. During the harvest of 1706, the Rev. Mr John Crakanthorp purchased 18 lb of sugar, and 70 lb of currants and raisins for the harvesters (in 1707 he purchased similar amounts, in addition to caraway seeds, ginger and pepper). By this time the price of sugar had fallen to 6–8d a pound, and by the mid-eighteenth century Richard Latham was paying about 4–6d a pound.[362] Cheap sugar was a very recent phenomenon in 1740, as it depended on the development of the slave trade, and the use of slave labour on Caribbean sugar plantations to supply the English market. It was extremely popular, and was one of the most common items Latham purchased. He bought sugar 1,065 times over the course of 43 years. In 1740 he probably bought about 30 lb.[363] By the end of the century sugar was commonly consumed, but most of it seems to have been drunk in tea by the poor rather than added to puddings. Both Eden and Davies complained that the poor used sugar in their tea and noted in their budgets that sugar was an almost universal item of consumption among labouring families, with consumption of about half a pound per week being common.[364] However, in terms of calories provided per penny (see Table 3.1), this was an expensive form of consumption, as both Eden and Davies were all too aware.

Before sugar became affordable, most labourers obtained sweetness from the beer they drank, which was used to flavour porridge and furmenty, as well as other dishes. However, as early as the late sixteenth century, imported currants and raisins were being sold for only 3–4d

[361] Thorold Rogers, *History of Prices*, VI, pp. 421ff.
[362] Fussell (ed.), *Robert Loder's Farm Accounts*, p. 153; Brassley and Saunders (eds.), *Accounts of the Reverend John Crakanthorp*, pp. 179, 218.
[363] Weatherill (ed.), *Account Book of Richard Latham*, pp. 42–5.
[364] Davies, *Case of Labourers*, pp. 37–8; Eden, *State of the Poor*, I, p. 535; III, cccxxxixff.

a pound and the price remained the same throughout the seventeenth century. This could have been afforded, as it was the same price as a pound of meat. Between 1563 and 1620 the amount of currants, raisins and spices imported into London also increased over fivefold, and by the mid-1590s over a million pounds of currants were being imported into London alone from the Levant, a figure which rose again to between 3 and 5 million pounds by 1620, or almost a pound per person in England. Possibly over 1,000 tons of foreign fruit, spices and groceries were being shipped into East Anglia each year by the 1590s.[365] The popularity of foreign groceries is shown by the fact that this figure represents possibly between 7 and 8.5 lb per person in Lincolnshire, Norfolk, Suffolk and Cambridgeshire.[366]

Salt was also ubiquitous and quite cheap at 2 lb per penny in the seventeenth century. This had risen to twice that price by the eighteenth century at 1d per pound, although Richard Latham sometimes bought cheaper salt at 3 lb for a penny. Latham usually bought his salt in 2–4d purchases at a time, and spent in the region of 5–9 s a year, implying that he used between 100 and 300 lb a year to salt meat.[367] After salt, pepper was probably used most commonly by labourers to flavour pottage and stews. In 1660 200,000 to 300,000 lb of pepper were being imported into London per year, or about 6 oz for every household in England.[368] The price of pepper dropped considerably from the Elizabethan period, when it was about 4s a pound, to 2s a pound by the late seventeenth and eighteenth centuries. Richard Latham usually spent less than a shilling on pepper per year, buying between 9 oz and a pound, but a pound of pepper could have lasted a long time. Other imported spices were more expensive. Nutmeg, ginger, cinnamon and cloves sold for about 6–8d an ounce between 1580 and 1700, but seem to have risen in price in the eighteenth century,

---

[365] N. J. Williams, *The Maritime Trade of the East Anglian Ports 1550–1590* (Oxford, 1988), p. 176.

[366] This calculation is based on the fact that, in 1811, these counties contained 9 per cent of the population of England. In the early 1590s this would have been about 351,000 people, which gives a rate of consumption of 8.5 lb per person. But the percentage of the population living in East Anglia was probably greater in the 1590s than in 1811, so the figure might have been lower. In addition, some of the groceries might have been transported into other counties. Williams, *Maritime Trade*, p. 176; Wrigley and Schofield, *Population History*, pp. 531, 621.

[367] The weight is not usually given in the accounts.

[368] London handled perhaps 80 per cent of imports around 1600, and some of the imports into East Anglia would have been re-exports from London. Clay, *Economic Expansion*, II, pp. 124–5, 165; Robert Brenner, *Merchants and Revolutionaries: Commercial Change, Political Conflict and London's Overseas Traders 1550–1653* (Cambridge, 1993), pp. 25–9.

and Latham only mentioned the purchase of cloves three times, and nutmeg fifteen times.[369]

Conclusion

I have gone into great detail in the sections above to show that what labourers ate was much more varied than we are often led to believe. In the next chapter I will look at some actual prescribed diets to measure more precisely how much food was eaten by individuals and families. I will also analyse some of the estimates made by historians of crop yields and the production of land to see if enough food was being produced to supply such diets. The amount of meat consumed, certainly, would seem to imply that pasture and fodder production was very efficient. It is much more difficult to know how an independent labourer's family with young children might have afforded to buy enough food, and in chapter 5 family income and expenditure will be examined.

In terms of nutrition, the amount of meat and cheese eaten would have provided protein and many vitamins. The consumption of apples would have provided vitamin C, as would the consumption of greens. Joan Thirsk has argued that one reason why the English never made sauerkraut, like other northern European countries, was that the winters were generally not harsh enough to limit the availability of some kind of fresh vegetables most of the year. Other vitamins would have been obtained from vegetables, but since most would have been cooked in stews the length of cooking would have reduced the available vitamin content. The low level of milk consumption in the south must also have been detrimental to children's growth, and could have led to vitamin A deficiency. Both in terms of milk consumption and the consumption of oatmeal instead of bread, the northern diet was healthier than that in the south. In years of bad harvests, shortages would have been exacerbated by lack of protein and some vitamins if meat and dairy consumption was curtailed. Moreover, of course, for the very poor, without enough employment or land to plant a garden or pasture a cow, poor nutrition and probably vitamin deficiency would have been constant.[370] However, before more widespread information became available on health in the nineteenth century, it is difficult to know what effect nutrition might have had on health, especially that of children. If a child was fed with

---

[369] Weatherill (ed.), *Account Book of Richard Latham, passim.* These prices are taken from Thorold Rogers and largely come from Cambridgeshire and Yorkshire. Thorold Rogers, *History of Agriculture and Prices*, VI, pp. 445ff.; VII, pp. 382ff.

[370] McClure, *Coram's Children*, p. 204; Clarkson and Crawford, *Feast and Famine*, chs. 8–9; Drummond and Wilbraham, *Englishman's Food*, pp. 121–68.

fresh cow's milk in porridge instead of beer they should have been stronger, and might have grown taller, and certainly in the south it is likely that the lack of milk would have had a detrimental effect on childhood nutrition. If more fresh vegetables and fruit were consumed raw more vitamins would have been available, but since health manuals all advocated cooking there might have been an adverse affect on health. All the information presented above certainly shows that healthy food was available, but it is difficult to say how it was consumed, especially by children. In the next chapter I will therefore focus on calories and energy, as the evidence for this is much more robust.

3   Calories consumed by labourers

Let such have ynough
That follow the plough.
Give servant no dainties, but give him ynough,
Too many chaps walking, do beggar the plough
Poor seggons halfe starved, worke faintly and dull
And lubbers doo loiter, their bellies too full.
        Thomas Tusser, *Five Hundred Points of Good Husbandry,* 1573[1]

You may not exede this proporcon whiche although it be slender yet
yt wilbe sufficient.
        Order for the Diet at the House of Correction at Westminster, 1561[2]

In the last chapter many examples were given of the amount of beer,
meat and other foods eaten by labourers. Here I will focus specifically
on contemporary examples of actual daily diets, and the number of calories they provided. This will be done in order to judge how much food
was available to perform the work needed to power the agricultural
economy. A wide range of household accounts from the mid-sixteenth
to the end of the eighteenth century survive which have information
on food served to servants and day labourers. These will be analysed
to determine how many calories were eaten on a daily basis by labourers. In addition, prescribed institutional accounts for soldiers and for
inmates in houses of correction, workhouses and hospitals will also be
looked at. However, apart from the diet provided by Jacob Vanderlint
for a London labourer and his family in the mid-eighteenth century
there are no earlier diets for entire labouring families comparable to
Eden and Davies. In order to overcome this problem I will use some
sample family budgets given by Eden and Davies, but apply them to
earlier years, substituting prices from those years. Some foods eaten
will also have to be changed, such as potatoes and sugar, which were not

---

[1] The editor of Tusser suggests that in the second line 'chaps walking' may be a misprint
   for 'chaps wagging', i.e. 'mouths craving'. Tusser, *Five Hundred Points,* pp. 171, 313.
[2] 'Houses of Correction at Maidstone and Westminster', British Museum, MS
   Lansdowne 5, reprinted in *English Historical Review,* 42 (1927), p. 260.

eaten before the mid-eighteenth century. Once the number of calories consumed has been established, it will be possible to make some estimations about how much work could have been done.

Before doing this we need to arrive at some reasonable estimates of the number of calories in different types of food, the results of which are presented in Table 3.1 below. This was done for beer on pages 79–80 above, using the amount of malt per gallon in a sample of recipes, and here I will look at other sources to do the same for bread, meat porridge, pottage and some other foods. For sugar, fruit, vegetables, cheese and eggs I have simply used modern measurements. But even if we know the amount of a certain food being eaten, estimating how many calories and nutrients it contained is often dependent on how it was prepared or manufactured. The amount of water added to bread dough during baking, for instance, affects the number of calories in the baked loaf, as does the amount of bran in the flour used. Estimating calories in

Table 3.1 *Calorific values of different foods*

Food	Quantity	Calories
Wheaten bread	1 lb (= 12 oz)	915
Rye bread	1 lb (= 12 oz)	900
Pease pudding/pottage	1 pint	900–1,000
Oatmeal	1 pint	900
Furmenty	1 pint	780
Plum pudding (no sugar)	1 pint	1,280
Thin soup	1 pint	350
Small beer	1 pint	200
Middle beer (ale)	1 pint	400
Strong beer	1 pint	600
Sugar	1 oz	112
Treacle	1 oz	71
Potatoes	1	75
Apples	1	50
Apple pie	1 piece	290
Egg	1	84
Milk	½ pint	200
Butter	1 oz	184
Hard cheese	1 oz	102
Beef	1 lb	1,000
Mutton	1 lb	1,000
Pork	1 lb	1,144
Chicken	1 lb	864
Bacon	1 oz	110
Fish	1 oz	34
Carrots	1 lb	150

meat is even more difficult, as this depends on whether the bone is included and how lean or fatty the cut of meat is. Even if these facts are known, the preparation of the meat, whether it is boiled or roasted, will affect the number of calories in what is actually eaten. With food such as porridge or pease pudding, the amount of water and milk added is obviously crucial to the calorific value of the portions served, and variation could be caused by personal taste or institutional practice, so only a rough estimation is possible. Even in the apparently straightforward case of things like fruit, for example, we cannot know for certain how much carbohydrate was present as fruit might have been smaller in the past before scientific breeding.

Calories in bread

To estimate the calorific content of a pound of bread I have relied primarily on the recipe given in *The Report of an Essay of Bread* of 1758 which states that 16 bushels of meal of all sorts of wheat will yield 12 bushels of whole-wheat flour of 56 lb each, which will then produce 12 bushels of bread of 69 lb 8 oz each, or an increase in weight of 23 per cent with the addition of water.[3] Frederick Eden, however, provided two different examples giving different proportions. The first came from a tract printed by the Board of Agriculture which estimated that 14 lb of household wheat flour 'well soaked' would produce 18.5 lb of bread, an increase of 25 per cent, while the second came from a Dr Charles Irving in a report to the House of Commons on the making of flour and bread in London using one-year-old flour. Here 3.5 lb of flour mixed with 2 lb of water produced 4 lb 8 oz of bread, an increase of 34 per cent, and a much moister bread than that given in the Assize pamphlet.[4] William Harrison noted that in his time bakers added 5 oz of water for every pound of flour.[5] In the early seventeenth century, Gervase Markham suggested using only 3 pints of water per bushel of flour (much less than a modern recipe). However, because the Assize pamphlet was supposed to represent the official method of baking I have relied on it.[6] This means that the number of calories in a pound of bread using the figures for modern wholemeal bread with 8.5 per cent fibre would be 996. However, for a loaf of modern white bread the calorific content would be 1,092, which represents a difference of 10 per cent.[7] Modern

[3] *A Copy of the Report of an Essay of Bread ...* (London, 1758), pp. 9, 15, 23, 24.
[4] Eden, *State of the Poor*, I, pp. 526, 533–4.
[5] Harrison, *Description*, pp. 133–4.   [6] Markham, *English Housewife*, p. 186.
[7] All modern estimates of calories in food have been taken from *The Composition of Foods* published by the British Ministry of Agriculture, Fisheries and Food and the

white bleached flour is undoubtedly finer than early modern stone-ground flour, and the household bread eaten by labourers probably had more bran in it. The Board of Agriculture calculated that in rye bread 8 per cent of the flour would be composed of bran, and William Ellis noted that, in Hertfordshire, for very fine wheat 10 per cent was removed as bran in the grinding process.[8] Also, since there is the possibility that the bread could have been moister, I have used a figure of 915 kcal per pound as a conservative estimate for household wheaten bread and 900 kcal per lb for rye, but this could well have been higher. I've also assumed that where bread is listed it is wheaten bread, since rye was little used and would have been noted as such.[9] When amounts of flour are listed in account books I have simply used the calories for a pound of whole-wheat flour. For the rarer occasions when oats or barley were ground into bread flour, I have used the following calculations. A labourer was said to eat 16 lb of oatmeal made into bread in a fortnight, which works out to 1,590 kcal per day for oat bread (see below, p. 147).[10] There is no equivalent measurement for ground barley flour, but one modern commercially produced barley bread contains about 1,430 kcal in barley flour per pound, which is the figure I will use.[11]

Calories in oatmeal, porridge, pudding and furmenty

Eden provided a recipe for oatmeal porridge, which he also termed hasty pudding. This involved boiling 13 oz of oatmeal in a quart of water with salt, which works out to 1,513 kcal in one quart, or about 800 kcal in a pint. However, he said the amount of water could be varied according to the consistency desired. This porridge was generally eaten with added butter, sugar, beer or milk, thus I will use a figure of 900 kcal for a pint of porridge, but this could obviously vary according to how thick the oatmeal was.[12] In 1719 William Hutton gave a recipe

Government Chemist, which is the standard source for the chemical composition of food. A. A. Paul and D. T. A. Southgate, *McCance and Widdowson's The Composition of Foods*, 4th edn (London, 1978).

[8] Eden, *State of the Poor*, I, p. 526; Ellis, *Country Housewife*, pp. 1–3. William Harrison claimed that, for the finest bread in his time, 22 lb of bran were removed for every bushel of meal, or 40 per cent, which must have been impossible. In modern wheat the bran forms only 14–15 per cent of the kernel, and even if strains at the time had more bran it is unlikely to have been 40 per cent. In an experiment of 1800 an extraction rate of 81.6 per cent was measured. Campbell *et al.*, *A Medieval Capital*, Table XXVIII, Appendix II, p. 191; Harrison, *Description*, pp. 133–4.

[9] On flour usage by labouring families, see Ellis, *Country Housewife*, p. 16.

[10] Eden, *State of the Poor*, I, p. 512.

[11] This is Hodgson Mill barley bread mix with the added sugars subtracted.

[12] Eden, *State of the Poor*, I, p. 497. On oatmeal also see Gibson and Smout, *Prices, Food and Wages*, pp. 136, 231–2, 236, 242.

for furmenty used in the Clerkenwell workhouse of 15 quarts of milk combined with 1s worth of wheat and 2.5 lb of sugar. Since a bushel of wheat cost 4s, roughly the average price at the time, this would be 14lb of wheat, equivalent to eight quarts in volume. If we assume this produced about 24 quarts of furmenty, using the modern calorific value of semolina its total calorific value would be 37,410 kcal, or 780 kcal per pint. Hutton also provided a recipe for plum pudding served in the workhouse consisting of 15 quarts of milk combined with 10 lb of suet and 10 lb of plums which contained a total of 61,725 kcal. If we assume this also made about 24 quarts it would be 1,280 kcal per pint.[13] A diet from the Bristol corporation for the poor states that there should be ½ pint of peas in a pint of pea soup or pottage, which would provide about 900 to 1,000 kcal.[14] Eden provided a recipe for a soup of which 1 pint contained 3 oz of meat (250 kcal) and an ounce of barley and oatmeal (100 kcal), giving about 350 kcal a pint.[15]

Calories in meat

Boiling reduces the food value of raw meat by about 30 per cent, but since the meat was often boiled with vegetables, if the broth was consumed there would have been no loss.[16] Roasting reduces the food value less depending on how rare the meat is cooked. A modern pound of raw dressed beef carcass with 23 per cent fat contains an average of 1,269 kcal, while a pound of raw beef brisket without the bone contains 1,134 kcal and a pound of raw forerib with the bone contains 1,305 kcal. A pound of lean mutton contains about 1,139 kcal and fat mutton 1,422. A dressed bacon carcass contains 1,584 kcal per pound, while a fatty cut of meat could contain over 2,000 kcal per pound. But bacon was normally eaten in smaller amounts once salted. From this it can be seen that in terms of calories, much more energy comes from the fatty than the lean part of the meat, which would affect its energy content.

Bones made up about 12–14 per cent of carcass weight depending on how fat the animal was, but would have contained marrow which would have been eaten. I have assumed that the pound of meat sold included the bone. In workhouse and other institutional diets where the meat is specified in ounces per day or meal it is much more difficult to determine what sort of meat this was, as in most cases it is not specified. When it is specified, however, it is said to be meat without bone,

---

[13] Hitchcock (ed.), *Hutton's Complaint Book*, pp. 1–2.
[14] E. E. Butcher (ed.), *Bristol Corporation of the Poor 1696–1834*, Bristol Record Society, 3 (1932), p. 68.
[15] Eden, *State of the Poor*, I, pp. 499, 525.   [16] See above, p. 108.

Table 3.2 *Daily diet at King's College, Cambridge, 1481–1664*

Food	1481	kcal	1562	kcal	1572	kcal	1664	kcal
Bread	1.1 lb	1,006 (22%)	1.1 lb	1,006 (26%)	1.5 lb	1,372 (37%)	1.8 lb	1,647 (35%)
Meat	1 lb	1,000 (22%)	1.9 lb	1,900 (48%)	1.5 lb	1,500 (40%)	1.5 lb	1,500 (32%)
Middle beer	7 pints	2,800 (45%)	2.2 pints	880 (17%)	2.6 pints	1,040 (20%)	4 pints	1,600 (25%)
Fish	1 lb	538 (11%)	0.4 lb	215 (5%)	1 oz	34 (1%)	3.5 oz	119 (2%)
Eggs	—	—	0.5 egg	42 (1%)	—	—	1 egg	84 (2%)
Butter	—	—	0.7 oz	129 (3%)	0.5 oz	92 (2%)	1 oz	184 (4%)
Total		5,344		4,172		4,038		5,134

as in Eden's description of the Oxford and Norwich workhouses, or the London Bridewell diet cited above.[17] This was also the case in Christ's Hospital in 1593, where the butcher was ordered to supply beef with the bones taken out, and in the Quaker workhouse in Clerkenwell, a diet from 1713 specifies '8 ounces boiled meat without the bone'.[18] Thus I have conservatively estimated that a pound of meat in the diets given below was from a carcass with bones, and contained 1,000 kcal for the purposes of calculating food energy. I have done this to account for the probability that cheaper cuts of meat and offal were bought by the poor, but it is certainly possible that more calories were consumed on some occasions.

Before going on to look at labouring diets, Table 3.2 is included to give an idea of how many calories one group of well-off people were eating. It is taken from the commons books of King's College, Cambridge. These books provide information on the number of people dining each week, together with the amount and cost of the food served for each of two meals every day.[19] The commons books are one of the few sources where the diet of relatively wealthy people can be measured on a day-to-day basis very precisely. Here I have picked weeks from the beginning of the Michaelmas term for a number of sample years from 1481 until the Restoration, when the series ends. The amounts eaten in other weeks from the rest of the year were similar, except during Lent, where

[17] See above, p. 92.
[18] Pearce, *Annals of Christ's Hospital*, p. 175; Hitchcock (ed.), *Hutton's Complaint Book*, p. 97.
[19] King's College Archives, KCAR/4/1/6, 12, 16, 18, 28, 30, 33. I would like to thank Matthew Westlake, who helped research these books.

the prohibition against meat was observed, at least in terms of fresh meat. Beef and mutton were replaced with mostly salted, but some fresh fish, as well as something termed 'salted animal'. Each week daily purchases and servings were listed, together with weekly expenditures on items from the college 'store' such as bread, beer, beef and fuel.[20] I have included the main food items of consumption, but other things like mustard, vinegar, currants and some sugar were present in small amounts. There were also feast days, where expenditure was significantly increased, but the books do not say if guests were present. Every week the numbers of fellows, scholars, the chapel choir and servants are listed, and I have included all and just divided by the total number of people present. This assumes that the servants were eating the same as the fellows, which seems unlikely, but it is probable that the difference was more one of quality than amount, as we shall see when we look at servants in other account books. But certainly choir boys would have eaten less than the adults, so these figures are somewhat abstract. Note also that, as in most accounts, greens are rarely listed. This is not because they were not eaten, but because they were grown in the college gardens and not costed. What this table shows, however, is that the daily calorific intake was much higher than we might expect for what was even then considered a fairly sedentary occupation. We should remember, though, that fellows and scholars would have had to walk everywhere, or ride a horse. Samuel Pepys, for instance, commonly walked most days from his residence near the Tower of London to Westminster and back, a distance of about 6 miles in total. The other thing that is immediately apparent is the importance of meat and ale or beer as sources of calories, although the amount of beer drunk was much less in the sixteenth and seventeenth centuries than in the fifteenth century, and the amount of meat and bread gradually increased over time.

In contrast, Table 3.3 shows the diets of soldiers, sailors and fishermen. Here I have used 400 kcal per pint for strong beer as it would not

---

[20] Measurements were sometimes given in 'fercula', or servings, which were a third of a stone, or 4.66 lb, but for the most part, measurements were given in volume or prices. When prices were given they have been compared to values given in the college accounts for purchase price of goods. To work out the amount of bread served, the price in the commons books has been compared to the price the college paid for wheat at the same time. For earlier dates this was compared to the Assize of Bread to work out the size of a penny loaf of the finest white bread, and then converted into pounds. Alternatively, I have converted the amount of wheat at the given price into flour (75 per cent) and then worked on the basis that a bushel of flour produces 69 lb of bread. Since the college baked its own bread, and brewed its own beer, I have assumed that the prices they give (in a section headed 'Stock') do not include labour costs, which would be in the servants' wages section of the accounts.

Table 3.3 Working diets

	1545		1565		1615		18th century		18th century
	English soldiers defending Boulogne[a]	kcal	Royal Navy sailors[b]	kcal	Fishermen sailors[c]	kcal	Navy rations, Tuesday[d]	Cal	Navy rations, Wednesday[e]
Bread	1.82 lb	1,665	1 lb biscuit	2,030	1 lb biscuit	2,030	1 lb biscuit	2,030	1 lb biscuit
Salt beef	1.26 lb[f]	1,260	2 lb	2,000	—	—	2 lb	2,000	—
Ale/beer[g]	7.2 pints strong	2,880	8 pints strong	3,200	8 pints strong	3,200	8 pints strong	3,200	8 pints strong
Honey	estimate	50	—	—	—	—	—	—	—
Bacon	—	—	—	—	4 oz	440	—	—	—
Oatmeal	—	—	—	—	3 oz	282	—	—	1 pint
Cheese	—	—	—	—	8 oz	816	—	—	4 oz
Butter	—	—	—	—	4 oz	736	—	—	2 oz
Total		5,885		7,230		7,504		7,230	

18th century Wednesday Cal values: Bread 2,030; Oatmeal 900; Cheese 408; Butter 368; Total 6,906.

Notes: [a] James Arthur Miller (ed.), The Letters of Stephen Gardiner (Cambridge, 1933), pp. 140–5.
[b] Michael Oppenheim, A History of the Administration of the Royal Navy and of Merchant Shipping in Relation to the Navy, I, 1509–1660 (London, 1896), p. 140.
[c] Drummond and Wilbraham, Englishman's Food, p. 465.
[d] Rodger, Wooden World, p. 83.
[e] Ibid.
[f] Alternatives to the beef are given as 1 lb of cheese or 0.5 lb of bacon and pease pudding, or 0.5 lb of butter and 5 herrings or half of a stockfish. Miller, Letters of Stephen Gardiner, pp. 141–5.
[g] Here I have used the strength of middle beer because consumption was so high.

Table 3.4 *London Bridewell diets, 1600*

	Men working in the hemp house or mill grinding corn	kcal meat day	kcal fast day[a]	Women spinning	kcal meat day	kcal fast day	Non-working	kcal meat day
Bread	2 lb	1,830	1,830	2 lb	1,830	1,217	1 lb	915
Meat	1.5 lb	1,500	—	1.5 lb	1,500	—	1.5 lb	1,500
Beer	4 pints	1,600	1,600	2 pints	800	800	2 pints	800
Porridge	1 pint (mess)	1,000	1,000	1 pint	1,000	1,000	1 pint	1,000
Cheese	—	—	400	—	—	400	—	—
Total		5,930	4,830		5,130	3,417		4,215

Note: [a] Cheese and butter were offered, but no fish.
Sources: Guildhall Library, London, Bridewell Court Book, IV, fos. 212r–v; Archer, *Pursuit of Stability*, pp.190–2.

have been the strongest, which was served at alehouses, but it had to be strong enough to last on ship and during the siege, and only strong beer had enough alcohol to preserve it over long periods of time.[21] The figures in the table represent huge numbers of calories, implying very hard work, fighting, carrying weapons, digging trenches or putting up and taking down sails and looking after ships. In the navy, the gallon of beer was only in practice an estimate, as by ancient custom the men drank as much as they needed. When beer, or the foods listed in the table were not available, especially in hot climates, the navy was obliged to provide equivalents such as a pint of wine or a ½ pint of rum instead of a gallon of beer, 4 lb of rice and stockfish instead of a gallon of oatmeal, or 2 lb of suet instead of a piece of beef.[22] It seems unlikely, though, that such huge amounts would have been eaten when less work was needed. But in the navy, at least, every officer and man was allowed the value of the standard ration even if they did not eat it, and would then be given credit by the purser for future food, or in their wages. In addition, in port wives and visitors were expected to drink the navy's beer freely.[23]

Tables 3.4, 3.5 and 3.6 show the diets from some sixteenth-century houses of correction for comparison. These were institutions designed to punish offenders who had committed misdemeanours. This was done

[21] Mathias, *Brewing Industry*, pp. 195–6, 204–9.
[22] Rodger, *Wooden World*, pp. 90–2.   [23] Ibid., p. 89

Table 3.5 *Diet at the Westminster house of correction, 1561*

	Men working in the mill grinding corn	kcal	Women spinning	kcal
Bread	16 oz	1,220	16 oz	1,220
Meat[a]	1 lb	1,000	0.5 lb	500
Beer	4 pints	1,600	2 pints	800
Pottage	1 pint (mess)	1,000	1 pint (mess)	1,000
Total		4,820		3,520

Note: [a] On fast days they received the equivalent in cheese and butter and fish. Note also that on fish days they were to be given the equivalent in 'Butter, Chese, heryngs, pescods [peas] & soche lyke'.
Source: 'Houses of Correction at Maidstone and Westminster', pp. 258–61.

Table 3.6 *Diet at the Bury St Edmunds house of correction, 1588*

Food	Non-fish days; standard	kcal	Working (est.)	kcal	Non-working	kcal
Bread	16 oz rye	1,200	20 oz rye	1,500	16 oz rye	1,200
Meat[a]	0.5 lb	500	0.5 lb	500	—	—
Beer	2 pints small	400	5 pints small	1,000	2 pints small	400
Porridge	2 pints	2,000	2 pints	2,000	2 pints	2,000
Total		4,100		5,000		3,600

Note: [a] On fast days they received 2/3 lb of cheese or 2 herrings and butter. Drummond and Wilbraham, *Englishman's Food*, p. 56.
Source: 'Orders for the House of Correction at Bury, Suffolk, anno 1588', in Eden, *State of the Poor*, III, p. cxliii.

through short periods of incarceration doing hard work in an attempt to inculcate the offender with the virtue of labour. The idea behind this was that they had been motivated to commit their crime because they were not engaged in honest labour. I will return to the theme of government attempts to create industrious workers in the last chapter, but the key thing to note here is that authorities thought this could not be done without supplying them with enough of the right sort of food. Although these examples do not provide as many calories as for sailors and soldiers, they still provide an amount large enough for very hard work. Even more interestingly they provide what to us seems like a very large amount of meat. The first example is for the Bridewell in London from 1600 (Table 3.4). This was the original house of correction, and it dealt with a large number of temporary inmates. This is a very valuable diet because it distinguishes between male work in a hemp house or corn mill, female spinning and non-work.

At the Bury house of correction (Table 3.6), the diet also differed according to whether the inmates worked. It was noted that this was a basic diet, and for those who 'applie theire worke, shall have allowance of beare and a little bread betwen meales, as … he doth deserve in his said worke', and 'they which will not worke shall have noe allowance but bread and beare onely, untill they will conforme themselves to worke'.[24] Such diets also included fasting day diets, where the eating of flesh was prohibited, which was all Fridays and Saturdays, all days in Lent, and on certain other days, or a total of 153 days in the year.[25] On these days, a 'like quantitie, made eyther of milk or pease or such lyke, and the thurd part of a pound of chese, or one good herringe, or twoe white or redd' was provided. The state attempted to justify such days, not on religious grounds but economic ones, as an attempt to get its subjects to eat more fish thus creating employment for fishermen and ensuring there would be a supply of sailors for the navy.[26] However, this legislation was unsuccessful in increasing the taste for fish, and by the eighteenth century these so-called fast days had been replaced by some days in the week when simply less flesh was eaten.

Although these diets are for correctional institutions, the number of calories they provide is still high, especially for work. What is more surprising is how high the Bridewell and Bury figures are for those who did not work, being not much lower than those for King's College. It is hard to see how an incarcerated sedentary person could have eaten so much unless they were doing some exercise, so perhaps they did not eat their full allowance. But in the case of the Bridewell, which was the most underfinanced of the London hospitals, such a diet must have been what the governors thought a poor person needed to eat if they were to learn how to labour hard.[27] The instructions to the governors of the house of correction in Westminster outlining the diet in Table 3.5 state that 'you may not exede this proporcon whiche although it be slender yet yt wilbe sufficient'. They were not being charitable, as the instructions go on to describe those to be incarcerated as 'desparate'

[24] Eden, *State of the Poor*, III, p. cxliii.   [25] Harrison, *Description*, p. 126 n.5.
[26] Rosemary Sgroi, 'Piscatorial Politics Revisited: The Language of Economic Debate and the Evolution of Fishing Policy in Elizabethan England', *Albion*, 35 (2003), pp. 1–24.
[27] Archer, *Pursuit of Stability*, pp. 190–1.

Table 3.7 *Robert Loder's family's daily consumption*

1612		kcal per person	1614	kcal per person
People (servants)	11 (6)		7 (5)	
Bread	1.4 lb	1,281	2.1 lb	1,922 (28%)
Meat	1.2 lb	1,200	1.8 lb	1,800 (26%)
Beer (malt)	1.1 lb	1,817	1.5 lb	2,478 (36%)
Fish	—	—	2.2 oz	75 (1%)
Cheese	1 oz	102	4 oz	408 (6%)
Butter	3.2 oz	589	1 oz	184 (3%)
Total		4,989		6,867

Source: Fussell (ed.), *Robert Loder's Farm Accounts*, pp. 44–5, 86–8, 106–7.

and ordered that shackles of iron had to be provided for 'the tamying of the wylde and lewde persons'.[28]

The accounts of St Bartholomew's and Christ's Hospitals from the late Elizabethan period also show that bread, meat and beer were all purchased in significant amounts for the patients and children residing in these institutions. At St Bartholomew's, for instance, in 1596 between £50 and £65 was spent each month to feed the patients or about 4d for each person a day, and at Christ's in 1556 the children received up to 1 lb of bread, 1.5 pints of beer and 5 oz of meat a day.[29]

It is much more difficult to find a diet for an agricultural labourer from this period. However, it is possible to use the incredibly detailed accounts of the Berkshire yeoman farmer Robert Loder of Harwell to get an idea of what his family, including his servants, were eating, since he describes who was resident in his household and how much they consumed each year.[30] In 1612, in addition to his servants and wife, his brother, his wife and their maidservant and probably his father were all living with him. In 1614 only he and his wife and their infant daughter remained in the house, together with their servants, who were listed as

[28] 'Houses of Correction at Maidstone and Westminster', p. 260.
[29] London Guildhall Library, Christ's Hospital Treasurer's Accounts, MS 12,819; E. H. Peirce, *Annals of Christ's Hospital* (London, 1908), pp. 28, 33–44, 173–9. St Bartholomew's Hospital Archives, HB1/2 Ledger 1562–1586, HB1/3 Ledger 1589–1614. Sir Norman Moore, *The History of St. Bartholomew's Hospital* (London, 1918), I, pp. 202–3, 225, 270, 284, 290.
[30] There is no way, however, of calculating how much extra food might have been consumed by guests at dinner. Given that hospitality was so important in this period, as the diary of Thomas Turner demonstrates, dinner quests would have been very common. But it would have been, presumably, just as common for Loder to eat at other farmers' tables, since hospitality was reciprocal. Thus it is probable that, over the course of a year, hospitality would not affect consumption figures that much. Pennell, 'Material Culture of Food', p. 232.

being a carter, a shepherd, a boy and two maidservants. Here I have just divided the total amount eaten per person not including the infant daughter. But the actual proportions eaten by men, women and children would have been different, with men consuming a greater percentage of the available calories (see below, p. 135).[31] The figures certainly show that a labourer working as a farm servant would have been eating enough calories for a great deal of work, as well as a great deal of meat. The adult men would also have been drinking a gallon of beer brewed at 2 lb of malt to the gallon each day.

It is possible that farm servants were provided with better diets than day labourers, who worked without food or board during the inflationary period in the late sixteenth and the first half of the seventeenth century. However, if this was the case, they would not have been able to do much work, and it would not have made sense for a farmer to pay day wages for someone to work at much less intensity than his own servants. A farmer would not save money in the long run if he only paid a day labourer wages which did not allow the labourer to buy enough food to do the work needed to make his farm profitable. Today, it would be like buying a car with no petrol tank. Also, as we shall see, labour input was one of the biggest factors in increasing farm yields. It is certainly possible that those who were underemployed or only working a small plot of their own were much less well fed, but not those hired for wages.

A great deal of work has been done on the calorific requirements for work in underdeveloped countries in the modern world, focusing on how far undernutrition, especially in agriculture, is an impediment to their further development. In many countries today, such as India, the availability of calories, as measured across the whole population, is much less than in the examples above.[32] The FAO has made extensive examinations of the calorific requirements of different types of work in tropical agriculture, but it has been noted that energy requirements in the tropics are quite different from those in Europe.[33] However, there is a much earlier literature, more relevant to us, from experiments largely carried out in Germany and Eastern Europe from the 1920s and 1930s

---

[31] The child would still have been breastfeeding at this time so she is not included in the calculations.

[32] See, for example, Peter Svedberg, *Poverty and Undernutrition: Theory, Measurement, and Policy* (Oxford, 2000).

[33] *Energy and Protein Requirements. Report of a Joint FAO/WHO/UNU Expert Consultation* (World Health Organization Technical Report Series 724, 1991), www.fao.org/docrep/003/aa040e/AA040E00.HTM. Fogel, 'New Sources', pp. 7–13; Fogel, *Escape from Hunger*, pp. 8–19; J. V. G. A. Durnin and R. Passmore, *Energy, Work and Leisure* (London, 1967), pp. 106–9; Derek Miller, 'Man's Demand for Energy', in Derek Oddy and Derek Miller (eds.), *Diet and Health in Modern Britain* (London, 1985), pp. 274–95.

on agricultural labourers working in ways that had changed little from the early modern period.[34] Working out the amount of calorific energy needed for work uses the principle of the basal metabolic rate or BMR, which is the amount of energy required to maintain the body at rest without doing anything, including eating. It varies between age, sex and body weight. Using the average height of men in the early modern period, as determined from skeletal evidence from London, of 5 ft 7.5 in and a weight of 140 lb this would give a BMR of about 1,500 kcal per day, which would be about 1,300 for a woman of the same age, with a height of 5 ft 2 and a weight of 120 lb.[35] Calories consumed for other essential activities are then expressed as a multiple of this basic survival amount. Eating and essential hygiene are calculated as 0.4 of BMR while awake. This would add up to a figure of 2,100 for the man in our example, and 1,900 for the women. Any other physical activity is then calculated at calories expended per minute of exercise such as walking or working, and then added up. Table 3.8 provides estimates of daily calorific expenditure for men and women engaged in different tasks for 8 hours and 10 hours of work, added to the basic 2,100 kcal for men and 1,900 kcal for women. To this I have added an estimated rate of 600 kcal expended walking over fields and tracks for 2 hours a day. The figures of calories per minute are all means, and depending on the size and strength of the person working, and the effort involved, these figures could vary by about 20 per cent. This table certainly shows that the number of calories provided in the working diets above were required given the tasks undertaken. Robert Loder was, in fact, very clear about this when one year he decided to try to save money by hiring his servants for wages rather than boarding them in his house, and discovered that it actually cost him more as he had to pay them enough to ensure that the work he required could be done.[36] Table 3.8 also shows that much agricultural work undertaken by women also required a high level of calorific consumption.

In Table 3.8 I have provided columns for eight and ten hours of hard work a day. The Elizabethan statute of labourers stated that in the summer labourers should arrive at work at 5.00 a.m. and leave between 6.00 and 8.00 p.m., with a half-hour break for breakfast, an hour for dinner followed by half an hour for sleep and half an hour in the afternoon for

[34] These studies together with many others on different tasks were brought together in Durnin and Passmore, *Energy, Work and Leisure*. For an example of experiments done in Budabest see G. Farkas, J. Geldrich and S. Láng, 'Neuere Untersuchungen über den Energieverbrauch beim Ernten', *Arbeits Physiologie*, 5 (1933), pp. 434–62.

[35] Lex Werner (ed.), *London Bodies* (London, 1998), p. 108.

[36] See below, p. 208.

Table 3.8 *Daily calorific expenditure for different tasks*[a]

Activity	Calories expended per minute	Eight hours of work	Ten hours of work
Mowing with a scythe	8	6,540	7,500
Binding sheaves (men)	7.3	6,204	7,080
Binding sheaves (women)	4	4,420	4,900
Stooking sheaves	6.8	5,964	6,780
Threshing (men)	5	5,100	5,700
Threshing (women)	4.5	4,660	5,200
Hoeing	5	5,100	5,700
Weeding	5	5,100	5,700
Ploughing	6.5	5,820	6,600
Digging ditches and shovelling	8	6,540	7,500
Cutting trees	8.4	6,732	7,740
Repairing fences	5.7	5,436	6,120
Forking sheaves	6.5	5,820	6,600
Working with an axe	8	6,540	7,500
Staking firewood	5.7	5,436	6,120
Heavy housework (women)	4	4,420	4,900
Light housework (women)	3	3,940	4,300
Milking by hand	3.5	4,180	4,600
Walking over fields and hills	5	5,100	5,700
Walking on streets	2.5	3,900	4,200
Grinding corn by hand	4.6	4,908	5,460
Carrying a heavy load	8	6,540	7,500
Building labour	6	5,580	6,300

Note: [a] One early modern task which was no longer practised by the 1930s was reaping with a sickle, which is why it has not been included in the table.
Sources: Durnin and Passmore, *Energy, Work and Leisure*, pp. 41–3, 51, 66–9, 72; *Energy and Protein Requirements*, Annexe 5, www.fao.org/docrep/003/aa040e/AA040E00.HTM.

drinking.[37] However, in Thanet it was reported that farmers made their servants go out into the fields at 6.00 a.m. and they returned home at 10.00 a.m. and did not go back until 2.00 p.m., from which time they worked until 6.00 p.m. before coming back for another drink in the evening.[38] Eden reported that in the late eighteenth century labourers

[37] Eden, *State of the Poor*, III, p. clvii.
[38] James Britten, *Old Country Farming Words* (London, 1880), p. 114.

worked from 6.00 a.m. to 6.00 p.m. with a 1–2-hour dinner break, and that they also had breaks at 10.00 a.m. and 4.00 p.m. to drink beer.[39] In the winter labourers generally worked through the hours of light, but day wages were often lower. About ten hours of work a day was probably normal in the summer, except for harvest, when more work would have been done, sometimes as much as fourteen hours.[40] However, it is unlikely that men and women worked continuously without slowing down. With some of the higher rates of calorific expenditure above 6,000 kcal a day it would have been difficult for men to continually work at this level, and breaks would have had to be taken, reducing the number of calories required.[41] Other factors such as keeping warm in the cold winters of the period might also have boosted the calories burned by women working in households.

Some idea of the pace of work in the early modern period can also be gained by comparing rates of pay for piece-work tasks to day wages. The source of such data will be discussed in chapter 6, when labour intensity will be considered, but here we can use it to get an idea of how much daily work was involved in the hours of work. On average a man reaped just under 2,000 square yards of wheat a day around 1700. At 10 hours a day this would have amounted to an area of 10 × 20 yards an hour, bending over and cutting with a sickle. In the Essex Easter quarter sessions rates from 1661, a haymaker could mow 0.8 of an acre of grass in a day with a scythe, or an area 10 × 40 yards an hour. The blades of tools in such constant use would also have dulled quite quickly, requiring more effort. Raking and cocking the same acre of grass, however, was 2 days' work for a man, and 2.4 days' for a woman. Reaping as well as cocking an acre of wheat or rye would take a man about 3.5 days. It was also expected that a man could dig a ditch about 34 ft in length, 4 ft wide at the top, 1.5 ft at the bottom and 3 ft deep in a day, or about 3–4 ft an hour.[42] In Kent in 1795, a labourer was expected to spread 43 cartloads of dung, of 24 bushels each, in a day, or to hoe a half acre of beans or peas in a day, or 0.3 of an acre of turnips. Digging an acre of hops was very labour intensive and took one man nine days.[43] Eden also provided some examples where industrious men earned up to twice the rate of day labour by doing piece-work. Such individuals must have been very strong and probably worked considerably longer hours.[44]

[39] Eden, *State of the Poor*, III, p. 822.
[40] Ibid., II, p. 293; Batchelor, *General View*, p. 110.
[41] Durnin and Passmore, *Energy, Work and Leisure*, pp. 124–6.
[42] Eden, *State of the Poor*, III, p. cii.   [43] Eden, *State of the Poor*, II, p. 293.
[44] Ibid., II, pp. 27, 78, 433, 548, 643–4; III, pp. 715.

We can also use the same calculations to look at the diets of three workhouses and St Bartholomew's Hospital from the eighteenth century in Table 3.9 below. The workhouse diets are for the young and the old doing lighter work. The figures for the Clerkenwell workhouse have been averaged over a whole week, so, for instance, 8 oz of meat without bones was served on three days of the week and 1 lb of plum pudding on one day, and so forth. As the orders for St Mary Whitechapel stated, no inmates were required to work beyond their strength. A boy of 12 would have a BMR of about 1,250, and if we assume that he worked for 10 hours making horse whips, which might be similar to tailoring, then he would have needed about 2,563 kcal. An old person of 60 sitting and winding cotton, however, would probably only have needed 1,875 kcal a day. Giving the excess to the children would result in them receiving 2,555 kcal, which would be just enough. The patients in St Bartholomew's were given more meat and milk porridge for their health, which provided them with more calories. Children at the Foundling Hospital received 8 oz of meat cooked with greens 5 days a week and meat broth thickened with rice as well as 8 oz of bread, 6 oz of cheese in addition to milk porridge, rice pudding thickened with treacle and small beer. Most of the meat was boiled except on Sunday, when they were served roast beef. The servants in the hospital were allowed 1 lb 1 oz of meat a day, and the washerwomen drank copious amounts of beer to combat the effects of heat.[45]

Although it is not an example of an agricultural labourer's budget, the next eighteenth-century diet comes from Jacob Vanderlint's pamphlet *Money Answers All Things*, one of the many pamphlets addressing the problem of the shortage of money to pay wages in the period.[46] Vanderlint argued that if 7/8 of the people in the country doubled their consumption, this would create consumer demand, thus stimulating the economy. He used his estimation of a London labourer's expenses as an example of what needed to be done. The total yearly budget for this London labouring family he put at £54 10s 4d, of which £36 8s (67 per cent) was spent on food, £6 9s on household goods, rent and schooling, £9 on clothes, and 10s for health care.[47] Vanderlint did not

---

[45] McClure, *Coram's Children*, pp. 198–201; London Metropolitan Archives, Foundling Hospital General Court Minutes, A/FH/K/01/1, 17th Dec., 1745, Steward's Account Book, Household expenses, A/FH/B8/7/1 (1758), General Committee Minutes, 11 April 1730, 18 Nov. 1747, 22 Jan. 1755, 3 Nov. 1762, 5 June 1776, 31 Dec. 1777, 9 Sept. 1778; A/FH/B8/6/2–3, Household Expenses 1742–54.

[46] Jeremy Boulton, 'Wage Labour in Seventeenth Century London', *Economic History Review*, 49 (1996), pp. 268–90; Jeremy Boulton, 'Food Prices and the Standard of Living in London in the "Century of Revolution", 1580–1700', *Economic History Review*, 53 (2000), pp. 455–92.

[47] Jacob Vaderlint, *Money Answers All Things: or an Essay to Make Money Sufficiently Plentiful* (London, 1734), pp. 70–7.

Table 3.9 *Eighteenth-century workhouse diets*

	St Albans 1724	kcal	St Mary Whitechapel 1725	kcal	Clerkenwell Quaker workhouse 1713	kcal	St Bartholomew's Hospital London 1715	kcal
People	20 men and women over 50 years old minding cotton, 10 boys making horse whips, 4 girls spinning		20 men and women 40–80 years old, 8 children 'Mostly Helpless'		c. 100 poor elderly people and children spinning		—	
Bread	0.6 lb	549	1 lb	915	1 lb	915	1lb	915
Meat	3.6 oz	300	3.8 oz	320	3.4 oz	213	7 oz	700
Beer	2 pints small	400	2 pints	800	3 pints	1,200	3 pints small	600
Porridge	—		0.6 pint	540	—		1.1 pints	1,000
Pease pudding	—		—		5 oz	312	—	
Meat broth	—		—		—		1.3 pints	296
Plum pudding	—		—		1.7 oz	136	—	
Milk	0.25 pint	100	—		0.3 pint	120	—	
Cheese	3.2 oz	326	2.5 oz	255	4 oz	408	0.6 oz	61
Butter	2.7 oz	497	—		—		0.3 oz	55
Sugar	2 oz	224	—		—		—	
Total		2,366		2,830		3,304		3,627

Sources: An Account of Several Workhouses for Employing and Maintaining the Poor (London, 1725), pp. 11, 65–6; Hitchcock (ed.), *Hutton's Complaint Book*, pp. xiv, 96–8; some other examples in *An Account of Several Workhouses* from the early eighteenth century provide much less meat in their diets. Moore, *History of St. Bartholomew's*, pp. 356; McClure, *Coram's Children*, pp. 199–201, 270–1.

describe the nature of this labourer's work, or that of any member of his family. Nor did he give a breakdown of the ages of the children, so it is difficult to know how their consumption might have been divided. The most common scale used to differentiate between the calorific needs of men, women and children is the Atwater scale, which breaks down consumption patterns according to age and sex. Simplified, this works out to average of 1 (man), 0.8 (woman) and 0.5 (child). The Atwater scale was calculated using detailed data from a sample of American families living in New York City in the 1890s.[48] I have used this breakdown in my calculations, but it is possible that women in the early modern period would have had to do heavier labour. The Bridewell diets, for instance, allowed a spinning woman almost 90 per cent of the man's rations if the beer was the same strength, or about 83 per cent if it was small rather than middle beer.

Compared to that of Loder's servants a century earlier, this diet provides many fewer calories in animal products, especially meat, but more in beer if it was home brewed. The calories supplied through this diet would have provided enough energy for the wife to wash clothes or spin, but the husband might have needed extra food or beer supplied at work if he was a building labourer or a porter. Earnings of £54 a year were also quite high. Wages were high in London, but even if he was working 312 days a year and his wife and children were earning a third of the family income he would have to earn 2s a day to live this well. But, as Vanderlint pointed out, this was rare. He claimed that most labouring 'mechanicks' were only able to work half this much as a result of lack of work and illness. Of course if they were not working their calorific requirements would have been much reduced, and £2–3 could be saved by eating rye bread, but they would still have had to purchase fuel and clothes and pay rent.

In comparison, to find out what an eighteenth-century agricultural labourer might have been spending, it is possible to use an example from Frederick Eden and then work out how much the cost would have been at sample years from earlier in the century. This is done in Table 3.11 for a relatively good harvest year (1744), and for a bad harvest year (1756). The example used here is for an agricultural labourer's family of nine from the parish of Streatley in Berkshire, which Eden visited in July 1795. The man was fifty years of age and three of his children were out at service and so not part of the family. Two others, twelve and fifteen years old, worked as ploughboys for neighbouring farmers, while the two youngest, aged five and seven, did not work. The wife earned

---

[48] Clarkson and Crawford, *Feast and Famine*, p. 173.

Table 3.10 *Jacob Vanderlint's budget for a labouring man, wife and four children in London, 1734*

	Weekly cost[a]	Weekly amount	Daily amount for man (×1) kcal	Daily amount for wife (×0.8) kcal	Daily amount for a child (×0.5) kcal
Bread	2s 7½d	44.6 lb (30s qrtr)	1,540	1,250	758
Meat	3s 6d	14 lb beef	520	420	260
Small beer	1s 9d	10½ gal. (21 gal. home brew)	(4 pints: 800)	(4 pints: 800)	(4 pints: 800)
Strong beer	10½d	2 gal. (3 gal. home brew)[a]	(2 pints: 1,200)	(1 pint: 1,200)	—
Milk	5½d	0.8 gal.	99	73	48
Cheese	5½d	1½ lb	105	70	46
Butter	10½d	8 oz	57	42	27
Roots, herbs, flour, oatmeal, salt, vinegar, pepper, mustard, sugar	10½d	—	50 (est.)	50 (est.)	50 (est.)
Total			4,371	3,905	1,989

Note: [a] Prices are from Ellis, *London and Country Brewer*, pp. 120–1.

1s 6d a week, but Eden did not say what she did. The man could earn 8s a week in winter, 12s in summer and 3s a day for 10 days during harvest. Altogether they earned £46 a year, and although Eden does not say how much the children earned, it would have been about £8 each. He claimed these were very high earnings, as this was a wealthy agricultural area on the banks of the Thames with good market connections to London, so there must have been continual employment. But their expenses were even higher. They spent what Eden termed the 'enormous' sum of £63 18s. He claimed this was the result of prices being over a third higher than they were in the previous year. As a result the parish paid their rent of £2 5s a year and £7 16s to pay for the cost of the two youngest, non-working children, indicating that the vestry did not regard this level of consumption as profligate.

In Eden's budget, £52 3s (82 per cent) was spent on food and £11 14s (18 per cent) on household goods, rent, fuel and clothing. No beer is included, and ½ lb of bacon is the only meat for the whole family in a week, reflecting the great increase in the price of bread. There is, however, more cheese and butter than Vanderlint provided. Thus in Table 3.11 I

Table 3.11 *Two mid-eighteenth-century diets abstracted from a well-employed Berkshire family*

	Weekly amount	Prices in 1744	Yearly cost	Prices in 1756	Yearly cost	Total daily calories	Daily amount for man (×1) kcal (24%)	Daily amount for wife (×0.8) kcal (19%)	Daily amount for each of four children (×0.6) kcal (14%)[a]
Bread	69 lb	21s qrtr wheat	£7 10s qrtr wheat[b] £5 qrtr rye	52s qrtr wheat 30s qrtr rye[c]	£18 wheat £10 9s rye	9,020	2,164	1,714	1,263
Meat	14 lb beef	2½d lb	£7 12s	3d lb	£9 2s	2,000	480	380	280
Small beer[d]	16 gal.	1d gal.	£3 9s	2d gal.	£6 18s	3,647	875	693	511
Table beer[d]	4 gal.	2d gal.	£1 14s	4d gal.[e]	£3 4s	1,829	439	348	256
Oatmeal	½ lb	40s qrtr[f]	2s 4d	40s qrtr	2s 4d	107	26	20	15
Milk	1 pint	7d gal.	4s	7d gal.	4s	57	14	11	8
Cheese	2 lb	5d lb	£2 2s	5d lb	£2 2s	466	112	89	65
Butter	2 lb	4½d lb	£1 18s	6d lb	£2 12s	841	202	160	118
Sugar	½ lb	9d lb	£1	8d lb	17s	128	31	24	18
Total			£24 13s 4d		£42 19s 4d	18,095	4,343	3,439	2,534

Notes: [a] Here 0.6 has been used rather than 0.5 as two of the four children were teenagers.
[b] Calculated from the Assize of Bread with 24 oz in a penny loaf.
[c] Thorold Rogers, *Agriculture and Prices*, VII, pp. 102ff.
[d] Eden does not include beer. Two ounces of tea is included. As argued above, beer was drunk, and certainly would have been earlier in the century when tea was less universal.
[e] With the price of barley being 28–30s per quarter this year, compared to 14s per quarter used in other calculations and taken from the *London and Country Brewer* (1733), p. 120.
[f] There are no prices for oatmeal for these years so this price is based on the market rate of oats of 19s a quarter, estimating that a quarter of oats produced about 55% its weight in oatmeal together with the milling cost. Swinton, *A Proposal for Uniformity of Weights and Measures in Scotland, by Execution of the Laws Now in Force* (Edinburgh, 1779), p. 52.
Sources: Eden, *State of the Poor*, II, pp. 15–16. The prices, as well as those in Tables 3.12 and 3.13, are taken from Thorold Rogers, *Agriculture and Prices*, VII, for the appropriate years.

have added beer and beef based on the amount suggested by Vanderlint, and I have reduced the amount of sugar to reflect earlier consumption patterns. From this table it can be seen that even in a bad year (1756) the cost of living was much cheaper earlier in the century, and in a good year (1744) it was only half the cost, including more meat and beer as well.

Tables 3.12 and 3.13 replicate this exercise for two much poorer families. One, provided by Eden, is from Cumbria, and the second is one of the very poor Berkshire families investigated by David Davies. In the Cumbrian example, the husband was an agricultural day labourer and the wife had five children, including a baby of six months, so presumably did little paid work. The first thing that is evident about this table is the exceptionally small number of calories the man was consuming, barely enough to keep him alive, let alone his family. These must be underestimates, as the family is not said to have been starving. The husband was also said to have been employed on farms and must have been supplied with beer and food by the farmer, as otherwise it would simply have been impossible to do even the amount of work suggested by Fogel. This was also one of the northern families whose dietary staple was cheap oatmeal porridge made with a lot of milk, praised by Eden. A small amount of barley was purchased, but no beer is listed in the diet, so some might have been purchased in an alehouse. The man's earnings in 1795 were given as £18 18s 6d a year, enough to purchase the quantities of food listed in the table, in addition to £5 16s 2d a year for salt, soap, fuel, rent, clothes, repairs and other household expenses. Fuel was stated to be cheap in this part of the country, as wood, peat and turf could be collected locally by the wife and children, and clothes were still often home-made.

The second example is from the parish of Barkham in Berkshire, southeast of Reading, and closer to London than Streatley. It is one of the budgets collected by David Davies, which were all for very poor families in his area. Here, the husband earned 8s a week working following a farmer's team of horses throughout the year. His wife also earned 8d a week, and they had three small children, one of whom was only an infant, which I have assumed was breastfeeding. The main cause of this family's more extreme poverty in comparison to the Berkshire family in Eden's example was that here all of the children were infants. In 1787 they earned £23 8s a year, but their expenditure on food, together with £7 for clothes, rent, fuel and other things, was £25. Again the amount of food given in this budget would have provided only an exceptionally small number of calories. If he was ploughing, harrowing and doing other team work he also must have been supplied with beer and food by the farmer, as it would simply have been impossible otherwise.

Table 3.12 *Two mid-eighteenth-century diets abstracted from a poor Cumberland family*

	Weekly amount	Prices in 1744	Yearly cost	Prices in 1756	Yearly cost	Total daily calories	Daily amount for man (×1) kcal (26%)	Daily amount for wife (×0.8) kcal. (21%)	Daily amount for each of four children aged 2–9 years[a] (×0.5) kcal (13%)
Barley	5.8 lb	18s qrtr	12s	29s qrtr	19s 6d	1,336	347	281	174
Wheat flour	6.5 oz	28s qrtr[b]	16d	69s qrtr	3s 3d	82	22	17	11
Bacon	4.6 oz	2d lb	2s 6d	2½d lb	3s 2d	72	19	15	9
Beef	4.9 oz	2½d lb	3s 4d	3d lb	4s	44	12	9	6
Oatmeal	9.3 lb	40s qrtr	£2 1s	40s qrtr	£2 1s	2,388	621	502	310
Milk	51 pints	2d gal.	£2 15s	2d gal.[c]	£2 15s[d]	2,900	754	609	377
Potatoes	6.1 lb	6d peck	11s 4d	6d peck	11s 4d	314	82	66	41
Butter	9.2 oz	4½d lb	11s 2d	6d lb	15s	242	63	51	31
Treacle	6.1 oz	2d lb	3s 4d	3d lb	5s	62	16	13	8
Total			£5		£6 16s 3d	7,440	1,936	1,563	967

Notes: [a] There was also a baby of six months, and an age of two has been estimated for the next youngest child.
[b] Worked out as 21s quarter meal × 33.5% for the price of flour.
[c] I have used 1d a quart, which is the price given in Eden, assuming it would not have been more expensive earlier.
[d] This is an estimation as there are few milk prices for this year.
Source: Eden, *State of the Poor*, II, pp. 104–7. Prices for goods in the north are much harder to come by than for the south, so might be different from those found in Thorold Rogers.

Table 3.13 *Two mid-eighteenth-century diets abstracted from a poor Berkshire family of four*

	Weekly amount	Prices in 1744	Yearly cost	Prices in 1756	Yearly cost	Total daily calories	Daily amount for man (×1) kcal (36%)	Daily amount for wife (×0.8) kcal (29%)	Daily amount for a child (×0.5) kcal (18%)
Flour	13.5 lb	27s qrtr	£2 6s	65s qrtr	£5 1s	2,752	991	798	495
Bacon	5.4 lb	2½d lb	£2 18s	3d lb	£3 10s	1,354	487	393	244
Small beer	2 gal.	1d gal.	9s	2d gal.	18s	342	123	99	62
Cheese	½ lb	5d lb	11s	5d lb	11s	116	42	34	21
Butter	1 lb	4½d lb	£1	6d lb	£1 12s	419	151	122	75
Sugar	1 lb	9d lb	£2	8d lb	£1 15s	255	92	74	46
Total			£9 4s		£13 7s		1,886	1,520	943

Source: Davies, *Case of Labourers*, pp. 11–15.

Since the cost of food was much less earlier in the century, and, in general, wages were only 15–20 per cent lower, living standards would have been much better. The diet of the Cumbrian family would have been exceptionally cheap earlier in the century. In 1744, if the labourer was earning £16, he would have had enough money to spend on food to raise the number of calories consumed to about 4,000 for himself. I will return to the question of living standards and earnings at the beginning of chapter 5, where the cost of the sample diet in Table 3.11 (Berkshire) will be extended back for sample years to the 1560s, and the amount of family earnings needed to purchase food as well as clothing and fuel, rent and household goods will then be estimated and examined in more detail. I now move from the particular to the general and attempt to see if agriculture was capable of producing the calories discussed here.

Global estimates of food production

Individual sample diets show how many calories were provided in specific instances, but they cannot tell us if the agricultural economy was actually capable of producing the necessary amount of food for the entire population to engage in such work. One way of approaching this question is to attempt to make rough global estimates of the total productive capacity of agriculture in terms of calories. Crop yields and average stocking densities can be combined with figures of total arable and pasture land at different dates and then converted into the number of calories produced per acre. These figures can then be divided by the population at the time to see if the amounts listed in the diets were feasible. Of course, precision is impossible, as no national surveys exist before the nineteenth century, but agricultural historians have made estimates of average yields per acre of different crops at different times and of animal numbers and their size.

Grain

Calculating the total calorific value of food grown and available for human consumption is a complicated procedure, so it will be necessary to go through the steps involved in the calculation quite carefully. The first step is to calculate the number of acres under cereal cultivation. For 1700 Mark Overton, who has worked most extensively on estimating seventeenth-century agrarian production, has adopted a figure of 9 million acres, with 1.8 million acres of this land lying fallow each year. This rose to 11.5 million acres under cultivation in 1800, with the same acreage of fallow land.[49] The next step is to calculate the percentage of ground sown with different crops. Reliable figures do not exist before 1801, so for earlier years I have relied on Overton's estimates taken from the crops found in samples of probate inventories from Cornwall, Hertfordshire, Oxfordshire, Worcestershire, Lincolnshire, Norfolk, Suffolk and Kent, together with Gregory King's estimates of national output in the 1680s. As Overton's samples show, percentages of different crops planted could vary greatly from place to place depending on soil. They could also vary from year to year, so any estimation is relative. However, what is clear is that barley was generally the predominant crop before the end of the eighteenth century, when much had been replaced by wheat, and that the percentage of rye grown declined throughout the period. In Table 3.14 I have used Overton's figures for the years 1700 and 1800. Unfortunately there are no estimates for the amount of land under cultivation in 1600 so I have reduced the cropped

---

[49] Overton uses a figure of 20 per cent for fallow. In King's calculations about beer he used a figure for fallow land of one third, but elsewhere he uses a figure of one quarter. It would seem that Robert Loder left as much as 50 per cent of his farm in Berkshire fallow, but he achieved a very high output per acre by doing so. His gross yield per acre of wheat and barley was generally over 25 bushels, twice the average found in probate inventories from the same time. Thus he was actually achieving a higher total yield by leaving an extra 25 per cent of his land in fallow. Overton, *Agricultural Revolution*, pp. 17, 76, 93–6, 99; King, 'Burn's Journal', p. 20; Thirsk and Cooper, *Seventeenth Century Economic Documents*, p. 782; Fussell (ed.), *Robert Loder's Farm Accounts*, pp. ix, xii–xvii, Table IV.

Table 3.14 Calories from global crop production

Year	Crop	Acres	Percentage	Yield	Total bushels	Percentage	Pounds per bushel	Calories per pound	Crop	Population	Calories per person per day
c. 1600	wheat	1,530,000	26	9.5	14,535,000	31	56	1,324	wheat	4,066,100	728
	rye	470,000	8	9.5	4,465,000	9	56	1,395	rye	4,066,100	236
	barley	1,780,000	30	9	16,020,000	34	48	1,206	barley	4,066,100	627
	oats	890,000	15	13	9,450,000	20	38	1,002	oats	4,066,100	243
	pulses	830,000	14	9	2,988,000	6	56	1,193	pulses	4,066,100	135
	other	500,000	8						other		
	fallow	2,000,000							fallow		
	total	8,000,000	100		47,458,000	100			total		1,968

Year	Crop	Acres	Percentage	Yield	Total bushels	Percentage	Pounds per bushel	Calories per pound	Crop	Population	Calories per person per day
c. 1650	wheat	1,600,000	22	12.5	20,000,000	31	56	1,324	wheat	5,220,613	780
	rye	520,000	7	13.5	7,020,000	11	56	1,395	rye	5,220,613	289
	barley	2,040,000	28	12	24,480,000	38	48	1,206	barley	5,220,613	746
	oats	1,060,000	15	14	9,328,000	14	38	1,002	oats	5,220,613	187
	pulses	980,000	14	11	4,312,000	7	56	1,193	pulses	5,220,613	152
	other	1,000,000	14						other		
	fallow	1,800,000							fallow		
	total	9,000,000	100		65,140,000	100			total		2,153

Year	Crop	Acres	Percentage	Yield	Total bushels	Percentage	Pounds per bushel	Calories per pound	Crop	Population	Calories per person per day
c. 1700	wheat	1,600,000	22	14.5	23,200,000	31	56	1,324	wheat	4,896,666	965
	rye	520,000	7	12.5	6,500,000	9	56	1,395	rye	4,896,666	285

		Acres	Percentage	Yield	Total bushels	Percentage	Pounds per bushel	Calories per pound	Crop	Population	Calories per person per day
	barley	2,040,000	28	16	32,640,000	43	48	1,206	barley	4,896,666	1,060
	oats	1,060,000	15	16	8,480,000	11	38	1,002	oats	4,896,666	181
	pulses	980,000	14	13	5,096,000	7	56	1,193	pulses	4,896,666	191
	other	1,000,000	14						other		
	fallow	1,800,000	14						fallow		
	total	9,000,000	100		75,916,000	100			total		2,682

Year	Crop	Acres	Percentage	Yield	Total bushels	Percentage	Pounds per bushel	Calories per pound	Crop	Population	Calories per person per day
c. 1770	wheat	2,957,200	32	17.5	51,751,000	34	56	1,324	wheat	6,405,166	1,646
	rye	635,440	7	19.5	12,391,080	8	56	1,395	rye	6,405,166	415
	barley	1,892,480	21	26	49,204,480	33	48	1,206	barley	6,405,166	1,222
	oats	1,295,320	14	32	29,578,240	20	38	1,002	oats	6,405,166	483
	pulses	1,197,560	13	16	7,664,384	5	56	1,193	pulses	6,405,166	220
	other	1,222,000	13						other		
	fallow	1,800,000	13						fallow		
	total	11,000,000	100	111	150,589,184	100			total		3,985

Year	Crop	Acres	Percentage	Yield	Total bushels	Percentage	Pounds per bushel	Calories per pound	Crop	Population	Calories per person per day
1800	wheat	3,104,000	32	18	55,872,000	31	56	1,324	wheat	8,606,033	1,322
	rye	97,000	1	23	2,231,000	1	56	1,395	rye	8,606,033	56
	barley	1,843,000	19	24	44,232,000	25	48	1,206	barley	8,606,033	817
	oats	2,522,000	26	32	67,136,000	38	38	1,002	oats	8,606,033	816
	pulses	1,067,000	11	19.5	8,322,600	5	56	1,193	pulses	8,606,033	177
	other	1,067,000	11						other		
	fallow	1,800,000	11						fallow		
	total	11,500,000	100		177,793,600	100			total		3,189

acreage for this date to 8,000,000 and increased the amount of fallow land to 2,000,000 acres because agriculture was less developed at that date.[50] For 1650 I have estimated that the area of land under cultivation was the same as in 1700, assuming that efforts at agricultural improvement, motivated by population pressure, had increased the land under cultivation by this date.[51] The acreage estimates for 1770 have simply been reduced by 500,000 acres from Overton's figure for 1800, assuming a gradual increase over the course of the century.

The next step in this process is to add estimates of yields per acre for all different crops, which have been taken from the work done on probate inventories, as well as the estimates made for the eighteenth century by Turner, Beckett and Afton from farm accounts.[52] The use of evidence from probate inventories was first developed by Mark Overton and has subsequently been modified by Robert Allen and Paul Glennie. It involves looking at listings of the value and acreage of a dead person's crops, and then estimating the production in bushels per acre based on the selling price of the grain, making adjustments for harvesting costs and the time of year the inventory was taken. Using a sample of 7,500 inventories from Hampshire, Glennie calculated average yields per acre of wheat, barley and oats through the seventeenth century by decade. His findings show that wheat yields rose 10 per cent (from 11.1 to 12.2 bushels) from 1600 to 1646, and then a further 30 per cent (from 12.2 to 15.8 bushels) from 1646 to 1689, before falling again in the 1690s, which suffered from a series of bad harvests. Similarly barley yields rose 15 per cent to 15.4 bushels an acre from 1600 to 1646, and 50 per cent before 1690 to 20.1 bushels an acre. In contrast, the production of oats rose only 18 per cent (from 18.7 to 22.1 bushels) over the whole century to 1690. Glennie also looked at a sample of inventories from Hertfordshire which show a more dramatic increase in the yield of wheat in the first half of the seventeenth century of 44 per cent between 1610 and 1639 compared to 1640–68, and a smaller increase of 10 per cent comparing 1640–68 to 1675–99. He also found a steady, but more dramatic, rise in yields of barley of 22 per cent and 44 per cent respectively for the same periods.[53]

[50] Overton, *Agricultural Revolution*, p. 92.
[51] Ibid., pp. 88–92; Eric Kerridge, *The Agricultural Revolution* (London, 1967), pp. 24–7.
[52] Overton, *Agricultural Revolution*, pp. 76–9. The methodology is summarised in Paul Glennie, 'Measuring Crop Yields in Early Modern England', in B. M. S. Campbell and Mark Overton, *Land, Labour and Livestock: Historical Studies in European Agricultural Productivity* (Manchester, 1991), pp. 255–83.
[53] Glennie, 'Measuring Crop Yields in Early Modern England', p. 273.

In Overton's samples of wheat yields from Lincolnshire, Norfolk and Suffolk, there was a 35 per cent increase in yields from 1600 to 1650 (from 11.7 to 15.8 bushels), no rise from 1650 to 1700 and a 28 per cent rise from 1700 to 1750 (from 15.6 to 20 bushels) in Lincolnshire.[54] In Norfolk and Suffolk he found a 21 per cent increase between 1600 and 1650 (from 12 to 14.5 bushels); a 10 per cent rise between 1650 and 1700 (from 14.5 to 16 bushels); a 25 per cent rise between 1700 and 1750 (from 16 to 20 bushels); and a 12 per cent rise between 1750 and 1800 (from 20 to 22.4 bushels).[55] Overton and Campbell show that in Norfolk alone barley yields increased by 40 per cent and oat yields by 45 per cent between 1710 and 1739 and in the 1760s, although this is based on a comparison of probate inventories used to obtain data for 1710–39 and Arthur Young's examples for the 1760s. This has possibly exaggerated the rise in this period, as Young was more likely to include more successful farms.[56]

The more recent work of Turner, Beckett and Afton, based on a wide selection of farm accounts from the eighteenth and nineteenth centuries, shows that wheat yields had reached 20 bushels per acre by the beginning of the eighteenth century and did not rise much before the 1820s.[57] However, their earlier estimates have been criticised for being based on fewer samples drawn from larger farms which might have had more capital to invest, and thus have achieved greater yields, whereas inventory evidence covers a much wider range of farm sizes.[58] Thus I have used a lower estimate of 17 bushels per acre for 1700. Similarly mean barley yields in Turner, Beckett and Afton's sample were 30 bushels per acre in 1700, and varied from 26.7 to 31.2 bushels per acre during the eighteenth century. In their sample, only the yield of oats increased significantly, from 22.1 bushels per acre to 36.5 bushels by the end of

[54] Unlike Glennie, Overton included the bad decade of the 1690s here.
[55] Overton, *Agricultural Revolution*, pp. 76–9. These are Overton's raw figures before being reduced by his Weighted Aggregate Cereal Yield algorithm, which is not used by Glennie and which I have chosen not to use here. Using it has the distorting effect of reducing the average gross yield of *all* of these grains combined by an enormous 60–65 per cent. The explanation given for the use of this calculation is that crops were planted in different proportions over time, and that every year yields of each crop would have varied differently according to the prevailing weather that year. Thus it is meant as a 'single integrated measure of the mean volume of output per acre'. However, it is unclear why this would not be captured by the random sampling of thousands of inventories over the range of years examined, nor why it results in reduction of the yields of all crops in every sample year. Overton and Campbell, 'Norfolk Farming', pp. 70–2, esp. n.86.
[56] Overton and Campbell, 'Norfolk Farming', pp. 70–2, esp. n.86.
[57] Turner *et al.*, *Farm Production*, pp. 128–37.
[58] I would like to thank Leigh Shaw-Taylor for this point.

the century. They also argue that in terms of wheat consumption, the bushels available per person per year actually dropped between 1750 and 1800 from 5.9 to 4.62 as population pressure overtook agricultural production.[59]

What all of this evidence shows is that gross yields of different crops rose continuously throughout our period, but at different rates at different times. In Table 3.14 I have tried to use what seem to be the best averages for the different periods, and for 1770 and 1800 I have relied on Turner, Beckett and Afton's figures. I have then subtracted a certain number of bushels which had to be kept back every year from a crop to be used as seeds for the next year's crop. For wheat and rye this was 2.5 bushels; for barley and pulses 4 bushels; and for oats 6 bushels per acre. Thus the figures in column five of Table 3.14 are net yields.[60] But it should be remembered that these are just averages and that yields could vary between places according to soil quality and farming methods, and as new land was brought into cultivation in the eighteenth century it was likely to be less fertile than land already under cultivation. Turner, Beckett and Afton, for instance, found there was a standard deviation of 4–6 bushels for wheat in the eighteenth century and 8–14 bushels for barley and oats. Yields also, of course, varied from year to year according to growing conditions, a theme we will return to later in the chapter.[61]

After working out the total yield of the land in bushels, these have to be converted to calories. Although the size of bushels could vary, the most common sizes were 56 lb for a bushel of wheat or rye; 48 lb for a bushel of barley; and 38 lb for a bushel of oats.[62] For wheat I will use the calories contained in 100 per cent whole-wheat flour. However, the calories contained in the ground flour would have been reduced by a number of factors, including loss of grain in storage and transport as a result of mice, damp and moulds such as smut, as well as waste during milling and the removal of bran from the flour. For the purposes of calculation I have used the number of calories contained in a pound of whole-wheat flour (1,431 kcal) and rye flour (1,508 kcal). Losses from milling were estimated in one pamphlet to have been 2.5 per cent, while Robert Loder calculated his losses to mice and mould of grain stored

[59] Turner *et al.*, *Farm Production*, pp. 218–19.
[60] Overton, *Agricultural Revolution*, p. 73; Turner *et al.*, *Farm Production*, pp. 166–72; Young, *Northern Tour*, IV, pp. 88–103.
[61] Turner *et al.*, *Farm Production*, pp. 129, 153, 158.
[62] Overton, *Agricultural Revolution*, p. xiv; John Swinton, *A Proposal for Uniformity of Weights and Measures in Scotland, by Execution of the Laws Now in Force* (Edinburgh, 1779), pp. 50–2.

over the winter to have ranged from little or nothing to as much as 10 per cent per year.[63] I have thus used a figure of 7.5 per cent to account for all losses, giving a final figure of 1,324 kcal for a pound of wheat and 1,395 for a pound of rye.

Calculating the calorific content of barley is even more difficult, as about 80 per cent was probably consumed as beer rather than flour. Thus the calorific content of the barley has to be converted into beer. Raw barley contains about 1,650 kcal per pound, but the barley husks are all lost in the brewing so have to be eliminated from the weight of the barley crop, which would be about 20 per cent.[64] In addition, as we saw, in the early modern period almost every brewing involved two to three worts to extract all the sugar from the barley so none would go to waste. Only large town-brewers would have made beer with only two worts, so it is much less likely that sugar was lost in this way, although some small beer would have undoubtedly spoiled if it could not be drunk in time. But there would also have been losses to vermin and in transport so I have used a figure of 27 per cent reduction of the calories in a pound of raw barley to account for all of these factors (1,206 kcal per pound).[65]

Calculating the calories for oatmeal is simpler, as the pamphlet *A Proposal for Uniformity of Weights and Measures in Scotland, by Execution of the Laws Now in Force* (Edinburgh, 1779) indicates that the weight of oatmeal produced from a bushel of oats was 60 per cent of the weight of the raw oats, and since a pound of oatmeal contains 1,805 kcal, then a pound of oats would have 1,083 kcal, from which I have subtracted 7.5 per cent for other losses.[66] For beans and peas, the weight of a bushel would be dry and thus the calorific content of a pound would have been roughly the same as modern dry broad beans and peas (1,290 kcal), from which I have also subtracted 7.5 per cent for other losses.[67] However, much of the oats and pulses would have been fed to animals as fodder. Overton and Campbell suggested that in 1700 50 per cent of oats were fed to horses. Although the number of horses in England at any one time is uncertain, work by Tony Wrigley and Paul Warde indicates there were probably about 75 per cent more horses in 1700 than in 1600, and 60 per cent more horses again in 1800 than in 1700.[68]

---

[63] Swinton, *Uniformity of Weights*, p. 50; Fussell (ed.), *Robert Loder's Farm Accounts*, pp. 29, 75, 175, 176; Ellis, *Country Housewife*, p. 4.

[64] John Palmer, *How to Brew*, ch. 12.   [65] See above p. 73.

[66] The oat hull would have weighed 30 per cent of the kernel, but the extraction rate was much lower. Swinton, *Uniformity of Weights*, p. 52.

[67] There might be more starch in modern varieties.

[68] Paul Warde, *Energy Consumption in England and Wales 1560–2000* (Istituto di Studi sulle Società del Mediterraneo, 2007), pp. 40–5; E. A. Wrigley, 'The Transition to an

Thus I have subtracted 50 per cent of the production of oats in 1700 and adjusted this figure accordingly for the other dates (I have assumed a 40 per cent increase in horses in 1770). I have also used a figure of 60 per cent reduction for pulses as it is clear from some workhouse diets that pease pudding was a common dish for the poor and that not all pulses were fed to animals, although it is possible that this figure should be higher. King estimated that horses consumed 11 million bushels of oats, peas and vetches in the 1680s, but my calculations provide much more fodder of 16,124,000 bushels of oats and pulses, for the same date.[69] In addition, for 1770 I have increased the percentage of wheat planted at the expense of barley, because consumption of beer, at least at alehouses, was declining by the late eighteenth century.[70]

What Table 3.14 shows quite clearly is a great increase in the availability of cereal calories per person in the roughly 100 years after the mid-seventeenth century. The greatest increase came in the early eighteenth century. According to the evidence from estate accounts in Turner, Beckett and Afton, significant rises in productivity of barley to 26 bushels per acre, and oats to 19 bushels per acre, had already occurred by 1720. As noted above, this increase might be somewhat exaggerated by their estate sample, but still it was enough to allow England to export surplus wheat and some barley from the beginning of the eighteenth century, which reached about 7–8 per cent of production by the 1740s.[71] The other striking result from these calculations is the increase in barley production, even as the number of acres of barley cropped went down. The figures from the excise tax show that continually between 24 and 27 million bushels of malt were produced to make beer between 1710 and 1770, whereas the figures in Table 3.14 show the production of barley was 32 million bushels in 1700, which if we subtract 20 per cent for bread leaves about 25.6 million bushels. However, this went up to almost 50 million bushels by 1770, 80 per cent of which would supply about 40 million bushels for malting. This would indicate that home brewers were much better at avoiding the excise than has previously

Advanced Organic Economy: Half a Millennium of English Agriculture', *Economic History Review*, 59 (2006), pp. 445–53.

[69] This is based on the advice of Paul Warde, who believes that if 1.2 million horses ate, as King reckoned, 11 million bushels of oats, vetches and peas, this makes for 348 lb per horse per year, less than a pound per day. Horses probably ate oats only as part of their diet, and in periods of heavier work, mainly in the spring and summer. But as they ate overall probably 15,000–25,000 kcal per day, even if oats were only part of the diet, King's figure is improbably low.

[70] See above in the section on beer, pp. 68–9.

[71] Overton, *Agricultural Revolution*, pp. 88–9; B. R. Mitchell and Phyllis Deane, *Abstract of British Historical Statistics* (Cambridge, 1971), pp. 94–6; David Ormrod, *English Grain Exports and the Structure of Agrarian Capitalism 1700–1760* (Hull, 1985).

been thought, although some barley would have been fed to pigs and poultry.[72] Finally, yields of oats went up dramatically in the eighteenth century, as did the acreage under cultivation. Since oats were a much more important part of the diet in the north this would have had the advantage of being able to feed many more people there.[73] Moreover, it is possible that some of the increased production in the south went to provide even more feed for horses than has been estimated here.[74]

Meat

Calculating meat production is much more difficult as not as much work has been done counting the numbers of animals in herds around the country. Most calculations about the size of animal herds and the amount of meat being eaten rely on Gregory King's figures for the 1690s.[75] He estimated that about 398,090,000 lb of meat was being consumed every year, of which the great majority was beef, mutton and lamb. In his calculations he provided estimations of the total numbers of livestock in England; the number slaughtered and consumed each year; the weight of a butchered carcass; and the average price of each animal. Given the doubts that have been cast on King's estimations, it is necessary to consider each of these categories carefully. To begin with, his estimate of the size of each cattle carcass (including calves) at 260 lb is undoubtedly too small. His figures have been criticised by B. A. Holderness, who has argued, based on examples from the eighteenth century, that even at the beginning of the century carcass weights must have been in the region of 400–500 lb.[76] Peter Bowden has also estimated that the size of live cattle would generally have been between 500 and 900 lb in the seventeenth century, and there is other evidence which supports this. The average size of oxen carcasses bought by Winchester College in the mid-seventeenth century was 588 lb, with some over 1,000 lb, which were purchased for about 2.5–2.7d a pound according to the weight of the carcass.[77] It might have been that the college

---

[72] Mathias, *Brewing Industry*, pp. 339–50, 372–3, 541.
[73] Crop percentages are given by county for 1801 in Overton, *Agricultural Revolution*, p. 96.
[74] Wrigley, 'Advanced Organic Economy', pp. 458–62.
[75] Thirsk and Cooper, *Economic Documents*, p. 783; King, 'Burns Journal', pp. 214, 243.
[76] Holderness, 'Prices, Productivity and Output', in *AHEW*, VI, pp. 152–3.
[77] Peter Bowden, 'Agricultural Prices, Wages, Farm Profits and Rents', in *AHEW*, V.II, pp. 10–11; Thorold Rogers, *Agriculture and Prices*, V, pp. 331–3, 347–50. Cattle in seventeenth-century America, however, seem to have been much smaller than this. Lois Green Carr, Russell R. Menard and Lorena Walsh, *Robert Cole's World: Agriculture and Society in Early Maryland* (Chapel Hill, NC and London, 1994), p. 335, App. 3.

was purchasing very large animals, but there also exists a broadsheet of 1691 in which one John Sellers attempted to compute the weekly consumption of London and Westminster. Here, cattle sold in Smithfield were said to be worth about £6 each, which would mean they would have provided 480 lb at 3d a pound or 576 lb at 2.5d a pound. This means the animals would have had to have been about 800–900 lb in weight when alive, given that the weight of a carcass is about 53 per cent of that of the animal. In 1610 an ox carcass weighing 600 lb was sold for £9 10s (expensive at 3.8d per pound), and a list of average market prices for meat for 1595 stated that a fat oxen cost £6 13s 4d, which at 2.2d a pound would have weighed 727 lb, while a lean oxen cost £4 6s 8d, which at the same price would have weighed 473 lb. A fat 'veale' cost 15s, which would been 82 lb in weight.[78]

Holderness estimated that over the course of the eighteenth century the weight of a cattle carcass might have increased to 600–700 lb by its end, and in the same volume of *AHEW*, R. J. Moore-Colyer found eighteenth-century examples of carcass weights of 600–1000 lb.[79] Turner, Beckett and Afton also examined examples of the weight of different animals in the eighteenth century and found examples within this range.[80] Frederick Eden claimed that bullocks slaughtered in London in the 1790s weighed 800 lb per carcass, and noted that in a report of a Select Committee to consider improvement of waste lands in the kingdom it was estimated that the size of cattle and sheep had increased by at least 25 per cent, while the numbers sold in Smithfield market had increased from 76,000 cattle and 515,000 sheep in 1732 to 109,000 cattle and 717,000 sheep in 1794.[81] Given this, it is probably reasonable to use an estimation of an average of 500 lb a cattle carcass including bones for the 1690s and 650 lb for *c.* 1770. However, at this later date there would have been a higher fat content in the meat, as one aim in eighteenth-century improvement in cattle weights was to increase the amount of fat in the meat.[82] The weight of a calf will be taken to be 100 lb for the 1690s and 130 lb for *c.* 1770, since Seller estimated the price of calves at a fifth of that of cattle in the 1690s.

---

[78] Eden, *State of the Poor*, III, pp. lxix, cxi.
[79] Holderness, 'Prices, Productivity and Output', and R. J. Moore-Colyer, 'Farming Techniques: Cattle', in *AHEW*, VI, pp. 152–3, 335–52.
[80] Turner *et al.*, *Farm Production*, ch. 6, esp. pp. 186–7.
[81] Eden compared this to the 1732 estimate and concluded that there had been a tremendous increase in the size of cattle in sixty years, but a more than doubling seems excessive. Eden, *State of the Poor*, III, p. lxxxviii.
[82] A. J. S. Gibson, 'The Size and Weight of Cattle and Sheep in Early Modern Scotland', *Agricultural History Review*, 36 (1988), pp. 163–5.

King also gives the weight of sheep and lamb carcasses as 32 lb, but most mature sheep carcasses purchased by Winchester College weighed about 40 lb, while sheep carcasses from the early eighteenth century weighed 48–64 lb. However, prices from 1595 indicate that a fat mutton costing 16s would have been 90 lb and a lean mutton worth 10s would have been 55 lb.[83] Eden cited figures from the same report mentioned in the previous paragraph of 80 lb for a sheep's and 50 lb for a lamb's carcass in the 1790s. Lambs were generally 70–80 per cent the price of mature sheep, but lamb was not eaten nearly as widely as mutton, even by the wealthy, since sheep were grown primarily for their wool, and ewe's milk was not widely used to make cheese. Thus, I have chosen averages of 50 lb for a sheep's carcass in the late seventeenth century and 68 lb for 1770. The weight of King's pig carcasses, not surprisingly, is similarly low compared to the size of hogs which Robert Loder fattened in 1613. Loder mentioned one fattened on peas and beans which provided 140 lb of meat, and another not fattened this way which provided 85 lb of meat. By the late seventeenth century, many of the boars listed by Thorold Rogers would have weighed well over 200 lb at 3d per pound, and some of the fattened boars (brawn) bought by All Souls College might have weighed as much as 600 lb or more.[84] By the end of the eighteenth century David Davies gave the weight of a fat hog bought by a poor family as 280 lb.[85] I will use an estimate of 200 lb for a swine in the 1690s and 260 lb for *c.* 1770 based on these figures and those provided in Turner, Beckett and Afton. For poultry, rabbits and wild animals I have just used King's figures for *c.* 1690 and increased them for *c.* 1770 to account for increase in oat production allowing for greater fattening of poultry and geese. But again King's weights, such as only 1 lb for a chicken, might be too low, but I have not been able to find any information with which to refine them.

Checking King's estimate of the number of animals in the kingdom is much more difficult. Some work has been done on the size of herds based on probate inventories together with Arthur Young's farm surveys. This information has been analysed in terms of stocking densities, and looks at the number of animals per acre of cropped arable land, or per acre of total farm size – including fallow and pasture.[86] In order to compare different animals' food requirements they are converted into what are termed livestock units, as follows: a horse = 1; oxen and

[83] Thorold Rogers, *Agriculture and Prices*, V, pp. 331–3, 347–50.

[84] Ibid., V, pp. 331–3, 347–50; VI, pp. 241ff.

[85] Davies, *Case of Labourers*, pp. 11, 84; Ellis, *Country Housewife*, pp. 96, 98.

[86] In probate inventories, since only cropped acres are included, total farm size cannot be estimated.

cows = 1.2; a calf = 0.8; a sheep = 0.1; a swine = 0.1. Information from Norfolk probate inventories shows that between 1584 and 1640 mean stocking density was 0.93 units per cereal acre, which rose to 1.02 units between 1660 and 1700.[87] On small farms, however, stocking density was, unsurprisingly, greater. Since Norfolk was composed primarily of arable land rather than pasture one would expect to find fewer animals recorded as a ratio of arable crops than in a more pastoral area of the country.

Unfortunately no similar study has been done for a pastoral county before the beginning of the nineteenth century, and since we know that large numbers of cattle were driven south from the pasture land of the north and southern Scotland, as well as imported from Ireland, densities must have been greater in the north.[88] At the Morval Barton and Golden Barton farms in southern Cornwall, where the arable land was much less productive and the amount of pasture greater, stocking density in the mid-eighteenth century was in the order of 1.92 and 2.36 animal units respectively per acre of sown crops (the size of pasture is unknown).[89] For Arthur Young's sample of farms, Robert Allen calculated stocking densities by the total size of the farm, as Young provided this information, and by this measurement densities varied between 0.2 and 0.46 per total farm acre.[90] However, in one of Arthur Young's hypothetical examples of a farm of 600 acres with 400 acres arable and 200 acres of pasture from his *Farmer's Guide in Hiring and Stocking Farms* the stocking ratio of livestock units is 1.3 per total farm acre.[91]

By way of comparison, if we convert King's estimate of the numbers of horses, cattle, sheep and swine to livestock units this results in a figure of 7,700,000 and if we divide this by 5,220,000 acres cultivated with

---

[87] Mark Overton and Bruce M. S. Campbell, 'Norfolk Livestock Farming 1250–1740: A Comparative Study of Manorial Accounts and Probate Inventories', *Journal of Historical Geography*, 18 (1992), pp. 386–7.

[88] Donald Woodward, 'Cattle Droving in the Seventeenth Century: A Yorkshire Example', in W. H. Chaloner and B. M. Ratcliffe (eds.), *Trade and Transport: Essays in Economic History in Honour of T. S. Willan* (Manchester, 1977), pp. 35–58; Donald Woodward, 'The Anglo-Irish Livestock Trade of the Seventeenth Century', *Irish Historical Studies*, 18 (1972–3), pp. 489–523.

[89] On Morval Barton 68 acres were sown with wheat, barley and oats in 1760, and in 1767 the farm possessed 74 head of cattle, 296 sheep, 9 horses and 31 pigs. At Golden farm 50–84 acres were under corn between 1748 and 1762, and in 1748 the Barton had 85 head of cattle, 406 sheep, 14 horses and 18 pigs. Pounds, 'Barton Farming', pp. 61, 70–7. Yields here per acre were very low compared to Overton's averages: ibid., pp. 64, 71.

[90] Allen, *Enclosure*, pp. 115–18, 194–8.

[91] Arthur Young, *The Farmer's Guide in Hiring and Stocking Farms* (London, 1770), II, p. 217.

wheat, rye, barley and oats this provides a stocking density of 1.5 per arable acre. If we divide the same number by 21,000,000 acres of the total arable and pasture land this results in a figure of 0.37. Table 3.15 combines King's estimates of animal numbers with estimates for 1770 made with the assumption that by this date pasture might have increased by 3 million acres to 15 million acres and arable to 11 million, giving a total of 26 million acres. I have increased the numbers of sheep according to contemporary estimates and added more cattle to achieve roughly the same stocking densities, although some contemporary estimates have lower estimates of cattle and swine.[92]

For 1695 this produces a raw average of 423 kcal or 5 oz of meat per person per day, and 579 kcal or 7 oz of meat in *c*. 1770. In terms of an age- and sex-specific distribution for 1695, when 30 per cent of the population were under the age of 14, if we assume that a woman ate 0.8 of the amount a man ate, and that children under the age of 14 ate 0.5 of an adult man's consumption, this works out roughly to 747 kcal per man, or 12 oz, 608 kcal per woman, or 9.6 oz, and 382 kcal per child.[93] In comparison, the daily consumption of meat in Great Britain in 1998 was 4.7 oz. When broken down by age and gender in 1770 the meat consumption for men fits with the evidence from farm accounts. However, the overall average is lower, and the early figure for the late seventeenth century is considerably lower than late sixteenth- and early seventeenth-century accounts suggested. It is also much less than that consumed by the wealthy. It might be that King's estimates are too low, as the evidence of stocking densities tentatively suggests. This implies that convertible husbandry was very widely practised, and that improvements such as floating meadows had considerably increased the productivity of pasture over the course of the seventeenth century. But even if this were the case, it also implies that many poor cottagers and day labourers' families ate much less meat than what was supplied by farmers to their servants, and had to obtain more calories from bread and beer. King, for instance, assumed that half the population were too poor to have eaten meat more than one or two days in the week.[94] This

---

[92] Holderness, 'Prices, Productivity and Output', pp. 149–51.

[93] Gregory King assumed that only children under the age of thirteen months did not eat an average amount of meat, and the children at the Foundling Hospital were served veal at a very young age, but the amount of meat consumed by the very young must have been much smaller than the average for an adult. Gregory King, 'Natural and Political Observations and Conclusions upon the State and Condition of England' (1696), in Laslett (ed.), *Earliest Classics*, pp. 54–5. See above, p. 135.

[94] Ibid., pp. 54–5.

Table 3.15 *Calories of meat consumed from estimates of numbers of animals slaughtered, 1695 and 1770*

1695

Animals	Carcass weight (pounds)	Consumption (pounds)	Total weight of consumption	Pounds per person per day	Calories per pound	Calories per day
Cattle	500	500,000	250,000,000	0.1403	1,000	140.3
Calves	100	300,000	30,000,000	0.0168	1,000	16.8
Sheep	50	4,000,000	200,000,000	0.1122	1,000	112.2
Swine	200	1,000,000	200,000,000	0.1122	1,114	125.0
Chickens	1	30,000,000	30,000,000	0.0168	864	14.5
Turkeys	4	1,200,000	4,800,000	0.0027	770	2.1
Geese	2	4,000,000	8,000,000	0.0045	1,436	6.4
Ducks	1	6,000,000	6,000,000	0.0034	1,526	5.1
Deer	80	20,000	1,600,000	0.0009	891	0.8
Total		47,020,000	730,400,000	0.4098		423.3
Milk*	300	1,100,000	330,000,000	0.1851	3200	474.0
Cider*		10,000,000		0.0919	2,080	191.2

1770

Animals	Carcass weight (pounds)	Consumption (pounds)	Total weight of consumption	Pounds per person per day	Calories per pound	Calories per day
Cattle	650	550,000	357,500,000	0.1533	1,100	168.7
Calves	130	350,000	45,500,000	0.0195	1,000	19.5
Sheep	68	6,680,000	454,240,000	0.1948	1,100	214.3
Swine	260	1,000,000	260,000,000	0.1115	1,214	135.4
Chickens	2	30,000,000	60,000,000	0.0257	864	22.2
Turkeys	6	2,000,000	12,000,000	0.0051	770	4.0
Geese	3	4,000,000	12,000,000	0.0051	1,436	7.4
Ducks	2	6,000,000	12,000,000	0.0051	1,526	7.9
Deer	80	20,000	1,600,000	0.0007	891	0.6
Total		50,600,000	1,214,840,000	0.5211		579.9
Milk*	400	1,100,000	440,000,000	0.1887	3,200	483.1

Note: * measured in gallons, not pounds.

suggests that being employed as a servant was a privilege, which will be explored later.

Unfortunately there is no way of making similar estimates for the earlier period. Measurements of cattle skeletons indicate that the great increase in the size of cattle over the medieval period had already occurred by the mid-sixteenth century, so animals were likely as large as in the seventeenth century, but we do not know how much pasture land there was.[95] Furthermore, if convertible husbandry was an innovation of the seventeenth century one would expect stocking densities to have been lower in the sixteenth century. Overton and Campbell's stocking estimates for the late sixteenth century are lower than their later means, but the figure for the early seventeenth century is the highest of all the periods they measured. In addition, the sixteenth- and early seventeenth-century houses of correction provided much more meat than the eighteenth-century workhouses sampled, so perhaps this is evidence that there was more pasture at the earlier date. The fact that the inflation of grain prices between 1540 and 1640 showed a rise of a factor of 4.6, while meat prices only rose by a factor of 2.3 during the same period, and the population grew by a factor of 1.2, also suggests that pasture was not being replaced with arable land. If it had been, one would expect the price of meat to rise more rapidly than that of grain.[96] Thus any earlier estimates must remain very tentative, and in general there seems to be a disjuncture between the evidence of meat consumed in account books and the potential productive capacity estimated from the still limited evidence of livestock production.

Milk, butter and cheese

In addition to meat, cows, of course, produced milk, butter and cheese, which formed an important part of diets on non-meat days, as we have seen. In Table 3.16 I have used King's estimates of the number of milk cows combined with the estimates of milk production per cow discussed on p. 253 below to arrive at a yearly figure of calories from the milk produced. However, in making cheese and butter about 30 per cent of the calories remain in the whey, which could be drunk by children, as in the case of the famous Miss Muffett, or put in porridge, but most seems to

---

[95] Juliet Clutton-Brock, 'British Cattle in the Eighteenth Century', *Ark*, 9 (1982), pp. 55–7; Philip Armitage, 'Developments in British Cattle Husbandry from the Romano-British Period to Early Modern Times', *Ark*, 9 (1982), pp. 52–3; Philip Armitage, 'A Preliminary Description of British Cattle from the Late Twelfth to the Early Sixteenth Century', *Ark*, 7 (1980), pp. 407–9.

[96] Clay, *Economic Expansion*, I, p. 49.

Table 3.16 *Total calories per day by sex and age*

	1600				1700				1770				1800			
	grain	meat	dairy	total	grain	meat	dairy	total	grain	meat	dairy	total	grain	meat	dairy	total
Average	1968	514	580	3062	2682	423	474	3579	3985	579	483	5047	3189	428	360	3977
men	2539	663	748	3950	3460	546	611	4617	5141	747	623	6511	4114	552	464	5130
women	2066	540	609	3215	2816	444	498	3758	4184	608	507	5299	3348	449	378	4176
children	1299	339	383	2021	1770	279	313	2362	2630	382	319	3331	2105	282	238	2625
												15141	9567	1284	1080	11931

have been given to pigs for fattening. A lot of milk was also used in furmenty and porridge, so not all was turned into cheese or butter. Thus in
Table 3.16 I have reduced the number of calories from fresh milk by 20
per cent to take account of the loss of whey fed to pigs, although this is
just an assumption, as there is no way of ever knowing what the proportion of milk consumed compared to cheese or butter really was.

There is also no way of knowing how many calories were obtained
from orchard fruit, but it would have been considerable. It has been
estimated that Devon alone produced 10 million gallons of cider annu-
ally in the mid-eighteenth century. Using the population of Devon
derived by E. A. Wrigley for 1761 of 298,855, this would work out to
about 191 kcal per person per day in the county.[97] Robert Loder's crop
of 9,482 lb of apples and 1,735 lb of cherries from 10 to 15 trees in 1616
would have provided in total 4,980 kcal per day for a year, without
losses due to rotting.

Table 3.16 is based on the calculation that a woman ate 0.8 of the calories of a man, and that children under the age of 14 ate 0.5, although
women working in the fields might have needed more calories than
this. It also assumes that children and youths under the age of fourteen
formed approximately one third of the population, and that sex ratios
were in balance, although there were probably more men in the population in 1600 and more women by 1700. It provides what I hope is a fairly
reasonable measurement of calories available in 1600, 1700 and 1770,
although the meat figure has had to be estimated for 1600, and the calculations leave out fish, which, as mentioned earlier, was not consumed
in great quantities by the poor, but perhaps another 50–100 kcal a day
should be added for fruit. Nor does it take grain exports into account,
as the aim here is simply to show *potential* availability, and certainly the
large figures for 1770 show why grain could have been exported in the
eighteenth century.

What do these figures then show about the number of calories available for work in comparison to the diets above? The figures for 1700
and certainly 1770 show that enough food was being produced to have
provided the number of calories suggested by the diets. But the calories
available in 1600 are still lower than those eaten by Robert Loder's servants, or those in the diets prescribed by the early workhouses, which
implies that there was a limit to the amount of work which could be
done at this date. However, we need to remember that about 9–10 per
cent of the population was of 60 years of age or older and would have

[97] Stanes, *The Old Farm*, pp. 61, 66; E. A. Wrigley, 'English County Populations in the
Later Eighteenth Century', *Economic History Review*, 60 (2007), p. 54.

consumed less food. It is also likely that much of the population who did not work as hard as labourers but were not wealthy, such as small shopkeepers like Thomas Turner, did not eat more than 3,300–500 kcal a day, leaving more available for labourers. In addition we need to take into account days of rest as well as days when less strenuous tasks were being done.

This reinforces what we know about the movement of grain prices in this period, but refines our knowledge. In years of good harvests in the early seventeenth century, apart from possible local scarcity, there would have been enough calories available to keep people in good health, but there would have been competition to obtain enough calories to do hard labour, leaving less available for those not working as much. Demand in years of good harvests would have been driven by need for work. This helps to explain increasing labour mobility and emigration in these years. If a disproportionate number of calories went to those working the hardest, such as servants in husbandry and day labourers who were hired regularly and rewarded with food for hard work, then there would have been fewer left for those lacking employment. This social distribution was increasingly worked out through the price mechanism of the market for labour, which we will examine in chapters 5 and 6.

However, in years of deficient harvest or dearth, the number of calories would have been reduced. E. A. Wrigley has made estimates of the likely relation between changes in the price of grain and its yield, and the lower the yield per acre, the greater the effect of a shortfall, as normally 2.5 (wheat), 4 (barley) and 6 (oats) bushels of every harvest must be reserved as seed for next year's crop, and this forms a much greater percentage of a yield of 9 bushels compared to one of 15 or 20 bushels. Thus Wrigley noted that the terrible harvest of 1596, when the price of wheat stood at 2.21 times its 30-year moving average, the shortfall of the gross yields would have been 28 per cent, but would have been 37 per cent when seed corn had been accounted for.[98] As yields went up over time the effects of a shortfall would have been less in percentage terms. According to Wrigley's calculations, between 1520 and 1659 16.25 per cent of harvests of wheat were more than 10 per cent below average, and 12.6 per cent were between 4 and 9 per cent deficient, while 27 per cent yielded more than 10 per cent of the average according to price. Between 1660 and 1789 only 11.4 per cent of harvests

[98] The method for calculating yields from market prices is explained in detail by E. A. Wrigley in 'Some Reflections on Corn Yields and Prices in Pre-Industrial Economies', in John Walter and Roger Schofield (eds.), *Famine, Disease and the Social Order in Early Modern Society* (Cambridge, 1989), *passim*, pp. 252–3.

were more than 10 per cent deficient, but in contrast 19.5 per cent now yielded more than 10 per cent of the average harvest.[99]

Thus in dearth years such as 1596–7, 1697, 1709 or 1740 calories available would have been reduced by 25–37 per cent. The 4,049 kcal available to a man in *c*. 1600 reduced by 37 per cent of grain calories is 3,077, which would certainly curtail the amount of hard work which could be done.[100] Of course less work would have been required in bringing in a deficient harvest, but the number of calories available to sow the next year's crop would also have been severely reduced, thus reducing the amount of labour available, which would have been exacerbated by a run of bad harvests.[101] This suggests that farmers would have had an incentive to keep servants so as to feed them from their crops to secure the labour to profit from next year's crops. However, those who worked by the day would have had their access to food squeezed disproportionately by the calories going to those fed by their masters. William Harrison described such years, where the poor were forced to eat

bread made either of beans, peason [peas], or oats, or of all together and some acorns among, of which scourge the poorest soonest taste, sith they are least able to provide themselves of better. I will not say that this extremity is oft so well to be seen in time of plenty as of dearth, but if I should, I could easily bring my trial. For albeit that there be much more ground eared [cultivated] now almost in every place than hath been of late yet such a price of corn continueth in each town and market without any just cause (except it be that landlords do get to carry corn out of the land only to keep up the prices for their own private gains and ruin of the commonwealth) that artificer and poor laboring man is not able to reach unto it and is driven to content himself with horse corn.[102]

Various poems alluded to the particular harshness of such a diet being the lack of meat, such as one which claimed:

Owre Englische nature cannot lyue by Rooats,
by water, herbys or suche beggerye baggage,
…
geeue Englische men meate after their old usage,
beiff, Mutton, veale, to cheare their courage.[103]

In 1596 the physician Hugh Platt published a pamphlet with a number of recipes for making flour out of vetches, acorns, parsnips and other

---

[99] Ibid., pp. 272ff.
[100] W. G. Hoskins, 'Harvest Fluctuations and English Economic History, 1480–1619', *Agricultural History Review*, 12 (1964), pp. 28–46; W. G. Hoskins, 'Harvest Fluctuations and English Economic History, 1620–1759', *Agricultural History Review*, 16 (1968), pp. 15–31.
[101] Wrigley, 'Corn Yields and Prices', pp. 245–9.   [102] Harrison, *Description*, p. 133.
[103] Drummond and Wilbraham, *Englishman's Food*, p. 51.

roots.[104] Using these sources of food for bread was advocated because bread was linked with sustenance for work. Contemporaries did not understand that energy came from foods with carbohydrates, but they picked on other foods which had some carbohydrate content, which undoubtedly had been learned through experience. In this way some energy could be gained for the work needed to plant next year's crop.

One other effect of such famine was that food like oats, peas, beans and lentils, which were fodder for animals, would have been consumed by people. Harrison noticed this when quoting the proverb 'hunger setteth his first foot into the horse manger', and this would have reduced the fuel for animal power.[105] One, theoretically, might expect this situation to lead to the increased slaughter of food herds, but it is curious that prices of meat did not seem to change much in famine years. In Rutland during the bad harvest of 1795 bread was made with both wheat and barley flour, but beef and mutton were actually sold at reduced prices to prevent too great a consumption of bread.[106] It must also have been the case that there were constraints on how many animals could be slaughtered because of the time it would have taken to regenerate the herds. But hay, which was the main fodder crop for cattle, grew better in wet years, which was the most common cause of bad harvest of grains, as in the 1590s.[107] In 1596, for instance, the price of livestock and animal products in Peter Bowden's price index actually fell.[108] But if people started to eat fodder for horses such as oats this must have created shortages of horses in following years, and a shortage of animal energy inputs into farm work.[109] This might be one reason why grain prices remained above 25s a quarter in the series of good harvests that followed the dearth of the late 1590s.

In other years of smaller shortfalls, grain could be stored over from good years, and in the eighteenth century exports could be halted to overcome the deficiency. But in runs of bad harvests such as those of the late 1640s or late 1690s grain stored from good years would have eventually run short.[110] However, as grain yields rose, even severe shortages would have had less effect. In the dearth of 1693, for instance, a rise in prices of 60 per cent would still have meant a shortfall of about 20 per cent, or a reduction in total calories available to 3,096, or 3,994 for a working man (see Table 3.16). By the deficient harvest of 1740, though,

[104] Hugh Platt, *Sundrie New and Artificiall Remedies against Famine* (London, 1596).
[105] Harrison, *Description*, p. 133.   [106] Eden, *State of the Poor*, II, p. 604.
[107] Hoskins, 'Harvest Fluctuations 1480–1619', p. 38.   [108] *AHEW*, IV, p. 849.
[109] See the discussion in *AHEW*, IV, pp. 624–6.
[110] Steve Hindle, 'Dearth and the English Revolution: The Harvest Crisis of 1647–50', *Economic History Review*, 61 (2008), pp. 64–95.

the price increase of 50 per cent for wheat indicates a net shortfall of 17 per cent, and if 17 per cent is subtracted from the grain calories for 1770 in Table 3.16, the harvest would still have supplied 4,431 kcal.[111]

From this work on diet I think we can safely conclude that, contrary to what Fogel proposed, there were enough calories available to do hard work, but that in the late sixteenth and early seventeenth centuries, and some subsequent years of high prices, these undoubtedly had to be rationed between individuals. This would have led to greater shortage among families with less access to work. In subsequent years, such pressures were much reduced, but certainly there were still local shortages during bad harvests in the eighteenth century, as the work on corn riots has pointed out.[112]

It has also been argued, on the basis of the much shorter stature of apprentices and labourers recruited into the army and navy after 1750 compared to the officer class, that wage labourers were undernourished as a result of poverty.[113] From the information analysed above it seems unlikely that, for those in regular employment, this was due to lack of calories. This certainly might have been the case for the underemployed poor, and it is possible that those attracted to the army and navy might have been those unable to maintain themselves in regular employment, and were thus less well nourished. But it is also possible that the shorter stature was the result of lack of milk or essential vitamins in the diets of children at the time. Work done by the Cambridge Group for the History of Population and Social Structure has demonstrated that in the period from about 1680–1750 there was a striking improvement in adult mortality, but no change in infant and child mortality apart from mortality in the first month of life, which fell in parallel with the sharp decline both in maternal mortality and stillbirths.[114] Especially in families more dependent on wage labour, it is possible that children too young to work might have had to be less well fed in order to supply enough energy for the parents and older children to continue to work hard enough to supply the family with food in years of high food prices. It would also be interesting to know if recruits from the north of

[111] Hoskins, 'Harvest Fluctuations 1620–1759', pp. 30–1.
[112] E. P. Thompson, 'The Moral Economy of the English Crowd in the Eighteenth Century', and 'The Moral Economy Reviewed', in *Customs in Common* (London, 1991), pp. 183–305; John Walter and Keith Wrightson, 'Dearth and the Social Order in Early Modern England', *Past and Present*, 71 (1976), pp. 22–42.
[113] Floud *et al.*, *Height, Health and History*, pp. 42–56, 217–24, 225–49, 287–91, 301ff.
[114] E. A. Wrigley, R. S. Davies, J. E. Oeppen and R. S. Schofield, *English Population History from Family Reconstitution 1580–1837* (Cambridge, 1997), pp. 280ff.

England were taller, as we know that more milk was consumed there. However the data have not been geographically disaggregated.

From both an economic and social point of view we cannot think of the working poor as simply poor, but as a resource of energy which drove the economy. The provision of food was bound up with notions of charity, but even for an improving farmer who was not charitable it would not have made sense to employ underfed labour, or for labourers to be fed what was considered unhealthy or culturally unacceptable at the time.[115] I think this gives rise to an important distinction between the employed and the underemployed in terms of what they ate. Another important result of this investigation seems to be that the idea of normal consumption was that needed for very hard work, just as 'normal' today means a sedentary middle-class office-worker. Thus we should think of poorer people who were not working as eating less, not those who were working eating more, as we might today. This has important implications. First it would mean that a dearth would have been a much sharper aberration, and would also have created an energy shortage. Second, complaints about hardship among the poor might have been about the lack of food to do work rather than absolute lack to survive, especially by the eighteenth century, if people were working harder. It also raises other issues about how far body fat was a store of energy, and how far conceptions of gluttony among the rich were related to work.

The other main finding which has come out of this part of the book is the great increase in energy available through calories: 17 per cent between 1600 and 1700 and another 41 per cent by 1770, before falling back to only an 11 per cent increase over the whole period by 1800, as a result of population growth after 1770. Such an increase in the availability of calories existed in a feedback loop. The labour market focused food energy towards the employed who worked harder to produce an increasing amount of food. Labour inputs into production led to increasing energy inputs into agriculture, creating more food to fuel more work, and this will be investigated in chapter 6. But before doing this we must now turn to labourers' houses to look at the sorts of material objects they possessed to get a broader picture of their material possessions and standard of living.

[115] Hindle, 'Campaign for General Hospitality', pp. 51–61.

4   Labourers' household goods

Although food comprised the greater part of a labouring family's expenditure over the course of a year, the family also, of course, had to pay for clothing, rent and fuel for heat. There were also medical expenses for sickness and childbirth. House rents could vary widely according to custom and the degree to which the landlord was charging market rents. Rent has been estimated to be about £1 a year in the late seventeenth century for a pauper, and about 30s for labouring families, rising to between £2 and £4 by the 1760s.[1] In the next chapter we will examine the changing cost of living based on the need to purchase such necessities, but labourers also, of course, had to purchase consumer goods to furnish their houses and to cook and eat with. In addition many labourers also possessed the farm equipment necessary to raise animals, grow crops and produce beer, milk, butter and cheese, either for home consumption or for sale.

Here we will analyse probate inventories taken after death, an excellent source which can be used to examine material goods. Probate inventories provide listings of rooms in a house together with their contents. They also list tools, production equipment, both in the house and in outbuildings or the yard, as well as farm animals and growing or harvested crops. In addition debts owed to the deceased were listed, and on rare occasions also the debts they owed to others. Occasionally clothing was also itemised and valued, and the average value of labourers' clothing in 382 inventories where apparel was listed separately, or where the clothing was itemised, was £1 2s. But since the clothing of the poor has recently been dealt with in John Styles's definitive study *The Dress of the People*, I will only touch on it here.[2] In this chapter the focus will be on the nature of the houses labourers lived in, the types of goods they possessed and how these things changed over time. Their

---

[1] Wrightson and Levine, *Poverty and Piety*, pp. 40–1. See the discussion below in chapter 5, for Table 5.3.

[2] Styles, *Dress of the People*.

farming and production activities to earn a living will be dealt with in the next chapter.

Here things like bedding, linen, chairs, mirrors, and so on will be examined in terms of the theory of the 'industrious revolution' put forward by Jan de Vries discussed in chapter 1. De Vries postulated that householders in early modern Europe worked harder to produce things for the market, or to sell their labour in order to also purchase things on the market. The best evidence for this increased purchasing power, he argued, came from the increasing numbers of goods in probate inventories. In England, as I demonstrated in an earlier book, this was certainly the case for middling-sort households in the late sixteenth century, where the numbers of goods increased dramatically between 1550 and 1580, as did goods in shops, indicating a great expansion in the market. The evidence for poorer households, however, suggested that they did not play a significant role in this early expansion.[3] In his original articles de Vries claimed that over the subsequent period (1600–1750) there was an increase of goods *across* the social spectrum which was crucial for his theory, as the poor formed the majority of the early modern population. For the first time a broad range of inventories made for individuals designated as labourers between 1550 and 1800 will be examined to see if this was true.

Probate inventories have now been used in a number of works examining consumption and household production. The two most of important of these for England are by Overton *et al.* and Weatherill. Weatherill used a national sample of 2,902 inventories to examine changes in the ownership of key consumer goods such as pewter, clocks, knives and forks, pictures and looking-glasses between 1660 and 1760, whereas Overton *et al.* examined a larger sample of 8,000 inventories ranging in date from 1600 to 1750, but only for the counties of Kent and Cornwall.[4] Overton *et al.*, however, used a computer software program which enabled them to analyse the entire contents of the probate inventory. Thus they could look at the number and contents of different rooms in households, as well as production of cloth, dairy products and beer among other things. They were also able to examine household wealth versus the value of crops, animals, farm equipment or shop goods. In both these studies, as well as in others, it has been noted that inventories have survived for much greater numbers of wealthier members of society than for poorer individuals, including day

---

[3] See above, pp. 14–15. Muldrew, *Economy of Obligation*, pp. 22–34.
[4] Lorna Weatherill, *Consumer Behaviour and Material Culture in Britain 1660–1760* (Cambridge, 1988), pp. 210–11; Overton *et. al., Production and Consumption*, pp. 179–80.

labourers.[5] In the sample used by Overton *et al.*, labourers formed less than 2 per cent in both Kent and Cornwall, and labourers and servants together formed less than 1 per cent of Weatherill's sample.[6] In his study of all surviving inventories for 20 parishes in Huntingdonshire Ken Sneath discovered a greater percentage of labourers' inventories (6 per cent), but in a comparison with baptism registers which listed occupations of fathers in 3 of those parishes Sneath found that while 14 per cent of the surviving inventories for just these parishes were for labourers, fully 34 per cent of the fathers listed in the parish registers were labourers.[7] Other estimates discussed in chapter 1 also support the figure that labourers formed about 30–45 per cent of the population of rural counties in the south. In aggregate terms, many fewer labourers were inventoried than individuals with other occupations, because in general they had fewer goods to bequeath, and the division of such goods was less likely to be complicated. In Cheshire, for instance, between 1550 and 1800, 82 labourers' inventories have survived compared to 3,624 husbandmen's, 11,764 yeomen's and 262 butchers' inventories.[8] However, given the sheer number of inventories which have survived from the sixteenth to the eighteenth centuries, the absolute number of labourers' inventories is still large enough to provide a statistically significant sample, but we will still have to consider how representative they were of the majority of labourers who were not inventoried.

Alan Everitt, in his pioneering study of the farm labourer in the fourth volume of *AHEW*, actually based much of it on probate inventories from the north, the east and the Midlands. But since he could not find enough inventories for labourers, he used 'all those which belonged to country people whose social status is not described, and were valued at under £5 before 1570, under £10 during the 1590s, and under £15 during 1610–40', without stating how many fell into this category. The exact number of inventories he used was also not given, but was probably about 300, and his survey stopped in 1640.[9] Given this

---

[5] See, for example, Carole Shammas's comparison of English and American inventories, Shammas, *Pre-Industrial Consumer*; Trinder and Cox (eds.), *Yeomen and Colliers*, pp. 1–188; Beverly Adams (ed.), *Lifestyle and Culture in Hertford ... Wills and Inventories 1660–1725*, Hertfordshire Record Society, 13 (1997), pp. viii–111.

[6] Overton *et al.*, *Production and Consumption*, p. 22; Weatherill, *Consumer Behaviour*, pp. 210–11.

[7] Sneath, 'Consumption, Wealth, Indebtedness', pp. 198–200.

[8] Cheshire Record Office, Wills Database Online, www.cheshire.gov.uk/recordoffice/wills/Home.htm.

[9] Everitt, 'Farm Labourers', pp. 413n.1, 431–2, 442–8. This point was brought to my attention by Leigh Shaw-Taylor, and is discussed in his paper 'The Nature and Scale of the Cottage Economy', which examines a sample of eighteenth-century

lack of precision it was decided to make a more comprehensive study here. Now, with many more inventories in county record offices catalogued according to occupation, it is possible, instead of using random sampling, to search out enough surviving inventories which have been catalogued as labourers'. More than enough have been discovered to provide a sample of almost 1,000 labourers' inventories between 1550 and 1800, providing a more empirically robust and long-term survey than Everitt's.[10]

Most inventories list an occupation for the deceased, and if they do not either the will or the administration bond does. To be listed by an occupation generally meant one was or had been married. As discussed in chapter 1, there is no straightforward contemporary description of what the occupational term 'labourer' meant, just as there was no precise demarcation between the farming activities of husbandmen and yeomen. Many labourers who worked for wages also had their own small farms and possessed animals and crops. Sixty-eight per cent of the inventoried labourers we will look at here possessed farm animals, while for 51 per cent there was evidence that they were growing crops. Robert Latham, examined above, hired himself out as a carter. The wealthier husbandman and father of the diarist John Cannon hired himself out to plough other people's fields for wages, while leaving his own farm under the care of a servant in husbandry.[11] Correspondingly, there exist some inventories where two different occupations can be found in the will, administration or inventory. The number of such individuals, however, was small. In the sample examined here, out of 972 inventories, 18 labourers were also termed 'husbandman', and 4 were listed as 'yeoman'. One was also listed as a woolcomber, although he did not possess any wool or combs. This implies that at different stages in the life cycle an individual might have worked for wages and gone on to become a self-sufficient farmer, or vice versa if a farmer went into debt and had to sell his land and work for wages. Furthermore, opinion on whether an individual was more of a farmer or a wage earner could differ depending on who was making up which document in the probate process. What does seem to be common is that working for wages was

Northumberland inventories and can be found at: www.geog.cam.ac.uk/research/
projects/occupations/abstracts/paper15. The examination of these labourers' inventories is the first fruit of a larger project Dr Shaw-Taylor and I are working on, funded by the British Academy, to compare the material wealth and goods of labourers, carpenters, weavers and husbandmen as represented in their inventories.

[10] Everitt, 'Farm Labourers', pp. 413–21, 443.
[11] Craig Muldrew, 'Class and Credit: Social Identity, Wealth and the Life Course in Early Modern England', in Henry French and Jonathan Barry (eds.), *Identity and Agency in England, 1500–1800* (London, 2004), pp. 162–3.

something individuals designated as 'labourers' on documents did, or had done, and thus using their inventories does give us a unified sample of labouring familes' household goods to study.

As with any source there are significant limitations in using inventories, and there is now a large body of work on their potential problems. This literature is rehearsed very effectively in Overton *et al.* and I will mention only the most salient points here.[12] As Margaret Spufford has shown, because only debts owed to the deceased are mentioned, and not the debts they themselves owed, we do not know their true state of wealth.[13] Given the ubiquity of credit in the early modern period financial wealth was dependent on the balance between inflows and outflows of payments, and what one could afford was dependent on one's credit. Thus it is possible that someone worth, say, £100 in goods and debts owing to him, might at the same time have £500 of debts he owed others, leaving the estate insolvent. This can only be discovered where probate accounts survive. But where they do, and have been analysed, it is possible to see that the value of household goods was generally related to an individual's financial credit, as it was this which enabled them to purchase more consumer goods.[14] Another serious omission is that inventories only list movable property or contracts such as debts or leases and not real estate. Thus we cannot tell how large a labourer's farm might have been from an inventory. In some cases this can be reconstructed from wills, and sometimes crops are listed as growing in a field of a certain size, but again such listings are seasonal. In addition, pigs and cattle could be slaughtered in the autumn, so there might be fewer in those inventories recorded for people dying in the winter.

Nor do we know at what point in the life cycle a person might have died, since no ages are given, or how many children were present in the deceased's household. Nor, without looking at the related wills, can we know how many wives outlived their husbands. There is also the possibility that many inventories were made for older people who might have accumulated more things over time. Alternatively, some old people might have given their estate to their children before they died so they

---

[12] Overton *et al.*, *Production and Consumption*, pp. 14–18. Also see Tom Arkell, 'The Probate Process' and J. and N. Cox, 'Probate 1500–1800: A System in Transition', in Tom Arkell, Nesta Evans and Nigel Goose (eds.), *When Death Do Us Part: Understanding and Interpreting the Probate Records of Early Modern England* (Oxford, 2000), pp. 3–37.

[13] Margaret Spufford, 'The Limitations of the Probate Inventory', in John Chartres and David Hey (eds.), *English Rural Society, 1500–1800: Essays in Honour of Joan Thirsk* (Cambridge, 1990), pp. 139–74.

[14] Overton *et al.*, *Production and Consumption*, pp. 138–9, 150; Muldrew, *Economy of Obligation*, pp. 103–7.

appear poorer than they really were. However, in a study of one parish, Milton in Kent, Overton *et al.* found that the survival of inventories there corresponded remarkably well with the age distribution of the population, with 14.5 per cent surviving for those under 26 years; 46.2 per cent surviving for those between 27 and 47 with children; 24.8 per cent between 48 and 59; and 14.5 per cent over 60.[15] If this single parish is typical then inventories do indeed represent a full range of individuals throughout the life cycle.

Finally, there is an inbuilt gender bias in that 'labourer' is an occupational title only for men, since women were always listed by their marital status. This means we cannot look at poor labourers' widows or single women who were the daughters of labourers who worked primarily in agriculture, as inventories for women do not give an occupation. We know from the work of Peter Earle and Amy Erickson that there were many single women who laboured for wages or did other work.[16] In addition, as we shall see below, many worked in agriculture as well. Inventories for poor women certainly exist: between 17 and 26 per cent of Overton *et al.*'s sample were for widows or single women.[17] But without the laborious hit-and-miss process of matching inventories with other sources such as witness statements in church court records or wage lists in account books, it is impossible to know how many inventoried spinsters and widows made their living primarily through wage earning.

There are other conventions which also limit the usefulness of inventories in some ways. Clothes and money, for instance, are usually simply listed together under the heading 'purse and apparel', so only in a limited number of cases is it possible to determine how much cash was possessed by the deceased or what sort of clothes they wore. There is also the possibility that certain goods would not be listed, such as those which the widow would continue to use. Even though, by the law of coverture, all property was in theory the husband's, women's clothing or jewellery was rarely listed in an inventory for the obvious reason that the widow continued to wear it. For similar reasons it is possible that distaffs or spinning wheels might also be under-recorded. More frustrating was the almost universal practice in all counties of pricing things in groups rather than individually. Thus, in one instance,

[15] Overton *et al.*, *Production and Consumption*, pp. 27–8.
[16] Peter Earle, 'The Female Labour Market in London in the Late Seventeenth and Early Eighteenth Centuries', *Economic History Review*, 2nd ser., 42 (1989), pp. 328–53; Amy Erickson, 'Married Women's Occupations in Eighteenth-Century London', *Continuity and Change*, 23 (2008), pp. 237–66.
[17] Overton *et al.*, *Production and Consumption*, p. 22.

'wooden dishes, spoons, 3 shelves, 1 wooden mortar, 1 salt box, 1 pair of bellows' were all listed together priced at 3s. Some have questioned the accuracy of the appraisers' pricing as a result of this practice, but where records exist of goods being auctioned off the prices have been checked and found to be quite accurate.[18] Another problem is that unless there is a qualifier such as 'new' or 'old' or 'joined' it is impossible to know the quality or age of a single good, which could, of course, affect the price. In addition goods would have been bequeathed and accumulated over time. Of course, this would have been a continuous process, already occurring before my period of investigation started.[19]

The labourers' inventories chosen for this sample have been drawn from Cheshire, Lincolnshire, Norfolk, Cambridgeshire, Kent and Hampshire. These counties all had sufficient numbers to study, and were chosen because the archives of probate material for each were well catalogued, and the numbers of labourers compared to other occupations could be judged. In addition, they represent a good cross-section of differing types of agricultural economies throughout the country. The Cheshire plain was predominantly pasture, providing some of the finest grazing in the country, and by the second half of the seventeenth century significant amounts of Cheshire cheese was being produced and shipped to London. Cereal crops were in the main only grown for local consumption, and low customary rents seem to have enabled many small family farms to survive into the mid-eighteenth century.[20] Lincolnshire contained a variety of areas, including the upland chalk wolds, the arable lowland areas and fenland marsh. The county was well known for the raising of sheep for wool on the uplands and for the grazing and fattening of cattle on the southern marshes for the London market. In addition, many of the farms in these arable areas practised convertible husbandry, mixing large flocks of sheep with cereal production from the seventeenth century.[21] The north of Cambridgeshire contained similar areas of fenland economy, while the south was suited to profitable market-orientated arable corn-livestock farming. Norfolk

---

[18] J. Cox and N. Cox, 'Valuations in Probate Inventories, Part I', *Local Historian*, 2 (1985), pp. 467–78; J. Cox and N. Cox, 'Valuations in Probate Inventories, Part II', *Local Historian*, 8 (1986), pp. 85–100, Carl Estabrook, *Urbane and Rustic England: Cultural Ties and Social Spheres in the Provinces, 1660–1780* (Manchester, 1998), pp. 130–3.

[19] Muldrew, *Economy of Obligation*, pp. 22–36.

[20] David Hey, 'The North-West Midlands: Derbyshire, Staffordshire, Cheshire, and Shropshire', in *AHEW*, V, pp. 129–58; Charles F. Foster, *Four Cheshire Townships in the 18th Century: Arley, Appleton, Stockton Heath and Great Budworth* (Northwich, 1992), pp. 11ff.; Charles F. Foster, *Cheshire Cheese and Farming in the North West in the Seventeenth and Eighteenth Centuries* (Northwich, 1998), pp. 3–35.

[21] Joan Thirsk, *English Peasant Farming: The Agrarian History of Lincolnshire from Tudor to Recent Times* (London, 1957), pp. 180–9, 220–36.

had a similar mix of arable pasture, and from an early date practised some of the most advanced profit-orientated agriculture in England.[22] Norfolk also had much employment in cloth production. Kent, too, was a wealthy agricultural county which produced much grain for export to the London market, but which also had significant areas of pastoral farming. There was also a cloth industry in the upland wealden area of the county in the sixteenth century, but this had already begun to decline by the early seventeenth century. Hampshire was predominately a corn-growing arable county with some woodland pasture in the New Forest, and it also had the naval docks in Portsmouth.[23]

For Cheshire, Norfolk and Hampshire all the surviving inventories were transcribed. Half of those which survived from Lincolnshire were used, while those from Kent and Cambridgeshire were sampled, with every second or third inventory being taken. It was intended to obtain a sample of roughly 1,000 inventories but as it turned out quite a few had to be rejected because they were illegible or incomplete, leaving a sample of 972.[24] In this sample 89 labourers resided in towns such as Cambridge, Nantwich, Chester or Great Yarmouth. But apart from 26 dock workers who resided around Portsmouth, who will be dealt with below, most of these labourers had animals and agricultural tools, and some had small crops, so were undoubtedly working in the surrounding countryside and for this reason it was decided not to exclude them from the sample. Labourers' inventories survive for other counties as well. Ken Sneath has studied a sample of 263 from Huntingdonshire, Leigh Shaw-Taylor has examined 60 from early eighteenth-century Northamptonshire and Paul Glennie has looked at Gloucestershire and Wiltshire.[25] I have used the ITEM program developed by Mark Overton to facilitate the input of the complete data found on each

[22] B. A. Holderness, 'East Anglia and the Fens: Norfolk, Suffolk, Cambridgeshire, Ely, Huntingdonshire, Essex, and the Lincolnshire Fens', in *AHEW*, V, pp. 197–238; Bruce Campbell and Mark Overton, 'A New Perspective on Medieval and Early Modern Agriculture; Six Centuries of Norfolk Farming *c*. 1250–*c*. 1850', *Past and Present*, 141 (1993), pp. 38–105.

[23] Brian M. Short, 'The South-East: Kent, Surrey, and Sussex' and J. R. Wordie, 'The South: Oxfordshire, Buckinghamshire, Berkshire, Wiltshire, and Hampshire', in *AHEW*, V, pp. 270–357.

[24] Cheshire Record Office, WS 1573–WS 1745, WC 1618–WC 1800, WI 1688–WI 1780; Lincolnshire Record Office, INV 8.140–INV 223.69; CRO, Vac 1–3, VC 19–46; NRO, DN/INV/3–44, ANW 23.1–21, ANF11, DCN 73; CKS, prc10.1–71, prc11.2–80, prc21.3–17, prc27.2–146; HRO, 1575b.66–1757a71.2, zim 65.d.3.799.

[25] Sneath, 'Consumption, Wealth, Indebtedness', p. 87; Shaw-Taylor, 'Cottage Economy', Table 3.2; Paul Glennie, 'Labouring, Smallholding and Poor Artisan Households in Early Modern England: Looking for Economic Boundaries', paper presented at the Economic and Social History of Early Modern Britain Seminar, University of Cambridge, 2004.

probate inventory in its entirety. This has the advantage of both simplifying data entry and also of enabling all the information available in each inventory to be machine-read and statistically analysed.[26]

As can be seen from Table 4.1 the largest number of labourers' inventories survive for the late seventeenth century, with very few surviving after 1750. In the analysis which follows, I have used equal periods of fifty years for convenience, as was done by Overton *et al.*, except for the eighteenth century, where, in most cases, I have put all the inventories together because too few exist after 1750 to form a statistically testable group. The value of the inventories in Table 4.1 represents the total sum of everything in the inventory including debts and leases. Table 4.1 also shows that the sample is dominated by inventories from Cambridgeshire and Kent because so many more have survived from those counties. Cambridgeshire is unusual in that no inventories have survived from before the Restoration. In addition, 75 per cent of Norfolk inventories survive from before 1650. This presents a possible problem in calculating change over time for the whole sample, since the average value of the labourers' inventories in Cambridgeshire was lower than all other counties except Norfolk. Thus in Table 4.6 I have calculated change over time for the total value of the inventories for the sample as a whole; without the Cambridge inventories; and then without the Norfolk inventories. As can be seen here, the rise in the value of the inventories is about the same between the periods 1550–99 and 1600–49, and the rise between the periods 1600–49 and 1650–99 is greater without Cambridgeshire and smaller without Norfolk, but overall the bias in the sample has the effect of slightly reducing the real rise in total inventory value over time.

In this discussion I shall analyse the sample as a whole, but hope to look at regional differences in the future. However, some general differences need to be pointed out here. In Table 4.1 it can be seen that the median value of the inventories in column ten is lowest for Cambridgeshire and Norfolk and highest for the southeastern counties. The median value of the Norfolk inventories is in part lower because so many of them are from before 1650. If we increase the value of all inventories from before 1620 by 25 per cent to account for inflation, the median value of all the Norfolk inventories becomes £14.07 and the median household value is £6.03. This makes Norfolk much more similar to Cambridgeshire, but still poorer than the other counties

---

[26] Overton *et al.*, *Production and Consumption*, pp. 19–21. I would like to thank Mark Overton for allowing me to use this software, and for his help in training me and my researchers in its use.

Table 4.1 *Inventory numbers, values and debts by county over time*

	1550– 1599	1600– 1649	1650– 1699	1700– 1749	1750– 1799	Total number	%	Average value of inventory
Cambs.	1	1	170	88	3	263	27	£24.60
Cheshire	7	20	32	17	4	80	8	£34.66
Hampshire	22	38	76	26	4	166	18	£39.00
Kent	48	64	112	37	0	261	27	£29.13
Lincolnshire	18	0	42	4	0	64	7	£29.03
Norfolk	24	77	12	23	0	136	13	£18.50
Total	120	200	444	195	11	970	100	£29.15

in total value. It is possible that the value of labourers' inventories in both Cambridgeshire and Norfolk was lower than in other counties because capitalist agriculture was more advanced there, allowing labourers fewer opportunities to inherit land at inexpensive rents. The other important point to note when comparing counties is that the median value of household goods in the different counties is much closer than the median total inventoried value, except for Cheshire, where the value of household goods was significantly lower that the total inventoried value. This is because the Cheshire labourers were owed many more large debts, which cannot be considered as increased consumption.

To give a general idea of what some of these documents contained I have listed a sample of five inventories below. The first two are for poor labourers, one from the sixteenth century and the other from the eighteenth century. The third, for Roger Potton of Impington, Cambridgeshire, is that of a fairly poor labourer with some land, while the fourth is a labourer of medium wealth and the last is an example of a wealthy eighteenth-century labourer with a significant number of household goods.

(1) Christopher Gyll, Kent, who died 15 March 1593[27]
      purse and girdle and apparel 2s. 4d.
      heifer £2 6s. 8d.
   chamber:
      1 cupboard 2s.
      2 chests 3s.
      2 rotten bedsteads 12d.

[27] CKS, prc21.12.482.

Median value of inventory	Average household value	Median household value	Average of debts to	Average of debts owed to divided by all inventories	Number of inventories with debts owed to
£16.16	£8.05	£6.45	£9.60	£4.60	66
£19.33	£8.07	£3.08	£22	£16.30	28
£22.37	£13.06	£8.01	£21.70	£14.40	83
£20.23	£11.07	£7.08	£14.60	£7.07	89
£19.92	£6.07	£5.08	£17.50	£6.30	16
£12.94	£8.08	£5.02	£13.10	£5.50	28
£18.49	£10.04	£6.07	£16.42	£9.03	310

> 7 old course sheets 8s. 9d.
> 1 old bolster and 1 old blanket 12d.
> hall:
> 3 old linen trendles and 1 old woollen trendle 4s.
> 1 bad table and 2 trestles and 1 small form 2s.
> 12 pieces small old broken pewter 3s. 4d.
> 3 small old tubs and 3 pails and 12 small wooden bowls 4s. 4d.
> 1 small spit and 1 old bad little frying pan 16d.
> other bad lumber 12d.
> sum £3 18s. 9d.
> debts he owed 16s.
> Widow Gyll for funeral costs 12d.

(2) William Wright, Linton, Cambridgeshire, who died 27 October 1707[28]

> dwelling house:
> 1 small featherbed and 1 bolster and 1 pillow and 1 blanket and 1 coverlet and 3 curtains and 1 bedstead £1 10s.
> 1 pair-old sheets and 1 pair-pillowbears 3s. 6d.
> 4 small pewter dishes and 1 flagon and 2 small saucers and 1 porringer and 1 pair-bellows 4s.
> 1 small kettle and 1 skillet and 1 chaffing dish 2s. 4d.
> 1 old cupboard and 2 old hutches and 2 chairs and 1 stool and 1 saltbox and 1 bracket 3s. 2d.
> 1 iron dripping pan 9d.
> yard:
> 1 cow £1
> 1 wheelbarrow 1s. 6d.

[28] CRO, VC 36.344.

1 fan and 1 sieve and 1 spade and 1 shovel and 4 rakes and
2 forks and 1 cutting knife and 1 hatchet and 1 flail and
1 grubbing axe and 1 old skip and 1 cobb 5s. 4d.

wood 10s.

2 old gates 1s. 6d.

barn:

0.5 load-straw 5s.

pocket and apparel 10s.

sum £4 17s. 1d.

(3) Roger Potton, Impington, Cambridgeshire, who died 13 October
1701[29]

Purse and apparel 1s.

1 old featherbed and bolster and 3 pillows and 1 coverlet 17s.

1 old flock bed and 1 bolster and 1 blanket 2s.

1 new coverlet bought at the fair 8s.

5 sheets and 1 napkin 6s.

2 old bedsteads and 2 hutches 5s.

1 old cupboard 2s.

4 brass kettles and 1 brass pot and 1 warming pan £1 10s.

2 pewter dishes and 1 tankard and 1 porringer and 1 saucer 4s.

3 small beer vessels 2s.

2 old keelers and 1 cheese press and 1 tub and 1 pail 4s.

2 old scythes and 2 frying pans and 2 pair pothangers 3s. 2d.

1 old coop and 5 old chairs and 2 old tables and 1 stool £4

1 old stand and 1 parcel earthenware 1s.

2 ladders and 1 pair tongs and things forgot 1s.

1 parcel-cheese and 1 parcel-wool 17s.

3 cows £4

1 sow and 4 pigs £1 10s.

2 sheep 7s. 4d.

0.5 acre-wheat in the barn £1

2.5 acres-barley and 1.5 roods-peas £2

1.5 roods-wheat and 1 acre-breakland £1

1 parcel-hay £2

sum £17 15s.

(4) Thomas Foreman, Faversham, Kent, who died 29 January 1731[30]

fire room:

1 old dresser and cupboard of drawers and shelves and 1 oval
table and 1 old square table and 1 joined stool and 6 old chairs
and 1 pair-coal grates and 1 fire pan and tongs and 1 poker

---

[29] CRO, VC 37.30.   [30] CKS, prc11.79.125.

and 1 sifter and 1 iron pot and pot hangers and 1 iron rack to keep the child out of the fire, and 1 gridiron and 1 sprat and 1 spit and logs and 1 fender £1 18s. 6d.

1 jill and weights and 2 spits and bellows and 2 brass candlesticks and 2 iron candle sticks and 1 box iron and heats and 1 stand and 1 save-all and 1 candle box and 1 tinderbox and 1 flour and pepperbox and 1 brass ladle and 1 brass egg slice and 11 pewter dishes and 24 pewter plates and 1 parcel-earthenware and drink pots and 1 brass warming pan and 1 runner £2 15s.

buttery:

1 kneading trough and sieves and 1 parcel-earthenware and 2 iron pottinger pots and 2 brass skillets 9s. 6d.

back kitchen:

1 small copper and 6 small tubs and pails £1 6s 3d.

cellar

3 firkins and 3 small cogs and 1 small brine tub and 1 stallder and 2 bushels-coals and 1 small parcel-brush faggots 18s.

chamber:

1 old clock £1

1 bedstead and 1 featherbed and 1 bolster and pillows and covering and old curtains £2 10s.

1 old couch and 1 squab and 6 old rush bottomed chairs 4s.

1 small drawer and 1 square table and 1 old trunk and 2 old chests and 1 small looking glass and window curtains and 1 parcel-earthenware and 2 pairs-brand irons and small creepers and 1 fire pan and tongs and 1 pair bellows £1 8s.

6 pairs-coarse sheets and 8 pillow coats and 2 small tablecloths and 12 napkins and 6 towels £2

little chamber:

1 old bed and old hangings £1 5s.

wearing linen and woollen apparel £2

unseen and forgotten things 1s. 6d.

sum £17 15s. 9d.

(5) John Hutson, Littlebourne, Kent, who died 25 March 1721[31]

fore room:

1 clock and 1 clock case and clock weights and clock line and 1 cupboard and 5 pewter dishes and 6 lb weights and 4 pewter porringers and 1 iron pot and pothooks and 1 brass pot and lid and 2 brass skillets and 1 brass mortar and 1 pestle

[31] CKS, prc11.76.38.

and 1 box iron and fetters and 1 pair-andirons and tongs and
1 fire shovel and pot hangers and 1 pair bellows and 2 bills
and 2 axes and 3 pails and 1 pot horse and 1 tin lantern and
4 earthen plates and 3 basins and 1 small looking glass and
1 saltbox and 1 mustard pot and 6 chairs and 1 cushion and
earthenware and 1 small table and 1 hanging table and 3
dishes and 3 spoons and 11 trenchers and 2 hammers and 2
irons and a gridiron £4 5s. 8d.

milk house
1 brine tub and 40 lbs-pork and 6 small barrels and stalling
and 3 wooden milk barrels and 3 wooden platters and flet-
ting dish and 1 churn and shaft and butter scales and weights
and 1 mousetrap and 1 butter basket and 1 linen wheel and 4
shelves and 4 lbs-crock butter and 4 lbs-hogsame and 1 bushel-
wheat and 1 meal bag £1 16s. 4d.

buttery:
1 washing trough and 1 small table leaf and 3 small stellings
and 9 small tubs and keelers and 1 galleon and 1 form and
2 shelves and 2 wooden bottles and 1 water pot and 2 small
baskets and 1 saw and 1 wooden funnel and 11 glass bottles
and 1 iron peel £1 8s. 7d.

washhouse:
1 small brass furnace and 1 brass kettle and 1 frying pan and
1 bucking tub and 1 ring tub and 1 old hand dish and sieve
£1 13s. 3d.

over the fore-room chamber:
1 furnished flock bed and 1 large chest and chairs and 1 trunk
and hooks and 1 sickle and 1 trivet and 6 sacks and 2 bags
and 1 brush and 1 fan and some scrappy corn and 2 iron
peelers and 1 small hatchet and 1 toss cutter and old iron and
7 pair-sheets and 4 tablecloths and 2 towels £3 5d.

best chamber:
1 furnished feather bed and 1 chest and 8 pieces new linen
cloth and 1 small looking glass £4 2s. 2d.

lodge:
2 ladders and 2 three-prong forks and 1 shovel and 1 rack
leaf 5s

barn:
2 pitchforks 4d.

lodge at the end of the house:
1 mattock and 1 spade and 2 hoe and 1 barn rake and threshing
tools and 1 garden rake and 1 grass scythe 3s.

yard:

> 2 cows and 1 grindstone and 1 stock and winch and 1 cloth and
> barrow and 1 crib and 1.5 loads of brush and poles and wood
> £7 15s.
>
> 5 roods-ploughed harrowed and sown wheat and 4 bushels-
> wheat seed £12s. 6d.
>
> 1 acres ploughed and furrowed beans and 5 bushels-bean seed
> £1 6d.
>
> 2 acres ploughed sowed oats and 8 bushels oat seed £16s.
>
> clover seed 5s.
>
> sum £31 13s. 9d.

The first inventory, for Christopher Gyll, is representative of the very poorest labourers in the sample. He lived in only two rooms, which were almost devoid of goods, and what he possessed was described as rotten or old. William Wright, a poorer eighteenth-century labourer, had more things, including what was described as a small featherbed with curtains and a dripping pan, implying that he roasted meat on occasion. His tools were also listed. The next labourer, Roger Potton, possessed about twenty more things, including what was described as 'a new coverlet bought at the fair', and had a small farm worth over £12. Thomas Foreman had significantly more household goods, including 'an iron rack to keep the child out of the fire', a pepperbox, a brass egg slice, a clock, a small looking-glass, and twenty-four pewter plates, together worth £17 15s, almost twice as much as the median value of all the sample. Finally, John Hutson possessed a standing clock, two looking-glasses and tools which he kept in the same room. However, he had a larger farm than most labourers, as well as a buttery and a washhouse. The statistical possession of these household goods will be dealt with below, and tools, crops and farm animals will be looked at in the next chapter. I've included these full inventories because it is useful to get a sense of what sort of possessions were located in which rooms and in yards.

Rooms

Although inventories cannot tell us how large labourers' houses were they can give us an idea of the minimum number of rooms they possessed, and what they were used for. Increasingly over time appraisers listed the rooms in which the deceased's goods were found, rather than just listing all the goods together. In addition, some inventories also listed outbuildings such as brew houses and barns. Before 1650 about 47 per cent of inventories listed items in rooms, which rose to 64 per cent after the middle of the seventeenth century. The median number

Table 4.2 *Number of inventories listing rooms in labourers'*
inventories sample over time

		Inventories with rooms listed	
Period	Number of inventories	Percentage	
1550–99	119	48	
1600–49	202	47	
1650–99	440	66	
1700–99	207	63	

Table 4.3 *Numbers of rooms in labourers' houses*

Rooms in house	Number of inventories	Percentage
1	62	11
2	146	26
3	157	27
4	113	20
5	55	10
6	25	4
7	4	1
8	5	1
9	1	—
Total	568	100

of rooms in the inventories where they were listed was only three for
the whole period. Over time, however, the average number rose from
2.7 before 1600 to 2.9 between 1600 and 1649, and from 3.2 between
1650 and 1699 to 3.6 in the eighteenth century. It is evident, though,
that in some cases appraisers did not always distinguish all the rooms
in a house if some were empty or only held a few low-value items, but
the number of such cases was small. However, the number of rooms in
labourers' houses was low in comparison to the sample examined by
Overton *et al.* for Kent, where the median number of rooms rose from
six to seven between 1600 and 1750 in Kent and remained constant
at six in Cornwall. Only 6 per cent of labourers' houses had so many
rooms. The number of rooms in these labourers' houses is also smaller
than suggested by Everitt, probably because he included poorer husbandmen in his sample.[32]

[32] Everitt, 'Farm Labourers', in *AHEW*, IV, pp. 413–21, 443.

Table 4.4 shows that the most common room was the hall, which since medieval times was the main room of the house, containing the hearth. Work on vernacular architecture in the sixteenth and seventeenth centuries has demonstrated that the houses of yeomen and wealthier husbandmen grew more complex in this period. First, halls were divided into two rooms with the addition of a chamber or parlour to the existing hall. Brick fireplaces with one chimney were then built into the middle wall to replace the old hall's open hearth. Then a kitchen or/and buttery could be attached with a separate hearth, and bedchambers or stage lofts would be added to second storeys.[33] This also happened in the houses of labourers, as can be seen in Table 4.4, where the percentage of inventories with rooms listed containing a hall declined from 89 to 52 per cent, while the numbers of kitchens, parlours and chambers rose significantly after 1650. In addition a new term, 'best chamber', came into being after this date, indicating a rise in quality and comfort. A best chamber was in essence a furnished bedroom containing a feather bed, often with luxury items such as window curtains or a mirror. For example, John Gibbon of Kent, who died in 1733, also had a table with a punch bowl in the best chamber.

When only one room was listed in the inventory, it was usually termed a hall, parlour or chamber. Sometimes it seems as if the dwelling was probably a room rented in a larger house. However, in other cases, such as that of John Suddabir of Linwood, Lincolnshire, who died in 1590, the dwelling was indeed a simple one-roomed building. He was listed as living in a parlour with three beds, a table with chairs and stools, as well as brass and pewter and a salting trough. But he also had a yard with 2 cows, hogs, hens and a 9-acre farm. No fireplace equipment was listed although he possessed furze for burning, so he probably had only an open hearth of some variety, on which food would be cooked in a brass pot.[34] Table 4.4 also shows that the functions of rooms were fairly clearly delineated between sleeping and cooking throughout the period, with over 85 per cent of parlours and chambers, and only 20 per cent of halls, fewer kitchens and almost no butteries, containing beds and bedding. In contrast cooking equipment could be found in most kitchens and butteries and in 73 per cent of halls as well, although cooking equipment could still be found in significant amounts in all rooms of the house wherever a hearth was present. There was some change over

---

[33] M. W. Barley, 'Rural Housing in England', in *AHEW*, IV, pp. 734–66; V, pp. 658–9; W. G. Hoskins, 'The Rebuilding of Rural England 1570–1640', *Past and Present*, 4 (1953), pp. 44–57; R. Machin, 'The Great Rebuilding: A Reassessment', *Past and Present*, 77 (1977), pp. 33–56.

[34] Lincolnshire Record Office, INV 78.33.

Table 4.4 *Types of rooms in labourers' houses*

Type of room or building	Number	Number of inventories listing rooms, containing certain rooms or buildings – before 1650	Number of inventories listing rooms, containing certain rooms or buildings – after 1650	Rooms containing beds, bedding and linen	Rooms containing cooking equipment[a]	Rooms containing working tools[b]
Total	571	150 (100%)	421 (100%)	20%	73%	26%
Hall	353	133 (89%)	220 (52%)	16%	85%	26%
Kitchen	244	35 (23%)	209 (50%)	6%	88%	17%
Buttery	151	42 (28%)	109 (26%)	89%	26%	9%
Parlour	198	25 (17%)	173 (41%)	86%	29%	18%
Chamber	223	29 (19%)	194 (46%)	100%	27%	0%
Best chamber	15	0	15 (4%)	100%	31%	20%
Bedchamber	35	18 (12%)	17 (4%)	—	—	—
Lodging chamber	29	3 (2%)	26 (6%)	—	—	—
Rooms noted as being on second storey	167	60 (40%)	107 (25%)	—	—	—
Cellar	21	2 (1%)	19 (5%)	—	—	—
Outbuildings	75	24 (16%)	51 (12%)	—	—	29%
Barn	35	2 (1%)	37 (9%)	—	—	—
Brew house/drink house	158	27 (18%)	131 (31%)	—	—	—
Dairy/milk house	11	2 (1%)	9 (2%)	—	—	—
Stable	3	2 (1%)	1 (.5%)	—	—	—
Malt house	13	1 (.5%)	12 (3%)	—	—	—
Wash house	142	15 (10%)	127 (30%)	—	—	11%
Yard						

Notes: [a] Cooking equipment here consists of pots and pans, as well as cutlery, plates and drinking vessels.
[b] Such tools are listed in Table 6.2 below.

time, though, with the number of halls containing beds declining to 11 per cent after 1650, although there was no concurrent decrease in cooking equipment in halls. Interestingly, working tools were found in 20 per cent of bedchambers but were rarely found in higher-status rooms like parlours or best chambers.[35]

The most common forms of labourers' houses consisted of either a hall, kitchen and some other type of chamber on a single floor-plan, or a house with two rooms on the ground floor and one or two rooms on a second storey. While Table 4.4 might seem to suggest that second-storey rooms were decreasing, it was simply becoming less common to designate a chamber as being on the second storey as two-storey dwellings became more numerous. Table 4.5 lists the presence of fire equipment in rooms, such as fire-irons or -dogs, fire-grates, pokers, spits, jacks, tongs, bellows, fire-shovels or trivets. The majority of hearths were equipped for burning wood with fire-irons of some sort. Coal-burning hearths required special design to successfully burn and carry away smoke, and possessed fire-grates to hold the coal.[36] Almost no labourers burned coal before the seventeenth century, but the numbers steadily increased thereafter.

It is surprising that fire equipment is not listed as being present in more houses, but much more surprising that its presence declined markedly in the late seventeenth century, before rising again in the eighteenth century. As we shall see, the value of other goods in labourers' houses went up in this period, so it is odd that they did not spend more on their hearths. One reason for this decline is the inclusion of Cambridgeshire inventories after 1650. In inventories from this county, only 40 per cent of households possessed fire equipment. However, 68 per cent possessed kettles, pots and pans, which would have been of no use without a fire. This suggests again that many households simply placed kettles on open hearths, which, perhaps, was more common in Cambridgeshire because turf from the fens was quite often burned. Comparison with hearth-tax data collected in the late seventeenth century also shows that some houses possessed hearths without such equipment.

---

[35] In comparison, Overton *et al.*'s study of room usage in Kent houses found that cooking equipment was found in 58–64 per cent of halls from 1600 and 1750, while beds were found in only 4 per cent of halls and in only a very small number of kitchens. Overton *et al.*, *Production and Consumption*, pp. 126–9.

[36] John Hatcher, *The History of the British Coal Industry*, I, *Before 1700* (Oxford, 1992), pp. 411–14.

Table 4.5 *Presence of fire equipment in labourers' houses*

Date	Inventories	Houses with one hearth	Houses with two hearths	Houses with three hearths[a]	Coal-burning hearths	Percentage of houses with hearths
1550–99	119	71 (60%)	6 (5%)	1 (1%)	3 (3%)	(66%)
1600–49	202	119 (59%)	15 (7%)	2 (1%)	17 (9%)	(67%)
1650–99	440	193 (44%)	27 (6%)	5 (1%)	42 (10%)	(51%)
1700–99	207	112 (54%)	36 (18%)	7 (4%)	37 (18%)	(76%)

Note: [a] Two houses had four rooms with fire equipment after 1650.

Value

Tables 4.6, 4.7 and 4.8 present information on the change in the value of labourers' inventories over time. Table 4.6 presents an analysis of the total value of everything in each inventory including debts, crops and leases in fifty-year periods, together with information on changes in the upper and lower quartile of inventories, and in the standard deviation. Table 4.7 refines this information by dividing the value of the inventories into household goods, outdoor goods and debts and leases, while Table 4.8 breaks the range of inventory values down from lowest to highest. Ideally, in order to measure consumption, it would be desirable to separate goods such as furniture, bedding or tableware from production equipment like spinning wheels, keelers for making beer or milk vats. Unfortunately, from the point of view of valuation, this is impossible because so much production equipment was found in kitchens and halls, and such items were valued together with furniture and other things we might think of as consumer goods, and are thus impossible to disaggregate. In addition, many items such as pots or barrels could be used for both beer and cheese production as well as for cooking and food preparation, so there is often no clear-cut distinction in any case. Thus the category of household goods includes all items of household furniture, clothing, money, bedding, cooking equipment, tools, brewing, baking and dairy equipment and preserved food such as bacon. The outdoor category includes anything which was generally listed separately from goods inside the household. Such things include crops, land, animals, harvested grains and legumes, wagons, carts, ploughs and their gear, firewood and animal hovels. However, many things found outside such as lumber and wood, tools and ladders were not included because they were also found in houses. In addition, some inventories are damaged on the edge or faded so it is not always possible to total their value. In

Table 4.6 *Total inventory and household values over time (pounds)*

Date	Mean total value	Median total value	Median total value without Cambridgeshire inventories	Median total value without Norfolk inventories	Mean outdoor value	Median outdoor value	Mean household value	Median household value	Mean debts	Mean money
1550–99	14.72	9.4	9.4	10.5	5.79	3.7	5.61	4	2.83	0.09
1550–99 (+ 25% inflation)	18.4	11.75	11.75	13	7.24	4.6	7	5	3.54	0.11
1600–49	21.3	15	15	16.5	6.62	2.75	8.58	5.39	7.2	0.51
percentage increase	*16*	*28*	*28*	*27*	*–9*	*–40*	*23*	*8*	*103*	*364*
1650–99	32.5	21.6	24.3	21.6	7.27	2.5	10.03	7.69	9.1	2
percentage increase	*53*	*44*	*62*	*31*	*10*	*–9*	*17*	*43*	*26*	*292*
1700–99	34	19.33	23.34	19.7	8.8	3	13.12	9.57	9.16	2.9
percentage increase	*5*	*–11*	*–4*	*–9*	*21*	*20*	*31*	*24*	*1*	*45*

Table 4.7 *Quartile inventory values over time*[a]

Period	Total inventories	Mean	Median	Lower quartile	Upper quartile	Max.	Standard deviation
1550–99	114	14.72	9.4	6.5	18.36	143.48	16.64
1550–99 (+ 25% inflation)		18.4	11.75	8.1	23	179.35	
1600–49	181	21.3	15	8.2	29	154.12	21.2
1650–99	429	32.5	21.6	11.37	36.16	542.6	45.45
1700–99	205	34	19.33	12	38.15	445.08	49.33
All	929	28.5	18.05	9.25	33.75	445.08	40.17

Note: [a]The total number of inventories used here is less because in a certain number of cases the total value was impossible to add up as a result of damage to the edges of the inventories.

the end it proved possible to use 810 inventories to compare household value, as broadly defined above, with total value.

In Table 4.6, even when inflation has been taken into account, it can be seen that there was a continual and significant rise in the median value of labourers' possessions between the second half of the sixteenth century and the end of the seventeenth century, rising from £11 15s, adjusted for inflation, to £21 7s by the century's end, and dropping slightly through the eighteenth century.[37] This represents a median rise of 28 per cent in the period 1600–49 compared to 1550–99, and then a further 44 per cent in the period 1650–99. However, for the last period, 1700–1800, the mean rose 5 per cent compared to an 11 per cent decline for the median because the number of unusually wealthy labourers increased in proportion to the rest. This can be seen in the maximum and standard deviation columns in Table 4.7. Table 4.7 also shows the change in total value for the poorest and wealthiest quartiles of the sample. Here we can see that between 1550 and 1649, in contrast to the total sample, the poorest 25 per cent of labourers saw no rise in the real value of their inventoried wealth during these years. Then, between 1650 and 1699, the same group's wealth rose 39 per cent, compared to a rise of 44 per cent for the wealthiest quartile.

Turning back to Table 4.6, looking at just the value of household goods, there was less of a rise between the first and second periods, but

---

[37] There was also a very dramatic rise in value after 1750 to £50 3s but only fifteen inventories have survived from this period, and it may be that since so few inventories survive from these years that these are unusually wealthy labourers, so I have treated the eighteenth century as one period.

then a continual rise throughout the entire period which continued into the eighteenth century. Overall, the rise in the median value of the total stock of household goods was 91 per cent compared to only 65 per cent for the total median inventory value. In contrast to this, the median value of outdoor goods declined by 35 per cent over the whole period, with the greatest decline occurring between 1550 and 1649. Debts owed to the deceased, however, more than doubled between 1550 and 1649, which fits with the rise in credit transactions in these years.[38] Debts rose again in the late seventeenth century but remained stable after that. Unfortunately we have no information on the level of these labourers' indebtedness to others. It stands to reason, however, that if the amounts they were owed by others went up so dramatically, then in all probability so too did what they owed others for the purchase of food, clothing or household goods.[39]

The decline in the value of crops, animals and farm equipment is not surprising, and supports what we know about the decline of the smallholder in the late sixteenth and early seventeenth centuries, as rising costs forced more poorer families to go into debt and sell their land. Given this, then, it is very surprising to discover that the material standard of living of these labourers, as measured in terms of the value of household goods, rose continuously. This is especially surprising in the period between 1550 and 1650, when real wages reached their lowest point, vagrancy and emigration increased and the national poor law was implemented in 1598 to deal with increased poverty. This was also something that Everitt found with his inventories, but it has not subsequently been commented on.[40] It is true that Table 4.7 does show that for the poorest labourers these years actually saw a reduction in their standard of living. But for others there seems to have been opportunity, albeit limited, and in the Restoration all seem to have benefited, some more than others, as the vast increase in the standard deviation indicates. How this was possible will be the topic of the next two chapters.

In Tables 4.8 and 4.7 we can see that 65 per cent of all labourers' inventories, where it is possible to arrive at an accurate total for things listed, were worth less than £25 in total value, and that the median value for all such inventories was £18. These trends can be compared to Overton *et al.*'s larger study. This work looked at changes in total value of samples of inventories from Hertfordshire, Lincolnshire and

---

[38] Muldrew, *Economy of Obligation*.
[39] Credit relations are discussed in more detail on pp. 200–5.
[40] Everitt, 'Farm Labourers', pp. 420–2.

Table 4.8 *Distribution of inventories by total wealth*[a]

Total value of inventory	Number	Percentage
<£2	17	2
£2–5	89	9
£5–10	157	17
£10–15	127	14
£15–20	123	13
£20–5	92	10
<£25	605	65
£25–30	51	6
£30–5	58	6
£35–40	48	5
£40–5	27	3
£45–50	23	2
£25–50	207	22
£50–60	29	3
£60–70	23	3
£70–80	12	1.5
£80–90	10	1
£90–100	13	1.5
£100–200	18	2
>£200	10	1
£50+	115	13
Total	927	100

Note: [a] This figure is not the total number of inventories used, as in some cases it was impossible to add up the total as a result of illegibility or damage to the document.

Worcestershire in addition to Kent and Cornwall, and in all of these counties the average of inventoried wealth was in the order of two to nine times as great as for the sample of labourers here. The mean value of the 2,902 inventories examined by Lorna Weatherill, which included only 26 labourers and servants, was £128, also much higher than that for the sample of labourers.[41] In Kent the median total value of inventories rose from £35 1s 7d between 1600 and 1629 to £75 5s between 1660 and 1689, and then to £99 5s between 1720 and 1749, a rise of 115 and 31 per cent respectively. Although there are no inventories from before 1600 for comparison, it appears that the rise in value of inventories in Kent was considerably greater than for labourers' inventories.

[41] Weatherill, *Consumer Behaviour*, p. 211.

Looking just at consumption goods, which are comparable to what I have termed household goods, the rise in the median value in Kent between the two periods 1600–29 and 1660–89 was 109 per cent, and 50 per cent between 1660 and 1689 and between 1720 and 1749.[42] Thus in the following discussion, it should always be borne in mind that these labourers were considerably poorer than the inventoried population in general. It is true that there was a significant minority of labourers worth more than £50. However, as will be discussed on pp. 200–5 below, almost all of their extra value consisted of debts and money.

Representativeness

Even though these inventoried labourers were poorer than most other inventoried occupations, we still need to try to determine if they were representative of labourers in general. As Ken Sneath discovered, for the parishes of Ramsey and St Ives in Huntingdonshire, while only 12 per cent of the surviving inventories were for labourers, 34 per cent of the fathers listed in the parish registers were recorded as labourers.[43] Thus it could well be the case that the bottom quartile of inventoried labourers were more typical of the labouring population as a whole. On the face of it this would seem plausible if we assume that it would be wealthier labourers who were inventoried. Since the probate process was designed to aid in the partition of an estate, the less one possessed, the less necessary such a process would be. Since so few labourers were inventoried it would make sense to assume that most were generally too poor to bother with the expense and effort of the probate process. This supposition can, however be tested in two ways. The first is through a direct comparison with the hearth taxes of the late seventeenth century. The second is by comparing the number and type of goods found in the labourers' inventories with those found in some pauper inventories analysed by Peter King.

The hearth tax was granted by an Act of 1662 (13 and 14 Car.II, c.10), and continued at intervals until 1689. It was designed to be a progressive tax, charging people with a higher standard of living more, as measured by the number of hearths in their households. As noted above, the increase in rooms and fireplaces was a significant development in the seventeenth century, and the tax was designed to use this increase in standards of living as a measurement of wealth. As a result, the surviving tax lists have often been used as a proxy measure of social

---

[42] In Cornwall, which was a much poorer county, the rise in value between 1600 and 1629 and between 1660 and 1689 was 58 per cent, which is closer to the figure for labourers. Also the accumulation of consumer goods remained flat and their value actually declined in some periods. Overton *et al.*, *Production and Consumption*, p. 140.

[43] Sneath, 'Consumption, Wealth, Indebtedness', pp. 198–200.

Table 4.9 *Labourers' inventories matched with hearth-tax entries for Cambridgeshire, Hampshire and Kent 1664–78*

	Number	Average inventory value	Median inventory value	Median outdoor value	Median household value	Debts owed average[a]	Debts owed number
Exempt	26 (37%)	£20.71	£15.62	£4.15	£7.04	£4.07	8 (36%)
One hearth	31 (44%)	£24.01	£15.76	£2.79	£7.02	£5.77	9 (27%)
Two and three hearths	14 (19%)	£26.83	£23.26			£8.08	9 (64%)
All labourers' inventories from these counties, 1662–90	273	£32.09	£21.04	£4.03	£7.62	£9.39	109 (40%)

Note: [a] Averaged over all inventories including those with no debts listed.

structure. Most importantly here, the tax provided for the poorest members of society to be exempted.[44]

As Table 4.9 shows, it was possible to match exactly half of the labourers' inventories from the counties of Cambridgeshire, Kent and Hampshire from the years between 1664 and 1678 with names in published hearth-tax lists for these counties, together with exemption certificates for Cambridgeshire held in the National Archives. The hearth taxes for both Cambridgeshire and Kent are from 1664, while the Hampshire tax is from 1665.[45] The exemption certificates for Cambridgeshire are from 1672 and were used in addition to the 1664 tax because there only 15.7 per cent of households were exempt compared to 32 per cent for Kent, a level of exemption which was more common in other counties.[46] It has been suggested by one of the editors of the Cambridgeshire hearth-tax volume that the assessors in this early tax simply neglected to list many households too poor to pay the

[44] Duncan Harrington, Sarah Pearson and Susan Rose (eds.), *Kent Hearth Tax Assessment, Lady Day 1664*, British Record Society Hearth Tax Series, 2 (2000), pp. xiii–cxii. The best general introduction is Schurer and Arkell, *Surveying the People*, Part I.
[45] The Cambridgeshire volume also has data from 1662. Nesta Evans and Susan Rose (eds.), *Cambridgeshire Hearth Tax Returns Michaelmas 1664*, British Record Society Hearth Tax Series, 1 (2000), Harrington, Pearson and Rose (eds.), *Kent Hearth Tax Assessment*; Elizabeth Hughes and Philippa White (eds.), *The Hampshire Hearth Tax Assessment 1665*, Hampshire Record Society, 11 (1991).
[46] Pound, *Tudor and Stuart Norwich*, pp. 42–3.

tax.[47] As can be seen from the table, 37 per cent of these labourers were exempt from paying the tax, while only 14 per cent lived in houses with more than one hearth and none had more than three. To put this in perspective, of the total number of households taxed in Kent in 1664, 32 per cent were exempted, 35.5 per cent had one hearth, 42 per cent had two or three hearths and 22 per cent had four or more.[48] As work by Margaret Spufford has demonstrated, householders with one hearth generally left inventories worth less than £30, and here, although the highest value for a labourer in a one-hearth household was £86, most were certainly worth less than £30.[49]

To be exempted under the provisions of the Act for the 1664 tax a household had to be worth less than £1 a year in rental value, and was supposed to have lands, tenements or goods worth less than £10. Alternatively, they were exempted if they were not eligible to pay church or poor rates. In addition they were not supposed to have more than two hearths.[50] In a detailed study comparing hearth-tax exemptions in two Warwickshire parishes with probate material, Tom Arkell found seventeen inventories which could be matched with exempt households. Only three of these were valued at less than £10, while ten fell between £10 and £20 and four were worth more than £20. In addition, a small minority were also discovered to be paying church or poor rates. Finally, by using the manorial survey of Chilvers Coton which listed rental payments of the poor, Arkell was able to show that almost no households paying less than £1 rent per annum were charged for a hearth, thus suggesting that this was the definition most likely to characterise the exempt.[51]

Unfortunately, in our sample of exempted labourers there is no way to examine what rent they paid, although William Harwood, who died in Hampshire in 1683, had a house and garden whose listed worth was £20, so he might have been paying rent of £1–£1 10s on this capital value.[52] Also, eighteen exempted households, or 69 per cent, were worth over £10, and, quite strikingly, the median of their inventoried and

[47] National Archives, Cambridgeshire Hearth Tax Exemptions 1672–3, E179, 84, 440. Evans and Rose (eds.), *Cambridgeshire Hearth Tax*, pp. xxvi, xxxviii–xlii; Harrington, Pearson and Rose (eds.), *Kent Hearth Tax*, pp. li–liii.
[48] Harrington, Pearson and Rose (eds.), *Kent Hearth Tax*, p. lxii.
[49] Although it was not impossible that individuals worth over £100 could reside in a one-hearth house. Evans and Rose (eds.), *Cambridgeshire Hearth Tax*, p. xxxii.
[50] Tom Arkell, 'Printed Instructions for Administering the Hearth Tax', in Schurer and Arkell, *Surveying the People*, pp. 39–40.
[51] Arkell, 'Incidence of Poverty', pp. 32–7.
[52] This was the rate Richard Latham paid in Scarisbrick, Cheshire. Foster, *Seven Households*, p. 145.

household value was almost identical to that of the taxed one-hearth labourers' households. A number of exempted households were worth significantly more than £10. Peter Fenford of Hampshire, for example, died with £50 of money in his possession, although he was living in very basic material circumstances. He possessed a grub-axe, three scythes, two bill-hooks and a chopping axe, which indicates that he was a typical farm labourer. The inventory gives no indication of how he was able to obtain such a large sum, or what he intended to do with it. Perhaps the money was an inheritance. Another labourer from Hampshire, John Brooker, was owed £55 in debts, while Edward Rampton had £22 worth of shovels which he was making for sale. James Williams of Kent was exempted, and when he died in 1670 his inventory was worth £34 19s. He was a fairly well-to-do labourer with over 200 things in his possession, 2 acres of wheat and grass, together with a pig, a cow, a dairy and a washhouse. Thus it is apparent that exemption must have had something to do with considerations other than simply material wealth. There are many such considerations, including being heavily in debt, not listed in the inventory, or being sick and out of work for other reasons. This might well have been the case for Thomas Rodgers, who died in Willingham in Cambridgeshire in 1673 owning only a bed and two chairs although he was owed £350 on forty-seven unpaid bonds, indicating that he had been someone wealthier who had gone broke because he had extended too much credit, and was forced to become a labourer.[53] However, on average, debts owed to the exempt were less than half that for the whole sample during these years, so this could not be common. A large number of dependent children might also be a reason for exemption.

If we look at the median total inventory value of both exempt labourers and those with one hearth, in comparison to all inventories from these counties between 1662 and 1690 as presented in Table 4.9, we can see that the former were indeed worth about 25 per cent less.[54] However, when only the median household value is considered, which is the best measure of material standard of living, the value of exempt and one-hearth households is almost exactly the same as for the whole sample. Those exempted were owed less than one-hearth households, and they had fewer farm goods, but they were not poorer in terms of having fewer material possessions. In addition, 44 per cent of exempt and one-hearth

[53] Muldrew, *Economy of Obligation*, pp. 274ff.
[54] Here the median is the more accurate figure because among these households there were some wealthier labourers such as Peter Fenford, worth £58 13s, who was exempted, and Thomas Doggett, charged on one hearth, whose inventory was valued at £84 19s.

households were valued at £15 or less, compared to 42 per cent in the whole sample from 1662 to 1690, and 70 per cent were valued at £25 or less compared to 65 per cent in the whole 1662–90 sample. So in terms of distribution there is also little difference. This suggests that when it came to exemption, assessors were thinking in terms of lack of access to capital such as crops and livestock or credit rather than a lack of household goods. Thus based on this sample, which is admittedly limited, it would be reasonable to assume that if exempt households were similar to those labourers who were not inventoried, then the latter had fewer farm goods and were more dependent on wages but were not significantly worse off in terms of the things they possessed than the inventoried sample here.

The second way of looking at the representativeness of the sample is to compare these labourers' inventories with the pauper inventories from Essex examined by Peter King. These were lists of goods taken by the overseers of the poor when people first became dependent on the parish, and as King has argued, they are one of the few windows into the household possessions of the poorest people in society who were not homeless. Such lists were taken in expectation that the goods would pass on to the parish, as was required by law when the pauper began to receive relief.[55] Unfortunately the overseers did not value the goods in many cases, but the number and type of goods can still be used for comparison. King used a sample of forty-one pauper inventories from between 1730 and 1799 in which goods were listed. Of these, nineteen exist from 1765 or before, and here the average number of goods in each pauper inventory was sixty-nine. In comparison, the average number of itemised goods in inventories drawn from my labourers' sample for the same time period was seventy-two. Because there were more instances in the larger sample of labourers' inventories where goods such as spoons were not individually counted, this figure should actually be higher for the labourers' sample, but since the great majority of items with a similar value were itemised, the difference would not be great. Table 4.10 compares the presence of individual items of unusually high value in the pauper inventories with labourers' inventories from the same period and, surprisingly, in all cases apart from chests of drawers, the paupers in King's sample were more likely to own such an item than were the labourers. If we look at a larger sample of labourers' inventories going back to 1700 the difference becomes even

[55] Peter King, 'Pauper Inventories and the Material Lives of the Poor in the Eighteenth and Nineteenth Centuries', in Tim Hitchcock, Peter King and Pamela Sharpe (eds.), *Chronicling Poverty: The Voices and Strategies of the English Poor, 1640–1840*

Table 4.10 *Presence of consumption goods in pauper inventories compared to labourers' inventories 1700–1800 (percentage)*

	Essex pauper inventories 1730–99 (41)	Labourers' inventories sample 1730–99 (40)	Labourers' inventories sample 1700–99 (207)
Looking-glasses	27	15	15
Clocks/watches	20	22	8
Candlesticks	49	35	21
Chests of drawers	32	38	24
Linen	68	45	56

more pronounced. It is possible that more of the paupers went on relief towards the end of their lives as they became more infirm, and therefore might have had the opportunity to accumulate more goods.[56] Overall, though, this, together with the hearth-tax evidence, suggests that the inventory sample here is broadly representative of the labouring population as a whole. There is no similar source to test the earlier inventories, but there is no reason to suspect that the motivation for inventorying someone was different in 1600 from what it was later.

Consumption

If we can reasonably assume that the inventory sample is representative of the working labouring population, then it seems likely that, if the value of household goods was rising over time, labourers were indeed spending more on consumer items, especially after the Restoration, when inflation ceased and the earning power of households increased for the first time in a century. The total number of things labourers possessed which were itemised in the inventories is given in Table 4.11, which lists the average number of goods in the inventories which were counted, together with the percentage of items in the inventory not counted, for both household goods and all goods listed.[57] This means that a listing of four napkins was counted, but a listing such as simply 'napkins' or 'brewing vessels' or 'things' was not. Chairs and tables, for

---

(Basingstoke, 1997), pp. 157–60. I would like to thank Thomas Sokoll and Peter King for letting me examine the original transcripts of these inventories.

[56] King, 'Pauper Inventories', pp. 166–72.

[57] This also includes such things as apparel, money and debts, which were rarely counted.

Table 4.11 *Itemised household goods per inventory*

Period	Average number of itemised household goods per inventory	Percent of total household goods not itemised	Average number of itemised goods per inventory	Percent of total goods not itemised
1550–99	67	19	88	23
1600–49	69	18	87	22
1650–99	51	25	63	31
1700–99	61	22	74	28
1550–1800	60		70	

instance, were itemised on 95 per cent of the occasions where they were present in an inventory. Linen, which was more likely simply to be listed in bulk, was still itemised in 82 per cent of cases. The most common goods not to be itemised were clothes, money and simply 'things' and its synonyms. Here we can see that the numbers of both household and total goods remained constant until the mid-century and then appear to have fallen in the period when the value of the inventories increased the most. The numbers then went up again in the eighteenth century. However, the percentage of goods not itemised jumped by 10 per cent at the same time, so it is likely that many small items previously counted were now not being itemised. Thus, it is likely, although impossible to prove, that the number of goods at least remained steady, and might have gone up in the eighteenth century.

In Table 4.12 I have examined the presence of certain categories of goods over time by fifty-year periods. There are certain things which the majority of inventories recorded such as beds, tables, linen, cooking equipment, tableware, and so on. For instance, Table 4.13 shows that most households possessed tableware such as dishes, plates, tankards and earthenware to drink out of, eat off and serve with, in quite large quantities. When something like a bed, for instance, is not mentioned, it is likely that this was an instance of someone old living with their children or renting a room from someone. But here I have chosen goods which labourers possessed where we would be most likely to see some sort of change in consumption patterns. Silver and gold items have not been included because so few labourers possessed any. One item, though, which was possessed by surprisingly high numbers of labourers from the very beginning of our period, was pewter. Already by the late sixteenth century three-quarters of labourers owned pewter goods, and this number remained quite constant throughout the period. For

Table 4.12 Possession of household goods by time period (percentage)

Period	Inventories	Beds	Feather beds	Pillows	Bed hangings	Linen	Pewter	Candlesticks	Stools	Chairs
1550–99	119	80	29	61	25	80	76	56	41	41
1600–49	201	91	35	62	31	79	78	43	50	61
1650–99	445	88	40	45	37	68	76	15	37	66
1700–99	207	84	34	33	41	56	71	20	33	71
All	972	87	37	47	35	66	73	34	42	64

Period	Inventories	Cupboards	Chests of drawers	Curtains	Looking-glasses	Clocks	Knives	Pewter dishes	Wooden dishes	Earthenware
1550–99	119	54	0	2	0	3	8	43	29	9
1600–49	201	61	1	3	1	1	7	35	29	13
1650–99	445	62	4	19	5	1	1	44	12	15
1700–99	207	38	23	20	14	6	5	57	9	28
(1750–99)	(15)	(33)	(33)	(20)	(33)	(40)	(20)	(45)	(0)	(33)
All	972	55	12	13	11	10	8	44	16	20

Table 4.13 *Ownership of tableware over time*

Period	Total	Percentage	Average number per inventory with tableware	Average number divided by all inventories
1550–99	119	87	19.4	14.3
1600–49	201	88	18.7	13.1
1650–99	445	81	13.5	7.7
1700–49	207	77	17.2	11.3
All	972	83	17.2	11.6

most things, though, Table 4.12 shows that labourers were obtaining more elaborate household goods over time. The ownership of chairs, for example, went up from 41 per cent to over 70 per cent by the eighteenth century. Very interestingly, we can see an obvious increase in the aesthetic quality of tableware as the itemisation of wooden dishes declined to almost nothing after 1700, while the number of labourers owning pewter dishes, and increasingly earthenware, went up. In the eighteenth century, the possession of chests of drawers, curtains and mirrors also became much more common, even if these items were owned only by a minority of individuals. Finally, although it is a very small sample compared to the other periods, the fifteen inventories from after 1750 show a large increase in the numbers of mirrors, clocks and knives, which are the classic items identified by Weatherill and Overton *et al.* as new luxury consumer goods.

However, the percentage of labourers with feather beds appears to have increased from 29 per cent in the first period to 40 per cent by 1700 and then decreased in the eighteenth century, which would appear to contradict a rise in living standards. A feather bed was what today would be thought of as a mattress filled with anything from 50 to 70 lb of feathers. It was one of the items identified by William Harrison in the sixteenth century as a marker of increased living standards among the yeomanry and middling sorts of his time, and it would be strange if fewer labourers possessed them while their tableware was increasing in quality.[58] In addition, the number of inventories mentioning pillows seems to go down even more precipitously. However, if we look at the number of labourers with beds listed in their inventories, we see that it remained at 85 per cent after 1700, and where the price of bedding is listed (Table 4.14), this also went up. Thus it is unlikely that fewer

[58] Harrison, *Description*, pp. 201–2.

Table 4.14 *Ownership of linen over time*

Period	Total	Percentage listing linen	Number of items per inventory with linen	Number of items divided by all inventories
1550–99	119	80	8.0	5.9
1600–49	201	79	9.3	6.6
1650–99	445	68	10.0	5.2
1700–49	207	56	14.7	5.5
All	972	71	10.5	5.8

labourers had feather beds or pillows after 1700. Moreover, with bed hangings, which were curtains on the side of a bed to add warmth as well as style, and which were fairly costly and more likely to be listed separately, ownership increased continuously from 25 per cent to 41 per cent over the whole period. What was actually occurring here was that appraisers were simply listing bedding more generically, as in 'a bed with bedding' or 'a furnished bed' rather than listing a bedstead with a feather bed, pillows, blankets, bed hangings, and so forth. The percentage of labourers owning feather beds was almost certainly much greater than these figures suggest, and this example shows that we need to be very careful when interpreting how information is presented in the inventories, since appraisers could lump a collection of things under one generic heading.

Linen might well also have been subsumed under such an entry, as in the case of John Gilby of Great Shelford, Cambridgeshire, who died in 1703. No linen was listed in his inventory, but the appraisers recorded '1 feather bed, 1 bolster, 2 pillows, 1 furnished bedstead with other goods' valued at £2 12s 6d. Obviously he would have needed linen for his bed, and it was most likely included among the 'other goods', given the relatively high value of this line in the inventory. Table 4.11 gives the percentage of goods listed which were not itemised, and thus not counted. As can be seen, the percentage of such listings increased after 1650, while the total number of goods went down. The itemising of linen, for instance, declined to 75 per cent. Table 4.14 looks just at inventories where linen was itemised, and here we can see that the number of pieces of linen almost doubled over the whole period.

The same process was undoubtedly occurring with candlesticks. At the beginning of our period most were made out of pewter and were high-quality display items. But as many more came to be made out of tin and iron in the eighteenth century, thanks to advances in metalworking,

Table 4.15 *Presence of roasting equipment over time*

Period	Total	Percentage listing roasting equipment	Number of items per inventory with roasting equipment	Number of items divided by all inventories
1550–99	119	49	2.7	2.5
1600–49	201	46	2.5	2.2
1650–99	445	33	2.2	1.2
1700–49	207	20	2.5	1.6
All	972	37	2.5	1.9

these items became cheaper and were simply listed under the heading 'things'.[59] Most inventories had unspecific listings for generally very small values of 'other things', 'hustlements', 'lumber' or 'other old trash'. In the later sixteenth century such terms could be found in 67 per cent of the inventories and were used with a frequency of 0.74 times per inventory. By the first half of the eighteenth century they were found in 80 per cent of inventories and used with a frequency of 1.55 times per inventory. The average value of such listings went up from 5s in the first period to 16s 5d by the eighteenth century. However, some things with a relatively high value undoubtedly did decline, such as cupboards listed in Table 4.12 or roasting equipment listed in Table 4.15. Cupboards might have declined as chests of drawers became more common, and the decline of roasting equipment reflected the changes in cooking practices discussed above in chapter 2.

If we compare this information to the set of wealthier inventories studied by Overton *et al.* we can see that some patterns of ownership are not dissimilar. In both Kent and Cornwall the ownership of chests of drawers increased as cupboards went out of fashion, although interestingly the labourers here possessed more chests than those in the Cornish sample of inventories. The percentage of feather beds owned by labourers was smaller than those possessed in Kent, but greater again than Cornish ownership. The number of pieces of tableware was similar, as was the percentage of knives owned. The Kentish sample owed about 10 per cent more pewter, and many more fire-jacks, although labourers had more skillets in the early seventeenth century. However, when we look at the classic luxury goods of the eighteenth-century 'consumer revolution', mirrors, clocks and window curtains, many more of the inventories from the Kentish sample list such things after 1690 than

---

[59] Maxine Berg, *Luxury and Pleasure in Eighteenth-Century Britain* (Oxford, 2005), ch. 5.

are found in labourers' inventories. Other items like books, which were common in Kent, were only possessed by thirty-four labourers; or pictures, which only twelve labourers had.[60] Although, again, the labourers had more of such goods than were found in Cornwall. This was also the case with the number of pieces of linen owned. While inventories from Kent listed a median number of twenty-eight pieces in the early sixteenth century this had risen to fifty by 1750, much more than what is listed in Table 4.14. Again, labourers were better off than the Cornish sample, who possessed only two to four pieces. This indicates that geography could be more important than occupation in determining relative poverty. All of the labourers in our sample came from more prosperous counties than Cornwall, and presumably Cornish labourers would have been even poorer.

Although it is difficult to identify the value of many individual items because they were most usually valued together with a variety of other items on one line, there are certain goods which were often listed separately. These are analysed in Table 4.16, where prices of individual items can be traced over time. This table shows that between the second half of the sixteenth century and the first half of the seventeenth the prices of linen, chairs, stools, tables and ironware rose in line with inflation of industrial products of about 25 per cent.[61] The price of labourers' apparel, where it was itemised, also rose in line with inflation of textile products of 55 per cent. Labourers, however, were certainly improving the quality of their bedding, as its value doubled between 1550 and 1650. Although the sample size is small, the value of labourers' pewter also went up.

More strikingly, the value of almost all these selected goods also went up after the mid-century. This is in contrast to the prices of individual items for a sample of 200,000 unit valuations of different goods in inventories drawn from Hertfordshire, Lincolnshire and Worcestershire from between 1550 and 1750 analysed by Mark Overton.[62] After 1650 the prices of the household goods looked at by Overton all fell. The price of pewter in Overton's sample fell by 38 per cent between 1650 and 1750, while the price of cupboards fell by about 50 per cent in Lincolnshire, and the price of linen also declined. Food prices also fell during this period, although not so dramatically. But industrial money

[60] Overton et al., Production and Consumption, pp. 91, 99, 109, 111. The percentages for Lorna Weatherill's national sample are similar to the Kent sample in Overton et al.; Weatherill, Consumer Behaviour, pp. 26ff.

[61] Clay, Economic Expansion, I, p. 49.

[62] Mark Overton, 'Prices from Probate Inventories', in Tom Arkell, Nesta Evans, and Nigel Goose (eds.), Until Death do us Part: Understanding and Interpreting the Probate Records of Early Modern England (Hertfordshire, 2000), pp. 120–43, 131, 140.

Table 4.16 *Average value per item*

Items	1550–99			1600–49				1650–1800			
	Number of instances	Price (£)		Number of instances	Price (£)	Percentage increase after 1600		Number of instances	Price (£)	Percentage increase after 1650	Total percentage increase
Linen	57	0.113		74	0.136	20		105	0.208	53	84
Chairs, stools, and tables	23	0.051		64	0.058	14		147	0.083	43	63
Bedding[a]	94	0.146		162	0.316	116		266	0.569	80	290
Pots, pans and ironware[b]	56	0.096		104	0.125	30		193	0.186	49	94
Pewter	8	0.024		19	0.042	75		18	0.097	131	304
Clothing	44	0.121		18	0.186	54		45	0.221	19	83

Notes: [a] Includes all bedding apart from linen such as hangings, covers, mattresses, bed stands, etc.
[b] Also includes skillets and fire irons.

Table 4.17 *Incidence of the use of adjectives to describe certain goods (percentages)*

Period	Inventories	'good'	'best'	'new'	'old'	'bad'	'joined'	'brass'	'iron'	'tin'
1550–99	119	2	4	5	66	5	13	50	19	2
1600–49	202	1	0	1	71	1	18	56	31	1
1650–99	444	3	0	3	52	1	23	45	45	4
1700–99	207	6	1	5	49	5	17	42	38	8
All	972	2	1	4	65	2	22	48	36	7

wages rose in line with agricultural wages, which implies that manufacturing costs must have declined.[63]

Although Hertfordshire and Worcestershire are different counties from those under consideration here, price trends of industrial goods (not including London) do not seem to have varied geographically as much as grain prices. The trends between Overton's three counties moved in broadly similar directions, so there is no reason to think price trends would have been different for goods in areas where the labourers resided. The only category which did not rise significantly after the mid-century was clothing. But clothing was very rarely itemised, and when it was, only the deceased's personal clothing was listed, not his wife's or children's. John Styles has looked at a much wider range of sources and has concluded that, indeed, labourers were purchasing more clothes in the eighteenth century.[64]

What this implies is that, instead of buying more things, labourers were instead buying better-quality items. This can be seen especially in the case of pewter, where the number of pieces remained about the same, but the value, and also the weight, when it was given, went up. More labourers also possessed pewter-cases to keep their pewter in. In addition, people were also replacing older, less expensive things like wooden tableware with new, more expensive goods. In Table 4.17 the adjective 'old', which was by far the most common description of labourers' goods, declined in usage over time, falling from being found in 66 per cent of inventories before 1600 to 49 per cent after 1700. Older goods probably came to be termed 'old lumber' or 'things' used in work spaces and not considered valuable enough to itemise anymore.

Wealthy labourers, debts and money

As we saw in Table 4.8, no fewer than 115 (13 per cent) of labourers' inventories were worth over £50, and 28 (3 per cent) were worth over

[63] Levine and Wrightson, *Industrial Society*, p. 245.
[64] Styles, *Dress of the People*, ch. 2.

£100. A small number of these were farming on a larger scale than most labourers. Some were more like husbandmen, such as Daniel Chadwell, who died in Kent in 1647 and whose possessions were worth £154. He possessed four cows, ten sheep, three hogs and £10 worth of wheat and hay and had household goods worth £28 2s. In addition he was owed £80.[65] But others were like Edward Lucas, who died in Hampshire in 1701 with crops, animals and farm equipment worth £98 9s. He had 25 acres under crop, as well as old horses, two ploughs, six harrows and a cart. However, his household goods were scanty and only worth £2 18s 4d. He had no money or credit listed, and his sheets were described as old and ragged.[66] He undoubtedly worked as a carter and ploughed for other people, which is why he was termed a labourer, but for whatever reason he was not successful as a farmer.[67] In total there were thirty-four inventories with an outdoor value of between £30 and £99, with a mean value of £50 8s and a median value of £47 10s. Many of them did live better than most labourers, as the median value of their household goods was £11 6s 10d, almost double the median of £6 12s 8d for the entire sample. There were a further eighty-eight inventories with a total mean outdoor value of between £15 and £30, with a median value of £20 0s 7d. Here the median value of their household goods was £9 19s. Thus most labourers who had larger farms were also able to afford more household goods than other labourers, but certainly not as much as the total sample of Kent inventories, where after 1660 the mean value of household goods was above £45 and the median above £25.[68]

However, the wealthiest labourers were not those more involved in farming, but individuals who had a lot of debts owing to them, or who possessed large amounts of money. There were 107 inventories of labourers who died being owed between £20 and £420, with 22 of these being owed £70 or more. The 27 labourers with inventories valued at £100 or more were owed on average £104 16s, and 6 of them possessed £826 in money. Some of these large debts might have been for legacies or portions. There were 153 debts listed as bills, bonds or other forms of written specialties, or 20 per cent of all the debts listed. Others were for wages and work, but most were simply listed as 'good', 'bad' or 'desperate' debts. Their household goods were also worth considerably more than the sample as a whole, with a mean value of £23

[65] CKS, prc11.14.155(2).   [66] HRO, 1701ad22.

[67] As Peter Bowden has argued, it was difficult to make a profit on such small farms. Peter Bowden, 'Agricultural Prices, Farm Profits, and Rents', in *AHEW*, IV, pp. 650–9.

[68] Overton *et al.*, *Production and Consumption*, p. 140.

Table 4.18 *Portsmouth dock workers' inventories*

	Mean	Median
Number	23	23
Number of goods	(12) 35	27
Animals and crops	£2 8s	0
Household goods	£12 18s	£7
Money	£16 8s	0
Debts	£41 2s	£20 3s
Bonds	£12 18s	
Desperate debts	0	0
Leases	0	0
Total inventories	£72 16s	£30 16s

and a median of £22 14s. This median is close to that of the Kent inventories, and although we do not know the reason for the debts owed to these labourers, they were assets which they could use to build a better standard of living.

As mentioned previously, among these wealthier labourers there were also twenty-three dockworkers who lived around Portsmouth and who were also owed a very large amount of money; their debts are listed in Table 4.18. Although these were not agricultural labourers it is interesting to examine them briefly for comparison.[69] Of these twenty-three individuals, twenty-two of their inventories were made between 1663 and 1711, and they were all owed a great deal of debts, largely in unpaid wages from the dockyard. Arrears of pay in the navy were notoriously common at this time.[70] A good example is Thomas Wild from Portsea, who possessed £74 in cash and was owed £36 on bond and £70 in wages. He was quite well dressed, with clothes worth £4, but he owned only what was described as an old bed, a chest and a few pots (sixteen things). The wages he was due were equal to about four years' pay at building workers' rates, and to put this in perspective might be worth almost £200,000 in contemporary terms. In addition, although many dockworkers only had a chest, overall they had household goods worth £12 18s on average. This was better than most labourers, but still much less than their total inventoried wealth would suggest.

Turning to look generally at debts, the amount of money owing to all labourers went up over time, as we saw in Table 4.7, and it jumped

[69] I have tested to see if these inventories added any bias into the sample, and they did not.

[70] Rodger, *Wooden World*, pp. 124–37.

Table 4.19 *Labourers' accounts from the national probate account database, 1600–1710*[a]

	All 1600–1799		1600–59		1660–1710	
	Avg.	Med.	Avg.	Med.	Avg.	Med.
Number	134	134	73	73	41	41
Number of debts owed by deceased	4.5	—	4	—	4.7	—
Charge	£36 4s	£25 14s	£35 13s	£27 5s	£37 5s	£29 16s
Balance	£20 12s	£11 4s	£22 4s	£16 9s	£20 14s	£13
Amount of debt owed by deceased	£15 12s (43% of charge)	£14 11s (57% of charge)	£13 10s (38% of charge)	£10 16s (40% of charge)	£16 11s (44% of charge)	£16 16s (56% of charge)

Note: [a] This information was taken from a national database of 28,989 probate accounts surviving from before 1710 collected by Professor Peter Spufford. I would like to thank Professor Spufford and Rosemary Rod for help using this database. The database is discussed in Peter Spufford, Matthew Brett and Amy Louise Erickson (eds.), *Guide to the Probate Accounts of England and Wales* (London, 1999).

an incredible 112 per cent in the early seventeenth century. This was undoubtedly caused by the general expansion of credit in this period, when labourers were owed more for wages and goods sold over longer periods of time.[71] Unfortunately, it is impossible to know how much labourers themselves owed others from these inventories. These were only listed in twenty-six inventories and were generally less than what labourers were owed. More information is contained in probate accounts, and 143 such documents survive for labourers from all over the country between 1600 and 1710. Probate accounts were a more advanced stage in the probate process, and here any debts owed by the deceased together with funeral costs and any costs of orphaned children were subtracted from the assets listed in the inventories.[72] These are listed in Table 4.19. In common with other estates for which probate accounts survive the value of the gross movable assets was generally more than average.[73] Here the median value of the deceased inventories, called a

[71] Muldrew, *Economy of Obligation*, pp. 25–6, ch. 4.
[72] Amy Louise Erickson, 'An Introduction to Probate Accounts', in G. H. Martin and Peter Spufford (eds.), *The Records of the Nation* (London, 1990), pp. 273–86.
[73] This is discussed in Muldrew, *Economy of Obligation*, pp. 103–7.

charge, was £25 14s. In these cases the debts owed were greater than what the labourers owed in the labourers' inventory sample used here, but since it was more likely for an account to be made if there were more debts owing we cannot simply assume from this that labourers were terribly indebted.[74] For instance, if we were to take just labourers whose total inventoried value was above £12, their median value was £26, which is comparable to the probate account sample in Table 4.19. If we measure the debts owed to these labourers, the average is £27 7s, and the median £14 2s. This median figure is similar to the median of debts owed in Table 4.19, and if the probate account sample is representative of debts labourers themselves owed others, this indicates that labourers at this level of prosperity were not particularly indebted. However, the much higher average of £27 7s owed to labourers in their inventories when compared to the average of £15 12s owed by them in the account sample, in contrast to the median (£14 2s), indicates that the wealthiest among them were actually accumulating significant savings, as it is unlikely that they would have been inheriting more from the generation that went through the terrible years of the 1590s. Moreover, lending on bond, which had been uncommon before 1600, rose rapidly afterwards. Before 1599 only 5 labourers possessed bonds, but 173 had bonds listed in their inventories after this date, 55 of which were from before 1650. Unfortunately, we cannot know if poorer labourers than this were more heavily indebted to others. What this does show is that labourers were fully integrated into credit networks.

Finally, eighty-six labourers' inventories (9 per cent) had money listed separately from apparel, the mean amounts of which are listed in Table 4.7. Before 1600 the mean was less than 2s, rising to 11s from 1600 to 1650.[75] After 1650 the mean amount of money listed separately rose significantly. This was the result of a very small proportion of labourers possessing unusually large amounts. Almost all of this rise can be accounted for by only fourteen labourers who possessed over £20 in cash each, whereas only one labourer possessed over £20 before 1650. Together these fourteen labourers possessed £1,169, or an average of £83 10s each. Labourers who possessed this much cash were also owed more; an average of £37 16s. Here, unlike labourers who were

---

[74] Ian Mortimer, 'Why Were Probate Accounts Made? Methodological Issues Surrounding the Historical use of Administrators' and Executors' Accounts', *Archives*, 31 (2006), pp. 2–17.

[75] Money was much more often listed together with apparel. In 271 inventories where this was the case, the average value of both together was £2.65. If the average value of apparel, where it was listed separately, is subtracted from this, the average amount of money possessed here was in the order of 11s 5d.

owed a lot of debts, we do not see their wealth leading to a substantial increase in the possession of household goods. Only one had any farm goods, and their median household value was just £7 14s 10d, so perhaps they were living partially on money lent out of legacies. Overall the financial wealth of these labourers was not reflected in more material household possessions, as there were only a small handful of inventoried labourers like John Hudson of Littleborne in Kent, who died in 1721 with over 300 things in his possession worth £31.[76]

Thus although this evidence does support an increase in consumption, it should not be overestimated. The number of things labourers owned hardly went up at all over the whole period covered here, and was small in comparison to the hundreds of goods owned by the middling sort. Already by 1580, in a sample of inventories from Southampton, the average number of household goods was 310. In Lincolnshire it was 175 by 1600, and in the parish of Chesterfield it was 212.[77] Labourers owned few or none of the common luxury items of wealthier tradesmen and artisans such as gold and silver tableware, Turkish carpets, tapestries, velvet cushions, virginals and imported carved furniture from Flanders and Italy. Their increase in consumption is best described as a modest trading up from households containing many things described as old, and possibly second-hand, to similar things of greater value. Apart from a minority in the eighteenth century who bought mirrors and clocks, their motivation was not the acquisition of new consumer goods, but simply a more comfortable standard of living.

Finally, Table 4.20 looks at a sample of the dates at which labourers were inventoried after death compared to the percentage of deaths by month in the national sample of parish registers taken from Wrigley and Schofield's *Population History of England*.[78] Of course parish registers and inventories are not directly compatible since deaths were recorded in parish registers almost immediately. Inventories were supposed to be taken soon after the death of the deceased, but no research has been done on how long this actually was in practice. But even with a lag of a week or two, the seasonal pattern would be roughly the same. As Wrigley and Schofield have shown there was a greater likelihood over the entire population of dying in the late winter and spring from winter respiratory diseases, but we can see that for labourers there was a much greater possibility of dying from these diseases than for the general population in the spring before the Restoration. Possibly this was due to lower nutrition in old age or during years of high prices. It

[76] CKS, prc11.76.38.   [77] Muldrew, *Economy of Obligation*, pp. 25–6.
[78] Wrigley and Schofield, *Population History*, pp. 293–8.

Table 4.20 *Inventory dates compared to national deaths by month of the year (percentages)*

Month of inventory	Month inventory taken, 1550–1660	Month inventory taken, 1661–1799	Wrigley and Schofield parish registers, 1550–1799
January	9	10	9
February	8	9	9
March	15	10	10
April	13	12	10
May	11	10	8
June	9	9	7
July	6	6	7
August	3	5	7
September	5	7	8
October	9	6	8
November	3	9	8
December	7	7	8
Total number of inventories with dates	281	612	—

might also have been the result of poorer housing offering less protection from the cold. However, after this date a definite improvement is evident, with deaths during March to May falling from 39 per cent to 32 per cent, only 4 per cent more than the population as a whole, which suggests a better standard of living.[79]

Thus after 1650, labourers in general were certainly benefiting from a more comfortable material standard of living. However, at this level of ownership it is difficult to say that they were motivated to purchase new consumer items because of the aesthetic or novelty appeal of the items themselves. This certainly might have been the case in individual instances, but the descriptive terms applied by appraisers are simply too limited to get any sense of this. The general sense one gets from the goods in the inventories is a move to purchase better-quality items when they could be afforded.

The evidence is also mixed on the degree to which goods that were purchased on the market were increasing. As Table 4.12 showed, the ownership of goods such as pewter, candlesticks, brass and ironware, as well as furniture such as beds and cupboards, which would have been purchased from specialist artisans, was already high by the second half of the sixteenth century. It is impossible to tell where such goods

---

[79] Ibid.

were manufactured, but port books do list cargoes of furniture and kitchenware being shipped from London to ports such as King's Lynn in substantial quantities before 1650.[80] What we can see is a growing tendency to purchase more specialised items such as mirrors, clocks or joined furniture, although in small numbers. The number of inventories containing sheets, towels and napkins described as being made out of hemp rather than flax also declined from 10 per cent to only 1 per cent over the period, while the number of inventories with evidence of hemp growing declined from 21 per cent before 1650 to 6 per cent after that date. This means that less clothing was being manufactured at home.[81] Since most flaxen linen was imported before the eighteenth century this represents more purchases on the market. The possession of earthenware increased as well, which was more likely to have been shipped from areas of specialised pottery manufacture such as Staffordshire.[82] Also, as we saw in the case of Richard Latham, more imported sugar and spices were consumed in the eighteenth century. From the perspective of market sophistication, therefore, more specialised goods were available at the local shop which had moved considerable distances from their point of production and manufacture, but this was a process which had already begun in the late sixteenth century.[83]

This could still be called an 'industrious revolution' from the point of view of work. However, it was one which was initially motivated not by consumer desire but consumer survival in the period before 1650, when food prices were going up more than wages; when rents were going up; when access to commons was falling; and when labourers' own farming activities were declining. Since the rise in quality began during this period, rather than after 1650, it is hard to see how the money, or credit, to purchase these better-quality goods could have been raised if the labourers' who owned them were not working more. What the nature of this work was will now be the subject of the last three chapters of the book.

---

[80] National Archives, E190, 440/3, 441, King's Lynn Port Books, 1684–86; Williams, *Maritime Trade*, pp. 179–80.
[81] Styles, *Dress of the People*, ch. 8.
[82] Lorna Weatherill, *The Pottery Trade and North Staffordshire 1660–1760* (Manchester, 1971), ch. 6.
[83] Muldrew, *Economy of Obligation*, chs. 1–2.

5   Work and household earnings

Memorandum that every one of these [servants] spent me in meat and drinke ... one with another another xii l. a piece & a little above. Soe that I judge it were good (in such deare years) to keep as few servantes as a man possibly can, by any meannes convenient. To effect which I know no other meannes, but by putting forth a mans land to tillage, or at a rent, or else keeping them [the servants] at borde wages.[1]

We have seen that labourers had to consume a lot of calories to do their work, and also that English agriculture generally supplied enough food in most years to maintain this consumption. In addition to this, most families managed to increase the value of their household goods as the price of food rose in the early seventeenth century. We now need to consider how labouring families afforded to feed themselves at such levels on the wages labourers were paid, especially when there was such a marked preference for foods which were more expensive per calorie such as wheaten bread, beer and meat. This is especially problematic for the period from 1550 to 1650, when nominal wages lagged significantly behind rising food prices.

As we saw in chapter 1, the most important work on estimating changes in real wages has been done by Phelps Brown and Hopkins and more recently by Gregory Clark. Clark has looked at a much larger sample of farm labourers' wages from all over England, in contrast to Phelps Brown and Hopkins, who largely based their series on building labourers' wages from the south of England.[2] The main differences produced by Clark's data set in comparison to Phelps Brown and Hopkins with respect to how real wages changed over time are that the fall in real wages from the mid-fifteenth century to 1600 was only of a degree of about 50 per cent rather than 60 per cent, and, more surprisingly, that real wages rose much less over the course of the

---

[1] Fussell (ed.), *Robert Loder's Farm Accounts*, p. 90.
[2] Phelps Brown and Hopkins, 'Seven Centuries', pp. 13–57; Clark, 'Long March', pp. 97–135; Clark, 'Farm Wages', pp. 477–505.

Table 5.1 *Change in day wage rates over time as estimated by Phelps Brown and Hopkins, and Gregory Clark*

| Dates | Wages in pence per day | |
	Phelps Brown and Hopkins	Clark
1550–80	6–8	6.5–7.5
1580–1626	8	7.5–8.8
1639–93	12	8.0–10.4
1701–30	14–15	11.2–10.2
1730–73	16	10.2–11.4
1776–98	19–22	11.4–14.5

Sources: Clark, 'Long March', pp. 131–4; Phelps Brown and Hopkins, 'Seven Centuries', pp. 28–31.

early eighteenth century.[3] The main reason for the latter difference is that in Clark's sample, nominal farm wages from 1660 to 1760 were significantly lower than those used by Phelps Brown and Hopkins. Clark used examples of winter wages, when they were at their lowest, from numerous farm accounts drawn from all over England, as well as from Arthur Young's various tours. He used winter wages as a constant measure, and he also chose examples which were likely to be for wages without board.[4]

Table 5.1 shows the differences between Phelps Brown and Hopkins's and Clark's measurements of changes in nominal money wages over time. Clark's figures are precise averages of many different samples. In reality, wages were paid in round figures of pence per day or shillings and pence per week, and Phelps Brown and Hopkins have given the most common round figures. Of the two series Clark's contains much more data drawn from more geographically diverse sources. But when using an average we must remember that wages paid could vary between villages only miles apart. In Howden, southeast Yorkshire, winter wages were 1s a day in the 1760s, whereas in Risby, just on the other side of the Ouse, they were 7s a week or 16.8d a day, while 30 miles further east on the coast at Holderness they were as much as 8s 6d a week or 20.4d a day. According to Young these higher wages were due to additional need for labour making drains and enclosures as well

---

[3] Clark, 'Long March', pp. 131–4; Phelps Brown and Hopkins, 'Seven Centuries', pp. 28–31.
[4] Clark, 'Farm Wages', pp. 482–3.

as building turnpike roads.[5] Thus the experience of labouring families could be significantly different depending on where they lived.

Another problem with the measurement of real wages over time is that it requires a constant basket of consumables to compare to the money wage. But as we have seen, in reality what the poor ate varied considerably according to time and place. For instance, in the north and in Cornwall oats formed a much higher percentage of the diet than elsewhere, and oats, as we saw, were much cheaper per calorie than wheat.[6] As a result money wages were often considerably lower in the north, especially in the early eighteenth century.[7] This is the main reason why Clark's average nominal wages are lower for the eighteenth century, but when calculating his real wage series a different northern oat-based diet was not used.[8] Similarly beer formed a much higher percentage of labourers' diets than Clark's estimate of 4.7 per cent and barley was also 56 per cent the cost of wheat in the same period.[9]

An even more serious problem is that in most farm accounts it is usually impossible to tell what sort of food perquisites might have been given in addition to the money wage. Monetary accounts of wages were generally kept in wage or general disbursement books. One needs to look at kitchen accounts to see if produce from the farm is being made into bread, meat and beer in enough quantities to feed labourers, as we saw in chapter 2. This means that using farm wages as a measure of real wages over time is much more difficult than using building wages, where feeding workers was less common.[10] In the second part of this chapter I will show just how much of a farm wage could be composed of non-monetary food perquisites, which were commonly used to

[5] Thorold Rodgers, *History of Agriculture and Prices*, VII, pp. 625–35; Young, *Northern Tour*, I, pp. 171–8, 235. For further examples of differences in wages see Wrightson, *Earthly Necessities*, pp. 312–13.

[6] Since a bushel of wheat produced 75 per cent of its weight in flour and a bushel of oats only 55 per cent in meal, more oats would have had to have been bought, but since a pound of oatmeal has more calories than whole-wheat flour this would only have amounted to about 10 per cent more. Paul and Southgate, *McCance and Widdowson's Composition of Foods*, pp. 38–9. Woodward's estimated consumption of oatmeal in Yorkshire seems very high. He estimates a consumption of 30 oz a day, which is much higher than Gibson and Smout's figures for Scotland. Woodward, *Men at Work*, pp. 276–82; Gibson and Smout, *Prices, Food and Wages*, pp. 248–60.

[7] Clark, 'Farm Wages', p. 496, Table 9.

[8] Ibid., p. 493; Clark, 'Long March', p. 107.

[9] Clark himself noted this, although he did not revise his estimate of beer consumed upwards enough. Clark, 'Long March', pp. 106–7, esp. note 14; Clark, 'Farm Wages', p. 496.

[10] Other perquisites such as wood chips might have been much more common. Woodward, *Men at Work*, pp. 142–9; Alan Hassell Smith, 'Labourers in Late Sixteenth-Century England: A Case Study from North Norfolk', *Continuity and Change*, [part I] 4:1 (1989), pp. 11–52; [part II] 4:3 (1989), pp. 367–94 here, I, pp. 23–5.

overcome the lack of cash in the economy. Simple money wages do not give an accurate idea of standards of living. For instance, in the large sample collected by Arthur Young he noted that many winter wages were supplemented with beer or sometimes food supplied at work.[11] As we saw in chapter 2 beer and cider were commonly supplied, and the practice is likely to have been more widespread than Young indicates, as he lists no cider being supplied in Gloucestershire whereas Eden claimed that unlimited amounts were supplied to workers.[12]

Furthermore, in calculating total yearly earnings we need to consider summer, and especially harvest, wages and their accompanying perquisites. Another reason why Clark's average wages are lower than Phelps Brown and Hopkins's series is that in choosing to use winter wages as a constant, he did not factor in the much higher harvest wages paid during July and August. Summer wages almost always included beer, and harvest wages came with board. Fortunately we possess a calculation of what such perquisites were worth from Thomas Batchelor's *View of the Agriculture of Bedfordshire*, listed in Table 5.2.[13] During the five weeks of harvest money wages were much higher because of the farmer's need to secure enough labour in order to make sure all the crops could be taken in.[14] Thus winter wages of 1s a day could rise to 1s 6d a day, or even 2s during harvest, depending on the demand for labour in the neighbourhood. In addition to this farmers also provided extra food, listed in Table 5.2. Bachelor also shows that extra money could be earned through carting and a wife's cooking for two to three days. In Batchelor's calculation harvest wages were 57s in 1808, while other earnings were worth 68s or 119 per cent of the money wages. In the rest of summer, what Batchelor termed the hay harvest, extra earnings were also worth 15s 6d or 26 per cent of money wages. Batchelor's estimate of earnings in 1808 was based on a winter wage rate of 1s 6d a day, and a harvest wage of 2s. This was after a period of inflation, and Arthur Young's examples of Bedfordshire wages from *c.* 1770 are much lower. However many of Young's other examples from the same date

---

[11] These were collected from Young by Thorold Rogers and can be found in Thorold Rogers, *History of Agriculture and Prices*, VII, pp. 624–35.

[12] See below, pp. 228–9.

[13] Here extra food was worth £2 13s 5d more than the wages. This was due to the much higher food prices of these years than earlier in the century when beef would have been 4d a pound and pork 5d. But the amounts of ale and meat given here are less than in many earlier diets. In addition, Batchelor stated that the food supplied was needed as 'the extra labour of that period cannot be supported by the ordinary quantity of food'. The total year's work given by Batchelor for a day labourer was 52 weeks of full-time work with an extra 2s per week from piece-work. Batchelor, *General View*, pp. 79, 108.

[14] See above, p. 43.

Table 5.2 *Batchelor's estimate of a labourer's earnings including harvest from 1808*

	£	s	d
Average month's pay including earnest	£2	8s	
One week finishing harvest and thatching		9s	
Two quarts of ale a day for five weeks		15s	
Extra ale, largess		2s	
Small beer		1s	10.5d
Meat, principally pork, 3.5 lb per week at 9d per pound (without bones)		13s	1.5d.
Cheese, 1 lb per weeks at 9d per pound		3s	9d
Brown bread or pudding, 1.5 lb per day		8s	9d
Plumbs, 1 lb for 8 days, at 8d per pound		2s	11d
Salt, mustard, etc., at ½d per day		1s	5.5d
Vegetables at ½d per day		1s	5.5d
Harvest home: food for the men's families, three persons each		3s	
Cooking: a woman's work for 12 men at 2s per day		5s	10d
Firing for 12 persons at 2s per week			10d
Wood carting		8s	
Total harvest	£6	5s	
Hay time, five weeks' pay	£3		
One quart of ale per day		7s	6d
Extra ale and food for working late		6s	
Small beer		2s	
Total haymaking	£3	15s	
Common farming labour, 42 weeks at 9s	£18	18s	
Small beer and milk at 3d per week	£1	1s	
Extra earnings by the piece at 2s per week for 30 weeks	£3		
Garden produce	?		
Total yearly earnings	£32	19s	6d

Source: Batchelor, *General View*, p. 80.

are in the region of 1s a day winter wages for forty-two weeks, 1s 6d a day during the first five weeks of summer and 2s a day during the five weeks of harvest.[15] If we then use the same percentage figures for perquisites that Batchelor estimated, total earnings would amount to £17 17s a year c. 1770 for an adult male day labourer working a full fifty-two weeks. However, it is probably more reasonable to subtract two weeks of winter wages for holidays and sickness, which would leave £17 7s.

Measuring standards of living of only those men who earned their living by the day also omits the importance of service, as well as extra

[15] Thorold Rogers, *History of Agriculture and Prices*, VII, pp. 624–35.

earnings from piece-work. Many labourers were hired as servants in husbandry by the year, where they would receive board if they were single and food if they were married with a family. Being hired for a year would have provided security against the potential loss of earnings for a day labourer if there was not enough work in a locality for all the labourers during the winter. Keith Wrightson and Donald Woodward have stressed that the amount of work available in a locality would determine how many days of work might in fact be available to day labourers.[16] In addition, many families who depended on day wages might well have financed part of their expenditure during periods of under-employment by carrying heavy debt loads.[17] Many labouring families purchased food from their employers in direct exchange for work, and this could alleviate rises in the cost of food during years of high grain prices. Many possessed small farms or animals as well as dairy and brewing equipment, and such produce could also add to household income, either by being sold on the market or providing grain, beer, hemp and dairy products for home consumption.

Finally, although male agricultural day wages are the most readily available source of data for measuring earnings, it has long been realised that they form only one part of a household's earning power. Women and daughters of a certain age could also work for wages in agricultural work. In addition, they spun yarn and did other tasks related to cloth manufacture, sewed, were employed as wet nurses or washed clothes. Boys and girls could also spin yarn and work in agriculture once they reached a certain age. As Thomas Sokoll has pointed out, the concept of dependency ratios is crucial to understanding how much a household might earn.[18] A family with a greater number of children under the age when wage earning could begin (usually about seven to nine in most parts of England) would have been poorer because they had to earn enough to feed and support their small children, while the wife's earning power was reduced by the time spent looking after the young children. Thus in the earliest years of marriage earning power was most dependent on the husband, but once the majority of children reached their teens the earning power of the household was at its maximum, as the children were able to earn almost as much as the adults and the wife had more free time. If only the father was working, and there were, say, three children below the age of nine, expenses would probably be about

[16] Wrightson, *Earthly Necessities*, pp. 195–7; Woodward, *Men at Work*, pp. 101–7, 131–42, 218, 283–4.
[17] Muldrew, *Economy of Obligation*, pp. 303–4.
[18] Thomas Sokoll, *Household and Family among the Poor: The Case of Two Essex Communities in the Late Eighteenth and Early Nineteenth Centuries* (Bochum, 1993), pp. 23–45.

25 per cent less, but without the children's earnings the family would be much worse off. Based on the cost of a child's diet from Table 4.11, in the mid-eighteenth century feeding a small child between the ages of 4 and 6 probably would have cost between £2 and £3 a year with 3 oz of meat a day and between £1 and £2 without.[19] Assuming a cost of another £1 a year for clothing, furniture and medicine means that it would cost about £21 to raise only one child to age seven. For most young labouring families savings from a time period spent as a servant would have been needed to begin a family to pay for this. Ann Kussmaul estimated that two servants marrying who had been in service from six to ten years could save between £27 and £60 together depending on their combined length of service and whether they were able to save half or two-thirds of their wages.[20] Thus a period in continual service while young was crucial to be able to afford to start a family.

The remainder of this chapter will examine all of the sources of earnings available to labouring families in an attempt to measure how much they might have been worth to families with different dependency ratios and how this might have changed over time. In order to do this we first need to go back to the budget looked at in chapter 3 for a family from Berkshire. There, the cost of living was calculated for 1756 and 1744.[21] Now I will go further to calculate the cost of living for the earlier sample years – 1568, 1596, 1625, 1680 and 1740 – so that the cost of living can be compared to potential wage earnings at different times. These calculations are presented in Table 5.3. Using these examples I can then determine how much extra family earnings would have been needed for the family to survive or to purchase more consumer goods during these years.

This example, it will be remembered, was of a family from the parish of Streatley, and was a household of six in which two children aged twelve and fifteen worked as ploughboys for neighbouring farmers, while the two youngest did not work. For the earlier years I have made estimates based on the same-sized family with children of the same ages, but I have adjusted the amounts and types of food eaten to accord with earlier sixteenth- and seventeenth-century diets. For instance, I have reduced the amount of bread eaten per day for a man from 2.3 lb to 1.5 lb, and added an equivalent amount of pease pudding instead. I have also increased the amount of meat and butter consumed based on Robert Loder's example and eliminated the oatmeal

---

[19] This calculation is based on the Atwater scale of a child's consumption being equal to 0.4 of adult food consumption with reduced small beer. See above, p. 135.
[20] Kussmaul, *Servants in Husbandry*, pp. 81–3.   [21] See Table 3.11 above.

Table 5.3 Labouring family budget estimates for 1568, 1597, 1625, 1680 and 1740 (based on Table 3.11)

	Weekly amount	Daily calories, man	Prices in 1568	Yearly cost	Prices in 1597	Yearly cost	Prices c. 1625	Yearly cost	Prices c. 1680	Yearly cost	Prices c. 1740	Yearly cost	Percentage of expenditure c. 1740
Bread (wheaten)[a]	45 lb	1,412	15s qrtr	£3 11s	50s qrtr	£11 14s	32s qrtr	£7 10s	32s qrtr	£7 10s	25s qrtr	£5 17s	17
Meat	16 lb beef	480	1½d lb	£4 11s	2d lb	£6 1s	2½d lb	£7 12s	3d lb	£9 2s	2½d lb	£8 14s	25
Small beer	16 gal.	875	Barley 10s qrtr	£2 6s	Barley 28s qrtr	£6	26s qrtr	£5 12s	18s qrtr	£3 17s	1d gal.	£3 9s	10
Table beer	4 gal.	914[b]	–	£1 18s		£4 19s		£4 12s		£3 3s		£1 14s	5
Pease pudding	25 lb	857	7s qrtr	18s	30s qrtr	£3 17s	22s qrtr	£2 16s	18s qrtr	£2 6s	12s qrtr	£1 10s	4
Bacon	½ lb	21	1½ d lb	3s	2d lb	4s	2d lb	4s	3d lb	4s	3d lb	7s	1
Cheese	2 lb	224	1.5d lb	£1 6s	2d	£1 14s	4d lb	£1 14s	4d lb	£3 7s	5d lb	£2 2s	6
Butter	3 lb	505	3d lb	£1 19s	5d	£3 5s	4d lb	£2 12s	6d lb	£6 12s	4½d lb	£2 10s	7
Total food		5,306		**£16 12s**		**£37 14s**		**£35 15s**		**£37 1s**		**£26**	**75**
Rent				£1 8s		£1 16s		£2		£2 10s		£2 10s	7
Fuel				13s		17s		£1 3s		£1 13s		£2	6
Clothing, lighting and other costs				£1 17s		£2 8s		£3 1s		£3 11s		£4	12
Total				**£20 10s**		**£42 15s**		**£40 9s**		**£43 18s**		**£34 13s**	**100**

Notes: [a] This calculation is based on the size of the penny wheaten loaf drawn from the coarse cocket. Powel, The Assize of Bread.
[b] Here the man is assumed to drink 50% of the strong beer, and the eldest sons the rest.

and milk, as pease pudding was generally eaten instead of porridge in earlier diets, and added bacon to be cooked in the pease pudding. Sugar has also been removed, as it was uncommon before the mid-eighteenth century. I have also reduced the amount spent on clothing and other goods to £4, as Eden commented that the family he looked at spent a great deal more than others. To estimate amounts spent on rent, fuel and clothing I have started with figures for 1740, based on Arthur Young's prices for the 1760s, and then I have deflated prices for earlier years based on Clark's index in his article 'Farm Wages and Living Standards'.[22]

In Table 5.3 the amounts of food have been kept constant for comparison, although certainly in the dearth of 1597 labouring families would have had to eat less meat and cheaper grains if they were available. During the seventeenth century money could also have been saved by eating less meat and more peas.[23] In addition, the figures for rent and fuel here are expensive as Berkshire is near London. In many other areas rent would have been less, and often fuel could be collected through common rights, as we shall see. In the north, where much more oatmeal was eaten, the cost of living would have been £2–3 cheaper per year. In 1610, for instance, the price of a quarter of oats was over three times less than wheat. Very importantly, we also have to remember that prices of grains could vary quite dramatically from year to year, while wages were what economists term 'sticky' in comparison. That is, they rose very gradually over time but did not vary much from year to year. For instance the building labourers' wages measured by Phelps Brown and Hopkins remained at 8d a day from 1580 to 1625, then rose to 12d a day from 1640 to 1690 and were at 15–16d a day from 1710 to 1770.[24] This means that without savings, based on wage earnings alone, a family's living standard would go up and down depending on the quality of that year's harvest and that some years would be better and some would be worse than this.

To begin the process of determining family earnings, Table 5.4 compares the costs of the budget presented in Table 5.3 to *only* male wage earnings of just the husband and the husband with two teenage sons

[22] The percentage of this budget devoted to meat and beer is much higher than in that used by Clark, but not dissimilar to the division used by Phelps Brown and Hopkins. Clark, 'Long March', p. 107; Phelps Brown and Hopkins, 'Seven Centuries', pp. 15, 20.

[23] However, if this family is assumed to have eaten as much meat as the earlier houses of correction diets recommended, around a pound per day for adults, this would have meant they would have been eating about 25 lb per week, rather than the 16.5 lb supplied here, which would have cost £5 10s more at 3d a pound.

[24] Phelps Brown and Hopkins, 'Seven Centuries', Fig. 2.

Table 5.4 *Male wage earnings over time*

	Winter wage (40 weeks)	Summer wage (5 weeks)	Harvest wage (5 weeks)	Husband's yearly earnings	Yearly earnings with two sons	Cost of living from Table 5.3	Deficit	Clark's real wage index[a]
c. 1568	7d	11d	14d	£10.5	£17.8	£20.5	−£2.7	87
c. 1597	8d	12d	16d	£11.9	£20.2	£42.75	−£22.5	51
c. 1625	10d	15d	20d	£14.9	£25.3	£40.5	−£15.1	65
c. 1680	11d	16d	22d	£16.3	£27.7	£43.9	−£16.2	70
c. 1740	12d	18d	24d	£17.8	£30.3	£34.7	−£4.4	75

Note: [a] Clark, 'Long March', pp. 131–5.

employed for 50 6-day weeks (300 days) without beer supplied during the winter for the same sample years. Later in the chapter I will add other family earnings after all potential sources of such earnings have been discussed. This calculation also assumes that the number of holidays taken or sick days amounted to only two weeks and that full employment was available. By the end of the eighteenth century agricultural writers like Eden, Young or Batchelor tended to assume that labourers worked a full year, and many account books show labourers working all year. But it has been argued that there may have been as many as forty-six days on which work ceased even as late as the mid-eighteenth century.[25] The availability of work will be dealt with in the next chapter, and the culture of industriousness versus leisure preference in the Conclusion, but here I will assume fifty weeks' employment as a standard.

At the very beginning of the period the earnings of the husband together with those of his two sons was almost enough to cover the living expenses of the whole family of six. Even earlier, in the 1540s wages were 25 per cent lower but wheat prices were about 40 per cent lower as well, so there would have been little deficit. The moving average of wheat prices began to rise more quickly in the 1580s to over 20s a quarter, but much of this was due to much higher prices in bad years such as 1586.[26] Things changed dramatically, however, with the two bad harvests of 1595–6 followed immediately by the terrible harvests of 1596–7. During these years shortage was so acute that there were dearths in some northern areas, and grain prices doubled while wages remained static. The potential shock of this great dearth comes out

[25] See below, p. 291. [26] Clay, *Economic Expansion*, I, pp. 36–51.

quite clearly here.[27] After this, the deficit between male earnings and expenses during the seventeenth century was considerable, before rising nominal wages and falling food prices almost closed the gap again by the mid-eighteenth century. The remainder of this chapter will be spent looking at the value of other different possible earnings, before returning to this calculation at its end to determine the extent to which these deficits could have been overcome.

Numbers of servants in husbandry compared to day labourers

Before looking at additional earnings for other sources of wages or piecework it is important to try to obtain some notion of just what percentage of labourers would have been working by the day, as opposed to being employed in service on yearly contracts. From Ann Kussmaul's work we know that service remained a vital part of social organisation in the early modern period, with 25–35 per cent of families in the seventeenth century containing servants, from one young inexpensive maidservant to more than a hundred servants with their livery in great households. Service was generally a life-cycle position whereby young boys and girls from poorer households would move to a different household to learn both housekeeping and the skills of husbandry.[28] At the time it was thought that the authority of strangers was much more appropriate than that of parents, who were likely to be too kind to prepare children to be independent and responsible for themselves. Most young women became maidservants within a household, while boys worked in agriculture, although wealthier households also required grooms and livery servants. Since most servants came from poorer families, by the end of the seventeenth century it has been estimated that 81 per cent of the labouring population had been or were in service. Thus for most families children did not need to be supported after fourteen.

Those boys who became agricultural servants became known as 'servants in husbandry'. Their conditions of employment were different from day labourers'. As servants, they became members of the master's household living under his or her authority; eating food and living in

---

[27] Andrew Appleby, *Famine in Tudor and Stuart England* (Liverpool, 1978); Steve Hindle, 'Dearth, Fasting and Alms: The Campaign for General Hospitality in Late Elizabethan England', *Past and Present* 172 (2001), pp. 44–86; Harrison, *Description*, p. 133.

[28] Sheila McIsaac Cooper, 'Service to Servitude? The Decline and Demise of Life-Cycle Service in England', *History of the Family*, 10 (2005), pp. 367–86. Some sons of yeomen, however, remained in their parents' household working as servants. *Men and Armour, passim.*

Table 5.5 *Percentage of the population in service age 15–29*

Men in service		Women in service	
15–19	35	15–19	27
20–24	30	20–24	40
25–29	15	25–29	15

Source: Sharpe, *Early Modern England*, pp. 210–11.

accommodation provided by the master. As we saw in chapter 3, surviving account book purchases show that servants were well fed, even in years when grain prices were high, in order that they could do the work required of them. It is much more difficult to know how comfortable their sleeping arrangements were, but they would have slept in the same dwelling as their masters, although perhaps on flock rather than feather beds.[29]

Because being a servant in husbandry was a life-cycle position, and was dominated by young men, Kussmaul argued that there was a quite sharp distinction between servants in husbandry and day labourers. But account books would seem to indicate that this distinction was in practice less sharp. Many adult labourers were hired for periods much longer than a day, often for a year or more, and their contracts usually included food and sometimes board for part of the year. Since the cost of food for a servant was borne by his master, to fully understand standards of living we need to have some idea of how many day labourers there were compared to servants in husbandry and, further, how they were hired.

Hiring servants for the year was the traditional means of providing employment, and was stressed by Tudor moralists as an expected display of the proper hospitality of yeomen and gentry towards their labourers, providing them with good food and shelter as well as security over the course of the year. However, the proportion of servants in the population fluctuated over time. Kussmaul has argued that since servants were most likely to get married in October, after their yearly contracts ended on the traditional date of Michaelmas, a decline in the number of October marriages recorded in parish registers is evidence of more young people either leaving service or not finding employment. In a sample of southern counties October marriages dropped by about 25 per cent between 1560 and 1650, because rising food prices and a surplus of labour made it logical for farmers to hire more young people

[29] Kussmaul, *Servants in Husbandry*, p. 41; Snell, *Annals of the Labouring Poor*, p. 69,

as day labourers rather than servants. This finding is supported by the fact that this was the period when the greatest number of young people took to the road and moved to London or emigrated to Ireland or America. Once this emigration had caused the population to fall, October marriages rose sharply again in the late seventeenth century, until 1750. Stagnant or falling prices for grain coupled with a labourer shortage as a result of the fall in population after 1650 meant that it was advantageous for farmers to keep servants to ensure enough labour for necessary work. In addition, it was cheaper now to feed them from their own produce, and since small change was scarce this also reduced the need to find cash to pay day wages.[30]

Keith Snell has also shown that because of the nature of the laws of settlement, which made a parish liable for the poor relief of anyone who worked there as a servant for more than a year, the practice of hiring servants declined rapidly in the very late eighteenth century as the cost of poor relief went up. From the evidence of settlement examinations, where poor individuals seeking settlement were asked about their work history, it can be seen that the percentage of individuals hired as servants for more than two years in all the southeastern counties dropped from about 50 per cent between 1701 and 1740 to under 20 per cent by the 1790s.[31]

But despite such fluctuations, there was always a need for farm servants or labourers hired on a long-term basis, which had a number of advantages over hiring labourers by the day. Most importantly long-term hiring provided a secure number of labourers available to do work at all times during the year, especially at harvest. At least one live-in servant was almost always necessary to be available to look after animals in the early morning, and for the same reason dairying remained a service occupation of housekeepers.[32] Providing food for a family, including a large number of servants, was also cheaper than having to give money to a number of individuals expected to find their own food. It also made accounting simpler, as most payment was in board, and the remaining wages were only usually paid from two to four times a year, rather than weekly, as was expected in the case of day labourers.

---

[30] Kussmaul, *Servants in Husbandry*. pp. 97–114; Craig Muldrew, '"Hard food for Midas": Cash and Its Social Value in Early Modern England', *Past and Present*, 170 (2001), pp. 96–7, 105–6; Craig Muldrew, 'Economic and Urban Development of Seventeenth-Century Britain', in Barry Coward (ed.), *The Blackwell Companion to Stuart Britain* (Oxford, 2003), pp. 155–8.

[31] Snell, *Annals of the Labouring Poor*, pp. 73–5.

[32] Kussmaul, *Servants in Husbandry*, pp. 22–7; Snell, *Annals of the Labouring Poor*, pp. 69–70, 103; Donald Woodward, 'Early Modern Servants in Husbandry Revisited', *Agricultural History Review*, 48 (2002), pp. 141–50.

But perhaps the most important reason for keeping servants was social and moral. Since servants were family members, and under the authority of their master, their behaviour could be monitored and skills and discipline could be taught and enforced. In the 1730s William Ellis still thought it best to keep young people as servants, which

must rebound to their Masters and Mistresses Profit, for according to their Management they may be made either serviceable or unserviceable. I never knew a farmer thrive that let his Servants stay long, or lie out nights, to go to common Dancing or Drinking Bouts, etc. ... to rise at Five is the way to thrive.[33]

Of course a master's discipline could also be cruel, or their housekeeping stingy, and for this reason many servants moved to different households a great deal, but many other masters were kind and formed bonds of affection with their servants.[34]

Although evidence is scarce, census-type lists exist for local areas which can be used to compare the numbers of agricultural servants with day labourers. The earliest is a petty sessions list from 1566 which survives for the village of Marsham in Norfolk. It lists all the employers, servants, labourers and craftsmen living there. At that date there were seven day labourers compared to eleven male servants and seventeen maidservants, as well as a thatcher who was also listed as being a day labourer.[35] Somewhat later in 1599 the well-known census of the village of Ealing near London listed only one day labourer, one ploughwright and one mole-catcher in comparison to forty-eight male servants in husbandry.[36]

There is an important early seventeenth-century occupational listing which lists male servants, the 1608 muster list for Gloucestershire of 'Able and Sufficient Men in Body fit for His Majesty's Service compiled by John Smith'. This is an unusually detailed muster list of all the adult males potentially capable of being soldiers, which lists both the person in question's occupation and their servants. The list includes 828 servants of yeomen and husbandmen. It does not distinguish between household servants and servants in husbandry. But since no women were

---

[33] Ellis, *Country Housewife*, p. vii. Arthur Young also said much the same thing. Snell, *Annals of the Labouring Poor*, p. 82.

[34] This can be seen in Ann Kussmaul (ed.), *The Autobiography of Joseph Mayett of Quainton 1783–1839*, Buckingham Record Society, 23 (1986), pp. 1–13, 70–1. Paul Griffiths, *Youth and Authority: Formative Experiences in England 1560–1640* (Oxford, 1996), ch. 6 ; Carolyn Steedman, *Master and Servant: Love and Labour in the English Industrial Age* (Cambridge, 2007), ch. 7; Tadmor, *Family and Friends*, chs. 1, 5.

[35] Jane Whittle, *The Development of Agrarian Capitalism: Land and Labour in Norfolk 1440–1580* (Oxford, 2000), p. 233.

[36] Kussmaul, *Servants in Husbandry*, pp. 11–14.

listed this is only a problem for gentry households, which would have had male livery servants, such as footmen or coachmen, in addition to servants in husbandry. If we assume that a quarter of the gentry's servants were household servants and that the remaining three-quarters were servants in husbandry, then we need to add another 563 servants. Finally, 383 sons of yeomen and husbandmen worked as servants for their fathers or other relatives. This gives us a total of 1,774 servants in husbandry. But since only men above the age of twenty are listed, it is not a total listing of servants in the county, as it is likely about half would have been below that age (see Table 5.5). Thus there might have been 3,548 male servants in husbandry compared to 1,831 labourers listed, or a ratio of 1.9 servants to every labourer, and there would have been many more maidservants as well.[37]

A further seventeen village and county surveys of population with information on occupation collected by the Cambridge Group for the History of Population and Society were analysed by Ann Kussmaul to compare the ratio of servants of both sexes to labourers and farmers. The earliest of these is for 1688 from Clayworth in Nottinghamshire, and there are another eleven censuses from before 1750, and six censuses from between 1777 and 1800. Before 1750, out of a total of 3,768 people listed, there were 357 servants of 253 farmers compared to 211 labourers.[38] Between 1777 and 1800, out of a population of over 3,500 there were 578 servants listed, compared to 444 labourers and 772 farmers. Thus in the first period there was only 1 labourer to every 1.7 servants, but this had dropped to 1 to 1.3 by the end of the century. However, there was also a difference between northern parishes in the sample (from Westmorland), and the remaining southern parishes. In Westmorland, in the early eighteenth century there was 1 labourer to every 4 servants, while in the south the ratio was only 1 labourer to every 1.4 servants. When the same comparison is done for the period 1777–1800, there was 1 labourer for every 2.3 servants in Westmorland and only 1 labourer to every 0.7 servant in the south. Thus while the overall ratio of servants to labourers remained high in the north, there was still a decline. In the south, though, servants had become only 42 per cent of the labouring population by the century's end.

[37] Tawney and Tawney, 'Occupational Census', pp. 50–3, 59–62.
[38] The places and the nature of the surveys are described in Kussmaul, *Servants in Husbandry*, pp. 11–14. As Kussmaul notes, here again some of the male servants of farmers might have been livery servants, but these would only have been in the houses of the gentry, or very wealthy yeomen, so would have formed only a tiny proportion of the total.

Table 5.6 *Numbers of servants compared to day labourers in the 1760s*

	National estimate	Percentage of total	Percentage of men	Numbers on a sample of 250 farms from the north	Numbers on a sample of 93 farms from the east	Estimated national earnings	Percentage of earnings for each group
Male servants	222,996	27	33	486 (28%)	205 (23%)	£3,899,639	27
Maidservants	167,247	20		268 (15%)	82 (9%)	£1,413,236	10
Boys	111,498	13	17	232 (13%)	103 (11%)	£1,070,380	7
Labourers	334,494	40	50	768 (44%)	525 (57%)	£6,160,262	42
Extra labourer	—	—	—	—	—	£2,053,420	14
Total	836,235	100		1754	915	£14,596,937	100
Total males	668,988	—	100	—	—	—	—

Sources: Young, *Northern Tour*, IV, pp. 236–46, 355–60, 364–5; Arthur Young, *The Farmer's Tour through the East of England* (London, 1771), IV, pp. 375–8.

The only national estimate for the number of agricultural servants was made by Arthur Young. He based this on an extrapolation of information he gathered on his visits to 250 farms in the north and 93 farms in the east of England in the 1760s. His data are presented in Table 5.6. He divided servants by sex, and also included the number of boys hired on a farm. Unfortunately he did not provide a definition of what he meant by 'boy' in terms of age, but presumably these would have been those boys younger than servants who would have been hired at lower wages, probably between the ages of seven and twelve. Presumably they were also boarded and not casual labour, since Young did not include the labour of female agricultural workers, which, as we shall see, was considerable in the summer months. If boys are included, the number of both male and female servants is greater than the number of labourers, with a ratio of about 1.5 servants to 1 labourer. More servants were employed in the north, although the ratio is not as high as the Westmoreland censuses cited in the previous paragraph. Also, since Young tended to visit larger, more productive farms which would have needed to hire more labour, his sample probably overestimates the number of labourers in relation to servants.[39]

---

[39] Ibid., p. 18; Robert Allen, *Enclosure and the Yeoman: The Agricultural Development of the South Midlands 1450–1850* (Oxford, 1992), pp. 212ff.

Taken together, these surveys would seem to indicate that until 1770, at least, most hired farm labour of all ages, including maid servants, was still being provided by servants and not day labourers. This can be explained in part because service formed a large part of the employment life cycle, and 35 per cent of the population was between the ages of seven and twenty-four. However, there were still older labourers who were also hired as servants in husbandry. Kussmaul found that 11 per cent of servants reported in settlement examinations that they married before leaving service. In the mid-seventeenth century Henry Best, of Elmswell, Yorkshire, for example, hired some married servants who only ate in his household.[40] In his famous table of the ranks and degrees of people in England in 1688, Gregory King classed labourers and 'out-servants' together, implying that some married labourers were definitely hired as servants.

Most farm accounts recorded a core of labourers being hired as yearly servants, including increasing numbers who were married but who lived separately in their own households. On the estate of Nathaniel Bacon at Stiffkey in north Norfolk between 1587 and 1597, eight to ten male servants in husbandry were employed. These, such as the bailiff, sub-bailiff and stockmen, were older married men with experience of farming who lived in accommodation provided by Bacon. Other servants were mostly young unmarried men who joined and left the household at any time of year, and often served for long periods of time. They also had their own lodging house in the estate yard. In contrast to this, in the year 1593–4, the employment of day labour amounted to only 418 days. This work was generally done in small amounts by twenty-six labouring smallholders who resided in the parish and who supported themselves through their own farming or by working for others.[41] When the Yorkshire farmer Richard Cholmeley hired his farm labourers in the first two decades of the seventeenth century, they were almost all hired as live-in farm servants for a year or half year with board and wages of 20–40s or thereabouts (one man was paid 7 nobles and another 4 marks). He had seven male servants and one maidservant when his wife arrived to live with him at Brandsby in 1604, and his notebooks record the continual hiring of servants thereafter, with wages generally being paid after he collected his rent. It is impossible to tell how many of them had families, but some were certainly small tenants who rented land from Cholmeley, and had part of their rent deducted from their wages. Occasionally labourers were hired for shorter periods of, say, five weeks,

---

[40] See below, p. 227.
[41] Hassell Smith, 'Labourers in Norfolk', I, pp. 15, 26, 44–6; II, pp. 367–91.

but only rarely did he record hiring extra labourers by the day.[42] When he did it was usually from a group of people, including John Marshall, Henry Watson, Thomas Fentyman, John Sickling, Ambrose Story and Ann Martin, whose hiring occurs repeatedly throughout the memorandum book.[43]

The account book of the Toke family for the Godinton estate in Kent, which covers the years from 1616 to 1704, shows that they mostly hired labourers as servants in husbandry. In 1628 they hired seventeen male servants at wages of generally £5–8 and three maidservants for £3 each. They also employed the services of fifteen day labourers over the course of the year, mostly for cutting wood and making poles, but also for lambing, mole catching, hedging and ditching, as well as harvest work. However, the greatest part of the farm's work was done by servants. In 1679 the Tokes were still hiring eighteen servants.[44] Henry Best commonly hired five to nine servants by the year at the Martinmas hiring fair, depending on his need for labour. He left lists of all the servants he hired between 1617 and 1643, and during those years 122 servants were hired. Sixty-nine per cent were hired only once, 17 per cent stayed for a second year and only 10 per cent for a third, although the average length of time spent in employment for those servants hired for a year was actually eighteen months. Again most of these servants lived in, some sleeping in the stables, but some servants were married when hired and only ate in the Best household.[45] Robert Loder also hired most of his labourers as boarded or semi-boarded servants (with some deduction in rent if the servant had a family), apart from harvest time, when many more of what Loder termed his 'taskers' were hired to do all the extra work needed.[46] In contrast to these examples, Thomas Cawton of Great Bentley in Essex hired many day labourers in 1631–2, including women, hired mostly in the summer for tasks such as carting, threshing, harvesting and weeding. But he still retained a core of four live-in servants.[47]

[42] *Memorandum Book of Richard Cholmeley of Brandsby, 1602–1623*, North Yorkshire County Record Office Publications, 44 (1988), pp. 40, 43–7, 50, 52, 53–4, 56–8, 62–6, 68, 73, 75, 79–80, 85, 87–8, 98, *passim*. Between 1776 and 1802 Parson Woodforde hired thirty-three people to fill his five service positions of farming man, farm boy, footman, housemaid and a cook-dairymaid. Kussmaul, *Servants in Husbandry*, p. 55.

[43] *Memorandum Book of Richard Cholmeley*, *passim*.

[44] Eleanor C. Lodge (ed.), *The Account Book of a Kentish Estate 1616–1704* (London, 1927), pp. xxxii–xxxiii, 108–16, 379–85.

[45] Woodward (ed.), *Farming Books of Henry Best*, pp. xxxvii–xxxix.

[46] Fussell (ed.), *Robert Loder's Farm Accounts*, p. 101.

[47] Wrightson, *Earthly Necessities*, pp. 195–6.

On the Thornborough estate in Yorkshire, from 1749 to 1773, there continued to be many live-in servants as well as day labourers.[48] At Golden Barton in Cornwall in the mid-eighteenth century the number of live-in labourers varied from three to eight depending on the season. At Morval Barton, where more work was required, there was a nucleus of ten labourers hired by the year who did not live on the farm but were tenants on the estate who had their rent reduced.[49] Randall Burroughes seems to have hired three or four men by the year, again providing free rent to those who were tenants, but he relied mostly on day labour, usually hiring between ten and fifteen men to do various tasks, and more at harvest time with board wages and other perquisites.[50]

Although the evidence is slender for the late sixteenth century it would seem probable that it remained most common to hire labourers as servants in husbandry by the year with board, or food and reduced rent if the servant had their own family. However, the earliest large-scale statistical evidence, that of the Gloucestershire muster list, which indicates in that county 66 per cent of the male agricultural workforce was hired as servants. The evidence of October marriages suggests that this percentage went down in subsequent years, but recovered after 1650.[51] This is supported by the other early eighteenth-century censuses and Arthur Young's figures, which suggest that 60 per cent of the agricultural workforce were servants. Since food, lodging and some clothing was supplied by the hiring farm in these cases, all of these labourers would have been insulated against rising food prices in the period before 1650.

Food, drink and other perquisites

It has already been noted how nominal day wages of labourers were augmented by drink and food supplied during the summer hay and corn harvests. But such provision was also common throughout the year in many places in order to ensure that the work farmers wanted done could be performed. In his pamphlet *Bread for the Poor*, published in Exeter in 1698, Richard Dunning provided a budget for a poor day labourer's family where he assumed that the husband was provided with

---

[48] E. W. Gilboy, 'Labour at Thornborough: An Eighteenth Century Estate', *Economic History Review*, 1st ser., 3 (1931–2), pp. 388–98, here, pp. 389–95.

[49] Pounds, 'Barton Farming', pp. 61, 73.

[50] Martins and Williamson (eds.), *Farming Journal of Randall Burroughes*, pp. 3–35, 108. On other farms rent was deducted from wage earnings in the farm account books. See for instance SRO, DD/WO/6.

[51] Kussmaul, *Servants in Husbandry*, p. 98.

all his food and drink at work.[52] The value of such food can be seen by examining wage assessments drawn up by Justices of the Peace. Under the provisions of the Statute of Artificers of 1563, JPs had the responsibility of drawing up maximum rates of wages in their locality. This was a continuation of government policy initiated in the fifteenth century which attempted to cap wages in an era when low population meant that farm labour was in demand and wages were high. But it was revitalised by the inflationary pressure on wages in the mid-sixteenth century. In the remainder of the sixteenth century the inflation of prices would far outstrip the growth of nominal wages, and there has been debate as to the degree to which the wage levels set under the provision of the statute were obeyed. But JPs did try to assess wages at the market rate, and as a result there are detailed lists of the rates for types of work at different times of the year.[53] These wage assessments stipulated the cost of a day's labour both with and without food and drink. Wages without food were higher and generally termed 'board wages'. Carole Shammas has looked at a large sample of such ratings, and the average amount of the value of meat and drink, as assessed by JPs, was 55 per cent of the total wage between 1560 and 1600, dropping to 51 per cent between 1721 and 1760.[54] This not only shows the value of food, but also means that when the labourer, though not his family, was supplied with food, much of the inflation of food prices was borne by the farmer, since wages with food and drink always rose in the same proportion to wages without food and drink.

For the sixteenth and seventeenth century, unfortunately, few farm accounts have survived which detail how many day labourers were paid wages with food supplied at work. At Stiffkey, in late sixteenth-century Norfolk, Nathaniel Bacon's day labourers were paid meat and drink wages, and the food provided was worth 5d a day per person according to the kitchen accounts. In contrast, the more highly paid building labourers took board wages.[55] Henry Best noted that he would feed poor thatchers 'that finde them not soe good a dyett' at work, as well as giving them 1–2d extra a day, implying that they were too poor to afford enough to feed themselves and their families on board wages.[56] On one occasion Richard Cholmeley hired some day workers to help fire bricks, and he supplied them with beer and tabling.[57]

[52] Richard Dunning, *Bread for the Poor* (Exeter, 1698), p. 5.
[53] Donald Woodward, 'The Assessment of Wages by Justices of the Peace, 1563–1813: Some Observations', *Local Historian*, 8:8 (1969), pp. 293–8.
[54] Shammas, 'Food Expenditure', pp. 93–5.
[55] Hassell Smith, 'Labourers in Norfolk', I, pp. 22–4, 27.
[56] Woodward (ed.), *Farming Books of Henry Best*, p. 142.
[57] *Memorandum Book of Richard Cholmeley*, p. 54.

By the 1760s, though, we have information collected by Arthur Young. In his series of wages almost all of the examples included beer and food, during the ten to twelve weeks of summer work, but rarely was food provided in winter by that time.[58] Gregory Clark, who has looked at the largest sample of wage accounts from farms all over England, concluded that by the late seventeenth century provision of food to workers in the south was rare, but continued to be normal in the north into the nineteenth century.[59] However, given the complexity of how wages were negotiated, counter examples can easily be found. Frances Hamilton provided food at work on her Bishops Lydeard farm in the eighteenth century, as did Nathaniel Brewer of Over Stowey, Somerset, in 1713.[60] Clark also cites an example from Cumbria where both types of wages were paid for threshing in 1732. The late eighteenth-century Norfolk farmer Randall Burroughes generally paid board wages (that is wages without food supplied), but on occasion provided board or dinner.[61]

For an adult labourer with children old enough to be employed themselves, a hiring with meat and drink would make a great deal of sense, if it were possible. But for someone with small children, the lower cash wages on offer would have made it difficult to help feed his children and pay for fuel and rent, in addition to what his wife could earn. Day wages of 8d a day with food provided, which were common in the early seventeenth century, would have provided about £10 a year to feed a family, only half of what board wages would have provided. This would also have been a problem for married servants in husbandry, as the average wage for servants older than twenty, from a sample of quarter sessions wage assessments examined by Kussmaul, was £5 15s. Bacon's adult servants in the 1590s earned only about £2 a year, and two married servants in husbandry hired by Henry Best in 1617 were paid £3 and £1 6s 8d a year, but they were still in employment in 1622, when their wages went up to £6 and £5 with house rent.[62] On such wages small children could only have been supported if the farmer helped out by providing a cottage or selling food cheaply, as described below, or if a labourer had savings from earlier boarded employment.

But even for labourers on board wages there is much evidence that the provision of beer or cider at work was a normal part of wages. The

[58] Thorold Rogers, *History of Agriculture and Prices*, VII, pp. 624–35.
[59] He used wages without food. Clark, 'Farm Wages', pp. 479–80.
[60] See chapter 2, note 243, and note 82 below.
[61] Martins and Williamson (eds.), *Farming Journal of Randall Burroughes*, pp. 46, 55, 59, 61, 65, 68, 79, 84–7, 123–4.
[62] Kussmaul, *Servants in Husbandry*, pp. 37–8; Woodward (ed.), *Farming Books of Henry Best*, p. xxxix.

value of such provision in the early to mid-eighteenth century could potentially vary from 2d to 10d a day if a gallon of strong beer was supplied. If we were to add the value of beer provided at work during the winter to wages, it would add £2 a year for every 2d of beer supplied per day. In Young's wage data beer was always included during the summer, and also listed as being included with winter wages in about a third of his examples.[63] However, there is evidence which suggests that provision of beer during the winter was more extensive than suggested by Young.[64] Although Frederick Eden generally looked on beer favourably as a source of nutrition, when describing diets in Gloucestershire he complained that:

a very pernicious custom takes place in this county, as in many others, of allowing labourers an enormous quantity of liquor. That the more they receive in liquor the less they receive in wages, there can be no doubt: in many parts of the county the labourer receives almost as much liquor as is equal to his day's pay; and is thus encouraged in a practice which is not more ruinous to his health, than prejudicial to his family.[65]

But none of the examples of wages given for Gloucestershire by Young included beer or cider, indicating that not every farmer reported the practice to him.

Henry Best noted how it was his practice, for labourers whom he hired without food, 'at noones to sende them, nowe and then a quart of the best beere to theyre dinners'. Eden, as we saw, noted that labourers normally broke work to drink beer at 10.00 a.m. and 4.00 p.m.[66] Wage bills for labourers employed in different counties for work on county bridges, buildings and roads frequently itemized 'drink to the labourers'.[67] In the late eighteenth century, Randall Burroughes almost always noted providing beer at work in addition to cash wages, as, for instance, in July 1796 when he paid 5 mowers 1s 6d and 3 pints of beer per day, or 5 days earlier when he paid 2s with 2 pints of beer per acre. This must have been strong beer, as he reckoned its value at 2d a pint, which was expensive even for the late eighteenth century.[68] At roughly the same time in Somerset, on her Bishops Lydeard farm, Frances Hamilton paid an extra 1s an acre for harvesting without beer or cider. It was said that

[63] Thorold Rogers, *History of Agriculture and Prices*, VII, pp. 625–35.
[64] Clark, 'Farm Wages', p. 480.   [65] Eden, *State of the Poor*, II, pp. 105, 511.
[66] Woodward (ed.), *Farming Books of Henry Best*, p. 140; Eden, *State of the Poor*, III, p. 822.
[67] Elizabeth Waterman Gilboy, 'Wages in Eighteenth-Century England', *Journal of Economic & Business History*, 2 (1929–30), pp. 603–29, 606–7.
[68] Martins and Williamson (eds.), *Farming Journal of Randall Burroughes*, pp. 46, 55, 59, 61, 65, 68, 70, 79, 84–7, 123, 124.

farms there that produced no cider found it hard to obtain enough day labour.[69] Such supply is also demonstrated by the finding of Overton *et al.* that the number of farmer's inventories with brewing equipment in Kent actually increased quite dramatically between 1650 and 1750.[70]

Another way in which day labourers could have helped to offset high food prices for their families was to either negotiate some extra payment in kind or to purchase food from their employers on credit or at a price lower than the market rate.[71] The potential value of such agreements can be seen in an example described by Robert Loder. In most of the years detailed in his account book he boarded his servants well and provided feasts for them. However, he estimated that each servant cost him about £10 5s a year in food and drink, compared to wages of between 15s 6d and £3, and he constantly complained that it would be cheaper to keep fewer 'unruly' servants and instead rely on wage labourers.[72] When writing up his costs and expenses for 1613 he calculated that if he only kept one maidservant and hired his other servants at board wages, he would save £5. But when he negotiated with his carter William Weston for board wages in 1617, he had to agree to pay £11 in money together with four bushels of wheat, three weeks' board at harvest, the keeping of Weston's hog by Loder and shorter working days in the winter, which Loder reckoned to be worth £13 9s 4d. He termed this 'exceeding great wages', and indeed it was little different from what a carter usually cost him with board provided.[73] It was also about 33 per cent greater than the standard wages of 8d a day without food would have provided. But despite his frustration at the cost of board, Loder could see no other way of getting his work done than by hiring his labourers as servants, which implies that he thought about £10 was the necessary cost of providing food and drink to run his farm efficiently and profitably. Given the extent to which he attempted to work out the cost and profit of all aspects of his farm in minute detail, there is no doubt this is correct.[74]

[69] Helen Speechley, 'Female and Child Agricultural Day Labourers in Somerset, *c.* 1685–1870', University of Exeter Ph.D. thesis, 1999, pp. 109–10.

[70] Overton *et al.*, *Production and Consumption*, pp. 58–60. In contrast, brewing equipment declined in inventories from Cornwall, although the Barton estates brewed a lot of their own beer on a large scale.

[71] Kussmaul, *Servants in Husbandry*, p. 39.

[72] Donald Woodward, 'The Means of Payment and Hours of Work in Early Modern England', in Carol S. Leonard and B. N. Mironov (eds.), *Hours of Work and Means of Payment: The Evolution of Conventions in Pre-Industrial Europe*, Proceedings of the Eleventh International Economic History Congress (Milan, 1994), p. 17; Kussmaul, *Servants in Husbandry*, p. 40.

[73] Fussell (ed.), *Robert Loder's Farm Accounts*, pp. 72, 90, 107–8, 137.

[74] Ibid., pp. 72, 90

Even with his live-in servants, Richard Cholmeley often negotiated extra payments in kind, such as the case where he supplied one with horse grass and 5 pecks of oats together with a pair of black breeches.[75] Feed for animals was a common extra supplied as part of wages. Henry Best, when describing the negotiations involved in the hiring of farm servants, noted that 'some servants will condition to have soe many sheepe wintered and sommered with theire masters … we account that equall to so many eighteene pences'. In 1622, he recorded paying one servant '£6 in money, 8 bushels of barley, 2 bushels of oats, and a peck of oatmeal, and a *frise* coat, and a stook of straw every weeke from Christmas to Lady Day in Lent', and another 'to have £5 in money, and 10 sheep wintered, and the rent of his house and garth the next year; and I to pay for his *cowjeast* on the *greets* next summer'.[76] At Dunster farm in Somerset, in addition to wages, labourers also received cider in the summer, the run of a pig, unlimited turf for fuel and milk in the winter.[77]

It was also very common for labourers, if the cash was not available to pay their wages, to turn them into a debt which the employer owed to the labourer. This debt could then be cancelled against a debt the labourer might incur to the employer for grain or meat purchased from, or rent owed to, the farmer for whom they laboured. Cholmeley paid some labourers to carry wood with corn, beer, ale and meat as well as cash.[78] To give just one example from the many found in the accounts of the Godinton estate in Kent, in 1699 Jacob Wootton had his wages for threshing, hedging and ditching cancelled in the accounts against the rent he owed his employer for his house as well as peas, barley and oats he purchased.[79] Accounts also exist from 1719 to 1754 for the Kingston farm in Wiltshire where James Flower and John Lacy had their yearly rent cancelled in the accounts against work done by the day, mowing, grubbing, working in the orchard and making faggots, as well as for butter they sold to the farm.[80] John Crakanthorp's accounts record continual sales of small amounts of grain to various labourers who worked for him, such as William Thrift, who in June 1706 bought 7 pecks of barley. He also exchanged his labour for the wintering of his cow for 21

---

[75] *Memorandum Book of Richard Cholmeley*, pp. 40, 43–7, 50, 52, 53–4, 56–8, 62–4, 65, 66–8, 73, 75, 79, 80–1, 85, 87, 98ff.
[76] Woodward (ed.), *Farming Books of Henry Best*, pp. 141, 169.
[77] Speechley, 'Female and Child Agricultural Day Labourers', p. 115n.8.
[78] *Memorandum Book of Richard Cholmeley*, p. 62.
[79] Lodge (ed.), *Account Book of a Kentish Estate*, pp. 474–7.
[80] WRO, 2533/1, f.1147, 198–9, 205, 209ff. Other examples for similar reckonings against wages can be found in the accounts of other farms. WRO, 1178/24; WRO, 415/86; WRO, 3238/49; SRO, DD/WO/6.

weeks on Crakanthorp's land worth 10s 6d.[81] This process can be seen very clearly in the double-entry accounts of Nathaniel Brewer, a farmer of Over Stowey in Somerset. In 1713, for instance, he listed debts due to him from a labourer for various sales of peas, barley and wheat worth about £3 15s. On the debit side he listed debts he owed the man for felling timber and sawing it.[82] On another occasion he paid a labourer and his boy board wages, but also exchanged various parcels of meat for his wages to feed his family. On the Tabor farm in late seventeenth-century Essex, the accounts demonstrate that there the day labourers were continuously paid with quite large quantities of meat in exchange for their work. William Dod, for instance, was paid with 23 lb of bull beef priced at 2d a pound as well as peas and 7 lb of mutton for threshing.[83] At this point in time the normal market price of beef was 3d a lb, so he was also receiving a discount.

Another example of a farmer supplying his trusted labourers with food or rent at reduced prices is when Henry Best simply paid one of his labourers £10 in 10 quarters of barley, which at the market price listed by Best would actually have been worth £13. Day labourers were also paid in kind with barley, cheese and oatmeal, in addition to money wages.[84] One labourer at Thornborough was often paid in mutton, beef and butter allowed at reduced prices.[85] Such exchanges could also be used to extend credit to some labourers in years of high food prices or when work was scarce, such as in the case of the labourer Leonard Goodale. In 1622 he purchased £3 12s 8d worth of barley, oatmeal and straw from Richard Cholmeley, but did only £1 11s worth of work.[86]

Practices like this remained common throughout the eighteenth century, and can be found in the wage book of the Somerset farmer Frances Hamilton from 1802 and many other estate accounts from the southeast and southwest, as well as Yorkshire and Northumberland in the north.[87] These sorts of debts had the advantage that they could be

[81] Brassley and Saunders (eds.), *Accounts of the Reverend John Crakanthorp*, pp. 172–5, 180–1.
[82] SRO, DD/DR 70 Part 1.
[83] Other labourers were paid with similar amounts of beef and pork. ERO, D/DTa/A1, 12 Nov. 1690–22 Sept. 1690; July 1784; 1, 22 Oct., 5 Nov. 1785.
[84] Woodward (ed.), *Farming Books of Henry Best*, pp. 169–73.
[85] Gilboy, 'Labour at Thornborough', pp. 392–3.
[86] Woodward (ed.), *Farming Books of Henry Best*, pp. lvi, 169–73, 175.
[87] This can be seen in the wage book of the Somerset farmer Frances Hamilton from 1802, and in a number of farm accounts from the eighteenth century. SRO, DD/FS 7/4; WYASB, Tong 5a/7, Tong 4b/23, Sp St/13/D83/1; NCS, Allgood Estate, ZAL 44/1; ZAL 57/26. Also see Vivienne Pollock, 'Contract and Consumption: Labour Agreements and the Use of Money in Eighteenth-Century Rural Ulster', *Agricultural History Review*, 43 (1995), pp. 19–34; M. Reed, '"Gnawing It Out": A New Look at Economic Relations in Nineteenth-Century Rural England', *Rural History*, 1 (1990), pp. 83–4, 91.

transferred to third parties, making the bargain more flexible, as in an instance where Richard Cholmeley paid a tailor for some work done for one of his servants as part of the wages he owed her.[88] Because of the close integration of their work with the local production of food this made the economic position of agricultural labourers crucially different from that of those working for wages in industry. Although miners, builders and cloth weavers generally earned higher nominal money wages, they were much more vulnerable to fluctuating food prices because they had to buy all their food on the market. As a result they relied more on credit and were vulnerable to going broke.[89]

Thus nominal wages were only the basis for more complex negotiable means of payment. They were meant to be the chief measure of the value of a labourer by time or task, and they remained 'sticky' because simple pence rates for work made accounting easier, and provided a price basis by which the value of the labour could be compared. However, this meant that bad harvests which raised the price of bread in effect lowered labourers' wages. It was not impossible that by law wages could have been tied to food prices, as was done later with the poor law.[90] But given the constant shortage of small change in the economy, it would have been difficult for farmers to actually find the cash to deal with the sudden rise in wages in years of bad harvests, or even over the course of higher winter prices. It would also have made accounting much more difficult, given the rudimentary nature of most farmers' bookkeeping at this time, if they kept accounts at all, and also more difficult for labourers to keep track of.[91] Instead day wages should be seen in a similar light to the penny loaf. They changed slowly so that they could be calculated and added up simply, and when food prices went up they were dealt with in the myriad ways discussed above, by selling food for labour or allowing a labourer to pasture an animal on an employer's field.

Family income

Even before entering service, between the ages of seven and nine, it was expected that boys would be hired at wages one half or less those of an adult. Any boys who did not go off to work as servants could be earning the equivalent of adult day wages by about the age of eighteen. In the

---

[88] *Memorandum Book of Richard Cholmeley*, p. 186.
[89] John Walter, *Understanding Popular Violence in the English Revolution: The Colchester Plunderers* (Cambridge, 1999), pp. 237, 247–8, 251–6; Wrightson, *Earthly Necessities*, p. 315.
[90] Daunton, *Progress and Poverty*, pp. 455–7.
[91] Muldrew, *Economy of Obligation*, pp. 60–5.

1760s Arthur Young estimated that there were 111,498 boys in employment. Using Wrigley and Schofield's age breakdown of the population in 1766, the eight to fourteen year age group comprised about 14 per cent of the total population. If the rural agricultural population at this date was about 45 per cent of the total population in England, as Wrigley has suggested, this means there would have been 202,122 sons of yeomen, husbandmen and labourers of this age at that time. If 70 per cent of these households were labourers this would imply that there were 141,478 sons of labourers.[92] Thus Young's figures suggest that about 80 per cent of labourers' sons were employed elsewhere, which seems a reasonable figure, given that many labouring families had small crops and animals to look after.[93]

Young girls could also start adding to the family income by spinning rough yarn from a similar age before becoming milkmaids or housemaids. They could also help their mothers in looking after children, thus freeing the latter to engage in labour to earn money.[94] In her work on women's and children's labour on a sample of Somerset farms, Helen Speechly discovered that children there normally started agricultural work at eight or nine, and that on the Nynhead estate in the 1680s, 16 per cent of the day labourer force comprised children. Both girls and boys could pick stones from fields, pick fruit or weed, while boys could drive sheep and cattle and lead ploughs. However, even children as young as three could be employed scaring birds with their rattles in a field. Boys at Nynhead were paid 4d a day in the 1680s; however, by the 1780s Frederick Eden reported that children of ten in the Kent parish of Meopham earned 6d a day; twelve-year-olds earned 9d; fourteen-year-olds 12d; sixteen-year-olds 18d; and eighteen-year-olds a full adult's wage of 24d. Elsewhere he noted that children could also earn money knitting or plaiting straw, going on errands or to market, and that many boys and girls earned money helping their mothers in spinning yarn. Such earnings could amount to between 1s and 4s a week.[95]

For young girls, from about the age of fourteen, there was always a great demand for maidservants and milkmaids. A very simple calculation suggests that if the population was about 1 million households around the beginning of the eighteenth century, and of these 30 per cent employed one female servant and 5 per cent two female servants,

[92] Wrigley and Schofield, *Population History*, pp. 528–9; Wrigley, 'Urban Growth', p. 170. For the percentage of labourers in the rural population see above, chapter 1, pp. 26–8.
[93] See below, pp. 246–56.
[94] Speechley, 'Female and Child Agricultural Day Labourers', pp. 157–60, 165, 167, 173, 179, 182, 185.
[95] Eden, *State of the Poor*, II, pp. 2, 81, 130, 287, 290, 357, 448; III, p. 752.

this would have provided employment for 400,000 girls and women. Thomas Batchelor claimed that 'in the management of a family, as in other cases, the housekeeper receives the highest wages, as the reward of skill and attention, rather than of labour'.[96] The production of dairy products was also very labour intensive. Gregory King estimated that there were 1,100,000 milk cows in England and that:

3 Dairy Women will manage 20 Cows and do much other work besides this the number of Dairy women is about ... 150,000 persons [whose] whole labour being worth £400,000 per annum comes to 53s. 4d. each per annum, And each such Dairy woman (whereof many are girls only) Requiring about £8 per annum for keeping and wages, the Business of ye Dairy must take up one third of their time in converting ye milk when milked into Butter or Cheese.

In the margin he calculated, 'Of these 150,000 Dairy women 60,000 are the mistresses or [?] of the family and 90,000 are servants', and at the bottom of the page he claimed that of the 90,000 servants a third earned 40s per annum, a third 24s per annum and a third 10s per annum. Following his own estimation, the number of dairy women should have been 165,000 rather than 150,000 so there could well have been more dairymaids.[97]

By the 1760s, Arthur Young estimated that there were 167,247 maid-servants on farms, although he did not estimate how many of the maid-servants he listed were involved in dairying. He also estimated their wages to be on average £3 9s each, and the value of their board at £5.[98] In the mid-1760s, the number of agricultural labourers' households probably numbered about 411,158 compared to 176,210 other rural households.[99] Here Young's figure seems to be much too low, as almost all wealthier households would have hired at least one maidservant just to look after household chores, and many more maids would have been needed for milking. In fact, many of Young's sample farms are not listed as employing any maids, and if we compare the number of cows these farms possessed to the number of maids they employed, there is no correlation. There were farms with twenty cows and no milkmaids, which strongly suggests that Young was counting only household maid-servants.[100] Young estimated there were 1,337,976 cows, which would

[96] Batchelor, *General View*, p. 79.   [97] Laslett (ed.), *Earliest Classics*, p. 214.
[98] Young, *Northern Tour*, IV, pp. 345, 356.
[99] This is based on the calculation of a population of 6,200,000, or 1,305,263 households of 4.75 members each, of which 45 per cent were involved in agricultural production (587,368), and of these it has been estimated that 70 per cent were labourers' households, based on the data in chapter 1, above. Wrigley and Schofield, *Population History*, p. 534; Wrigley, 'Urban Growth', p. 170
[100] Young, *Northern Tour*, IV, pp. 208–18, 236–46.

Table 5.7 *Yearly earnings of dairymaids in
1808, from Thomas Batchelor*

	£	s	d
Superintendence of house and dairy	5	4	0
Dairy work (15 cows)	19	5	2
Cooking at 7s a week	18	5	0
Management of beds and other furniture	2	2	0
Washing their own clothes	3	0	10
Total	48	7	0

mean that every one of his female servants would have had to both do housework *and* milk eight cows as well. Using King's estimation of one dairymaid to about seven cows means we should probably at least double Young's figures. A century later Batchelor calculated that in 1808 a family of seven persons keeping fifteen dairy cattle would need a housekeeper and maid to do all the house and dairy work *exclusive* of washing clothes, which he assumed would be sent out at this time. The earnings he listed for this date, given in Table 5.7, were considerably higher than previously, even taking wartime inflation into account.[101]

Dairying was very labour intensive, and must have provided a great deal of employment for women, and as Batchelor shows it could be rewarded well (see pp. 271 and 273 below). Many girls from labouring families would, of course, also have gone to work as domestic servants in artisans' and tradesmen's houses both in the country and in towns, especially London. Indeed, the sex ratios of eighteenth-century towns were significantly skewed towards women, owing to the numbers of female domestics employed.[102]

Like men, women were also employed as day labourers for weeding, picking stones, mowing and other harvest work. In twenty-five of the seventy parishes where Frederick Eden described the nature of agricultural work, he mentioned women's work, in contrast to only three parishes where he pointed out that the women did not work at all.[103] For adult women, both Helen Speechley and Joyce Burnette have done work which demonstrates the importance of female labour for late seventeenth- and eighteenth-century agriculture. In the account book of

[101] Batchelor, *General View*, p. 79.
[102] P. J. Corfield, *The Impact of English Towns, 1700–1800* (Oxford, 1982), pp. 126–30; Tim Meldrum, *Domestic Service and Gender 1660–1750: Life and Work in the London Household* (Harlow, 2000), pp. 12–24.
[103] Eden, *State of the Poor*, II–III, pp. 1–904, *passim*.

Richard Bagshaw for the Oakes farm of about 92 acres in Derbyshire in the 1770s, the total percentage of female day labour hired over the course of a year varied from 17 per cent to 19 per cent. On the Somerset farms examined by Helen Speechley female day labour made up 20 per cent of hired work. On the Golden Barton farm in Cornwall, where the accounts list both women's and men's work by the day very thoroughly from 1754 to 1755, 34 per cent of the work was done by women.[104]

On the Oakes farm, however almost all of the women day labourers were hired during the hay harvest, where 47–54.5 per cent of days worked were by female labour. In 1772, at the Oakes, an unspecified number of women and girls worked a total of 444 days over 7 weeks during the summer. Only one woman, Ann Parkinson, worked more regularly at other times of the year.[105] She worked 122 days of the year, which was still less than the 5 men, who worked over 300 days of the year. One reason for this was that the farm was clearly geared towards pastoral production of animal products, selling cows, calves, tallow, hay, wool and lambs. There were undoubtedly cows for home dairying, but the work involved would have been done by live-in dairymaids.[106] On the Somerset farms again, most female labour was employed in the summer, but in these mixed arable farms, many more women were hired earlier in the summer to do weeding as well as for the hay and corn harvests. At the Nynhead farm in Somerset 45 per cent of female employment occurred during the summer, while at Chancellor's farm women were employed only between May and September.[107]

The breakdown of female day labour as a percentage of the total day labour hired over the year at Crowcomb Barton farm in Somerset for 1756–7 is given in Table 5.8.[108] Here the average amount of female labour hired between May and October was 25 per cent, compared to only 8 per cent during the winter. Similarly, on the Golden Barton farm, women's work was done almost exclusively from May to September, when large numbers of women were hired, first to weed, then in haymaking, then for the harvest and finally in picking apples and making cider. This farm was primarily given over to stock rearing, especially sheep; possessing 85 head of cattle, 18 pigs and 406 sheep in 1748, compared to 50–84 acres under arable cultivation between 1748 and

---

[104] Speechley, 'Female and Child Agricultural Day Labourers', p. 57; Pound, 'Barton Farming', pp. 61–3; Joyce Burnette, 'Labourers at the Oakes: Changes in the Demand for Female Day-Labourers at a Farm near Sheffield during the Agricultural Revolution', *Journal of Economic History*, 59 (1999), p. 56.
[105] Burnette, 'Labourers at the Oakes', p. 48.   [106] Ibid., pp. 46–7.
[107] Speechley, 'Female and Child Agricultural Day Labourers', pp. 57, 73.
[108] Ibid., p. 74.

Table 5.8 *Percentage of work done by women at Crowcombe Barton farm over the course of 1756–7*

January	5
February	5
March	10
April	5
May	20
June	25
July	35
August	32
September	20
October	15
November	10
December	12

1762. It still, however, required a great deal of female labour input into what arable land was cultivated and for the hay harvest. During the summer months at Golden Barton there was enough work to employ between six and thirteen women working full-time and many more part-time.[109] Similarly the accounts for labour on the Thornborough estate in Yorkshire from 1749 to 1773 list women hired for many of the same tasks, supporting William Marshall's claim that 'here it is almost equally rare to see a sickle in the hand of a man; reaping ... being almost entirely done by women'.[110]

Arthur Young calculated that the owner of a small arable farm of 40 acres with 25 acres under wheat, oats and barley, together with 7 cows and 2 horses, would have to hire enough labour for 266 days of weeding, mowing and harvesting in the summer, or 39 per cent of the total yearly labour required on the farm.[111] Although Young gives no indication of which gender might be hired for this work, it does show that the potential for women's labour would be the same or greater on more heavily arable land. Over the winter women also helped manuring fields, fencing, cutting wool, clearing roads and picking stones, apart from dairying and housework.[112]

Women's wages, though, were generally only about half those of men. In the mid-eighteenth century, whereas men could be paid up to 16d

[109] Pound, 'Barton Farming', pp. 61–3. For the employment of women in the late sixteenth century see Hassell Smith, 'Labourers in Norfolk', I, pp. 29–30.
[110] Gilboy, 'Labour at Thornborough', p. 391.
[111] Young, *The Farmer's Guide*, II, pp. 123ff.
[112] Speechley, 'Female and Child Agricultural Day Labourers', pp. 57, 73.

a day women generally earned 6–7d.[113] In some cases this was because of gendered wage discrimination, but as Joyce Burnette has argued in many cases it was due to the fact that women spent less time in paid work during the day because they were responsible for so many tasks at home, such as preparing and delivering meals, cleaning and dairy production.[114] In other cases, such as heavy lifting, it was because the men could do more work in the same amount of time.[115] In Yorkshire it was noted that women generally started work one to two hours later than men, and if they had small infants to look after in a field this would have taken a certain percentage of their time.[116]

Eden commented that in Broomfield, Cumbria women did most of the work, but were paid only half as much as men, claiming that it was 'not easy to account for such a striking inequality; and still less easy to justify it', which sounds like obvious wage discrimination.[117] However, he noted that elsewhere many women were paid 8–12d a day for weeding by the 1780s, and women could earn more in harvest, generally 10–12d. Also some women were paid as much as men. Eden noted that in Kirkoswald, Cumbria, women were paid 22d a day with victuals, and in Seergham in the same county both men and women earned 10–12d a day. In Market Weighton, Yorkshire, they could earn 18d a day burning sods. One female labourer in Somerset was paid 2s a day digging at piece-work rates, and in Hothfield, Kent, an industrious woman was said to be able to earn 30–36d a day picking hops.[118] In addition to wages, women and children could also earn money gleaning after the harvest, which has been estimated to have been worth 4–6 bushels of grain.[119] In one instance 25s was earned gleaning.[120] Taking these rates, if a woman worked a month weeding at 8d a day at hay harvest and 6 weeks at 12d, together with another 6 weeks doing other odd jobs at 8d, this would provide earnings of £4 16s for 109 days' work. At Nettlecombe in Somerset in 1802 three women worked 176, 143 and

---

[113] Speechley, 'Female and Child Agricultural Day Labourers', pp. 120–2; Eden, *State of the Poor*, II, p. 73.

[114] Joyce Burnette, 'An Investigation of the Female–Male Wage Gap During the Industrial Revolution in Britain', *Economic History Review*, 50 (1997), pp. 257–81, esp. p. 268; Joyce Burnette, 'The Wages and Employment of Female Day-Labourers in English Agriculture, 1740–1850', *Economic History Review*, 57 (2004), pp. 664–90.

[115] Laslett (ed.), *Earliest Classics*, p. 213; Eden, *State of the Poor*, II, p. 419.

[116] Gilboy, 'Labour at Thornborough', p. 396.   [117] Eden, *State of the Poor*, II, pp. 47–8.

[118] Ibid., II, pp. 65, 67, 73, 81, 84, 90, 139, 287, 290, 390, 404, 471, 544, 548, 596, 652, 692; III, pp. 723, 744, 794, 863.

[119] Jane Humphries, 'Enclosures, Common Rights, and Women: The Proletarianisation of Families in the Late Eighteenth and Early Nineteenth Centuries', *Journal of Economic History*, 50 (1990), p. 35.

[120] Speechley, 'Female and Child Agricultural Day Labourers', p. 115.

114 days each during the summer at 7d a day, earning between £4 6s and £6 12s.[121]

It is possible to get a very rough idea of how much demand there would have been for female agricultural labour by using the number of days worked by women at the Oakes and on the Golden Barton farms described above as an example. This can then be divided by the farm size and multiplied by the amount of cultivated land in England. At the Oakes in 1772, women worked a total of 426 days and the size of the farm was about 92 acres, which works out to 4.6 days per acre on an almost entirely pastoral farm.[122] At Golden Barton in 1754–5, women worked a total of 754 days during May to September weeding and harvesting hay and corn, which works out to 11.3 days per acre (using an average of 67 arable sown acres). Given the number of animals at Golden Barton, using information on stocking densities discussed in the last chapter, the farm would probably have contained about 130 acres of pasture in addition to the 50–84 acres of arable land.[123] Since no milking was mentioned in the accounts this task must have been done by maidservants. If we assume that hay, which would have been used to feed animals over the winter, was grown on the pasture, and since 31 per cent of women's work was haymaking, this leaves 7.8 days work per acre of arable land.

In 1700 it has been estimated that there were 9 million acres of arable land compared to 12 million acres of pasture. At this time there were about 814,000 rural women between the ages of 15 and 59, of whom 569,862 (70 per cent) would have been members of labouring households.[124] If we use the ratio for the Oakes of 4.6 days per acre as an

---

[121] Ibid., pp. 119–21; Burnette, 'Labour at the Oakes', p. 48.

[122] Burnette, 'Labour at the Oakes', pp. 46–7, 50. The figure for days worked is taken from her Table 4 and has been reduced by 25 per cent to account for labour at Wormhill farm, which was included in this table (see the top of p. 43).

[123] Two hundred and forty-five days were spent harvesting hay, and according to the wages appointed by the Justices at the Essex Easter session in 1661, a woman could mow 0.45 of an acre of grass a day. Raking and cocking the same acre of grass, however, took 2.4 days for a woman. Although, as we shall see, rates of work measured in this way could vary in different places, these Essex rates are very detailed and allow this calculation to be made for a woman. (This is discussed in more detail on pp. 267–70 below.) If we add another day for loading wagons, this implies there were also about 63 acres of hay in addition to summer pasture and the arable land under cultivation. In the mid-eighteenth century it has been estimated that there were 10 million acres of arable to 15 million acres of pasture. This works out to be about 1.8 days of work haymaking per acre of pasture, in comparison to 2 days of women's work per acre in the hay harvest at the Oakes. Pounds, 'Barton Farming', pp. 61–3. Burnette, 'Labour at the Oakes', p. 52.

[124] Assuming a population of 5,057,790 and a sex ratio of 50:50 in the absence of accurate national figures, of which 55 per cent were rural agricultural families. Wrigley and Schofield, *Population History*, pp. 528–9; Wrigley, 'Urban Growth', p. 170.

average for female employment on pastoral land and the Golden Barton ratio of 7.8 days' work per acre as an average for arable land, this works out to a potential of 157 days' full daily employment for each rural woman in this age range per year, or 224 days' full employment just for women from labouring households. These estimates are much higher than the three to four months of summer employment indicated by the examples cited above.

Moreover, by 1750 demand would have increased as the acreage of cultivated land was increasing, while the total population had not grown much, but the percentage engaged in agriculture had declined to 45 per cent.[125] However, since this estimation is based on all the land in the country, it also includes work female labourers would have done on their own family farms if they possessed any land. But at the same time, it leaves out dairy work, which, as we saw, was considerable. Of course any generalisation based on just two farms is at best highly speculative, and the high estimates of labour required suggest that these farms might have been unusual. Still, they do imply that there was a good opportunity for women to earn wages in agriculture, and that they must have been in great demand during the summer.

Women in rural areas could also earn money working on roads for the parish for wages similar to those available for agriculture.[126] Money could also be made washing. Thomas Batchelor reported that, 'male servants generally pay from 4s. to 5s. per Quarter to some person in the Neighbourhood for washing, etc. but in the case of female servants, it makes a part of their annual expense, as ... they perform it themselves, their master must allow leisure for that purpose: the expense may be averaged at 1d. a day or £1 10s. 5d. per annum'.[127] One penny a day in 1808 would work out to at least an hour's worth of daily work for a woman for each male servant employed, and many large households needed to hire extra labour for washing. In 1678 the Earl of Ailesbury paid two washerwomen 1s each a day for 4 days' work.[128] In addition, wet nursing, nursing, sewing, straw plaiting, lace making and cooking all provided other forms of female employment.[129]

Much more important, though, was the employment provided by the cloth industry, primarily in spinning wool and then flax. Millions of

[125] Wrigley, 'Urban Growth', p. 170; Overton, *Agricultural Revolution*, p. 76.
[126] Gilboy, 'Labour at Thornborough', p. 607.   [127] Batchelor, *General View*, p. 78.
[128] Sara Mendelson and Patricia Crawford, *Women in Early Modern England* (Oxford, 1998), p. 273.
[129] Ibid., pp. 274–5, 285; Hassell Smith, 'Labourers in Norfolk', I, pp. 28–9. Sue Wright, '"Chumaids, Huswyfes and Hucksters": The Employment of Women in Tudor and Stuart Salisbury', in Lindsey Charles and Lorna Duffin (eds.), *Women and Work in Pre-Industrial England* (Beckenham, 1985), pp. 103–21; Meldrum, *Domestic Service*, pp. 127ff.

yards of thread were needed to make clothing and to manufacture cloth for England's largest foreign export. Almost all of this spinning was done by women and children in the winter months, when there was less demand for agricultural labour. Estimating how much money a family might make from spinning is an even more difficult task than for agriculture, especially with the shift from the so-called old draperies to the lighter new draperies in the 1630s and 1640s which required finer, better-spun thread.[130] Rates of spinning were variously estimated, and although the spinning for old draperies was paid at a lower rate, more could be spun in a week. Frederick Eden estimated that a single woman could spin about a pound of wool per day, and a married woman 2.5 lb per week if she also had housework and children to look after. But he did not say what quality of yarn this produced, only that the average earnings were 1s to 1s 2d a pound.[131] This also accords with the report of a clothier of Bradford in the late eighteenth century who claimed that the spinners he used could spin 2.5 lb of 20-count yarn at 1s per pound. Another Yorkshire clothier reported that girls aged 14–15 could spin 2.7 lb a week at 2s.[132] This implies that skilled adults could have spun the same weight of finer yarn for more money, as is indicated by some of Arthur Young's estimates given in Table 5.9. However, children of six to fourteen would have spun more slowly and less frequently, and were consequently paid less. Arthur Young gave various estimates of children's earnings of 1–2s a week in comparison to 2s 6d to 6s for adult women.[133]

Eden's and Arthur Young's figures can be combined with earlier contemporary estimates and actual rates paid to women by clothiers for spinning for both the old and new draperies in order to determine how much a woman could earn. Because yarn of different fineness was spun at different speeds, this means that wages are best measured as weekly wages. Although it is not often explicitly stated, it is clear that almost all such estimates were for married women's rates of weekly work. The

---

[130] This is explored in more detail in Craig Muldrew, '"Th'ancient Distaff and Whirling Spindle": Measuring the Contribution of Spinning to Household Earnings and the National Economy in England 1550–1770', *Economic History Review* (in press).

[131] Eden, *State of the Poor*, III, p. 796.

[132] The quality of the yarn was measured by its fineness. This was done by specifying the length of yarn to be spun from a pound of wool, which was measured by the number of times it could be wound around a reel returned by a spinner. Each revolution was termed a 'thread', and the number of revolutions was termed either a 'hank' or 'skein'. A very low count would be between ten and twenty and a high count was generally above thirty, but counts above fifty were possible. Norman Biggs, 'A Tale Untangled: Measuring the Fineness of Yarn', *Textile History*, 35 (2004), pp. 120–9. John James, *History of the Worsted Manufacture in England* (London, 1857), pp. 324–5.

[133] Young, *Northern Tour*, III, pp. 133–6, 163–4, 192; Young, *Eastern Tour*, II, pp. 78–81.

Table 5.9 *Earnings from domestic spinning c. 1770,*
taken from Arthur Young's tours

Place/cloth	Weekly earnings
Sudbury worsted	2s 9d
Witney wool	4s 6d to 5s 6d
Romsey worsted	2s 6d
Norwich worsted	2s 6d to 3s
Leeds worsted	3s 6d to 4s
Kendal stocking yarn	3s
linsey-woolsey	4s 6d to 5s
Warrington sailcloth	1s
sacking	6s
Manchester cotton	2s to 5s

Source: Rule, *Albion's People*, p. 192.

sheer numbers of women involved imply that most spinning was done
by married women and their children, since widows and adult single
women were unlikely to have formed more than around 12 per cent of
the population. But again we need to assume that such estimates will
only ever be averages, as a woman with one child would have had more
time to spin than one with a larger number of small children under
the age at which they themselves could begin to spin or do other work.
The earliest estimates for the Yorkshire old draperies would provide
earnings of about 1s 3d per week, which remained roughly the same
until the 1630s. By the end of the seventeenth century this had risen to
about 3s a week and by the 1770s had further increased to an average
of 4s, as shown in Table 5.9. Table 5.10 shows the change in a married
woman's potential earnings from spinning, assuming that she spun for
thirty-five weeks in the winter, with the remainder of the year taken up
with agricultural work.

Rates of spinning not only rose because of the greater skill required
to spin finer yarn, but also because of increasing demand for cloth.
In the late seventeenth and early eighteenth century there was a great
increase in cloth production, largely driven by exports of English woollen manufactures and increased home demand. Table 5.11 is an attempt
to estimate the potential employment of spinners in England based on a
complex set of calculations used to determine how much thread would
have had to be spun to make all of the cloth produced at different dates
for both home consumption and export. It is based on rates of spinning
for married women as a standard. These are only approximate figures,

Table 5.10 *A married woman's potential earnings from 35 weeks of spinning*

Date	Earnings
1580	£2 4s
1615	£2 12s
1690	£5 5s
1760	£7

Table 5.11 *Estimates of total earnings from spinning at different dates*

Date	Employment	Total earnings
1580	225,083	£744,462 (£443,132 + 68% to account for inflation[a])
1615	338,427	£877,647 (£765,503 + 14% to account for inflation)
1700	481,564	£2,604,057
1741	651038	£4,560,754
1770	785,627	£5,499,389

Note: [a] Clay, *Economic Expansion*, I, p. 49.

since single women spun more and children spun less. Furthermore, employment opportunities for spinning would be much greater in areas where cloth making was concentrated such as East Anglia, the area around Gloucestershire and Wiltshire and increasingly Lancashire and Yorkshire.

It is also possible that the number of weeks worked in a year increased in the eighteenth century, when demand rose quickly because of increasing exports. Many complaints were made at this time that it was hard to find good maidservants because so many women were spinning full-time. A woman earning 4s a week in the 1760s could have earned £10 a year if she spun for a full 50 weeks. Also many poor households had elder daughters spinning as well, like that of Richard Latham, or some of the households noted by Young, Eden and Davies. If there were two daughters in the family between the ages of 8 and 14 who could earn, say, £4 between them, then the female contribution to the family income would have been increased even more. As John Styles has shown, in the years from 1742 to 1754 when the Latham daughters entered their teenage years and remained at home earning money from cotton spinning, the average annual household expenditure went up from about £16 to £28, while expenditure on clothes trebled.[134] In addition to this there is much evidence than English linen production expanded from a very small industry to something quite substantial by the mid-eighteenth century. At a rate of spinning of 6 lb a week for a married woman, flax and hemp spinning might have provided employment for another 714,286 wives in 1750. Since much of this was probably low-grade spinning it was not worth as much as spinning wool, but even at a rate of 6d a pound this would have been worth £3,750,000 in earnings.[135] Taking wool, linen and hemp spinning together, the potential employment by 1770 could have been in the order of 1,500,000 married women. If we were to add to this figure 100,000 women employed in hand-knitting stockings, this would have provided employment for about 75 per cent of *all* women over the age of 14 in the country.[136] Of course, some proportion of this would have been done by younger children, so total employment would have been less, but this still represents a huge demand for labour.

Almost all sources are in agreement that spinning was primarily an occupation for women and children in poorer families. John Haynes, for instance, described woollen manufacture as the chief employment of the poor, and in the Ipswich census of the poor from 1597, 68 per cent of poor women listed their work as spinning or knitting, which provided 47 per cent of their income.[137] The fact that so many workhouses employed their inmates in spinning is further evidence of the role of spinning in the income of the poor. It was noted in the early seventeenth century that 'yarn is weekly broughte into the market by a great number of poor people ... [who] weekly buy their wool in the market by very small parcels according to their use, and weekly return it in yarn and make good profit having the benefit both of their labour and merchandize and live exceeding well'.[138]

---

[134] John Styles, 'Custom or Consumption? Plebeian Fashion in Eighteenth-Century England', in Maxine Berg and Elizabeth Eger (eds.), *Luxury in the Eighteenth Century: Debates, Desires and Delectable Goods* (Basingstoke, 2003), pp. 107–9; Weatherill (ed.), *Account Book of Richard Latham*, pp. xiii, xxii.

[135] N. B. Harte, 'The Rise of Protection and the English Linen Trade, 1690–1780', in N. B. Harte and K. G. Ponting (eds.), *Textile History and Economic History* (Manchester, 1973), pp. 104–5.

[136] Wrigley and Schofield, *Population History*, p. 529.

[137] John Webb (ed.), *Poor Relief in Elizabethan Ipswich*, Suffolk Records Society, 9 (1966), pp. 119–40; John Haynes, *Great Britain's Glory: or An Account of the Great Numbers of Poor Employed in the Woollen and Silk Manufactures* (London, 1715), pp. 1–5; James, *Worsted*, pp. 311–12; Eric Kerridge, *Textile Manufactures in Early Modern England* (Manchester, 1985), p. 207; Alice Clark, *Working Life of Women in the Seventeenth Century* (London, 1992), pp. 100–4.

[138] Clark, *Working Life*, p. 108.

This overwhelmingly demonstrates the necessity of adding female earnings to male wages if we wish to trace change in earnings over time. There certainly seems to have been enough demand to add £7 or more female income to a household a year, depending on its location and the number of children spinning. If we also add potential earnings from embezzlement this rises to £8 2s.[139] Eden, for instance, reported that in South Tawton, Devon, a labourer's wife could earn £9 2s 6d a year in the 1780s.[140] This figure was over three times what a woman could earn in the late sixteenth century, while a male agricultural worker's money wage had only gone up from 8d to 11–16d. This means, as we shall see, that the rise in family earnings was much greater than indicated by male real wage series.

Home production

In addition to working for wages many labouring families also engaged in some form of home agricultural production. Here, the probate inventory sample examined in chapter 4 can be used to evaluate how labourers could augment their income through home production. Farm animals, growing or stored crops and all sorts of farm and food production equipment were all listed in inventories. Unfortunately, land, being real property, fell under the jurisdiction of customary not testamentary law so was not required to be listed in an inventory. As a result it is impossible to determine the size of farms.[141] Only the acreage of crops actually growing in the field when someone died was listed.[142] Out of the total sample of 972 labourers' inventories, 624 mentioned fields or some kind of crop.[143] Table 5.12 provides information on such crops. Here, the percentage of inventories with any sort of crop noted as either growing or present in harvested form in the house or barn is listed in column one. However, these percentage figures do not necessarily indicate that the labourer in question was growing his own crops, as much of the grain listed in houses was only very small amounts, which could

---

[139] John Styles, 'Embezzlement, Industry and the Law in England, 1500–1800', in M. Berg, P. Hudson and M. Sonenscher (eds.), *Manufacture in Town and Country before the Factory* (Cambridge, 1983), pp. 175–7.

[140] Eden, *State of the Poor*, II, p. 139.

[141] Land was bequeathed in wills but only the names of farms were listed, not size or value.

[142] The significant literature discussing how the value of crop acreages in probate inventories can be used to determine crop yields, which was discussed above on pp. 144–6. This is summarised in Glennie, 'Measuring Crop Yields', pp. 255–83.

[143] There were 174 from Cambridgeshire; 6 from Cheshire; 88 from Hampshire; 238 from Kent; 36 from Lincolnshire; and 79 from Norfolk. See Table 4.1 for the total number of inventories from each of these counties in the sample.

Table 5.12 *Labourers' inventories mentioning crops in the field*

Period	Percentage of inventories mentioning crops or grain	Percentage of inventories with crops in the field (number)	Percentage of inventories with crops in the field, March to July	Average size of crop in acres
1550–1649	57	20 (65)	30	2.3
1650–99	51	20 (87)	30	2.6
1700–50	42	13 (27)	20	4.3

also have been bought on the market. Out of the 138 listings of grain by the bushel, only 38 (28 per cent) were for amounts greater than 5 bushels. The largest amount of any harvested crop listed was for 26 quarters (1 quarter = 8 bushels) of hemp. For wheat it was 14 quarters, and only 6 inventories listed over 10 quarters of any crop. Other amounts were listed by parcel, pound, stack and load, but few were for large amounts.[144]

Table 5.13 shows the types of crop mentioned in the inventories (both growing and stored). The largest crop was hay or grass to feed cattle and sheep, which will be discussed below. The next largest grain crops were wheat and barley.[145] Oats and rye were mentioned relatively rarely. Since most of the inventories in the sample survive from the south, where these crops were rarely eaten, this is not surprising.[146] Also, since fewer than 30 per cent of labourers owned a horse, they were less likely to grow oats as horse fodder. The large number of inventories with hemp is perhaps surprising (although this crop was not found in the sample from Hampshire). This indicates that hemp was grown by labourers to make cheaper cloth which could be used as sheets and tablecloths or more rarely shirts. It was also commonly used for sacking and rope.[147] The accounts of Sarah Fell show that she grew hemp on her Yorkshire farm and continually had it spun and woven into cloth.[148] However, the presence of hemp was much more common

---

[144] Both the 26 quarters of hemp and the 14 quarters of wheat were owned by labourers from Kent, who died in 1568 and 1682 respectively. CKS, prc10.3.469–70, prc27.29.161.
[145] 'Corn' simply refers to grain.
[146] Unfortunately, only six of the inventories from Cheshire mentioned crops, so a comparison of these inventories with those from the south is not possible.
[147] Styles, 'Clothing in the North', pp. 144–51.
[148] Norman Penney (ed.), *The Household Account Book of Sarah Fell of Swarthmoor Hall* (Cambridge, 1920), pp. 25, 29, 37, 41, 43, 69, *passim*.

Table 5.13 *Types of crops, harvested food and fuels mentioned in labourers' inventories*[a]

Crop	Number of times mentioned
Hay and grass	241
(Wood, faggots, firing)	207
Wheat	206
Barley	134
Corn	110
Hemp	106
Peas	69
Oats	46
(Turf)	38
Rye	36
(Malt)	31
(Coals)	29
Beans	27
Hops	19
Saffron	11
Maslin	9

Note: [a] Firewood, turf and coals are in parentheses and are included here for comparison, since the gathering of firewood was an activity contributing to household income.

before 1650, being found in 21 per cent of inventories before that date, and in only 6 per cent afterwards, which again is indicative of the rising standard of living after that date. The number of inventories containing sheets and so forth described as being made of hemp also declined from 10 per cent before 1600 to only 1 per cent after 1700.

One gets a better sense of labourers' arable agriculture by looking just at crops growing in the field, listed in the third column of Table 5.12. Here only 20 per cent of labourers had such crops before 1700, falling to 13 per cent afterwards. In addition, it can be seen in Table 5.14 that the areas of crops under cultivation were very small. Almost half were under 1.9 acres. However, since crops were much more likely to be listed in inventories from the spring and summer, between planting and the harvest, we need to look specifically at these months to get a more accurate figure. Table 5.15 compares the dates of the inventories listing crops in the ground to the dates of the whole sample. The first column on this table shows that indeed most crops were listed in inventories of people who were inventoried between March and July. If we just compare the numbers of labourers with crops who were inventoried between

Table 5.14 *Size of crop acreages listed in labourers'*
inventories

Acres	Number of inventories	Percentage
≥ 10	7	4
5–9.9	20	12
2–4.9	61	36
≤ 1.9	83	48

Table 5.15 *Monthly totals of inventories by date*

Month of inventory	Percentage of inventories with crops in the field	Percentage of total inventory sample[a]
January	9	10
February	3.5	8.5
March	12	12
April	17.5	12
May	17.5	10.5
June	16	9
July	9	6
August	3.5	4
September	3	7
October	3.5	7
November	2.5	7
December	3	7
Total number	171	894

Note: [a] Seventy-six inventories had no date, or the month was illegible.

March and July to the total number of labourers who were inventoried
in these months (Table 5.12, column five), the proportion with crops
rises to 30 per cent before 1700, before falling to 20 per cent thereafter.[149] But this still means that, even in the sixteenth century, the great
majority of labourers did not farm their own land. This not only confirms the historiographical argument about the decline of the labouring
smallholder in the seventeenth century, it also suggests that it might
have begun earlier.[150] If smallholders were more prevalent in the late sixteenth century, they were not being called 'labourers' by their assessors,
and thus in all probability not supplementing their income working for

[149] Only twenty-eight inventories had crops listed before 1600.
[150] Wrightson, *Earthly Necessities*, pp. 186–90; Spufford, *Contrasting Communities*, ch. 2.

Table 5.16 *Ownership of animals over time in labourers' inventories*

Period	Total	Cattle[a] Percentage with cattle	Cattle Number per inventory with cattle	Cattle Number divided by all inventories	Cows Percentage with cows	Cows Number per inventory with cows	Sheep Percentage with sheep
1550–99	119	62	3.8	2.3	52	2.6	36
1600–49	201	52	3.2	1.7	46	2.4	21
1650–99	445	55	4.4	2.4	51	3.3	23
1700–99	207	46	4.3	1.9	44	3.3	21
All	972	54	3.9	2.1	49	3.1	25

Note: [a] Includes cows.

others.[151] This reinforces what Peter Bowden demonstrated in the *AHEW* that it was simply uneconomical to labour on such small farms.[152]

Tables 5.16 and 5.17 show that pastoral agriculture was clearly more important to labourers than arable production. More than half of the inventories in the sample listed cattle, most of which were cows. However, this evidence also shows that labourers had many fewer animals than suggested by Alan Everitt.[153] The potential importance of cow-keeping to a labouring family's earning in the eighteenth century has been stressed by Leigh Shaw-Taylor.[154] A cow could provide food for the family or earnings through the sale of milk and cheese. William Harrison's comment that 'white meats, as milk, butter, and cheese', despite their dearness, were food of the 'inferior sort' indicates that this was equally the case during Elizabeth's reign.[155] In chapter 2 we saw that milk and butter were certainly staples of northern labourers' diet, being used in porridge and gruel. The number of labourers possessing cows was also higher in the sixteenth century than in the seventeenth century, and this percentage continued to drop in the eighteenth century to 44 per cent.[156]

[151] Together with Dr Leigh Shaw-Taylor I intend to examine a sample of husbandmen's inventories to investigate this question.
[152] Peter Bowden, 'Agricultural Prices, Farm Profits, and Rents', in *AHEW*, IV, pp. 649–62.
[153] Everitt, 'Farm Labourers', pp. 413–21, 443.
[154] Shaw-Taylor, 'Labourers, Cows, Common Rights', pp. 95–126; Shaw-Taylor, 'Cottage Economy', Table 3.10, p. 31. See also Humphries, 'Enclosures, Common Rights', pp. 23–9.
[155] Harrison, *Description*, p. 126. On the importance of butter see Moffet, *Health's Improvement*, p. 129.
[156] The number of labourers possessing cows in Cheshire, however, was not higher than for the sample as a whole.

Sheep	Sheep	Pigs	Pigs	Pigs	Horses	Poultry
Number per inventory with sheep	Number divided by all inventories	Percentage with pigs	Number per inventory with pigs	Number divided by all inventories	Percentage with horses	Percentage with poultry
15.6	5	51	2.9	1.4	21	42
10.2	2	41	2.7	1.1	20	28
12.5	2.7	42	2.5	1.23	24	9
13.4	2.7	34	1.9	0.64	29	3
12.9	3.1	42	2.5	1.1	24	16

Table 5.17 *Value of animals in labourers' inventories*

Period	Number of inventories used	Average value of all animals
1550–99	92	£3.15 (+ 69% inflation, £5.32)
1600–49	165	£4.70
1650–99	348	£5.01
1700–99	164	£4.80
All	769	£4.42

In addition, although grass and hay were mentioned more often than any other crop, only four crops of grass were listed as growing, implying that most hay was either cut from common land, bought or received as wages. Since inventories do not list real property we cannot know whether these labourers owned copyhold pasture, but leaseholds were considered a chattel, and were supposed to be listed in inventories by appraisers. Only thirty-five labourers' inventories had leases listed as assets, and many of these were for houses rather than fields. If a significant number did have pasture, we would expect to find more crops of grass, given the obvious need for hay over the winter. Most of the cows mentioned must have been pastured either on commons or on pasture leased from landlords. It is impossible to tell from this evidence how many had access to common grazing rights, but the decline in numbers of labourers possessing cows would certainly seem to support Shaw-Taylor's argument that by the late eighteenth century more labourers had to rent pasture ground.[157] For poorer labouring families with less

---

[157] Shaw-Taylor, 'Proletarianisation, Parliamentary Enclosure and the Household', pp. 654–59.

access to employment, this would have represented a loss of income, but since the living standards of most inventoried labourers went up between 1650 and 1750 it might also indicate that more money could be earned by working for wages.

Pigs were owned by 50 per cent of labourers in the sixteenth century, but only by 34 per cent by the eighteenth century. They were also owned in smaller numbers than cows, and the number per inventory also dropped over time. This is despite both Eden and Davies noting the economic advantage to a labouring family of raising a pig for bacon to put in pottage rather than buying meat at the butchers.[158] However, pig-keeping was often reliant on having a cow, as the skimmed milk was used to feed pigs.[159] Sheep were kept by many fewer labourers, although the number owned was greater, as it has been estimated that ten sheep could graze on the same area as one cow.[160] The possession of poultry, while quite common in the sixteenth century, declined precipitously thereafter. One reason for this could be that appraisers simply neglected to list poultry because the value was too small, but in the sixteenth and early seventeenth century, when the birds were listed, they were not valued at insignificant amounts. One inventory from Kent for 1583 listed two geese, twelve ducks, four hens and two cocks valued at 8s, and one from Hampshire in 1582 listed three hens, one cock, eight chickens, one goose, one gander, four ducks and one mallard worth 5s. In the mid-eighteenth century the price of a goose ranged from 1s to 2s, a duck was worth about 8d and a chicken 6d compared to 4d for a pound of beef.[161] Poultry was not considered as particularly appropriate food for labour, and since it had to be fed on grain, when grain prices went up in the 1590s perhaps it was considered to be too expensive. But still eggs were needed for cooking, and the absence of poultry from the inventories is odd. Probably many labouring families continued to possess one or two hens which were kept by wives after their husband's death and thus not valued.[162]

Overall, the number of households with animals declined over time, as did the total number of animals possessed, although the latter decline was not as pronounced for cattle. In all cases the decline in ownership was most pronounced when comparing the period 1550–99 to 1600–49. During the hard years of the 1590s labourers must have either slaughtered many of their animals for food or sold them to buy bread. The

[158] Davies, *Case of Labourers*, p. 11; Eden, *State of the Poor*, I, p. 531.
[159] Humphries, 'Enclosures, Common Rights', p. 26.
[160] Allen, *Enclosure and the Yeoman*, p. 198.
[161] Thorold Rogers, *History of Agriculture and Prices*, VII, pp. 303–4.
[162] Moffet, *Health's Improvement*, p. 8.

further decline of pigs and cattle in the eighteenth century could have
been due to declining common rights. The one animal whose possession actually rose, however, was the horse – from 20 per cent before
1650 to 24 per cent between 1650 and 1700, and then to 29 per cent
in the eighteenth century. This suggests that once labourers were able
to earn more, they purchased a horse, which would allow them to earn
more carting dung, stones, and so on, or ploughing as Richard Latham
did. It also supports the argument of E. A. Wrigley that horse use went
up in the eighteenth century.[163] Finally, if we look at the twenty-three
inventories which were exempted from the hearth taxes on the grounds
of poverty, they had fewer sheep and horses, but more pigs and about
the same amount of cattle. The numbers are too small to make anything much of this, except to say that exempt households did not possess fewer animals.

It remains to estimate what value the possession of animals was to
labourers. Both Gervase Markham in the 1620s and Arthur Young in
the 1760s estimated that a typical cow could produce between 300 and
400 gallons of milk a year, although with rich pasture and a lot of hay
in the winter, a good cow could produce over 600 gallons.[164] A number
of contemporary estimates from 1796 to 1801 show that the revenue
from butter, milk and calves of one cow was in the range of £7–9 a year.
With rights to common land, most of this would have been profit after
subtracting the cost of the cow and hay in the winter. However, by this
time, most authors included rent of pasture and the cost of hay, which
was variously estimated at about £4 per annum.[165] Also, as we saw, the
price of milk had more than doubled by these years. In the 1760s gross
profits would have been more in the region of £4, although rents were
probably about 70 per cent cheaper as well. So perhaps net profits were
in the region of £1 10s to £2 by the early to mid-eighteenth century.[166]

Such profits work out to about 7–9d a week. Arthur Young reckoned
in his survey of over fifty farms that produced milk, that the average
number of cows per dairymaid was nine. If one milkmaid could look
after nine cows over the course of a day this might roughly work out to
one hour per day per cow. Looking after just one or two cows would
be less efficient, as the butter- or cheese-making equipment had to be

---

[163] Wrigley, 'Advanced Organic Economy', pp. 458–62.
[164] Markham, *English Housewife*, p. 141; Young, *Northern Tour*, IV, pp. 149–68. Ellis stated
that a good cow gave 3 gallons of milk a day. Ellis, *Country Housewife*, p. 172; Overton
et al., *Production and Consumption*, p. 60.
[165] Humphries, 'Enclosures, Common Rights', pp. 24–8.
[166] Young noted that about 2½ gallons of milk made 1 lb of butter. Robert Loder made a
similar estimate in the early seventeenth century. At this time when butter sold at 3–4d
a lb this would amount to 18s to £1 19s revenue a year for a cow producing 350 gallons

cleaned very regularly and it would have taken time walking from the pasture to the dairy, and thus the total time spent might have been on average two or more hours a day.[167] Given this, we might assume that looking after one cow, and making milk and cheese, took the equivalent of about fourteen hours' work a week for a labouring family's wife. Such wages work out to the equivalent of 4½d for an eight-hour day, which is probably less than a woman could earn from spinning or agricultural work by the late seventeenth century. Looking after a cow would also have required constant attention, while spinning work was more flexible. Thus it might have made economic sense by this time to work for wages, where demand for work was high enough, and this might have been another reason why the ownership of cows declined in the eighteenth century.

In addition, many labourers might have only been able to achieve smaller milk yields if they fielded their cows on common land. Robert Loder was only able to get 132 gallons a year, milking from Whitsuntide to Michaelmas on common land, but it should be added that he also only provided a diet of straw in the winter.[168] But whatever the yield, a cow, as long as it remained healthy, would have provided employment for a wife with small children if the pasture was reasonably near the cottage or house, and would have been security against lack of demand for the labour of the wife and children.[169]

Moreover, by the 1790s when the price of milk had risen so dramatically, a cow would have been much more valuable, as both Davies and Eden noted. Once the rapid inflation of food prices began in the 1780s the lack of a cow meant a lack of access to milk. The price of a gallon of milk rose from 4d to 6d between 1770 and 1785, and was more than 10d a gallon by the beginning of the nineteenth century. By the 1780s in Berkshire, Davies complained that the poor could

---

of milk a year, in addition to the value of the calves produced. However, rent of pasture would have been much cheaper. Loder charged 6s rent for one cow on his grassland. Fussell (ed.), *Robert Loder's Farm Accounts*, pp. xxi, 156.

[167] Young, *Northern Tour*, IV, pp. 149–67. In comparison, Gregory King estimated that a dairymaid could look after six cows. However, Thomas Batchelor stated that, in 1808, dairy work for a maid looking after 15 cows cost £19 5s a year for milking and £5 4s for looking after the dairy. This works out to 19d a day for 312 days. However, in his section on the expenses of grassland, he estimated the cost of 'Dairy expenses, maid, etc., milking, hazard, etc.' to be £3 13s per cow, which for 15 cows would work out to £54 15s. This implies that the earnings stated in the earlier section do not include feed for the cows. Still, his estimates also imply that the cost of dairying had increased dramatically over the course of the late eighteenth century. Batchelor, *General View*, pp. 79, 157. Constant time spent cleaning was vital if the butter was to be good. Batchelor, *General View*, p. 526.

[168] Fussell (ed.), *Robert Loder's Farm Accounts*, pp. xxi, 156.

[169] Shaw-Taylor, 'Cottage Economy', pp. 12–14.

Table 5.18 *Brewing and dairy production in labourers' inventories (percentage)*

Period	Cows	Cows and pigs	Dairy equip- ment	Cows and dairy equipment	Brewing equip- ment	Cows and sheep	Barley and brewing equipment
1550–99	52	68	26	61	35	64	41
1600–49	46	59	35	57	40	50	46
1650–99	51	62	35	60	31	55	38
1700–99	44	53	29	52	37	51	39

no longer afford to drink enough milk. He asked the question, even if a poor labouring family could afford to buy a cow; 'where could they find pasture for her? The commons are so covered with the rich farmer's herds and flocks, that the poor man's cow would soon be starved there. And the little ground about their cottages is barely sufficient for garden stuff.'[170] Eden also noted that, by the late eighteenth century, cottagers in the south did not keep cows, because the expense of keeping a cow was too great where the rent of grassland was high.[171] This undoubtedly led to less milk being available in porridge for growing children, and was perhaps one reason for the decline in average heights of army recruits born at this time and analysed by Floud, Wachter and Gregory.[172]

Table 5.18 shows that many labouring households possessed dairying equipment which could be used to make butter and cheese. There was a significant rise in such possession from the sixteenth century, reaching 35 per cent in the seventeenth century, indicating that more cheese and butter were being made. However, the number of such households dropped to 29 per cent in the eighteenth century. This is less than the 48 per cent of households in Cornwall and 59 per cent in Kent which possessed dairying equipment in the Overton *et al.* sample, but still demonstrates a significant level of production.[173] Overall, there were 218 references to cheese-making equipment, such as presses, moulds and boards, and 184 to butter churns, baskets and firkins. Also, cheese (69 references) and butter (40 references) were the most commonly

---

[170] Davies, *Case of Labourers*, p. 37.
[171] Because of this he argued that poor cottagers in the south should have been provided with a garden to cultivate potatoes and turnips to feed a cow. Eden, *State of the Poor*, I, p. 531.
[172] Floud *et al.*, *Height, Health and History*, pp. 135–54, 259–60.
[173] Overton *et al.*, *Production and Consumption*, p. 37.

occurring stored foodstuffs, after bacon (104 references), in the labourers' inventory sample. One surprising feature of this data is that not all
households which possessed dairying equipment also possessed a cow.
It is possible that they had possessed a cow before and had sold it on,
but it might equally be possible that they were purchasing milk and
profiting from their labour.

The production of cheese and butter was also valuable, because a pig
could be kept on left-over skimmed milk together with brewing waste
and other garden produce. This was estimated to be worth £3–4 profit in
the examples from *c.* 1800 cited by Humphries, which would have been
worth about £2 earlier in the century. David Davies cited one example
of a poor family which was sold a fatted hog weighing 14 score (280 lb)
at 1s per score under the market price by the farmer from whom they
rented their dwelling, instead of them having their own pig or poultry.
This animal was worth £4 11s, and was said to last the family a whole
year.[174] But pigs fatted with food such as beans could weigh up to 400 lb
or more, which would provide meat worth over £6.[175] For sheep a fleece
of 5 lb of wool at 8d a pound would be worth 3s 4d. If income from the
manure, which could be sold as fertiliser, and the meat, which was worth
about 9–15s, are added to this then a sheep might be worth about £1.
Ewe's milk could also be drunk or made into cheese, although William
Harrison was somewhat dismissive of it as a food.[176] However, Henry
Best estimated that feed for a sheep for a year cost 18d in 1641, so the
profit would be slim compared to the profit of a cow.

Table 5.18 shows that many labouring families were also saving
money by brewing their own beer for family use rather than having
to purchase it at the alehouse. It was also possible for families to make
some extra money selling beer to neighbours, as John Cannon did during a period of financial distress.[177] The presence of brewing equipment
in inventories remained fairly constant, with between 30 and 40 per
cent of inventories possessing it, and many labourers also grew barley.

The rights to wood could be worth £1 18s a year after the labour of
cutting it was subtracted, and again if work was scarce this could be
vital, and would have been something which attracted families to wood
pasture districts.[178] Most labouring families relied on wood cut from
hedges and local woods for heating, as is evidenced by the large number

[174] Davies, *Case of Labourers*, p. 11; Ellis, *Country Housewife*, p. 101.
[175] Ellis, *Country Housewife*, pp. 47, 96.
[176] Thorold Rogers, *History of Agricultures and Prices*, VI, pp. 350–8; Thirsk, *Food*, pp. 4–5;
Harrison, *Description*, p. 311.
[177] Muldrew, 'Class and Credit', p. 159. Clark, *English Alehouse*, pp. 41–55, 80–2.
[178] Humphries, 'Enclosures, Common Rights', p. 33.

Table 5.19 *Estimates of all other family earnings compared to male wages*

Date	Earnings for wife's spinning	Wife's agricultural work	Children's work	Cow and pig	Glean-ing and fuel	Beer at work	Total	Deficit of male earnings from Table 5.4	Balance
1568	£2 4s	£3	£2	£2	£1	£1	£11 4s	−£2 14s	+£8 10s
1597	£2 4s	£3	£2	£2	£1	£1	£11 4s	−£22 10s	−£11 6s
1625	£2 12s	£3 10s	£2	£3	£1	£1 10s	£13 12s	−£15	−£1 8s
1690	£5 5s	£4	£3	£4	£2	£2	£20 5s	−£16 4s	+£4 1s
1760	£7	£4 10s	£4	£4	£2	£2	£23 10s	−£4 8s	+£19 2s

possessing wood in the probate inventory sample. Table 15.13 shows that firewood was listed 207 times – more than any crop except for hay, and much more than coal, which was found only 29 times. Wood-cutting equipment was also the most prevalent type of tool owned by labourers, especially bill-hooks, which were used to cut branches. This is evidence that many labourers obtained their own firewood through common rights, pilfering or through agreement with their employers to take wood from hedgerows in exchange for their maintenance. Since fuel costs in the budgets listed in Eden were normally between £1 and £2 a year, access to wood from hedges could have provided enough fuel for a family.[179]

Finally it remains to add up all of the potential earnings we have discussed above to compare them with the deficits of male earnings presented at the beginning of this chapter, which has been done in Table 5.19. This calculation assumes the work of one child between the ages of seven and twelve, working about eighty days of the year, together with the two teenage sons whose work was included in Table 5.4, but if more children were working earnings would have been greater.[180] The rise in the value of cows, pigs, fuel and beer is based on rises in the prices

[179] Thomas Batchelor claimed that a good double-row hedge would produce sufficient wood to make 120 faggots for every 14 poles every 12 years, or 10 faggots a year. This works out to about 1 faggot per 22 feet per year. A faggot equalled 26 in × 36 in of sticks. Making faggots cost 3s per hundred and they cost about 3–4d each on the market in the eighteenth century. £1 18s worth would be 2,280 faggots or 9.5 miles of hedgerow. If there were 422,600 miles of hedgerow this would provide fuel for only 44,487 families, which seems a low yield. Batchelor, *General View*, p. 114; Warde, *Energy*, pp. 32–40.

[180] This calculation does not include families with only infant children, as most were expected to save from their period in service (see p. 214 above); however, for those without enough savings there would have been a larger deficit.

of the relevant products. For families with access to common rights, or who possessed a small farm with a low rent, earnings would have been greater. However, for those families without a cow, and without access to spinning or some other form of industrial work, earnings would have been less. Nonetheless, these figures give some indication of possible additional earnings. Finally, no attempt has been made to estimate the value of any of the possible wage perquisites discussed on pages 230–3 above, apart from beer provided at work.

Here we can see the importance of adding family earnings to the husband's wages. Looking at the earliest date on the table, 1568, there was a healthy surplus which could have been used to cushion the impact of higher foods prices or to purchase household goods or more expensive foods. Next, in the terrible harvest years of the late 1590s, a significant deficit still remained, demonstrating how important charity and borrowing must have been to enable labouring families to survive these harsh years.[181] However, the figure for 1625 is closer to a general average for the early seventeenth century, though still in deficit. This shows that families were unlikely to be earning enough to pay for basic maintenance, let alone household goods or new commodities like tobacco. Looking back to the probate inventory evidence and the question posed at the end of the last chapter, it does not explain how labourers' households in the early seventeenth century managed to actually increase in value. We might expect households whose life course included the years 1594–7, and subsequent years of high prices through much of the 1620s and 1630s, to have had to reduce spending on household goods. Instead, as we saw, the median value of goods went up by 10 per cent. Households were also owed much more, indicating that they were earning more wages. This implies that many householders were reacting to the higher cost of living by working more in an attempt to stave off a decline in their standard of living. Table 5.19 also shows there was not yet much scope for improved female earnings in the cloth industry, which was in a depressed state before 1650. Increased earnings in the first half of the seventeenth century would have had to come from extra agricultural work, as farmers attempted to improve the productive capacity of their land in order to profit from rising food prices, as we will see in the next chapter.

In contrast to the situation before 1650, by 1690 family earnings show a surplus which then potentially quadrupled by 1760. Thus rising earnings can clearly be seen as an explanation for the rising material standard of living found in inventories after 1650. Although Table 5.4 shows

---

[181] Hindle, 'Dearth, Fasting and Alms', pp. 44–86; Muldrew, 'Hard Food', pp. 94–5.

that the cost of living declined by about 20 per cent between 1680 and 1760, the rise in the value of inventoried wealth occurred in the period between 1650 and 1700, indicating that the cause of the increase in the value of labourers' household goods was increased earnings more than falling prices. This also suggests that family earnings might have risen more quickly in the late seventeenth century than suggested here. This is certainly possible if we think that population remained low compared to expanding cloth and agricultural output.

The greatest jump in earnings was from spinning. Comparing 1740 with 1625, women's income went up by almost £10 by 1760 while male earnings went up £5, and grain prices declined by 20–25 per cent. In addition, after 1650, more young people were working as servants for longer periods, increasing young people's savings, which would have helped them buy more household goods when they finally married.[182]

Thus there is certainly evidence to support the part of de Vries's thesis which argues that increasingly family labour was adding income to family earnings. By the eighteenth century, increased earnings, combined with falling prices, allowed labourers to continue to improve the quality of their household goods and clothing, as well as to purchase other new foreign goods such as tea and sugar. Much of this came from increased demand for spinning in the cloth industry, which provided new opportunities for female and children's employment. But dairying and other agricultural work continued to provide increased opportunities for women. Unfortunately there is simply not enough information to determine how many hours in a week any single housewife might have had free from cooking, cleaning and rearing children to spend spinning, dairying, gardening or working for agricultural wages, but the opportunity to expand work certainly existed. Fortunately, the intensity of male agricultural work can be measured, and this is the subject of the next chapter.

---

[182] Kussmaul, *Servants in Husbandry*, pp. 98ff.

6 Agricultural labour and the industrious revolution

> Great earnings operate, as I have already explained, in bringing
> people to work who otherwise would have continued idle ...
>
> It is for these reasons, which are founded upon the most simple of all
> principles, the common emotions of human nature, that no industri-
> ous nation need ever fear a want of hands for executing any the most
> extensive plans of public or private improvement.
> Arthur Young, *A Six Month Tour through the North of England*[1]

Since most labourers' work came from farming it is important to attempt
to try to estimate how much demand there was for agricultural labour
and how it changed over time. Labourers could only have worked more
days, or increased the intensity of their work, if the demand for work
was there. The earnings worked out in the last chapter represent fairly
full employment, but many day labourers appear in account books
working fewer days. Of course they might have been working on their
own farms or moving between farms as labour was needed, but this
cannot be reconstructed from accounts. However, a global estimate of
demand for labour can be made by estimating the number of days of
labour required per acre to produce crops and animal products, and
then multiplying this by estimates of the number of acres devoted to
pastoral and arable farming in England, as was done earlier for women.
In addition, the numbers of labourers employed on a farm per year
listed in account books can be divided by the acreage of the farm and
then multiplied by national estimates of farmed land. With this information, provisional estimates of the national labour force required can
be made. But we also need to know if this requirement went up over
time, which would create opportunities for more work and potentially
greater family earnings.

This is also relevant to the previous discussion of calorific consumption and contemporary writings on diet, where it was argued that the

---

[1] Young, *A Six Month Tour through the North of England*, I, pp. 176–7.

hard work required by agriculture required large levels of daily food consumption. Increasing the amount of food produced also required increasing the amount of food consumed by the workers producing it. There were many tasks requiring hard labour on a farm. In the extract quoted on page 44 above, William Ellis described the amount of work involved in a harvest day, but even in the winter much work was required. Gervase Markham described a typical winter day's labour: the servants and farmers rose at 4.00 a.m., foddered the cattle, cleaned the stable, rubbed down the cattle, curried the horses, watered and fed the beasts and breakfasted at 6.00 a.m. They ploughed from 7.00 a.m. until 2.00 or 3.00 p.m., came home for dinner, and returned to the stables at 4.00 p.m. to repeat their pre-breakfast tasks. Supper was taken at 6.30 p.m., and then servants mended shoes, beat hemp, stamped apples for cider, ground malt, threshed corn, sharpened the plough irons or repaired ploughs until 8.00 p.m., when they returned to the stables to clean the stalls and replace the straw in them.[2]

Fields needed to be ploughed, sown, weeded, harvested, gathered and threshed to produce grain. Hay also needed to be harvested and gathered. Horses needed to be fed and looked after. Cattle and sheep had to be pastured and fed in the winter, and their health had to be attended to. Sheep had to be dipped and sheared, and cows milked. At home beer had to be brewed regularly, and butter and cheese made. Gardens had to be hoed and tended, and fruit had to be picked. Roads, fences, hedgerows and drains had to be maintained. All of this required a lot of hard physical work. Additional labour inputs into agriculture could be increased in many ways. More ploughing and breaking up of the soil could increase productivity, as could more intensive weeding in the summer. Drains could be constructed to both irrigate land and to create floating meadows, thus increasing grass yields. The enclosure of fields involved the construction of fences and the planting of hedges. The adoption of convertible husbandry (or up-and-down husbandry – folding sheep on fallow land to fertilise it) or new crop rotations involving growing and harvesting clover on land instead of leaving it fallow, all required more ploughing and other labour. As a result of improved productivity, more labour would then be required during the harvest. Finally the reclamation of waste land added to the area under cultivation or pasture, which further increased demand for labour, both for clearing and then working the new land.[3] At the same time, however, the conversion of arable to cattle grazing and for meat

[2] Cited in Kussmaul, *Servants in Husbandry*, pp. 34–5.
[3] Overton, *Agricultural Revolution*, ch. 3; Kerridge, *Agricultural Revolution*, chs. 3–10.

production (but not dairy farming) could reduce labour, as this sort of animal husbandry required considerably less work. Also, Robert Allen has argued, the growth in the number of very large farms in the second half of the eighteenth century led to labour shedding through economies of scale.[4]

All of these factors are aspects of what is generally termed the agricultural revolution, and the degree to which they were put into practice at different times is still hotly contested and debated. As we saw in chapter 3, yields have been measured by examinations of crops listed in probate inventories.[5] Production and agrarian practice can also be looked at using agricultural accounts from farms and estates, but these are much rarer for the seventeenth century than the eighteenth, and almost non-existent for the sixteenth century.[6] Note too that farms which practised accounting were more likely to be large farms, or farmed by those such as Richard Loder, who kept his accounts precisely because he was interested in innovation and increasing profit through better production. Finally, late eighteenth-century authors such as Arthur Young or William Marshall who were interested in promoting productive innovations toured the country and wrote about what they saw.

Taken together, this work shows that a great expansion of production took place which enabled England to export grain in the beginning of the eighteenth century and feed a rapidly expanding population after 1770, even if dramatic rises in its price after this date indicate that supply was tight. The question of most importance here, and the one which has been most debated, is when this expansion of production took place. On page 144 we saw that crop yields of wheat and barley went up variously but continually by about 70–100 per cent, between 1600 and 1750, in the counties of Hertfordshire, Lincolnshire, Norfolk and Suffolk. Yields of different crops rose continuously throughout our period but varied according to quality of the soil, and yields of wheat and barley rose more quickly in the seventeenth than in the eighteenth century. However, understanding yields per acre is only part of the question of total food output. The amount of land under cultivation is also important. Between 1700 and 1800 the amount of arable land increased from 9 million acres to 11.5 million acres, and the amount of meadow and pasture increased from 12 million acres to 17.6 million acres, as more marginal land was brought into cultivation and used as

---

[4] Allen, *Enclosure and the Yeoman*, ch. 11.
[5] The best summary of this method is found in Glennie, 'Measuring Crop Yields', pp. 255–83. A good summary of the data on yields for wheat from this work can be found in Turner *et al.*, *Farm Production*, pp. 117–23.
[6] Farm accounts are discussed extensively in Turner *et al.*, *Farm Production*, ch. 2.

pasture. Unfortunately there are no estimates for the amount of land under cultivation in 1500, but there is much qualitative evidence to show that as population increased, more waste land was brought into cultivation in the sixteenth century, and eventually pasture was converted to arable land.

All of these improvements in productivity required more work, which could have been done by employing more people, improving labour productivity or both.[7] Creating water meadows or improving drainage involved a great deal of digging and banking, as well as the hauling of mud, slates or wood.[8] Adding more fertilisers to the soil such as sand, marl, ash, ground bones or lime involved much carting, spreading and digging over. Added ploughings and more weeding also required more labour.[9] The process of enclosure meant a great deal of work planting hedges and building fences of posts or stones and then maintaining them. Running a sheep-fold also involved more work shepherding and moving fences. The increased use of horse power also helped increase production because it allowed more ploughing, but more importantly it allowed fertilisers such as marl, lime or dung to be carted over long distances – a task which would have been impossible to achieve economically by hand carrying. But this also required labour to drive ploughs, to load and drive carts, as well as to look after the horses.[10] Bringing more marginal land into cultivation required an even greater effort in terms of labour; cutting wood, moving stones and adding fertiliser. If all of these things were occurring then it stands to reason that there would have been more demand for labour per acre once they were implemented than previously.[11]

According to Wrigley's figures, between 1655 and 1770 the ratio of productive land to the rural population increased significantly from 5.3 acres to 8.8 acres per person as the amount of agricultural land increased and the rural population remained roughly the same.[12] Also, as Overton has

[7] Allen, *Enclosure and the Yeoman*, pp. 150–9: Kussmaul, *Servants in Husbandry*, p. 122.
[8] Joan Thirsk, 'Farming Techniques', in *AHEW*, IV, p. 181.
[9] Bowden, 'Agricultural Prices, Wages, Farm Profits and Rents', pp. 90–2; Joan Thirsk, 'Agricultural Innovations and Their Diffusion', in *AHEW*, V.II, pp. 590ff.; Turner *et al.*, *Farm Production*, pp. 81–8.
[10] E. A. Wrigley, 'Energy Availability and Agricultural Productivity', in Bruce M. S. Campbell and Mark Overton (eds.), *Land, Labour and Livestock: Historical Studies in European Agricultural Productivity* (Manchester, 1991), pp. 326ff., esp. n.10.
[11] Kerridge, *Agricultural Revolution*, chs. 3–6.
[12] This is based on Wrigley's figures for rural agricultural population divided by the acreages used above. Wrigley, 'Urban Growth', p. 170; Wrigley and Schofield, *Population History*, pp. 532–4. Also, according to Overton *et al.*'s calculations, the percentage of non-agricultural occupations in inventories in Kent and Cornwall also involved in some farming activity declined between 1600 and 1750. Thus it is unlikely that

argued, the introduction of nitrogen-fixing clover and the cultivation of crops like turnips as feed for cattle did not occur until the mid to late eighteenth century, and that convertible husbandry had only a limited effect in releasing old stored nitrogen. If this was the case, then the seventeenth-century productivity gains in bushels per acre must have been achieved by some part of the population working harder, manuring, marling and liming fields, ploughing fallow fields often to reduce weeds, surface ditching to improve drainage and through the employment of women and children in summer weeding and scaring birds.[13] Certainly the higher than expected amount of meat consumption indicates that the use of manure to fertilise arable land was an extensive practice.[14] Walter Blith in his *English Improver Improved* discussed the advantages of using sheep, horse, swine and poultry dung, but considered the spreading of cattle manure so common and well known as to need no comment.[15]

Probate inventories provide direct evidence on the type of work labourers engaged in through listings of tools they owned. Of course this is not an inclusive guide to all that they did, as farmers who hired them often also supplied them with tools, especially if they were hired for long periods of time. Good quality, sharp implements meant that the work was more efficient and went faster.[16] If the quality of tools increased over the course of the period this could also have potentially increased labour productivity. Unfortunately the inventories say little about whether cutting tools were made of steel or iron, so there is no evidence of change over time. There was also little change in the average price of tools when given. Little work has been done on tools in the early modern period, but we do know that it was not until the early nineteenth century that steel scythes became strong and sharp enough to be used to cut wheat, which previously had required using a sickle, thus taking much longer.[17]

---

extra agricultural work was being undertaken by craftsmen engaged in agricultural by-employments. Overton *et al.*, *Production and Consumption*, pp. 66–70, App. 3.

[13] Gregory Clark, 'Yields Per Acre in English Agriculture, 1250–1860: Evidence from Labour Inputs', *Economic History Review*, 44 (1991), pp. 445–6. Gregory Clark, 'Productivity Growth without Technological Change in European Agriculture before 1850', *Journal of Economic History*, 47 (1987), p. 432. Overton, *Agricultural Revolution*, pp. 16–18, 80–4.

[14] Kerridge, *Agricultural Revolution*, pp. 240–4; Overton, *Agricultural Revolution*, pp. 108–11.

[15] Walter Blith, *The English Improver Improved or the Survey of Husbandry Surveyed* (London, 1652), pp. 144–9; Edward Littleton, *The Groans of the Plantations: or a True Account of Their Grievous and Extreme Sufferings by the Heavy Impositions upon Sugar* (London, 1689), pp. 18.

[16] Davies, *Case of Labourers*, p. 181.

[17] Overton, *Agricultural Revolution*, pp. 12, 122–4; E. J. T. Collins, 'Harvest Technology and Labour Supply in Britain, 1790–1870', *Economic History Review*, 22 (1969), pp.

Table 6.1 *Numbers of labourers' inventories recording tools*

Period	Percentage of inventories with tools	Average number of tools per inventory with tools
1550–99	64	6
1600–49	65	6.9
1650–99	35	4.2
1700–99	39	4.8

Labourers who worked their own land, or had access to common rights, however, definitely needed their own tools. Tables 6.1 and 6.2 show that before the mid-seventeenth century 65 per cent of inventoried labourers possessed tools of their own, a percentage which dropped significantly afterwards, as did the average number of tools they possessed. Most of these tools are familiar to us today, such as spades or axes. The most common, however, was the bill, or bill-hook, a hand-held cutting tool with an 8–10-in handle and an 8–12-in blade which curved at the end and was about 3 in wide at the curve. This was used for cutting off small branches, especially in hedges. Another very common tool, the mattock, was like a pickaxe but with a wide, flat blade used for dislodging soil and stones. A wimble was a boring tool to make holes for fence posts. By far the greatest number of tools consisted of wood-cutting and digging tools, attesting to the importance of hedging and ditching as sources of work. This type of labour was also more often paid by piece-rates than other agricultural work, so it is more likely that labourers would possess their own tools, as they moved around doing day work. The most common harvest tool was the scythe. Most of these were owned by those labourers who possessed cattle and horses so that they could cut hay for winter feed. In comparison to hedging and digging tools, such harvesting and farming tools declined more after 1650, which is what would be expected, since labourers' landholding and animal possession was also declining.[18]

To date, two methods have been used to attempt to measure change in labour intensity. One focuses on comparing piece-rates with day wages to see if labour intensity changed over time. The other involves looking at potential increases in the number of days worked in a year.[19] Many

453–73; J. A. Perkins, 'Harvest Technology and Labour Supply in Lincolnshire and the East Riding of Yorkshire 1750–1850', *Tools and Tillage*, 3 (1976–7), pp. 46–58, 125–35.
[18] See pp. 250–3 above.
[19] Overton, *Agricultural Revolution*, pp. 80–4, 121–8; Voth, *Time and Work*.

Table 6.2 *Types of tools in labourers' inventories*

Hedging and wood cutting	
Bill	127
Axe	108
Hatchet	95
Hook	79
Wedge	56
Prong	16
Pike	6
Total	487
Digging:	
Spade	130
Shovel	111
Mattock	77
Hake	36
Pickaxe	21
Scavel	9
Total	384
Mowing and reaping	
Scythe	108
Rake	74
Sickle	41
Total	223
Other agricultural	
Pitch fork	29
Hoe	21
Total	50
Fencing:	
Auger	20
Wimble	14
Total	34
Carpentry	
Hammer	36
Crow	6
Saw	2
Total	44

tasks, such as digging and hedging, were paid at piece-rates, allowing labourers to increase their earnings through more work in addition to their day labour. Gregory Clark has attempted to measure changes in labour inputs into reaping, mowing and threshing by comparing piece-rates for these activities at different times with day wages, to determine how many man days such tasks took. If, for instance, workers were paid

5s to reap an acre of wheat, and the day wage for agriculture in the same area was 2s a day, then the time it would take to reap an acre of wheat can be calculated to be 2.5 man days. Using a sample of 70 wage assessments drawn up by JPs of the type described on page 227 above between 1561 and 1768, together with data from Arthur Young and the Board of Agriculture for the period from 1768 to 1810, Clark argued that while man days per acre in reaping rose from 1.86 to 2.9, or by 56 per cent over this period, yields probably doubled. Since there was little technological change before the introduction of sharper scythes, which could be used to replace sickles after 1810, he argued that reapers must have worked harder to harvest more grain as time progressed. Only 15 per cent of this increase had taken place before 1600, 30 per cent occurred in the seventeenth century and 40 per cent in the eighteenth century.[20]

However, when looking at rates of threshing, Clark, together with Ysbrand van der Werf, has come to a different conclusion, arguing that a comparison of piece-rates with day wages shows little evidence of increased labour intensity.[21] But since threshing was done in the winter when demand for labour was at its lowest, there might have been less incentive for harder work. Moreover, when different wage assessments are compared, the differences between assessments is much more striking than any change over time. Table 6.3 presents rates of labour for different tasks from a sample of published wage assessments, calculated by dividing piece-rates for each task by the published day wage. This table would seem to show that labourers in Middlesex in 1665 were able to work over twice as hard at mowing than their counterparts in Wiltshire two years earlier, which is unlikely. The harvest work in Lancashire in 1725 is unfeasibly slow if worked out this way. In 1725 the wages set there were only 1s a day for reaping, whereas by the piece an acre paid 7s, implying that only a seventh of an acre was cut in a day.[22] By comparison, in Essex in 1651, the official wage rate for a male reaper was 22d a day without food, and the reaping, binding and stooking of an acre of wheat rye or maslin (mixed) was 3s without food, implying that all of this could be done in 1.6 days.[23] As we saw earlier, day wages could differ significantly from place to place depending on levels of rents and access to other entitlements. It is likely that the setting of piece-rates also reflected these other concerns as well as local demand for the labour involved.

---

[20] Clark, 'Yields per Acre', pp. 448–59.
[21] Gregory Clark and Ysbrand van der Werf, 'Work in Progress? The Industrious Revolution', *Journal of Economic History*, 58 (1998), pp. 830–43.
[22] Eden, *State of the Poor*, III, pp.cvi–cix.   [23] Ibid., III, pp. xcviii–ci.

Table 6.3 *Rates of work calculated from wage assessments*

Task in acres per day	Wiltshire 1603	Norfolk 1610	Wiltshire 1655	Northamptonshire 1667	Middlesex c. 1665
Reaping and binding wheat	.5	.63	.6	.5	.33
Mowing barley	2	1.4	2.6	.66	1.7
Mowing oats	2.5		3	.66	1.7
Harvesting beans	.8	1	1.3		.8
Mowing grass	1	1.2	1.3	.66	.8

Task in rods (16.5 ft) per day					
Ditching	1.2	1	1.2		1.2
Hedging	3.5		3.5		
Fencing	.7				

Threshing in bushels per day					
Threshing wheat	5.6	4	4	5.3	5.3
Threshing barley	8.8	6.4	9.3	8	9.1
Threshing oats	8.8	8	9.3	8	9.1

Notes: [a] Both Essex wage rates also give rates for reaping barley and oats which were much slower. This suggests that reaping was practised here rather than shearing.
[b] For Lancashire the acre is said to be one of 7 yards a rod instead of 5.5, so to make the wages comparable to the other areas I have reduced them by 21%.
[c] Batchelor gives his threshing costs per acre, so I have calculated the cost per bushel using the mean yield figures for 1810 from Turner *et al.* of 21 bushels for wheat, 39 bushels for oats and 30 bushels for barley. However the rates are suspiciously low, so it is probable that Batchelor was assuming larger harvests than this. Turner *et al.*, *Farm Production*, pp. 129, 153, 158.

Sources: B. H. Putnam, 'Northamptonshire Wage Assessments of 1560 and 1667', *Economic History Review*, 1 (1927–8), pp. 124–34; J. C. Tingey, 'An Assessment of Wages for the County of Norfolk in 1610', *English Historical Review*, 13 (1898), pp. 522–7; T. S. Willan, *A Bedfordshire Wage Assessment of 1684*, Bedfordshire Historical Record Society, 25 (1943), pp. 129–37; Elizabeth Waterman, 'Some New Evidence on Wage Assessments in the Eighteenth Century', *English Historical Review*, 43 (1928), pp. 398–408; Historical Manuscript Commission Reports, no. 15, *Report on Manuscripts in Various Collections*, I (London, 1901), pp. 160–75; William Cunningham, *The Growth of English Industry and Commerce in Modern Times* (Cambridge, 1929), Part 2, pp. 887–93; Eden, *State of the Poor*, II, pp. 293, 452–53; III, pp. lxxxix–cx. For Young and Batchelor see discussion in text, below.

Essex 1651[a]	Essex 1661	Bedfordshire 1684	Lancashire 1725[b]	Lancashire 1725	Kent 1795	Arthur Young c. 1770	Batchelor 1808[c]
.55	.46	.45	.14		.81	.4	.3
1.3	1.3	2	(Shearing) .21		3	1.3	.7
1.3	1.3	2	(Shearing) .18		3	1.3	.7
.5	.5	.8	.21		2.5	.33	
.9	.8	.9–1.2			4.3	4 Clover grass)	.7
.85	.85	.7					

			Best labourer (12d a day)	Ordinary labourer (10d a day)			
4.4	4.4		4	3.3	5.3	4	2.6 (?)
9.6	9.6		5.3	4.4	9.6	8	4.7 (?)
9.6	9.6		8	6.7	9.6	8	3.75 (?)

To test this, we can compare these rates to some actual examples. Henry Best thought that in 1641 a good shearer could shear ten stooks of winter corn a day, but ordinary shearers only eight a day, for which he paid 8d a day without food, stating that the 'stookinge of Winter-corne is a mans labour and requireth … ability and toyle'. These were very low harvest wages, but this was not unusual in the north. (By comparison, in 1615 Robert Loder paid his harvest 'taskers' the equivalent of 14d a day in money and food.)[24] Best's stooks comprised twelve sheaves each (an armful about a foot in diameter), of which there were thirty to a land.[25] Although the size of a land could vary, it seems to have been about 1.5 acres. If this was normal, then his good reapers were finishing half an acre in a day, which is what we would expect from the majority of the wage assessments. However, Best claimed that those who were able to mow corn with a scythe could do an acre and a half in a day, earning 3s 9d a day, which was five and a half times what he paid his

[24] Fussell (ed.), *Robert Loder's Farm Accounts*, pp. 100–1.
[25] Woodward (ed.), *Farming Books of Henry Best*, p. 45.

best shearers. Since mowing corn requires much more strength than reaping it, these must have been very strong, hard-working men.[26]

It is also possible to work out some rates of mowing hay, ditching and hoeing turnips from Randall Burroughes, although not for reaping. His workers were able to mow from 0.8 to 1.2 acres of grass a day, depending on the size of the crop. They hoed 0.17 acres of turnips a day and did almost 25 ft of ditching. These are also close to the official rates, but show that the amount of work that could be achieved in a day depended very much on the nature of the crop, the soil being dug, and the wetness of the season. On one occasion Burroughes agreed to pay his men more than he had bargained for reaping wheat, as the crop was 'remarkably thick and extremely well & clean picked' although it is impossible to determine how fast they worked from his journal.[27]

Clearly, what this shows is that rates of labour could vary from place to place, and that comparing official rates from different areas is very misleading. A more profitable route for determining labour productivity lies in comparing contemporary estimates of how long different tasks took to complete with the number of days' worked listed in estate wage books, and then working out days worked per acre of land. By the late eighteenth century, agricultural writers had begun to attempt to determine how much time certain tasks took in order to help farmers arrive at the most accurate way to estimate potential profits from different sorts of farming. The best-known of these was Thomas Batchelor, who worked out the total costs of growing different types of crops in different rotations on various qualities of soil in 1808.[28]

Tables 6.4 and 6.5 summarise Batchelor's figures. His method was to express certain tasks in terms of the cost of labour per acre, in order to give farmers an idea of expense. To convert these figures into labour per day we need to divide them by an average winter day wage. Batchelor noted that this was 18d for a man in Bedfordshire, the county he was writing about. This was a wage without the provision of food, and is quite close to the average of 20.7d a day from Gregory Clark's dataset for the Midlands from 1805 to 1809.[29] As we saw in Table 5.2 above, during both the hay and corn harvest wages were much higher, both nominally and because of the extra food supplied. This meant that the expense of hiring a man for the hay harvest was 30d a day and for the corn

[26] Ibid., pp. 40, 42–4, 114–15; Eden, *State of the Poor*, III, p. xcix.

[27] Martins and Williamson (eds.), *Farming Journal of Randall Burroughes*, p. 65.

[28] Batchelor, *General View*. I would like to thank Robert Allen for informing me of the value of this source.

[29] Here labour costs, being estimated at the height of the great wartime inflation, were much higher than earlier. Clark, 'Farm Wages', p. 485.

Table 6.4 *Batchelor's costing of labour expenses per acre[a]*

Task	Fallow	Wheat	Barley	Oats
Fallow ploughing	2s			
Other ploughing	6s	2s	2s	2s
Heavy harrowing	2.75d			
Harrowing	4.5d	9d	6.25d	9d
Rolling	1.5d	2.5d	1.5d	1.25d
Carriage of manure	10d			
Turning and spreading	3s 1.25d			
Weeding		2s	3s	3s
Couch burning, clodding		1s 6d	1s	1s
Reaping or mowing		10s	2s 2d	2s 2d
Cocking		3s 3d	2s 8d	2s 8d
Thatching		1s	1s	1s
Harvest carriage		4s 6d	5s 6d	5s 6d
Threshing		12s.35d	12s.65d	12s
Expense of sale	1s	1s 7.25d	1s 7.25d	1s 7.25d
Attendance of sheep	1s	1s	1s	1s
Extra	6d	6d	6d	6d
Total	15s 2d	41s 2d	33s 7.5d	33s 3.5d
Number of days work per acre	10.1	19.4	17.6	17.4

Note: [a] For a five year clover rotation. Batchelor, *General View*, p. 117. In this table wages are 18d a day and harvest wages 51d a day, as used by Batchelor and given above on p. 212.

harvest 51d per day.[30] The total year's work given here for a day labourer was fifty-two weeks of full-time work, with an extra 2s per week earned through piece-work.

Batchelor did not provide separate day wages for a female day worker, presumably because the cost per task would have been the same, but the hours worked would have been shorter, although this can only be inferred as it is not stated. However, he did provide costs for female live-in servants. He estimated that a housekeeper would earn wages of £10 10s a year and consume food worth 4s a week or £10 8s a year, which, together with the costs of cooking, lodging and washing would cost a farmer £26 16s a year. A dairy- or kitchenmaid would cost £21 11s as she earned £5 5s less.[31] This works out to 20.5d and 16.5d a day for a 312-day year, which is very similar to the day labourer's wages.[32]

[30] Batchelor, *General View*, p. 108.
[31] Ibid., pp. 78–9.   [32] See Table 5.1 above.

Over the winter Batchelor calculated that one man could plough three-quarters of an acre in a day at 2s an acre. Fallow clay fields had to be ploughed three times, light land five times and other fields once a year.[33] Further scuffling, harrowing and rolling could be done at three acres a day's work per man for each process.[34] Although Batchelor advocated that sowing should be done by the farmer rather than by servants, to ensure maximum efficiency, he calculated that it cost 4d an acre, implying that about four acres of wheat could be sown in a day. However, fewer acres of barley and oats could have been sown in the same time, as twice as much seed was needed.[35] Weeding crops was a time-consuming process and was estimated to cost 2–10s an acre for wheat, 3s 6d for barley, 3s for oats and 1–2s for a fallow field of clover. Beans and peas cost from 5s to 8s an acre to weed. Batchelor did not say how often fields needed to be weeded, but he claimed that in light soils a man could hand-hoe a third to half an acre in a day. Presumably the varying cost depended on how often the weeding needed to be done. Adding manure or other fertiliser to a field occupied three drivers and four men filling and spreading the manure, which at sixteen loads an acre amounted to 4s 8d, implying that they could do about two acres a day.[36]

During harvest half an acre of wheat or rye could be reaped in a day, while barley and oats, which were mowed with a scythe, could be done at the rate of two acres a day. Peas could be harvested at the rate of two-thirds of an acre a day. Carriage to the barn, or rickyard, was also expensive. For corn ten persons were employed: four to five at the stack and three drivers – two to drag after the cart and one to drive it. Ten men could clear five acres of barley, oats or peas in a day, which works out to 4s 4d per acre. For peas, thirteen people needed to be employed to glean after the cart, but for wheat sometimes only eight people were needed.[37] The cutting of wheat stubble and gathering the leftover stems into cocks cost 2s 3d an acre. Barley and oats were cheaper, because they were cocked at the same time as they were mown, and five men could clear ten acres per day.[38]

[33] Batchelor, *General View*, pp. 101–3. In the following examples all costs are for labour only. They are also slightly different than Table 6.4 as these are his averages of different field rotations.

[34] Ibid., p. 102.   [35] Ibid., pp. 106–7, 117–19.

[36] Ibid., pp. 105–6. This figure is higher than that of 3s 1.25d given in Table 6.4 because Batchelor made the assumption that only two-thirds of fallow land was manured, and so he divided his cost of manuring 20 acres on his model farm by the full 30 acres of fallow.

[37] Ibid., p. 109. It would appear from this that Batchelor assumed that gleaning was no longer a perquisite of the labourers.

[38] Ibid., pp. 110–11.

Batchelor calculated that in five weeks of harvesting one labourer performed all the work belonging to 10.38 acres, although he noted that some farmers assigned 12–14 acres to each harvest man. He also noted the difficulty in finding enough labour to complete the harvest, claiming that 'much wheat is reaped by acre-men; those who are only hired for a month, frequently return [to their previous occupation] before the ricks are thatched, and sometimes leave much corn in the field in wet weather'. After the harvest was over, Batchelor also included the cost of 'wadding', the gleaning of beans, which was tedious and cost as much as 6s an acre, as well as 'clodding' or breaking the soil into small pieces in the autumn, which could cost as much as 2s 6d to 5s per acre for wheat, although Batchelor only accounted for it as costing 1s per acre, as it was not always done.[39] Finally, threshing was the most expense activity in the production of grain. Bachelor also included the cost of taking the grain to market and sheep-folding on the arable land, as well as extra costs as a result of bad weather. Folding a herd of 182 sheep occupied 1.5 hours setting the fold and driving the sheep forwards and backwards.[40]

In Table 6.4 I have added up all of the costs of growing and harvesting wheat, barley and oats and converted the cost of labour input into days worked per acre in a year. As can be seen, wheat required the most labour, owing to the time spent reaping, but the difference between crops is not that great. In comparison to this the cost and labour needed to raise animals for slaughter was much less, as is shown in Table 6.5, where it can be seen that an acre of grass required only five days a year when pasturing animals and thirteen days a year when hay was grown. If we simply assume that half of pasture land was planted with hay for winter feed and to supply towns, this works out to an average of nine days' work an acre.[41] However, as we can see in Table 6.8, the employment per acre on the primarily pastoral farms visited by Arthur Young was higher than this. This is because the most expensive and labour-intensive form of food production by far was the keeping of milk cows, as can be seen from the very large amount of labour required per acre on small dairy farms. Indeed, Arthur Young commented on the dairy farms he observed in the 1760s, saying that he could not 'possibly discover wherein ... lies the profit of these dairies'. Batchelor commented that 'The luxury of butter is obtained at a very great expense of human labour, viz. nearly 4½d. per pound.'[42] This can be starkly shown in

---

[39] Ibid., pp. 105–6.   [40] Ibid., pp. 94, 111–13.

[41] In 1626 John Stafford estimated that tillage maintained four times as many people as pasture. Here he must only have been considering summer pasture. Thirsk, *Economic Policy*, p. 104.

[42] Young, *Northern Tour*, V, p. 167; Batchelor, *General View*, p. 157.

Table 6.5 *Batchelor's costs of pasture per acre*

Task	Animal grazing[a]	Hay	Hay and milking
Weeding, banking, cleaning	5s	5s	5s
Mowing		3s	3s
Haymaking		3s 6d	3s 6d
Loading, staking and thatching		5s[b]	5s
Spreading dung	1s 6d	1s 6d	1s 6d
Marketing and extras	2s	2s	2s
Milking			31s 3.5d
Attendance at pigs			3s
Total	7s 6d	20s	54s 3.5d
Days per acre	5	13	34

Notes: [a] For land used primarily in the raising of animals for butchering, Batchelor worked out that an acre of land could produce 124 lb of beef or mutton, which would have produced much less profit than grain, even after the lower cost of labour is taken into account. Batchelor, *General View*, p. 84.
[b] Harvesting a crop of clover cost 2s 1d. This cost included beer, 3 turnings at 6d an acre, the carrying by 10 men at 6 acres a day of 7 hours at 1s 4d and one man thatching at 6d acre. Harvesting a crop of clover involved 3 turnings, cocking and ragging, involving 10 men working 5 acres. Carriage was done by 10 men at 6 acres per day. These calculations by Batchelor were based on a 7-hour day, but this assumption was made for convenience, as workers often worked much more in harvest. Batchelor, *General View*, p. 110.

cost per calorie. Whereas wheat flour bought at 4s a bushel provided 1,670 kcal per penny spent, butter bought at 3d a lb provided only 82 kcal per penny. This reinforces how valuable a cow was to a labouring family in terms of utilising the labour of the wife and daughters to gain value from the sale of butter, and also shows how expensive it was as a foodstuff.

We must also remember that these costs account only for the production of crops, all of the other labour on the farm, such as ditching, fencing, carrying stones, tending to gardens and orchards, was not dealt with by Batchelor. The only other labour he discussed was that involved in hedging and road repair. The latter, however, was very expensive, costing £1 6s 4½d for every 1,210 yards of road 4 yards wide (based on an acre of 220 poles = 0.7 mile), and levelling cart ruts cost 5s per acre.[43]

---

[43] Batchelor stated that dairy work for a maid looking after 15 cows cost £19 5s a year for milking and £5 4s for looking after the dairy, which works out to 19d a day for 312 days, of which nominal wages would form 4.5–7d. Batchelor, *General View*, pp. 78–9.

A horse-keeper also earned 2s more a week as he had to put in extra hours of attention to the team early in the mornings and on Sundays.[44]

Arthur Young also provided a more comprehensive, although more abstract, account of all the labour needed, calculated in days, to run a small arable farm of 40 acres in *The Farmers Guide in Hiring and Stocking Farms* (1771). This hypothetical farm had 12.5 acres under wheat, 3 acres under oats, 9 acres under barley, 12.5 aces sown with beans and 3 acres of clover, together with 7 cows and 2 horses. In his model Young calculated the amount of labour needed on the farm provided by the farmer, his family and hired day labour. This labour is listed in Table 6.6. Young's farm employed a modern Norfolk crop rotation. The cows provided manure, and there were 3 acres of clover for winter feed, although the amount of summer pasture needed was not given.[45] In addition, neither garden nor dairy work is included, presumably as it was done by the wife and family, but since pasture is not mentioned we do not need to consider this work here. The amount of labour needed here works out to about eighteen days per acre of arable land, which is very similar to what Batchelor calculated.

In comparison to these ideal calculations, there are also examples of farms where actual employment per acre can be worked out. In his tours around England, Arthur Young provided information on the number of servants, labourers, maids and boys hired by farms, together with the total acreage, value and land use.[46] Robert Allen has used this information to work out total employment per acre for different sizes of farms. He did this in order to demonstrate how the move towards larger farms in the late eighteenth century resulted in less total employment for farm labour thanks to increasing economies of scale. As Table 6.8 shows, the smaller farms Young looked at all provided employment for more people than indicated by either Young's (40 acres) or Batchelor's (150 acres) example farms. The labour required on a small pastoral farm was incredibly high because the time needed to milk a few cows and to make butter and cheese was proportionally much higher than for a larger herd. In addition, these figures do not include the farmer's own labour, which, as Young's model indicates, would be a considerable portion of the total on a small farm. Young tended also to visit more successful, efficient farms, so, if anything, the figures for the labour requirements on his farms are probably on the low side. However, they still indicate that considerably more labour was employed than both Young's and later Batchelor's abstract models indicate.

[44] Ibid., pp. 81–2, 87.   [45] Young, *Farmer's Guide*, pp. 120–4.
[46] See p. 223 above.

Table 6.6 *Labour on Arthur Young's model farm*

Month	Work done	Cost of hired labour[a]	Days	Days of hired labour
October	Ploughing 12.5 acres of wheat		13	
	Ploughing last year's stubble		13	
	Sowing wheat	6s 3d		6.25
	Water furrowing	12s 6d		12.5
November	Threshing 13 quarters of wheat		26	
December	ditto		26	
January	Ploughing fallow		13	
	Water furrowing		6	
	Sundry work		7	
February	Threshing 7 quarters of wheat		14	
	Threshing 26 quarters of spring corn		13	
	Manuring	25s		25
	Ditching 50 perches	£2 10s		50
March	Ploughing 12.5 acres of bean land (the fallow)		13	
	Ploughing 12.5 acres last year's bean land for barley and oats		13	
	Sowing 12.5 acres of beans	12s 6d		12.5
	Water furrowing	12s 6d		12.5
	Threshing 12 quarters of spring corn	12s		12
April	Ploughing 12.5 acres of barley and oat land		13	
	Threshing 12 quarters of spring corn		12	
	Small articles		2	
	Sowing 12.5 acres of spring corn	3s 1d		3
	Water furrowing	6s 3d		6.25
	Threshing 25 quarters of beans	25s		25
May	Ploughing between beans		7	
	Manuring		8	
	Hand-hoeing 2.5 acres of beans		10	
June	Ploughing between beans		7	
	Hand-hoeing 4 acres of beans		15	
	Carting 3 acres of clover hay		5	
	Hand-hoeing 6 acres of beans	30s		30
	Mowing 3 acres of clover	12s		12
	Carting	6s		6
	Weeding 25 acres of corn	25s		25
July	Ploughing between beans		7	
	Carting and other jobs		20	
August	Carting 12.5 acres of wheat		4	
	Carting 12.5 acres of barley and oats		9	

Table 6.6 (*cont.*)

Month	Work done	Cost of hired labour[a]	Days	Days of hired labour
	Carting 12.5 acres of beans		9	
	Small articles		5	
	Reaping 12.5 acres of wheat	£3 2s 6d		31.25
	Reaping 12.5 acres of beans	£3 15s		37.5
	Mowing 12.5 acres of barley and oats	18s 9d		9.4
	Turning, harvesting and carting	£2 10s		25
September	Mowing and carting 3 acres of clover		10	
	Ploughing the bean land and throwing it up		13	
	Carting 12.5 acres of stubble			
	Chopping and raking 12.5 acres of stubble	18s 9d		18.75
Total		£23 3s 11d	313	360

Note: [a] Worked out at winter wages of 12d a day and harvest wages of 24d. Young, unlike Batchelor, did not account for the cost of food during harvest.

Table 6.7 *Profits of Arthur Young's model farm*

Produce	Yield per acre	Value
12.5 acres wheat	21 bushels	£50
9 acres barley	33 bushels	£27
12.5 acres beans	16 bushels	£37 10s
7 cows		£35
Total		£149 10s
Expenses		£127 18s
Interest		£11 11s
Profit		£10

We also have examples of employment on actual farms. Employment between 1772 and 1774 on the largely pastoral 92-acre Oakes farm near Sheffield, examined by Joyce Burnette, works out to 22–24.5 days per acre of employed day labour, including the female labour discussed.[47] There would also have been at least one maidservant, and possibly one or two men hired in addition to the farmer's own labour, which

[47] Burnette, 'Labourers at the Oakes', pp. 45–6, 56.

Table 6.8 *Employment per acre in the 1760s, based on Arthur Young's data*

Acres	Days of employment per acre: arable	Days of employment per acre: pasture
0–50	34	129
50–100	27	22
100–150	21	16
150–200	18	13

Source: Allen, *Enclosure and the Yeoman*, pp. 159–60, 212–18.

would increase the labour input per acre to around thirty-six days for this pastoral farm.[48] Labour input per acre can also be calculated for the Golden, Keveral and Morton Barton farms. These farms have the advantage that the type of labour was broken down in the account books. At Golden Barton, 50–84 acres were cropped each year (average 67) and stock consisted of 85 head of cattle, 406 sheep, 14 horses and 18 pigs, and the farm employed 3–8 labourers doing various tasks. Haymaking accounted for about 10 per cent of the labour done on the farm. It is impossible to measure the amount of labour engaged in the pastoral part of the farm since no acreage is given, but if some of the 85 head of cattle on Golden Barton were cows, maidservants must have been employed Since no labourers are recorded as looking after the cattle or sheep, then at least one shepherd must have been employed as a servant. But, even without this work, the hired labour input for the arable land here works out to thirty days per acre.[49]

At Keveral Barton farm an average of 68 acres were sown each year, mostly with barley and oats. Yields were very low; only between 5–8 bushels per acre for wheat and 5–14 bushels per acre for barley. The number of days spent on various different types of tasks is listed in Table 6.9, and the total labour input works out to thirty-eight days per acre of arable land. But since 27 per cent of the labour was for mowing and looking after cattle and sheep, this implies that there was also a considerable amount of grassland as part of the farm.[50] Again no dairying is mentioned, implying that there were servants hired as milkmaids. However, the number of days of hired work per arable acre can be calculated by subtracting the days spent mowing and looking after cattle and sheep, resulting in a total of twenty-eight days per acre.

[48] Ibid., p. 45.   [49] Pound, 'Barton Farming', pp. 57–63.   [50] Ibid., pp. 64–6.

Table 6.9 *Farm labour at Keveral Barton*

Activity	Days worked	Percentage
Carrying and spreading lime, sand, ashes and manure	333.5	13
Preparing soil, weeding	254	10
Ploughing, sowing, harrowing	292.5	11
Harvesting	395.5	15
Threshing	320	13
Haymaking	450	18
Orchard	62	2
Cattle and sheep	243	9
Hedging	141.5	6
Miscellaneous	75	3
Total	2567	

At Morval Barton, again sixty-eight acres of crops were grown each year, and yields were also very low. Ten labourers were hired throughout the year, and all were smallholders who bought grain from the farm and sold it their manure. Here, however the amount of pasture is known. There were eighteen fields consisting of fifty-seven acres of grass, although cattle were also summered on moorland, where they were looked after by local families, not the farm labourers. On this farm labour input was much greater, working out to sixty-one days of work per acre of arable, including the gardening, and eight days per acre of pasture, without dairy work. The greatest cause for the extra labour was the attempt to improve the land: spreading lime and sand, picking stones, weeding, as well as clearing new land.[51]

Using these figures, a rough calculation of the total hired labour requirements for all of England *c.* 1770 can be made based on the rates of work just discussed multiplied by the total acreage of arable and pasture land estimated by Overton. The same procedure will be used here as earlier when measuring demand for just women's work in agriculture (see above, pp. 240–1), but here it will be done for *all* hired labour, both male and female. The difficulty here is choosing average figures for the days of work needed per acre, given the differences in the examples we have examined. Considering arable land first, clearly both Batchelor's and Young's model farm rates of seventeen to nineteen days of work per acre seem too low when considering the examples of real farms, and thus must be considered ideals of industriousness. Golden, Morval

[51] Ibid., pp. 69–74.

Table 6.10 *Farm labour at Morval Barton*

Activity	Days worked	Percentage of days
Carrying and spreading lime, sand, ashes and manure	675.5	15
Ploughing, sowing, harrowing	343.5	7
Driving horses and oxen	279	6
Preparing soil, weeding	471.5	10
Cutting and carting timber and furze	180	4
Clearing fresh land	123	3
Harvesting	514.5	10
Threshing	486	11
Haymaking	418.5	9
Gathering apples and making cider	74	2
Cattle and sheep	53.5	2
Hedging	180	3
Gardening	298	6
Cultivating turnips	37	1
Miscellaneous	546	12
Total	4630	

and Keveral Barton required twenty-eight to sixty-one days of work per acre, and all but the largest farms visited by Arthur Young required over twenty days of work per acre. In the following calculation, for *arable* land, I will assume that the labourer input was thirty-one days an acre by simply taking the difference between the figures for 0–15-acre farms and 50–100-acre farms from Arthur Young's surveys found in Table 6.8. In Allen's survey of estate data from the south Midlands most farms were still under 100 acres before the end of the eighteenth century. There were, however, also some large enclosed farms which would have been more efficient in terms of labour requirements, but if we assume that there were also many more less efficient farms not visited by Young, like the Oakes and the Cornwall Bartons, then a figure of thirty-one days of work per acre is probably a reasonably conservative figure to begin with. By 1770 the amount of arable land under cultivation would probably have been about 10.5 million arable acres requiring 325,500,000 days of work, enough for 1,043,269 people working full 312-day years.

Working out the labour input in pasture is more difficult because much pasture would have been part of mixed arable farms, and the amount of labour involving in dairying decreases rapidly with the size of a farm. Land farmed and animals pastured by labourers themselves would also have required much more labour input per acre, especially for cows, as was demonstrated by Batchelor, and is the reason why small

Table 6.11 *Percentage comparison of the size of farms in a sample of south Midland estates*

Acres	Early seventeenth century open	Early seventeenth century enclosed	Early eighteenth century open	Early eighteenth century enclosed	About 1800 open	About 1800 enclosed
5–60	63	44	59	43	29	35
60–100	25	9	19	19	15	12
100–200	9	17	19	30	26	25
200+	2	30	3	8	30	28
Total number	328	23	398	84	145	327

Source: Allen, *Enclosure and the Yeoman*, pp. 72–4.

arable farms in Table 6.8 required so much labour. As we saw, 49 per cent of labourers with inventories possessed cows, which would have required a considerable amount of labour to look after. However, larger cattle farms would have employed much less labour. The simplest way to approach the problem is to use the figure of 22 days per acre from Arthur Young in Table 6.8 for farms of between 50 and 100 acres as an average, although we might wish to keep in mind that on the Oakes this figure was as high as 36 days. If there were 15 million acres of pasture in 1770 this would require a further 330,000,000 work days, or work for 1,057,692 people working full 312-day years.

Combined with the estimate for arable land this indicates a potential labour requirement of 2,100,961. By 1770 the population had grown to 6,447813 people, and the rural agricultural population stood at about 45 per cent of this total. Of this figure about 70 per cent were members of labouring families.[52] Of these 23 per cent were children below the age of 9, so there would have been 1,563,917 people above this age.[53] Thus the labour requirement, measured this way, was more than the total available male and female labour at this date working a full 6 days a week for the whole year. This figure includes the elderly, too, some of whom would have been too old to work. In addition, as we have seen, women and children did not work full-time in agriculture. Children would also have gone to school in some instances, or would have been spinning and helping around the house. Previously I calculated that the availability of work for women in agriculture might have been as

[52] See above, p. 234.   [53] Wrigley and Schofield, *Population History*, pp. 529.

high as 157 days a year, although these would have been shorter days to allow time for childcare, housework and gardening. There is no way of knowing what percentage of their time women spent in cloth work and washing, but it must have been considerable. If we subtract, say, 60 per cent of the labour of women and a further 50 per cent of that of boys between 9 and 14 years of age, this leaves only 1,055,644 available workers expressed abstractly as labour equivalents working a full 312-day year. This amounts to a shortage of 12.8 days per acre with the labour requirements worked out above. This certainly implies that on many other farms labour intensity must have been greater, which suggests that many were perhaps actually closer to Batchelor's and Young's examples by this time. But what this shows, with a great deal of certainty, is that there was no labour shortage at this time. In their budgets, neither Davies nor Eden mention underemployment as a widespread problem causing low wages, and Arthur Young argued just the opposite: that demand for labour had led to higher wages. All the budgets assume full-time work of fifty to fifty-two weeks a year, with some instances of time lost to sickness.[54] Furthermore, in 1797, one farmer noted that, in general, farmers desired local labourers not to have animals or crops of their own because they needed their labour.[55]

However, it must be stressed that the need for labour was seasonally unbalanced, with perhaps two to three times as much labour being required in the summer as in the winter, which is why women needed to work during the summer. The amount of labour required could also vary from place to place, depending on the balance of arable to pasture land. Bad weather could reduce the number of days available to work, as would a bad harvest. Further, a farmer might create a need for labour by improving or clearing land, which would then drop off once the tasks had been completed. Many day labourers recorded in estate accounts did not work for an entire 312-day year. The same labourers appear and disappear for some months before reappearing when they were needed again.[56] The labourers in question might have gone on to do the same work for another farmer, or had some land of their own to work, but it is impossible to know how many days they managed to fill in a year. But certainly demand for agricultural labour was more stable than that for building work or industrial employment

---

[54] Population had risen, but the percentage involved in agriculture had fallen. See the discussion in Overton, *Agricultural Revolution*, pp. 80–1.

[55] Humphries, 'Enclosures, Common Rights', p. 29.

[56] Wrightson, *Earthly Necessities*, pp. 196–7; Gilboy, 'Labour at Thornborough', pp. 392–5.

like weaving, which were heavily dependent on market demand, which could fluctuate greatly.[57]

We must now attempt to see if this was equally the case at earlier dates. In 1700, it has been estimated that there were 9 million acres of arable and 12 million acres of pasture land. Yields, however, were lower at this time than in 1770, as can be seen in Table 3.14 above, and thus the amount of labour needed for harvest and threshing per acre would have been proportionally lower when yields were lower because there were fewer, or weaker, stalks to reap and gather as straw, and less grain to thresh.[58] From Table 3.14 we can see that the average yield of all grains and pulses was 35 per cent lower in 1700 compared to 1770. Since harvest and threshing costs of corn made up 40 per cent of the day labour on Arthur Young's model farm in Table 6.6 (263 days), labour requirements on an arable farm might have been 14 per cent lower. There are no comparable estimates of grass yields for hay production, so I will simply assume that hay yields were similarly lower, and required 14 per cent less labour to harvest. Using these assumptions, and the same figures of 31 days worked per acre of arable land and 22 days' work for pasture, then in 1700 arable land would have required 239,940,000 work days, or enough to employ 769,039 people, and pasture land would have required a further 227,040,000 work days, or work for 727,692 people employed for 312 days a year. This gives total employment on arable and pasture for 1,496,731 people.[59] If the rural agricultural population of England was 55 per cent of the total population of 5,026,877, or 2,764,782, in 1700 and approximately 70 per cent of these were labouring families or servants in husbandry, this would be 1,935,348 people. Further subtracting the 20 per cent of the population who were under the age of 9 amounts to a potential labourer force of 1,548,278. If we make the same reductions for women and children as was done for 1770, this becomes 1,045,088.[60] The difference between these two figures amounts to 6.7 days of work per acre of the total 21 million acres under cultivation in 1700. This again implies that there was enough aggregate demand for labour, and that labour intensity had increased, but not as much as later in the century.

Going back further in time to the early seventeenth century, the grain yields used in Table 3.14 were 55 per cent lower than in 1770, which

[57] Woodward, *Men at Work*, pp. 131–42.   [58] Clark, 'Yields per Acre', pp. 452–4.

[59] If we use King's estimate that there were 1,100,000 milk cows at the end of the seventeenth century at 9 cows per milkmaid this would provide employment for 122,222 women. King, 'Burns Journal', p. 214.

[60] Wrigley, 'Urban Growth', p. 170; Wrigley and Schofield, *Population History*, pp. 532–4.

means that labour requirements would have been about 22 per cent lower (since harvest work was 40 per cent of total farm labour). It is impossible to know how much land was under cultivation as no figures exist, but much effort had already gone into converting more marginal land to husbandry in the sixteenth century. But if we assume for the sake of calculation that there were 8 million acres of arable land, this might have provided work for 620,000 people working 312 days a year.[61] Then if there were 10 million acres of pasture this would have supplied work for 550,000 people. This gives a total potential employment on arable and pasture for 1,170,000 people. In 1620 the population was 4,634,570, but at this time the rural agricultural population was closer to 70 per cent of the total population. This leaves 3,244,199 people, and if labourers and servants formed 70 per cent of this figure, this amounts to 2,270,939 people, of whom 22 per cent were under 9 years of age, which leaves us with 1,771,333 people in labouring families. Thus the rural agricultural population actually consisted of over 200,000 more people than worked in agriculture in 1700! Making the same subtractions for women and for children aged 9–14 as for 1700 would leave us with 1,195,650 people available to work 312-day years.

At this date it is also the case that, on average, labourers could not have worked at the same intensity as later, given that fewer calories were available. For labourers hired as servants this might have meant that more labour would actually have had to be employed to do the same amount of work. In addition, more farms were smaller at this time, which would have increased labour requirements in comparison with later periods. However, as we saw, this was a time when farmers were hiring fewer servants and instead relying on day labour. In such cases, the fewer calories available would have resulted in *less*, not more employment, as they would have been rationed to a smaller number of the hardest-working labourers. In addition, there was much less work available from spinning in 1600 (see Table 6.11) so women and boys would have had more time available for farm work. This means that at this date there would almost certainly have been a labour surplus. Population also continued to rise to over 5,200,000 in the mid-1650s, which means the labour supply would have increased by 12 per cent.

The most compelling evidence of a labourer surplus at the time is the amount of emigration which took place. The years from 1630 to 1660 saw the greatest rate of emigration before the nineteenth century. As positions in service became fewer in the years after 1600, many

---

[61] This was worked out subtracting 18 per cent for smaller labour requirements during the harvest. Clark, 'Yields per Acre', pp. 452–7.

young men and women chose to seek their fortunes elsewhere. Every year 6,000–10,000 new immigrants arrived in London from the countryside looking for new work.[62] Many died owing to the high death rates in the capital, but many found work in industry, trade and service. Many others among the young men sought their fortune outside the country altogether, first in Ireland and then in the Caribbean and the Chesapeake, where labour was in demand. The labour market quickly adapted itself to this demand through the process of indentured service and the activities of colonial agents in London and Bristol willing to profit from the shipping of largely masculine labour out of the country.

The most recent estimates indicate that somewhere in the region of 530,500 people emigrated from England in the seventeenth century. Of these, 180,000 went to Ireland, 190,000 went to the West Indies, 116,000 to the Chesapeake and 21,000 to New England. Most of the emigration to Ireland occurred between 1610 and 1660, and while a few thousand settlers emigrated to Virginia in the 1620s, large-scale Atlantic emigration did not begin until the 1630s. If the population going to Ireland is added to that emigrating to the Americas it means that about 120,000 Englishmen left each decade between 1640 and 1660, which gives a figure of about 6 per cent of the male population over the age of 15 leaving the country every decade. In the 1630s this accounted for 32 per cent of the decade's population growth, and had risen to 51 per cent of population growth by the 1640s and well over 100 per cent of population growth for the next two decades, reducing the population of England by about 5–6 per cent. Further, between 75 and 95% of emigrants were male, given that the labour involved was heavy field work. While higher wages were certainly an incentive for emigration to the Caribbean, lack of work must have driven many to leave the country.[63]

However, as we saw in Table 4.6, there was a rise in the median value of labourers' possessions recorded in their probate inventories between the second half of the sixteenth century and the years 1600–50. The median value of the labourers' inventories studied went up by 28 per cent, while the median value of their household goods rose by 8 per cent. At the same time the value of animals and farming goods possessed by labourers declined by 40 per cent from £4 12s to £2 16s. The reason why the total value of the inventories rose was that the average

[62] A. L. Beier and Roger Finlay (eds.) *The Making of the Metropolis: London 1500–1700* (London, 1986), pp. 9–10.

[63] Muldrew, 'Economic and Urban Development,' pp. 156–7.

amount owed to labourers when they died went up by 103 per cent from £3 12s to £7 4s. Although the nature of the debts is not often stated, when it was, unpaid wages was a much more common reason than the sale of agricultural produce. This implies that more of the inventoried labouring households were spending a greater percentage of their time working for wages rather than farming for themselves. Wages at this time were most likely further in arrears because farmers were finding it difficult to obtain money to pay their workers thanks to a shortage of small change.[64] However, as we saw on page 204 above, some labourers were still managing to accumulate their wages as savings, which indicates that for some there must have been more opportunity to work.

As shown in Table 3.14, there were continual rises in the yields of most crops from the beginning of the seventeenth century, and since yields were beginning to increase, we can also assume that extra labour must have been required to dig ditches to improve drainage, and to cart manure, marl and lime to improve soil quality. This is dramatically demonstrated by the example of Morval Barton, where the labour input of sixty-one days per acre of arable was a result of the extra labour needed in the attempt to improve the land by spreading lime and sand, picking stones and weeding as well as clearing new land.[65] In addition, as J. R. Wordie has shown, 28 per cent of enclosure took place between 1600 and 1760, requiring more digging and planting of hedgerows.[66] In Adam Moore's *Bread for the Poor*, written in the 1620s but not published until 1653, the great need for labour in agricultural improvement was noted when the author made one of the first arguments for employing the poor in productive work:

And touching imployment for the poor (wherewith this Land so infinitely aboundeth) such means thereof would be for them in the manurance of each sort of these *Wastes* enclosed (as by *Diking, Hedging, Fencing, Setting, Sowing, Reaping, Gleaning, Mowing, Making hay*, and what not? Which is all *Bread for the Poor*) that from the noysome and deboist [debased] courses of *Begging, Filching, Robbing, Rouging, Murthering*, and whatsoever other Villainies their unexercised brains and hands undertake, they would (even gladly) be reclaimed and refined to loyall and laudable courses, as well for their own contenting relief, as the unspeakable comfort and honour of the whole State, who now (as a wretched and needy mother) is enforced to make continuall Massacres of them, for those misdoings which even their want of bread urgeth them to commit.[67]

[64] Muldrew, 'Monetary Scarcity', pp. 392–3.
[65] Pound, 'Barton Farming', pp. 69–74.
[66] Wordie, 'Chronology of English Enclosure', pp. 494–5.
[67] Adam Moore, *Bread for the Poor* (London, 1653), p. 30.

This extra labour must have been performed by those labourers who were able to increase their wealth, which created a situation in which there was competition between labourers to secure favoured status with the farmers willing to extend all of the advantages described in the last chapter – hiring them as full-time servants or offering them discounts on rent or food. These inventories were made for a portion of the population who were probably valued as hard workers, and who were able to maintain their earnings by increasing their labour. In contrast, the poorest 25 per cent of inventoried labourers experienced no rise in the real value of their inventoried wealth during these years. These would have been the less competent, less fortunate or less obedient labourers unable to secure as much local employment. The most important result of this situation was in the way it affected the social structure of the rural economy, with those favoured labourers fitting into a system of reciprocal obligations, while others who were less productive, preferred more leisure or were unable to get a foot in the door of opportunity when they came of age, took to the road or survived on waste land in increasing poverty.

It was through such conditions that competition for work led to social differentiation based on ability and application to work – what came to be called industriousness. Such labourers who were considered to be hard working were those chosen to work more days, as well as for piece-work, thus increasing their earnings. The same wealthy farmers and estate owners who sat on vestries and petty sessions juries and made decisions about poor relief and social discipline also hired labourers as their servants and day workers, and they could decide who was most deserving and capable of being given more work or better 'wages' in the form of payment negotiations.

In his description of the hiring of servants, Henry Best noted that when hiring for a year, a farmer first needed to find out what kind of labour the servant could do, but then he was to go to his former master or a neighbour and 'know of them wheather he bee true and trustie, if hee bee a gentle and quiet fellowe'. He also noted how the wages offered for the year could vary between 30s and 50s depending on how many different tasks he was reputed to be sufficient at. 'Lusty maidservants' were also valued highly, and he noted in 1640 that their wages had risen from 18s with a 1s 6d godspenny (a contractual down payment) to 28s per annum. Very interestingly, he also noted that servants who stayed with him over a number of years were given substantial rises every year. One maidservant's wages rose from 18s in the first year to 24s in the second year, 28s in the third year and 38s in her fourth year. He also described how hirings took place in different towns at the time when the chief constables would use the wage rates set by the Justices to 'set down a reasonable and indifferent wage' between any masters and servants who had disagreements and could not agree about a proper arrangement for parting from their initial contract. It was at one such hiring that Best heard a servant make a rhyme:

> I can sowe,
> I can mowe,
> And I can stacke,
> And I can doe,
> My master too,
> When My master turns his backe.

Best does not say if he hired the man, but he obviously thought it humorous enough to write down.[68]

Best shows how yearly wages could rise substantially after the initial hiring. Richard Cholmeley also did this, often augmenting the wages he paid with perks such as clothes or pasture rent.[69] But yearly wages set down by statute could vary as well. In the sessions of the peace held in Chester in 1596, servants in husbandry were even divided into the best sort, the second sort and the third sort, with yearly wages ranging from 20s down to 8s a year after board. This was also the case in Oakham in 1610, where a 'man servant, for husbandrie of the best sort, which can eire, sow, mow, thresh, make a ricke, thacke, and hedge the same; and can kill a hog, sheepe, and calfe' was to be paid £2, in contrast to 'A meane servant, which can drive plow, pitch cart, and thresh, but cannot expertly sow and mow', who was to be paid only £1.[70]

During harvest time, in particular, a good worker was especially valuable and could earn more. In Hertfordshire, William Ellis claimed that men were hired long before harvest 'by Way of Security' and they were paid 30–36s for a month (although they could be kept up to two months if the harvest required) besides victualling and lodging, which was done not so much as an added incentive but as a means of ensuring they started early in the morning. Ellis claimed that a good servant was 'better worth ten Pounds a Year Wages than some of the more ignorant, slow and careless are half ten Pounds; for such a right Workman, with us, is up first in Harvest-time, blows his Horn to awake and get ready the rest ... on his diligent, careful, nimble Performance, depends in a great measure the more Work of the rest that follow him'.[71]

---

[68] Woodward (ed.), *Farming Books of Henry Best*, pp. 138–42.
[69] *Memorandum Book of Richard Cholmeley*, pp. 77, 87, 204.
[70] Eden, *State of the Poor*, III, pp. xciv–xcvi.   [71] Ellis, *Country Housewife*, p. 73.

As we saw on pages 224–6 above, many farmers hired good workers as servants for longer periods of time to secure their service. Wage books exist in eighteenth-century farm accounts and these can reveal how often day labourers worked on larger estates and how much they were paid. These accounts can tell us how many labourers were in full employment and when days off were taken, but they cannot tell us if workers who did not work full-time were working elsewhere or on their own farms when not employed on the farm in question. One excellent set of labour accounts is that for the Harewood House estate in Yorkshire from 1789. In this book, records were kept for every day of the year for all labourers, as well as for extra boys and women hired on the farm. In addition, the nature of the work done every day was also described. On Thursday 5 March, for instance, ten men were employed loading stones and making a road, two men were loading hay, one was loading turnips to feed cattle, two were hedging and dressing hedge stakes, two men and two boys were spreading dung and one man was brewing. Over the course of the year this estate hired 45 different men, of whom 4 worked a complete 312-day year with no holidays at all besides Sundays. Another 4 worked more than 295 days, and a further 5 worked more than 275 days a year. Most of the rest of the workers worked five or six days a week, but worked for fewer weeks in the year. There were some labourers who did work fewer days at odd times, but there was no one who always worked only four or fewer days a week. Nor is there evidence of specific workers consistently taking St Monday off.[72]

Figure 6.1 shows the total number of days worked on the estate every week by men, boys and women. Here we can see the great need for extra labour in the summer months, which was met by hiring some extra men but primarily through employing more boys and especially large numbers of women. The figure also shows that Easter, above all, was the holiday season when most labourers took days off, followed by the first week of the year and then Michaelmas and All Souls' Day. When individual workers took a day or half a day off, it must have been for personal reasons, as other labourers did not follow suit.

A good set of accounts also exists for the Blackett family estate of Matfen, Northumberland, for 1758.[73] Here fifty-two labourers were hired over the course of the year, together with a number of female shearers during summer and fall. One man worked an entire 312-day year and another 307.5 days, while a further 3 worked between 270 and

---

[72] WYASL, WYL 250/3/197. On the practice of taking St Monday as a holiday, see Douglas A. Reid, 'The Decline of Saint Monday 1766–1876', *Past and Present*, 71 (1976), pp. 76–101.

[73] The period 17 March–9 June has been disaggregated equally. NCS, ZBL 283/1.

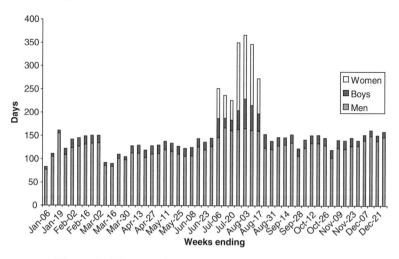

Figure 6.1 Harewood House labourers' work, 1789

285 days. In total 24 men worked over 125 days a year. Here there were some labourers who worked fewer days per week throughout the year, as well as some who worked full weeks irregularly. Figure 6.2 shows that at this farm less work was done in the winter than at Harewood House. As for holidays, many men took Monday 5 September off, but more men worked over New Year than in December; unfortunately the weeks including Easter were aggregated and so it is impossible to count them separately. At the Oakes farm, discussed in the last chapter, there were 5 day labourers in 1772 who worked over 300 days of the year, compared to 4 who worked 21–43 weeks out of the year and 7 casual workers, in addition to the boys and the female workers discussed above.[74] On all of these farms, then, a small group of labourers were hired in what amounted to full-time employment paid by the day. At the same time, a large number of other labourers made up their employment working here and there and probably for themselves as well.

What is most interesting about these wage accounts is that they show that there were no holidays when all labourers took time off, or if they did their employers continued to pay them for this time. But in the Harewood House accounts, where the nature of work was recorded for each day, it can be seen that those men paid every day were indeed working. By the end of the eighteenth century agricultural writers like Eden, Young and Batchelor tended to assume that labourers worked a

---

[74] Burnette, 'Labourers at the Oakes', p. 48.

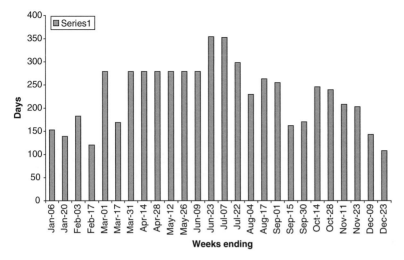

Figure 6.2 Blackett family estate labourers' work, 1758

full year, and these accounts show that some day labourers were in fact being hired as full-time employees. The only time when a significant number of labourers took time off was over Christmas and Easter.

However, as Robert Malcolmson has shown, there were local wakes, football matches and other sports where agricultural servants and day labourers did indeed take some time off to attend in the eighteenth century. Parson Woodforde often gave his servants leave to take a holiday to attend St Faith's fair, and Nicholas Blundell, of Little Crosby in Lancashire, also reported letting his servants go to fairs and dances.[75] Using a sample of court depositions for evidence of work activity on different days, Hans-Joachim Voth found that in London, and in more limited evidence from Northern Assize depositions, that there may have been as many as forty-six days on which work ceased, even as late as the mid-eighteenth century.[76] Certainly it was recognised that labourers needed recreations on Sundays, and celebrations on other days of the year as well, to break the monotony of daily work. As the author of an article published in the *London Magazine* in 1736 put it:

'Tis well known that such Diversions are chiefly enjoy'd by the common People; who being fatigued by labouring continually for a sorry Living, find

[75] Malcolmson, *Popular Recreations*, pp. 20–3, 25, 28–31, 39–51, 60.
[76] Hermann Freudenberger and Gaylord Cummins, 'Health, Work and Leisure before the Industrial Revolution', *Explorations in Economic History*, 13 (1976), pp. 1–12. Using a sample of court depositions for evidence of work activity on different days, Hans-Joachim Voth found that in London in 1760 there was less likelihood of people

a Relaxation highly necessary for them ... Then, think they, we shall not only rest from our mean Employments, but shall act the Part of richer and more Creditable People; we shall appear with our best Clothes, and with the Help of our Savings not only live well, but divert ourselves with the merry Humours of Harlequin and Punchanello.[77]

In addition, some labourers must have slept during work hours or spent time gossiping.[78]

Many eighteenth-century commentators, in fact, complained that workers spent too much time on leisure activities, arguing that once workers had earned enough money to maintain a standard of living which they found acceptable, they would then take days off to spend in recreation or in the alehouse. This has come to be termed 'leisure preference' by economists, and John Hatcher has argued that it continued to exist well into the early nineteenth century.[79] Robert Malcolmson has also noted that many of the contemporary commentators who complained of workers taking time off for leisure were also proponents of 'industriousness', which will be discussed in the next chapter. These pamphleteers and employers battled against what they saw as lost productive capacity when workers took time off for leisure or holidays.[80] Most of these complaints were directed against industrial workers who earned higher wages, and who, more importantly, earned *cash* wages which allowed them to take days off once they had enough to spend on leisure. It is a striking fact that almost all of the examples historians have found of leisure preference existed in industry.[81] In agricultural work, by contrast, higher 'wages' often took the form of more perks on offer from farmers, such as meals and rights to pasture and feed for animals. Thus farmers would have had more bargaining power to encourage workers to work more days, in contrast to the weavers and coal workers discussed by Hatcher who could take a day off after they had received their wages. In addition much farm work was seasonal and the

working on these days, but that this had disappeared by 1880. In evidence from Northern Assize depositions there was more tendency to work on these days earlier in the century. Voth, *Time and Work*, pp. 100–5; Wrightson, *Earthly Necessities*, pp. 194–8.

[77] Malcolmson, *Popular Recreations*, pp. 70–1.   [78] See below, p. 312.
[79] Hatcher, 'Labour, Leisure', pp. 64–114; F. S. Furniss, *The Position of the Laborer in a System of Nationalism: A Study in the Labor Theories of Later English Mercantilism* (New York, 1965).
[80] Malcolmson, *Popular Recreations*, pp. 90–100.
[81] See, for instance, *Considerations on Taxes as They Are Supposed to Affect the Price of Labour in Our Manufactories* (London, 1765), pp. 17–19, 42–3, 48–9; John Clayton, *Friendly Advice to the Poor; Written and Published at the Request of the Late and Present Officers of the Town of Manchester* (Manchester, 1755), pp. 9–16; Hatcher, 'Labour, Leisure', pp. 69–70, 86–92; Eden, *State of the Poor*, II, p. 357; III, p. 848.

rhythms of work would in some part be determined by this, although there would always be stones to be picked, roads to mend and fences to be repaired when other work was finished. As one author put it:

In the Country the Plowman, the Labourer, and the Artificer, are satisfied with their Holydays at Easter, Whitsuntide, and Christmas. At the two former they enjoy their innocent Sports, such as a Cricket-Match, or a Game at Cudgels, or some other laudable Trial of Manhood, to the Improvement of English Courage. At Christmas they partake of the good Cheer of that Season, and return satisfy'd to their Labour: But in this Town [London], Diversions calculated to slacken the Industry of the useful Hands are innumerable: To lessen therefore the Number of these, is the Business of the magistrate.[82]

Malcolmson argued that while campaigners against holidays began to have an effect in reducing the amount of leisure time taken in industrial employment by the beginning of the nineteenth century, rural employments were less affected.[83] However, the wage accounts cited here certainly show that for some agricultural labourers industry was already more important than leisure time. There is also an example given by a Berkshire agricultural labourer in a settlement examination from 1763, where 3s was deducted from his wages for going to Tadley Revel without his mistress's consent for three days. On his return she scolded him and did not employ him for three or four days, but eventually took him back into service.[84] Hans-Joachim Voth has also found that more people were working on former holidays by the late eighteenth and early nineteenth century.[85]

But hard work and leisure could also be connected. Harvest celebrations were a reward for what was often over a month of particularly hard labour.[86] In a very interesting example, Nicholas Blundell recorded in great detail the celebrations he organised after an intense effort on the part of his labourers marling his fields in the spring of 1712. Over the course of two weeks he was very busy making caps, costumes and flowered garlands for his marlers and some sword dancers. On 9 July:

The six Garlands etc: were carried by Young Women in Prosestion, the 8 Sword Dancers etc: went along with them to the Marl-pit where they Dansed, the Musick was Gerard Holsold and his Son and Richard Tatlock, at Night they Danced in the Barne.

On 15 July he baited a bull in the marl pit and finally on 23 July he held a large celebration for his workers, neighbours and tenants where

---

[82] As cited in Malcolmson, *Popular Recreations*, p. 161.
[83] Ibid., pp. 160–3.   [84] Durrant (ed.), *Berkshire Overseers' Papers*, p. 8.
[85] Voth, *Time and Work*, pp. 100–5.
[86] Malcolmson, *Popular Recreations*, pp. 58–60.

presents were exchanged and the marlers, spreaders and carters were ceremoniously paid before more dancing took place.[87]

However, the number of times holidays were taken with a master's or employer's consent is impossible to quantify. It is equally impossible to know how many days labourers took off who were listed in account books as working only part of the year. But given that there was more demand for labour in the eighteenth century, perhaps some labourers were able to work less intensely and still find enough work. Equally, others certainly took advantage of the greater demand to earn more through hard work to improve their standard of living, as the inventory evidence shows. Thus it certainly seems sensible to assume that some labourers worked full years, while others chose to earn less and engage in more recreations.

Finally, we need to ask ourselves what relationship there was between labourers and the poor law. As many authors have noted, the national poor laws were created just after the terrible years of the late 1590s, when poor families could no longer support too many small children, or the elderly and sick. However, it has also been noted that the number of doles paid out rose most quickly in the period after 1690, when demand for employment was increasing most rapidly. This increase in poor rates probably reflects rising expectations on the part of the main beneficiaries of the poor law, who continued to be the sick, elderly and dependent young.[88] But it has been estimated that rarely did those on relief form more than 5–6 per cent of parish populations at any one time.[89]

There certainly were working labouring families who found themselves in need of relief at some point in their life course, as can be witnessed in the stories told in eighteenth-century settlement examinations. This period saw the increase of what Paul Slack has termed 'shallow poverty'. This refers to working families who needed occasional relief at some point in their life cycle owing to temporary need. This could be caused by the survival of a large number of small children too young to work, by a local work shortage or by high food prices

[87] Ibid., pp. 62–4.
[88] Slack, *Poverty and Policy*, pp. 188–92. Steve Hindle, 'Power, Poor Relief, and Social Relations in Holland Fen, *c.* 1600–1800', *Historical Journal*, 41 (1998), pp. 80–3; W. Newman-Brown, 'The Receipt of Poor Relief and Family Situation, Aldenham, Hertfordshire, 1630–90', in Richard Smith (ed.), *Land, Kinship and Life Cycle* (Cambridge, 1984), pp. 405–22; Richard M. Smith, 'Ageing and Well-Being in Early Modern England: Pension Trends and Gender Preferences under the Old Poor Law *c.* 1650–1800', in Paul Johnson and Pat Thane (eds.), *Old Age from Antiquity to Post-Modernity* (London, 1998), pp. 64–95.
[89] Hindle, *On the Parish*, pp. 271ff.

in some years. Unemployment could also result from labourers disagreeing with their employers. In addition there were many pastoral woodland areas of the country where labourers remained small farmers whose production was often too small, and continued poverty was the result. One such example was the parish of Eccleshall in Staffordshire analysed by Margaret Spufford and James Went.[90]

Settlement examinations to determine which parish was responsible for paying poor relief often provide work histories of some labourers, as settlement was transferred to a new parish if an applicant worked a full year in a parish other than where they had been born.[91] Many of these documents show that there were labourers who found themselves having to apply for poor relief in the middle of their lives, such as the following example from Berkshire:

16 May 1799. Exam of Thomas Hopson [x], labourer ... He is aged 45 and was b[orn] in Chieveley where parents were leg[itimately] sett[led]. Has lived in divers services. 8 years ago at Newbury Hiring Fair was hired by Mr Osmond of Upton Farm, Vernham Dean, Hants. He served 2 years at £7 and 7½ gns. He m[arried] before his last year and sometimes slept at his master's and sometimes with his wife in Hurstbourne Tarrant [Hants]. He possessed a cottage house and garden in Chieveley by virtue of his grandfather's will. Has lately sold the house and garden to his sister for the sum of £19 4s 0d. He has a wife, Elizabeth, and 3 children now residing with him in Chieveley, Jane aged 5, Ann 3 and Giles 1.[92]

Unfortunately, no one has attempted to quantify how many labourers who might have found themselves in such circumstances were recorded in settlement certificates. In order to examine the length of service discussed above in chapter 5, Keith Snell counted 1,317 labourers' certificates for all the southeastern counties, but this ranged from 1701 to 1840, only about 9 a year on average. Norma Landau has argued, against Snell, that many more migrant workers were examined than is reflected by the survival of the certificates, but it is unclear how many would have been applying for relief at the time. In her view, examinations were more concerned with surveillance of the mobile

---

[90] Spufford and Went, *Poverty Portrayed*, pp. 14–24. David Rollison, *The Local Origins of Modern Society: Gloucestershire 1500–1800* (London, 1993), ch. 1.

[91] Settlement examinations contain a history of where the examinant was born, where they worked and for how long. They were made before two Justices of the Peace when someone applied for poor relief from the parish, but did not possess a certificate of settlement. This needed to be done to determine which parish was responsible for paying the relief under the legislation of 1662. For a description of these records, see Durrant (ed.), *Berkshire Overseers' Papers*, pp. ix–xxii, 157–198. Also see Snell, *Annals of the Labouring Poor*, ch. 2.

[92] Durrant (ed.), *Berkshire Overseers' Papers*, p. 89.

poor by parish vestries in an attempt to keep themselves from becoming financially responsible for potentially burdensome individuals and families.[93]

However, since the debate between Snell and Landau, little work has been done on these documents. It would also be useful to know what percentage of agricultural labourers were recorded as finding themselves in need of relief in comparison to industrial workers. If it was possible for industrial workers to earn high wages and take time off when demand was high, it was equally possible for these workers to find themselves unemployed during slumps in demand. Many of the pamphlets arguing against leisure preference complained that workers did not save enough by working more in good times to help in bad, because they were able to rely on the poor law to support them in hard times or when they became old.[94]

On the other hand, Thomas Turner actually gave an example which shows how some farmers could use the poor law to manipulate labour markets by *increasing* the number of workers in a parish in order to lower wages through competition:

As I were this day a-considering of the particulars that passed at the vestry yesterday, I think nothing sinks so deep in my heart as Dame Burrage's affair, to see a poor woman supplicating our charity with 6 poor helpless children (all small) deserted by a husband (who was well-known to be a more than common industrious man and also one who did not spend his money, but readily and with cheerfulness shared it in his family) and who has been eloped from his family about 10 days. Sure the thought of it must pierce any heart ...

Many of the richest and leading men of our parish (though I think not the wisest) have long since been endeavouring to pull down the price of this and some more poor men's wages (though not a man of 'em can say he ever asked more for a day's work than he earned) by bringing in many poor into the parish from other parishes, some with certificates and some without, until the parish is full of poor, and those wise gentlemen's scheme almost come to take effect ...

[93] Norma Landau, 'The Laws of Settlement and the Surveillance of Immigration in Eighteenth-Century Kent', *Continuity and Change*, 3 (1988), pp. 391–420; Norma Landau, 'The Regulation of Immigration, Economic Structures and Definitions of the Poor in Eighteenth-Century England', *Historical Journal*, 33 (1990), pp. 541–71; Keith Snell, 'Pauper Settlement and the Right to Poor Relief in England and Wales', *Continuity and Change*, 6 (1991), pp. 375–415; Norma Landau, 'The Eighteenth-Century Context of the Laws of Settlement', *Continuity and Change*, 6 (1991), pp. 417–39; Keith Snell, 'Settlement, Poor Law and the Rural Historian: New Approaches and Opportunities'. *Rural History*, 3 (1992), pp. 145–72. See also Peter M. Solar, 'Poor Relief and English Economic Development before the Industrial Revolution', *Economic History Review*, 2nd ser., 48 (1995), pp. 1–22.

[94] Clayton, *Friendly Advice to the Poor*, pp. 14–15, 24–9.

Oh, cruel and inhuman usage, oppression, fraud and grinding the face of the poor are our guilt![95]

Turner was an overseer of the poor and a member of the parish vestry and had much to do with the administration of the poor laws, both in keeping track of collection and in providing goods from his shop to be doled out to poor families. He described the administration of the poor laws in great detail, and when discussing the reluctance of his wealthier farming neighbours to pay their full rates, or their attempts to drive down wages, he inevitably sympathised with the plight of the poor, often identifying more with them than those he dined with, albeit through the prism of his reading of eighteenth-century texts on sensibility.

If it is impossible to measure how many agrarian labouring families were vulnerable to Slack's shallow poverty, and at what points in their life cycle, there is certainly enough evidence to argue that it is a great oversimplification to equate labour with poverty. Although the labour market concentrated resources towards fewer harder working individuals in the countryside between 1600 and 1650, after this date almost all families seem to have benefited from a rise in their standard of living as measured by the accumulation of goods over the life course. As we saw in chapter 4, the lower quartile of labourers' inventories rose in value 39 per cent compared to a rise of 24 per cent for the wealthiest quartile. But as the vast increase in the standard deviation indicates, there were also more relatively wealthier labourers by the end of the seventeenth century, indicating that a new, much greater degree of social differentiation existed between labourers in terms of material wealth. In the final chapter of the book the development of the ideology of 'industriousness' will be charted to show how differences in effort could affect social structure.

---

[95] Turner continued: 'NB: I do not any ways commend Burrage for leaving his family, for I think it a very unjust and imprudent thing in him, and more particularly so, as he the night before he went away received of Mr. Jer. French £3 and which he carried away with him. The only thing I endeavour to point out is the motive which occasioned him to abscond.' Vaisey (ed.), *Diary of Thomas Turner*, pp. 67–8. See also ibid., pp. 82–3, 91, 130–1, 176, 318–19.

And hence must arise a kind of Competition amongst the people who shall farm or purchase Land, when the Revenue of Land is certain, and grows higher daily, as the Treasure and People increase, which must cause Land to rise as well in the years' purchase, as in the years' value; nay, the very Earth must receive an inevitable *Improvement* by their Industrious numbers, whilst every one will be able and willing to possess and manure a greater or lesser part, according to his occasions; there is hardly any Land in *England* but may be improved to double the value, and very much to treble and more.

William Petyt, *Britannia Languens or a Discourse on Trade*[1]

The main spur to Trade, or rather to Industry and Ingenuity, is the exorbitant Appetites of Men, which they will take pains to gratifie, and so be disposed to work, when nothing else will incline them to it; for did Men content themselves with bare Necessaries, we should have a poor World.

The Glutton works hard to purchase Delicacies, wherewith to gorge himself; the Gamester, for Money to venture at Play; the Miser, to hoard; and so others. Now in their pursuit of those Appetites, other Men less exorbitant are benefitted; and tho' it may be thought few profit by the Miser, yet it will be found otherwise ... for if he labours with his own hands, his Labour is very beneficial to them who imploy him; if he doth not work, but profit by the Work of others, then those he sets on work have benefit by their being employed.

Dudley North, *Discourses upon Trade*[2]

Where there is no Servants, there can be no Masters: It's Labouring People must improve our Land, raise us plenty of Food, Clothing, and other Necessaries, and by what they raise, increase our Trade at home and abroad; acquire us Riches by raising more than

---

[1] William Petyt, *Britannia Languens or a Discourse on Trade* (London, 1680), reprinted in McCulloch (ed.), *Early English Tracts on Commerce*, pp. 291–2.
[2] Dudley North, *Discourses upon Trade; Principally Directed to the Cases of the Interest, Coynage, Clipping, Increase of Money* (London, 1691), pp. 14–15.

we spend, for the Increase of Posterity, and the Support of the Government.

John Bellers, *Essays about the Poor, Manufacturers, Trade, Plantations and Immorality and of the Excellency and Divinity of Inward Light*[3]

In this final chapter I wish to shift from an empirical investigation of work and living standards to look at how these changing patterns of work affected the place of labourers in the social order. The economic and social relationships between employers and labourers and masters and servants included both mutualities and differences.[4] It was in the interest of farmers to secure reliable, honest labourers to make their farms profitable, and to feed and treat productive labourers well. Equally it was in the interest of labourers to secure long-term security of work as well as the best earnings possible. Furthermore, because there were so few secure institutions which enabled poor servants to save for the future to support young children in the early years of a marriage, many would have had to trust to their masters to do this for them, which would require cordial relations.

The major changes in the period can be encompassed by considering the rise of the concept of 'industriousness', which emerged in the mid-seventeenth century and was used to distinguish industry from idleness, as in the case of William Hogarth's famous series of prints.[5] I will look at the emergence of this language and its relationship to improvement, as well as to poverty and employment. Certainly it is well understood by now through the work of Paul Slack and Steve Hindle that this was how those deserving poor relief were judged, but here I will try to discover how those labouring families who worked less were described in comparison with those who worked all the time.[6] Did labourers form part of the 'poor' in general when poverty was discussed abstractly, or did contemporaries think of the poor as those who could not work because of age, infirmity or lack of application?

The key terms in describing labourers in a positive light were 'honest', 'industrious', 'laborious' and 'painful'. Of these terms, 'honest' was probably the most commonly used over the whole period, and was a general reference to the reliability of labourers and servants in husbandry,

---

[3] John Bellers, *Essays about the Poor, Manufacturers, Trade, Plantations and Immorality and of the Excellency and Divinity of Inward Light* (1699), reprinted in George Clarke (ed.), *John Bellers, 1654 to 1725, Quaker Visionary: His Life, Times and Writings* (York, 1993), pp. 35, 64.

[4] Keith Wrightson, 'Mutualities and Obligations: Changing Social Relationships in Early Modern England', *Proceedings of the British Academy*, 139 (2006), pp. 157–94.

[5] Hallett and Riding, *Hogarth*, pp. 184–9.

[6] Hindle, *On the Parish*, pp. 379ff.; Slack, *Poverty and Policy*, pp. 17–32.

in relation to both their creditworthiness and diligence in performing their tasks. As we have seen, day labourers' wages were often paid in arrears, forcing them to rely on credit to buy things. This was much less important for agricultural labourers, who often bought food from their employers, than for industrial workers. However, all labourers would have bought things from shops such as salt, clothing and household goods, and if debts went unpaid then a reputation for honesty would be lost. Just as important, as Jennifer Richards has argued, was the fact that honesty in this period was more than just a reputation for truthfulness, it was an aspect of behaviour in conversation which permitted trust, and in the case of labourers this was an acceptance of subordination to their employers.[7] It has been well documented that many poor families resorted to petty crimes which were hard to detect, such as the embezzlement of wool by spinners or the theft of wood and fruit from landowners.[8] Such crime, whether it was prosecuted or not, led to a reputation for dishonesty, as is shown in Richard Gough's description of one labourer from his parish of Myddle in Shropshire:

This Richard was an untowardly liver, very idle and extravagant, endeavouring to suply his necessytyes rather by stealeing than by his honest labour. Hee was bound over to appeare att the Assizes for stealeing a cow from one of his kinsmen.[9]

A reputation for honesty was important in such a legalistic society, where labourers were often asked to stand as witnesses on oath. Two witnesses appearing before the church courts in Salisbury in 1665 claimed that 'a poor man may be an honest man as well as a rich man', while in 1637 a Kentish husbandman stated, 'true it is that his estate is not much worth yet he lives in good and honest repute amongst his neighbours'.[10] Just as being termed a gentleman came to rely on the opinion of one's better neighbours – those who already had the reputation of gentlemen or the titled gentry – being an honest labourer was also based on reputation, especially with those likely to provide employment.[11]

Similarly, 'painfulness' referred to one's application to work in the sense of the modern survival, 'painstaking', as when Thomas Tusser referred to servants as 'both painefull and good'.[12] But increasingly after the mid-century, these terms came to be supplemented, and then

---

[7] Jennifer Richards, *Rhetoric and Courtliness in Early Modern Literature* (Cambridge, 2003), pp. 27–9.
[8] Hindle, *On the Parish*, pp. 81–92.   [9] Gough, *Myddle*, p. 237.
[10] Shepard, 'Poverty, Labour', p. 90.
[11] Henry French, *The Middle Sort of People in Provincial England 1600–1750* (Oxford, 2007), ch. 4.
[12] Tusser, *Five Hundred Points*, p. 166.

dominated, by the concept of 'industriousness'. Although the term 'industry' had been used previously to refer to diligence and application, it was initially used to refer more to intellectual rather than manual pursuits, as in this definition of Sir Thomas Elyot's:

they that be called industrious, do most craftily and deeply understand in all affairs what is expedient, and by what means and ways they may soonest exploit them. And those things in whom other men travail, a person industrious lightly and with facility speedeth, and findeth new ways and means to bring to effect that he desireth.[13]

William Harrison also described the industry of brewers and skilled artisans, but not labourers or the poor.[14] However, we can see the meaning of the word beginning to change when used by Sir Thomas Smith, the Tudor humanist and adviser to Queen Elizabeth, in his *Discourse of the Commonweal of This Realm of England*, which was written in 1549 and published in 1581,

Is it not an old saying in Latin, *Honos alit artes*, that is to say, 'profite or aduancement nourisheth euery faculty' … For what lawe can compell men to bee industrious in trauayle or labour of body, or studious to learne any science or knowledge of the minde? to these thinges they may bee well prouoked, encouraged, and allured: if they be industrious and painefull, bee rewarded well for their paines: and bee suffereed to take Gaynes and wealth as rewardes of theyr labours.[15]

A few years after the publication of Smith's work we see 'industriousness' being used by Richard Hakluyt in the sense in which it would become common in the seventeenth century. This was in a manuscript tract entitled *Discourse of Western Planting* written in 1584, which set out arguments for why England should aggressively pursue a policy of imperial colonisation in the western Atlantic. Much of the tract was concerned with reducing or challenging the power of the Spanish empire. English colonies would potentially be a source of equal or better commodities, while also providing a platform for attacking the Spanish in the western Atlantic. In one chapter Hakluyt argued, on economic grounds, that England could best challenge the strength of the Spanish, not by discovering equal amounts of gold and silver, but by 'planting' colonies of people on the Atlantic seaboard north of Florida to exploit resources such as timber, fish, tar, resin, animal hides and

---

[13] Thomas Elyot, *The Boke Named the Governour* (London, 1531), fol. 87r–v.
[14] Harrison, *Description*, pp. 31, 40, 54, 56.
[15] Thomas Smith, *Discourse of the Commonweal of This Realm of England* (London, 1581), fol. 22v. I wish to thank David Harris Sacks for this reference and that in Hakluyt below.

anything else of value. But he also argued that, as these colonies grew, they would provide new markets for English woollen goods and other things manufactured in England, thus putting the poor to work.[16]

He also linked his argument to contemporary concerns about vagrancy and unemployment caused by the rising population of the time. Many writers in the late sixteenth century were concerned with the growing problem of poverty and the migration of poor people looking for work, and many were aware that this was caused by population outstripping the availability of work.[17] William Harrison, for instance, claimed:

There is no commonwealth at this day in Europe wherein there is not great store of poor people, and those necessarily to be relieved by the wealthier sort, which otherwise would starve and come to utter confusion. With us the poor is commonly divided into three sorts, so that some are poor by impotence, as the fatherless child, the aged, blind, and lame, and the diseased person that is judged to be incurable; the second are poor by casualty, as the wounded soldier, the decayed householder, and the sick person visited with grievous and painful diseases; the third consisteth of thriftless poor, as the rioter that hath consumed all, the vagabond that will abide nowhere, but runneth up and down from place to place (as it were seeking work and finding none), and finally the rogue and the strumpet.

He went on to qualify his last category, arguing that many migrant poor had been thrown off their smallholdings by enclosing landlords, but argued that the wisest of them had forsaken the realm for other countries in search of a living. But still among them were what he termed 'creatures abhorring all labour and every honest exercise', who needed to be punished.[18]

However, Hakluyt was more perceptive in that he saw that punishment would not increase employment if new work was not provided for the unemployed, as lack of work was the main cause of idleness:

But wee for all the Statutes that hitherto can be devised, and the sharpe execution of the same in poonishinge idle and lazye persons for wante of sufficient occasion of honest employmente cannot deliver our common wealthe from multitudes of loyterers and idle vagabondes. Truthe it is that throughe our longe peace and seldome sicknes (twoo singuler blessinges of almightie god) wee are growen more populous than ever heretofore: So that nowe there are of every arte and science so many, that they can hardly lyve one by another, nay rather they are readie to eate upp one another: yea many thousandes of idle

[16] Richard Hakluyt, *Discourse of Western Planting* (London, 1584), in E. G. R. Taylor (ed.), *The Original Writings and Correspondence of the Two Richard Hakluyts*, Hakluyt Society, 2nd ser., 77 (1935), pp. 211–13, 218–39.

[17] A. L. Beier, *Masterless Men: The Vagrancy Problem in England 1560–1640* (London, 1985); Slack, *Poverty and Policy*, pp. 91–102.

[18] Harrison, *Description*, pp. 180–3.

persons are within this Realme, which havinge no way to be sett on worke be either mutinous and seeke, alteration in the state, or at leaste very burdensome to the common wealthe.[19]

In contrast to this situation in England, the new discoveries had 'so many honest wayes to sett them on worke as they rather wante men than meanes to ymploye them', and in this way people 'shalbe kepte from idlenes, and be made able by their owne honest and easie labour'. These colonies would then, in turn, provide markets for manufactured goods made in England, especially clothes, which would create employment at home, with the result that

when people knowe howe to lyve, and howe to maynetayne and feede their wyves and children, they will not abstaine from, mariage as nowe they doe … I dare truly affirme that if the nomber in this Realme were as greate as all Spaine and Fraunce have, the people beinge industrious, industrious I say, there shoulde be founde victualls ynoughe at the full in all bounty to suffice them all.[20]

Although there were many other so-called 'projectors' who provided arguments for improving the production of manufactured goods made in England at this time, Hakluyt was unusual in putting stress on the employment of labour. In his *Discourse of Trade* from 1621, for instance, Thomas Mun discussed the industry of merchants in commerce, but not of labour.[21] But if writings about industry and trade neglected labour, the question of work was central to the relief of the poor. The Elizabethan statute which defined the poor laws (39 Eliz. I, c.3) stipulated that those able to work, but with no trade, were to be put to work on 'a convenient Stocke of Flaxe Hempe Wooll Threed Iron and other necessary Ware and Stuffe', in an attempt to create employment. But since most of these work schemes involved cloth manufacture of some sort, they proved to be expensive failures. The cloth trade was depressed throughout most of the early seventeenth century until the introduction of the new draperies, and the sale of the cloth made by the poor rarely offset the start-up cost of buying materials and providing training.[22] Nothing was said in this statute about the promotion of industriousness, and although idleness was certainly considered as parish authorities sought to define who should be relieved using the division outlined

[19] Hakluyt, *Discourse of Western Planting*, p. 234.   [20] Ibid., pp. 234, 236–7.
[21] Thomas Mun, *Englands Treasure by Forraign Trade*, in McCulloch (ed.), *Early English Tracts on Commerce*, pp. 125, 127, 178–9, 194. In his *Lex Mercatoria*, Gerald de Malynes did not use the term at all. Gerald de Malynes, *Consuetudo vel lex Mercatoria* (London, 1622), while Edward Misselden used it only three times in his *Circle of Commerce*. Edward Misselden, *The Circle of Commerce* (London, 1623).
[22] Hindle, *On the Parish*, pp. 171–86; Slack, *Poverty and Policy*, pp. 152–4.

by Harrison above, the terms used to describe the undeserving were 'unthrifts' or the 'dishonest', while the deserving were the 'painful and honest poor'.[23] In the late 1620s Stephen Burridge, a husbandman, referred to several of his co-witnesses in a church court case as 'very poor, indigent & necessitous persons', but added that he could say no more against them because they were all 'painstakers & such as by their industry and labour indeavor themselves to live in the world in honest courses'.[24]

It was not until the Commonwealth period that what can reliably be termed a discourse of 'industriousness' appeared. This began in the so-called Hartlib circle during the early years of the Commonwealth and continued throughout the second half of the seventeenth century. This moment also saw the beginning of the genre of pamphlets advocating 'improvement' in order to advance national wealth conceptualised in terms of labour and goods rather than money, and then eventually conceptualised as happiness.[25]

This transformation involved an effort to promote new agricultural techniques, and the importation and development of artisanal skills into England to develop industries such as linen making, cloth finishing and dying and paper manufacture among others, so that British consumers would not send money out of the country by purchasing foreign goods such as cloth from Flanders or French paper and Italian glass. At the same time it was also realised that new industries and improved agriculture could not develop without skilled labour, and increasingly writers began to advocate addressing the problem of poverty by teaching the unemployed poor skills in houses of industry and through parish apprenticeships.

The early phase of the first transformation was discussed by Joan Thirsk in *Economic Policy and Projects: The Development of a Consumer Society in Early Modern England*. There she focused largely on the proposals and initiatives of private projectors with connections to the court, but many pamphlets advocating similar things were published after the civil war.[26] In a book published in the same year as Thirsk's, Joyce Appleby looked at what many of these pamphlets on economic improvement had to say about employing the poor as a productive resource for the nation in her interpretation of how economic thought progressed in the seventeenth century. More recently, Paul Slack has added to the analysis of Appleby and provided a more subtly contextual analysis of how ideas

---

[23] Hindle, *On the Parish*, pp. 96, 125–7.   [24] Shepard, 'Poverty, Labour', p. 90.
[25] Paul Slack, 'Material Progress and the Challenge of Affluence in Seventeenth-Century England', *Economic History Review*, 62 (2009), pp. 576–603.
[26] Thirsk, *Economic Policy*.

about poverty were transformed in the mid-seventeenth century.[27] He termed this transformation one from 'reformation' to 'improvement.'[28] Whereas before the civil war, the so-called able-bodied poor and sturdy beggars had to be morally reformed through punishment, after 1650 much more effort was put into promoting improvement of skills and morals through education.

The key moment in this transformation was the influence of the Hartlib circle during the initial years of the interregnum. Here ideas about how agrarian 'improvement' could benefit England, most famously in the pamphlets of Walter Blith, were linked to projects for public education. For the first time, teaching the poor skills was seen to be a way of improving the country's economy by increasing production of food and industrial products. Many pamphlets were published throughout the Restoration arguing that improvements in industry as well as agriculture would lead both to more employment for the poor at home and to increased wealth from exports. These pamphlets began to employ the terms 'industry' or 'industrious' to describe either the benefit to the working poor of more employment or the need to educate the idle or unemployed poor with skills beneficial for the nation. They were mentioned twenty-seven times in Lewis Roberts's *The Treasure of Traffick* (1641) and thirty-three times in William Petyt's *Britannia Languens* (1680). Although idleness continued to be excoriated, labourers, as a group, were generally seen in a much more positive light as individuals now actively seeking work which was in short supply.

In *A Discourse Touching Provision for the Poor* written by Chief Justice Matthew Hale towards the end of the Commonwealth period but not published until 1683, the theme of improvement through industriousness was fully developed. In this work, he argued that the provisions of the current poor laws to put the able-bodied poor to work were ineffective, and he proposed that the laws should be reformed to require JPs to divide counties into jurisdictions and to collect money 'for the raising of a Stock to set the Poor within those precincts on work, and to build or procure a convenient Work House for imploying the Poor, if need be, in it, and for lodging Materials, and for instructing Children in the Trade or Work'.[29] This would bring

People and their Children after them into a Regular, Orderly, and Industrious course of life, which will be as natural to them as now Idleness, and Begging, and Thieving is.

---

[27] Appleby, *Economic Thought and Ideology*, ch. 6.
[28] Slack, *Reformation to Improvement*, chs. 4–5.
[29] Matthew Hale, *A Discourse Touching Provision for the Poor* (London, 1683), p. 9.

By this means the Wealth of the Nation will be increased, Manufactures advanced, and every Body put into a capacity of eating his own Bread, for upon what imaginable account can we think, that we should not be as able to improve our Populousness to our Wealth, as well as Holland, and Flanders, and Barbadoes, if we had but their Industry, and orderly Management? If it be said, their Disposition is more industrious than ours; it is true, in that condition that matters are ordered; but, if we had the same industrious Education, we should have the same industrious Disposition.[30]

Hale was much harsher than Hartlib in his attitude towards the poor, and he made a very marked distinction between the 'Poor that do their work well, and are honest and industrious', who, he claimed, 'cannot want work when any is to be had in the Country, and those that are not imployed are either such as will not work, or cannot tell how to work, or will steal or purloin their work'. The industrious were also described as the 'honestest Workmen', while those who were 'dishonest in their Work' were to be educated out of their dishonesty by the experience of the workhouse, and punished for it if they could not be disciplined by the experience.[31] Hale, in fact, mentioned 'industry' or 'industriousness' twenty times in this short twenty-six-page pamphlet.

In 1700, James Puckle claimed, 'The Time of labouring and industrious People well-employed, is the best commodity of any country', and in 1694 Humphrey Mackworth argued, 'there is no doubt, that the Consumption of the People is not so much, as the product of their Labourers, which is the real strength of the Nation'.[32] William Petyt put it best, stating that

our *People* are strong and able for Work at Home, generous and adventurous abroad, and such as all the rest of the World *have* most coveted to commerce with, and naturally as ingenious, industrious, and willing to labour as any part of Mankind, so long as they can have a reasonable fruit of their Labours.[33]

Application to industry on the part of labourers would lead to a competition between them to do better and earn more, which would in turn lead to general prosperity. This can be seen in John Houghton's *England's Great Happiness or, A Dialogue between Content and Complaint* (1677):

But our height puts us all upon an industry, makes every one strive to excel his fellow, and by their ignorance of one anothers quantities, make more than our markets will presently take off; which puts them to a new industry to find a foreign Vent, and then they must make more for that market; but still having some over-plus they stretch their wits farther, and are never satisfied till they ingross

---

[30] Ibid., p. 12.   [31] Ibid., pp. 15, 24.
[32] Appleby, *Economic Thought and Ideology*, pp. 137, 155.
[33] Petyt, *Britannia Languens*, p. 313.

the trade of the Universe. And something is return'd in lieu of our exporta-
tions, which makes a further employment and emprovement.[34]

Similar sentiments were echoed in the passage quoted from Petyt's
Britannia Languens of 1680 at the start of this chapter.

By the eighteenth century, 'industriousness' seems to have entered
into common usage, based on the evidence of Richard Gough's history
of his Shropshire parish finished in 1701, *The History of Myddle*, and
John Cannon's memoirs. Gough used the term 'industry' to describe
the success of one farmer:

> This Mr. William Watkins is now (1701) owner of this farme, and very happy in
> that it hath pleased God to give him such skill, care, and industry in good hus-
> bandry as his grand-father and father had, for hee is not inferiour to eyther of
> them therein. Hee is alsoe happy in a prudent, provident and discreet wife who
> is every way suitable for such an husband. They live very loveingly togeather,
> very loveing to their neighbours, and very well beloved.[35]

However, when describing the fortunes of labourers, he preferred the
similar term 'laborious', as in following case: 'Samuel Chidlow and his
wife were both provident and laboriouse persons, and gott an estate in
money', or Robert Davies, who was described as 'an honest and laboriouse person', his wife 'beeing a fashionable, modest woman, they were
likely to live well'.[36] Gough commented of another poor labourer that,
'Hee built a pretty lytle house on this tenement, and lived in a good
condition for many yeares. Hee was alwayes a sober man, and a painefull laborer; but his wife is now blinde, and hee is old and indeed an
object of charity.'[37] Cannon, who often described social mobility in his
diary, mentioned the importance of industriousness on many different occasions, often in the form of small proverbs: 'I humbly caution
all young people when in profitable places to be careful, frugal and
take the example of the industrious Ant or laborious Bee.' He also told
the story of Ignatius Jordan, who became Mayor of Exeter and who
would tell stories of those with 'small beginnings [who] afterwards by
being industrious & charitable arrived to Competent Estates and would
instance himself saying: "I came with 6 pence in my purse to this City.
Had I had a Shilling in my purse I had never been Mayor of Exeter."'[38]

Almost all of the late seventeenth-century pamphlet writers agreed
that England had become under-populated by that time, and more

---

[34] John Houghton, *England's Great Happiness or, A Dialogue between Content and
Complaint* (London, 1677), p. 7.
[35] Gough, *Myddle*, pp. 114, 126.   [36] Ibid., pp. 101, 152, 244.   [37] Ibid., p. 145.
[38] John Cannon's Memoirs, pp. 36, 189, 421–3. See also other references on pp. 20–1,
37, 51, 170, 230–31, 331, 448.

people were needed to supply bodies for work to increase the nation's wealth. As the empirical work of Wrigley and Schofield on parish registers has shown, the population of England did indeed drop from about 5,280,000 in 1657 to under 4,900,000 by the early 1680s and did not rise above 5,300,000 again until the 1720s.[39] Carew Reynal, for instance, in a pamphlet entitled *The True English Interest* published in 1674, claimed that complaints about 'the small vend of commodities' in the country proceeded 'especially from want of people', which was due to deaths in the Civil Wars, plague and most importantly emigration to the American colonies 'because they have employments and estates for all people, and no poor among them, which encourages people to come from abroad'.[40] Or, as William Petyt wrote:

these *Plantations* may be Considered as the true Grounds and Causes of all our present Mischiefs; for, had our Fishers been put on no other Employment, had those Millions of People which we have lost or been prevented of by the *Plantations* continued in *England*, the Government would long since have been under a necessity of Easing and regulating our Trade; the common Wants and Cryes of our People would infallibly have obliged it; but much of the Industry of the Nation being turned this way, and the *Plantations* affording room and hopes for Men of *necessitous and uneasie Conditions* ... they have deserted the Nation Continually, and left us intricated and fettered in private Interests and destructive Constitutions of Trade.[41]

Many now saw the motivation of those who emigrated to the colonies as improving their living standards through higher wages, rather than being forced to leave through lack of work. As Roger North, the brother of the merchant Dudley North, wrote in the 1680s:

Now what an Ease were it for the industrious Part of Mankind, if they might transplant themselves where their Labours would yield most ... For if Men have Limbs, the World is wide, and they may ... find Employment, and ought to do it, else, they should starve and not be pitied. No Place is so barren but will employ Men.[42]

[39] Wrigley and Schofield, *Population History*, pp. 532–3.
[40] Thirsk and Cooper (eds.), *Seventeenth-Century Economic Documents*, pp. 758–60; Mildred Campbell, '"Of People Either Too Few or Too Many" The Conflicts of Opinion on Population and Its Relation to Emigration', in William Appleton Aitken and Basil Duke Henning (eds.), *Conflict in Stuart England: Essays in Honor of William Notestein* (London, 1960), pp. 186ff. Appleby, *Economic Thought and Ideology*, pp. 136–7.
[41] Petyt, *Britannia Languens*, pp. 414–15.
[42] Roger North, *A Discourse of the Poor* (London, 1753), pp. 62–3. Although published much later, this tract was based largely on rough notes penned in the mid to late 1680s entitled 'Some Notes Concerning Ye Laws for the Poor'. George D. Choksy 'The Bifurcated Economics of Sir Dudley North and Roger North: One Holistic Analytical Engine', *History of Political Economy*, 27 (1995), pp. 477–8.

However, population growth continued to be slow, and this combined with the eventual success of industry and agriculture in creating more employment in England led to rising wages. This, in turn, led to a change in attitude among pamphlet writers. Increasingly, writers now complained that higher wages were eroding motivation for more industriousness. Although it is impossible to date precisely when it was written, Roger North described how competition for labour now worked to the advantage of all labourers rather than just the industrious:

That of late Years, the Enhancing of Labour is one of the greatest Burthens the landed Interest of *England* hath groaned under, will easily be granted: For it is notorious that both Year and Day-Men's Wages are risen almost as much as the Profits of Land have fallen; and chiefly in the Tillage Countries, where the Labour of Men is absolutely necessary for carrying on the Husbandry of the Country: And, in some Places, Men are not to be had upon any Terms; but, with much Trouble and searching in remote Places, some are found and far fetched, and no sooner arrive, but find themselves so necessary, that they fall to imposing in Wages and Diet, as well as lazy Working, that nothing shall content them: and their Insolence, as well as their Knavery, is intolerable to a poor Farmer.
It follows, that Scarcity of People must make Labour and Servants Wages dear; for, there being much Work and few Hands in the Country, the Labourer will set the Dice, and cannot fail to understand his Advantage, for all will court and invite him to their Work, and overbid each other ... For, granting we had People enough and to spare, the Price of Labour is such as they can make a good Living of two or three Days Work in a Week: And why more, say they?[43]

Many others wrote in a similar vein, that high wages were actually sapping industriousness as workers chose to take days off rather than to increase their wealth or savings.[44] Although most of these tracts imply that this practice was most common in industrial work (see above, p. 209), which was higher paid, another who did not was Daniel Defoe. He implied that agricultural labour was also affected. The title of one of his pamphlets clearly shows his opinion: *The Great Law of Subordination Considered or, The Insolence and Insuffrable Behaviour of Servants in England Duly Enquired Into*, published in 1724. Here he argued that not only were high wages making servants and day labourers work less, but they were also enabling them to disregard their subordinate place in society. A closer examination of Defoe's pamphlet reveals that it was really a lengthy complaint, with a series of examples, about the impudence of both household servants and servants in husbandry. It seems

---

[43] North, *Discourse of the Poor*, pp. 58–9, 60, see also pp. 17, 32, 36, 42.
[44] Appleby, *Economic Thought and Ideology*, pp. 145–7; Hatcher, 'Labour, Leisure', pp. 69–71.

to have been motivated especially by the latter. Just before writing it, Defoe, after a career as first a merchant who went bankrupt and then a political journalist, had bought himself a farm near Colchester, and for the first time in his life became a farmer. In many ways the work is an interesting illustration of the difficulties which someone from London had in adapting to the social negotiation needed to employ servants and labourers on a farm – including the problem of one servant who suspected his wife of having an affair with the estate steward and came to Defoe for some paternalistic negotiation but instead got a lecture on English liberty.[45]

However, both here and in an earlier pamphlet published in 1704, *Giving Alms no Charity and Employing the Poor*, he blamed what he termed the 'sauciness' of labourers and servants on high wages. In the earlier pamphlet he presented an argument which confirms the empirical conclusion I presented earlier, that there was a labour shortage. He, however, focused on the move of labour into new manufacturing jobs, as evidenced by the rise in customs revenue:

1. I affirm, That in England there is more Labour than Hands to perform it. This I prove,

1st. From the dearness of Wages, which in England out goes all Nations in the World; and I know no greater Demonstration in Trade. Wages, like Exchanges, Rise and Fall as the Remitters and Drawers, the Employers and the Work-men, Ballance one another.

Trade, like all Nature, most obsequiously obeys the great Law of Cause and Consequence; and this is the occasion why even all the greatest Articles of Trade follow, and as it were pay Homage to this seemingly Minute and Inconsiderable Thing, The poor Man's Labour.

… all that's valuable in a Nation, as to its Figure in the World, depends upon the Number of its People, be they never so mean or poor; the consumption of Manufactures encreases the Manufacturers; the number of Manufacturers encreases the Consumption.[46]

Defoe went on to agree with the view that wages were high because of the shortage of labour, and from this he concluded that

… 'tis plain, if there is more Work than Hands to perform it, no Man that has his *Limbs* and his *Senses* need to beg, and those that *have not* ought to be put into a Condition not to want it.

So that begging is a meer scandal in the General, *in the Able* 'tis a scandal upon their Industry, and *in the Impotent* 'tis a scandal upon the Country.

---

[45] Defoe, *Law of Subordination*, p. 60.
[46] Defoe, *Giving Alms No Charity and Employing the Poor* (1704), in W. R. Owens and P. N. Furbank, *Political and Economic Writings of Daniel Defoe* (London, 2000), pp. 174–5.

Charity, he thought, should be directed at poor families with numerous children or where a parent had died, but others should be made to work for lower wages:

and I affirm of my own knowledge, when I have wanted a Man for labouring work, and offer'd 9 s. *per* Week to strouling Fellows at my Door, they have frequently told me to my Face, they could get more a begging, and I once set a lusty Fellow in the Stocks for making the Experiment.[47]

In *The Great Law of Subordination* he developed this theme to show how increased demand for work in the manufacture of cloth was taking labour from agriculture. This was making servants and day labourers challenge their subordinate place in society, thinking that they were the equal to their employers as co-participants in the contract for labour:

That the Encrease of Trade and Wages is real, and the Fact true, you may take it thus in a few Words, *viz.* The rate for spinning, weaving, and all other Manufacturing-Work, I mean in *WOOL*, is so risen, that the Poor all over *England*, can now earn or gain near twice as much in a Day, and in some Places, more than twice as much as they could get for the same Work two or three Years ago: Particularly in *Essex*, *Suffolk*, and *Norfolk*, *Eastward*; and in *Wiltshire*, *Somerset*, and *Devon*, *West*; the Poor Women now get 12 *d* to 15 *d* a Day for spinning, the Men more in proportion, and are full of Work.

... If we go out of the Manufacturing Towns into the Country-Villages, there they feel the same thing another way; the Farmers Wives can get no Dairy-Maids, their Husbands no Plowmen, and what's the matter? truly the Wenches answer, they won't go to Service at 12 d. or 18 d. a Week, while they can get 7 *s* to 8 *s* a Week at spinning; the Men answer they won't drudge at the Plow and Cart, hedging and ditching, threshing and stubbing, and perhaps get 6 *L.* a Year, and course Diet, when they can sit still and dry within Doors, and get 9 or 10 *s.* a Week at Wool-combing, or at carding, and such Work about the Woollen Manufacture.

... And what now is the Consequence of this? not Diligence, not Thankfulness, *I assure you*; less is it enriching the Poor, or furnishing themselves with Conveniences, Cloaths, and Necessaries; *least of all* is it attended with a provident laying-up for a time of Scarcity; when Work may be wanting and Wages abate again; as 'tis very likely may be the Case hereafter: No, *No*, just the contrary; This Prosperity introduces Sloth, Idleness, Drunkenness, and all manner of Wickedness; instead *of making Hay while the Sun shines*, they slight their Work, and bully their Employers; perhaps they will work two or three Days, or it may be a Week, till they find a few Shillings jingle and chink in their Pockets; but then, as if they cou'd not bear that kind of Musick, away they go to the Alehouse, and 'tis imposible to bring them to work again, while they have a Farthing of it left.[48]

---

[47] Ibid., pp. 176–7.   [48] Defoe, *Subordination*, pp. 85–6.

... that Part of their Virtue, which I call Gratitude, and which is the brightest Part of an honest Man, is in a manner quite sunk among them ... Here indeed, they verifie what was by a late Author made part of their Character.

'The Lab'ring Poor, in spight of double Pay,
Are saucy, mutinous, and Beggarly.'[49]

It did not occur to Defoe that he himself might have been responsible for not being able to find labourers who would be willing to work harder for him by treating them properly.

Fifty years later another wealthy tradesman who decided to turn his attention to farming, although in a much more systematic way, was William Marshall. He eventually became the most prolific writer on agricultural practice and reform in the late eighteenth and early nineteenth century, and was responsible for the establishment of the Board of Agriculture created in 1793. However, when he first started farming he was a novice who hoped to learn from 'EXPERIMENT and OBSERVATION'. As Ann Kussmaul has pointed out he expected his servants to teach him, but the servants understood his predicament. They were not co-operative and almost certainly took advantage of him. Marshall was placed 'by the law of *right*' in a position of authority, but was at the mercy of his servants. He reflected that 'A THINKING SERVANT is very valuable; but rarely to be met with.'[50]

These two examples are of novice farmers who had bad relations with their workers, but aptly demonstrate how demand for labour left them unable to force their workers to behave as they wished. Much of the recent work on servants has stressed a more positive, mutually dependent aspect to relationships between servant and master.[51] The Somerset farmer Frances Hamilton noted on one occasion in 1788 that one of her labourers had drunk too much to do any work, but she did not punish him. Instead she offered an extra 1s an acre wages to anyone who would work without liquor.[52] Parson Woodforde relied on Ben Leggett, a servant in husbandry whom he called his 'farming man', to look after his glebe farm of some 46 acres. He kept him employed at a wage of £10 a year from 1776 to 1803, when Woodforde died. With close servants who were considered members of the master's family, such relationships were very emotional and could survive numerous disputes.[53] A good example

---

[49] Ibid., p. 84, see also pp. 57ff.   [50] Kussmaul, *Servants in Husbandry*, pp. 45–7.

[51] Steedman, *Master and Servant*, pp. 1–12. Tim Meldrum has recently stressed that the experience of domestic servants is much too varied to generalise. But there were equally cases of very good relations with trusted servants and workers. Meldrum, *Domestic Service*, ch. 4.

[52] Speechley, 'Female and Child Agricultural Day Labourers', p. 110.

[53] Winstanley, *Parson Woodforde*, pp. 187–9. Thomas Turner also had extensive relations with the poor family from which his longstanding servant Hannah Marchant came.

is the more troubled relationship Woodforde had with his servant Will Coleman. Coleman was nominally a footman, but also engaged in other household and agricultural tasks. However, he had been a servant to Woodforde since the age of fifteen, before Woodforde came to Norfolk in 1776. He came from a poor labouring family whose members had all worked for the Woodforde family in the West Country, but he was unreliable and did not shy from arguing with Woodforde in the same manner that Defoe complained of. This eventually led Woodforde to dismiss him in 1785, but as the following entry in his diary makes clear, the decision caused him much turmoil:

April 12
My Servant William Coleman was out all the Evening till just 11. o'clock – came home in Liquor behaved very rudely and most impudently to me indeed, I told him that I was determined never more to bear with such Behaviour, &c that he shd certainly go to Morr'.
April 13
I got up between 5. and 6. o'clock this morning had Will before me as soon as possible, paid him his Wages and dismissed him before 8. o'clock ... I threw him down a Couple of Guineas for him to have the remaining, but he would not take one farthing more than the above 1:17:9 – Being so much hurried last night and this morning made me quite ill all day – vomited a good deal at night ...

Will left the next morning and found work in a neighbour's garden but soon returned to Woodforde:

April 25
Will: Coleman came to us this morning as we were walking in the Garden, and said that he could not be easy after his late bad behaviour, till he had spoke to me and asked pardon for it – I then told him that I would employ him as a Gardner and give him a shilling a Day and his Board for 2. Days in a Week – but that he must get a Lodging from my House, and if he can somewhere in the Parish – He appeared then quite happy and went directly about his work in the Garden.[54]

Eventually Woodforde helped him return to Somerset and set up as an independent labourer, where he had a large family before dying in 1832.[55]

A very similar situation can be found in the journal of Timothy Burrell, a rural lawyer and small farmer in early eighteenth-century Sussex. He turned his footman Thomas Goldsmith away for theft in

Vaisey, *Diary of Thomas Turner*, pp. 256–8, 265, 334. Tadmor, *Family and Friends*, pp. 30–3.
[54] R. L. Winstanley and Peter Jameson (eds.), *The Diary of James Woodforde: 1785–1787*, 17 vols., Parson Woodforde Society (1999), XI, pp. 28–32.
[55] Winstanley, *Parson Woodforde*, p. 194.

1698. Burrell reported that, 'After a ramble to London, being almost starved, he came again as footman.' This was accompanied by a surprising rise in wages to £4 a year. Subsequently Goldsmith again left Burrell's service before repenting, and returning 'half-starved' and apparently married. Goldsmith continued to cause trouble, and on another occasion Burrell was forced to redeem his servant's shirt from a pawnbroker. Goldsmith was reported as rambling about all night, 'frequently drunk with brandy, and spent all the money I got for him in half a year's time besides his wages'. However, he remained in employment until 1706.[56]

But an argument with an employer could just as likely end in an immediate dismissal, as in the case of John Cannon, who was sent to work for his uncle Robert Walter as a 'hynd and Servant' on his farm. After two years' work, his relationship with his uncle broke down primarily over an argument about the best way to plough a field together. Cannon told Walter that since he had been raised as a baker, while Cannon had been trained by his father as a ploughman, he knew best. This led to a fight in which they struck each other with their tools, after which Cannon was immediately dismissed from his service.[57]

In the early seventeenth century labourers and servants in husbandry would have potentially been in a much more precarious position. Defoe claimed that on his various tours through the country, eventually published the year after *The Great Law of Subordination*, he had travelled with a learned and ancient unnamed gentleman who told him that

about the Year 1634 to 38, when he began to be conversant in the World on his own Account, the common People were plain, fair-dealing, sober, open-hearted, courteous, humble; that generally speaking, they were very honest in their dealing, and in many Places religious and conscientious in their Conversation; that the Servants were modest, humble, mannerly, and very subservient to those who entertain'd and employ'd them ... were laborious, and work'd hard for their Masters Benefit, having their Eyes at the Time.[58]

In Defoe's account the old man then goes on to blame the Restoration and subsequent Parliamentary elections after the Glorious Revolution for an increase in general drinking to excess among labourers. There is no evidence that this old man was real. It is likely he was a fictitious character invented to voice Defoe's own opinion. This account is undoubtedly exaggerated to make a point about the disobedience of labourers and servants in his own age, but it contains a grain of truth

[56] Blencowe (ed.), 'The Journal and Accounts of Timothy Burrell', pp. 133, 135, 140, 145, 150.
[57] Muldrew, 'Class and Credit', pp. 162–3.   [58] Defoe, *Subordination*, pp. 69–75.

in that labourers would have been much more subject to dismissal or unemployment when demand for labour was less.

A good example of someone from the end of this former period is Edward Barlow, the son of a poor husbandman from Prestwich, Lancashire, who was born at the beginning of the Civil Wars in 1642. In his journal, written at sea once he had become a sailor and learned to read and write, he noted the lack of work in his locality:

My parents were but poor people with six children to provide for (three sons and three daughters) and their living was but small – about £8 or £9 a year. My father being a husbandman and for work about the ground, which he could do himself for it was not much, was unable to put us, his children, all to trades.

[I] was forced to go to work with our neighbours sometimes when they had any need of me as in harvest or making hay and suchlike work, and sometimes going to the coalpits, for we have many of them in our country and coals are very cheap. I used to go with our neighbours' horses and fetch horse-loads to burn; paying them a horse-load three halfpence and two pence and two pence halfpenny for the best, and receiving two pence and three pence a day for my pains and victuals which were nevertheless but small wages.

Yet with that and suchlike work I made shift to buy me some clothes, and then I went to church on Sunday, which I never could do before for want of clothes to go handsome in. My father being poor and in debt could not provide us with clothes fitting to go to church in (so we could not go to church) unless we would go in rags, which was not seemly.[59]

Although Barlow's father managed to send his son to school, he was forced to leave school at about twelve years of age and go to work in the local fustian trade, whitening the cloth, which he described as:

A hard-working trade, for when we had done a day's work at the trade we had another to do about the cattle that we kept, looking after the horses and cows, dressing them and foddering them; and when we had no other work, as in the winter, for then they worked but little at the trade, then we must thrash and hedge and ditch and do all other country work.[60]

Eventually Barlow's father, who was ambitious that his son should do well, managed to arrange a potential apprenticeship with a master 'whitster' in Manchester, and Barlow went to work there for a fortnight at what he termed 'a-liking', to see if he and the master could get along. However, another young journeyman working for the master complained that working conditions were not good, and Barlow was also unhappy with the eating arrangements.

I considered their manner of keeping two tables of victuals. Though we all ate together, yet at the upper end of the table, where my master and dame and

---

[59] Lubbock (ed.), *Barlow's Journal*, I, pp. 15–16.   [60] Ibid., p. 16.

the children did sit, there was a great difference of victuals, namely a pudding with suet and plums; but at the lower end of the table one without both, though there might be a little strong butter to eat with it, melted and poured upon it: and at the upper end a piece of fat beef, but at the lower end a piece of 'sorloine' next to the horns: there was always something or other which we had not. We also had meat broth two or three times heated, which would never have vexed me had I eaten and drunk of the same as they did, though I had not sat at table with them.[61]

Soon afterwards, Barlow decided that he would rather travel to London, where he had an uncle and a brother, to seek work there. After working as a tapster and other domestic work, he eventually decided he was unsuited for it. After once again complaining of his food, 'for we ate sometimes salted mutton, which was a thing that I had never eaten salted before though it was good and wholesome victuals, yet I could not well relish it', he decided to seek his fortune at sea.[62] Although by the 1650s Barlow seems to have found work relatively easy to come by despite his poverty, his story of unsatisfied ambition must have been typical of many young people in the fifty years before his journal began. But his story also reinforces the theme of the second chapter of this book. It shows that even someone so poor in this period expected good meat and hospitable behaviour in return for hard work, and that it was dissatisfaction with such things, not hunger, that drove him onto the road.

Unfortunately, there are few other autobiographical accounts which we can draw upon to discover the feelings and experiences of labourers in the early seventeenth century, but perhaps the experiences of Joseph Mayett, a day labourer from Quainton in Buckinghamshire, suffering under the extremely high price of provisions around 1800, would have been similar to those of a labourer in the early seventeenth century, when grain prices were also high. His autobiography is valuable in that it shows, like Thomas Goldsmith and John Cannon mentioned above, how even in a period when there was a demand for labour, someone could lose employment by not getting on with a master:

I did not very well like my master for he was a very odd man but my mistress and her neice was both very good to me/but I was not troubled with master long for when I had been there just a month he came to me in the stable on the Sunday morning and told me he thought I should not suit him and paid me for my time and told me to take my Cloths and go but he never told me the reason nor he and I never disagreed. so I Came away and went to the overseer for work and he sent me one week to a master in the parish to work and gave me eight pence per day

---

[61] Ibid., pp. 17–18.   [62] Ibid., pp. 22–30.

and the next week he sent me to another master at the same price or wages. this was the first time that the Cares of the world laid hold on me ...

during this time through the dearness of provision I was obliged to live cheifly on barley bread and hog peas except when my master gave me my dinner when I went out with the team. this I was not very fond of but it being winter and provisions dear and many servants out of place I could not extracate myself from it.

However, even in these desperate straits Mayett devised a scheme to get himself hired as a servant in husbandry:

in the begining of the year 1801 I found my master entended to keep me on but in Consequence of the dearness of provision he would not hire me servant so long as he could have me at four shillings and sixpence per week this Caused me to begin to devise a scheem to get him to hire me.

This scheme, which was successful, involved making the master think another farmer was interested in hiring him: 'my master hearing this began to think if he had me he must hire me or else he should loose me for work'.[63] In these examples we can see how Mayett could both suffer from the hierarchy a conservative like Defoe held so dear but also use his wits to manipulate the labour market to obtain work with a master more likely to be sympathetic.

Mayett's example shows that even for one person there could be many experiences of work and working relations. It is hard to discover any single attitude to work. There were labourers who worked full 312-day years, as well as those who took holidays to go to fairs and/or the alehouse. There were also undoubtedly some who were naturally ambitious, and others who were goaded into working harder by parish officials and masters. There were also masters who let their servants sleep under trees, and those who docked wages for time spent not working.[64] The idea of leisure preference being a general attribute of labourers is really something which comes from negative comments by observers like Defoe and cannot be generalised to the labouring population as a whole. There were many different attitudes to work, as well as opportunities. However, all labourers would have had to adopt strategies for dealing with their masters. As the examples of Defoe and Marshall demonstrate, they were capable of great stubbornness and resistance,

---

[63] Kussmaul (ed.), *Autobiography of Joseph Mayett*, pp. 10–12; Peter King, 'Social Inequality, Identity and the Labouring Poor in Eighteenth-Century England", in Henry French and Jonathan Barry (eds.), *Identity and Agency in England, 1500–1800* (London, 2004), pp. 60–86.

[64] Defoe has a discussion of how a friend of his supposedly watched a workman talking instead of working. He then accused him of robbing him of his time. Defoe, *Subordination*, pp. 148–52.

and many like John Cannon or Joseph Mayett chose to disagree and incur poverty rather than be submissive. But, certainly by the eighteenth century, industriousness had entered popular discourse as a quality of moral good which many aspired to achieve. Whatever the degree of poverty the ploughboy John Cannon had to go through, by the time he came to compose his memoirs in the 1740s he could still comment that:

As Idleness is the rust and bane of all human virtues so on the contrary Industry and diligence in business are conquerors in all difficultys.[65]

[65] John Cannon's Memoirs, pp. 421–2. See also the comments in Keith Thomas, *The Ends of Life: Roads to Fulfilment in Early Modern England* (Oxford, 2009), pp. 91ff.

Conclusion

In this book I have argued that employed labourers ate more and better food than has previously been assumed. This made it possible to supply the economy with the necessary energy to produce enough food to feed the country and then to eventually feed an expanding number of people working in manufacturing as well as an increased number of workhorses. However, before this the country went through a very difficult period of high food prices and labour surplus before agricultural output and employment rose. This confirms much historiography which describes the period before the Civil Wars as one when it was hardest for day labourers to make ends meet. Although contemporary diets suggest that for those in employment, food remained sufficient and continued to contain a surprising amount of meat, for those day labourers searching for work conditions were hard, and in these years poverty and emigration increased.

But this was rapidly turned into a situation of potential labour shortage after 1650 as farm production expanded and other industries grew in size, attracting labour, while population growth remained sluggish. The evidence of probate inventories shows that this led to a general rise in standards of living for labourers, but, more importantly, that it led to a significantly widening gap between the poorest and wealthiest labourers. Thus I think it is fair to say that the evidence points to a more optimistic view of labourers' standards of living in the period from 1650 to 1770. However, it would be blind to suggest that this covers the whole experience of labourers in this period. Although aggregate demand for labour might have been growing, there is certainly evidence that there were areas of local under-employment. Employment opportunities could also rise and fall in a parish according to how much improvement was taking place, whether roads needed repair or more yarn needed to be spun. Labourers could also become sick or lame, or they could have too many children to be able to support them all. It is by now well documented that the amount of money spent on poor relief rose in this period at the same time as living standards were also rising.

It remains nonetheless the case that over the period from roughly 1650 to 1780, the output of English agriculture increased substantially while employing a smaller percentage of the population than it had formerly. This in turn, as E. A. Wrigley has argued, allowed a greater number of people to be fed while being employed in secondary or tertiary employments such as metalwork or shop keeping. This productive achievement was especially acute during the period before 1750, when population growth was slow. In 1750 the population of England was only 9 per cent greater than it had been in 1658, and 23 per cent greater by 1770.[1] The productivity gains in agriculture required more labour, which provided more opportunity for employment. The scale of this opportunity would have varied over time and by place, and is impossible to measure precisely, but the calculations in chapter 6 show that it was there. This raises the interesting question as to why population growth remained slow in this period, compared to the period 1540–1658, and more especially the very rapid growth which started in the 1770s. It is possible that this demographic situation allowed labourers, as well as English society in general, to build up capital for consumption and investment which otherwise would have been spent on feeding more people. But, more importantly, it created a demand for labour which allowed the 'industrious' labourer to benefit.

This was the origin of the high-wage economy, which Robert Allen has recently argued created the conditions whereby initially expensive investment in mechanisation to increase production made sense, and eventually led to the industrial revolution.[2] However, it also eventually led to increased fertility, and in the years after the date at which I have chosen to end this investigation, population started to rise rapidly and had reached 9,000,000 by 1805. In addition, in 1796, 38.8 per cent of the population was under fourteen, younger than it had been at any time since 1540. This was one reason why Malthus was worried the poor law was creating population growth by supporting such a large number of small children. In 1686, by comparison, only 30 per cent of the population were under fourteen.[3] This once again put pressure on the food supply, leading to the very high food prices of the period from 1790 to 1820.

The introduction of mechanisation in spinning also led to a reduction in family earnings after 1780. Sarah Horrell and Jane Humphries

[1] Wrigley and Schofield, *Population History*, pp. 532–3.
[2] Robert C. Allen, *The British Industrial Revolution in Global Perspective* (Cambridge, 2009), ch. 2.
[3] Wrigley and Schofield, *Population History*, pp. 528–9.

found that women's and children's labour accounted for only 10.5 per cent of family income in high-wage agricultural budgets and 18.4 per cent for low-wage agricultural families after 1787, compared, generally, to more than 35 per cent for outwork families engaged in weaving, knitting, shoemaking, and so forth for the same period.[4] As Eden noted on a number of occasions, the invention and application of the various forms of spinning machinery, from Hargreaves's original spinning jenny to the spinning mule introduced in the late 1770s, had vastly reduced the demand for labour needed to spin both wool and cotton. Eden quoted a pamphlet of 1788 which estimated even by that date there were over 20,000 machines with 80 spindles or more *just* for the spinning of cotton, but 25 years before all of this would have had to be spun on single wheels or distaffs.[5] When describing the economy of the parish of Seend in Wiltshire Eden described the effect this had on the household economy:

Since the introduction of machinery, which lately took place, hand spinning has fallen into disuse, and for these two reasons; the clothier no longer depends on the Poor for yarn which they formerly spun for him at their own homes, as he finds that 50 persons (to speak within compass,) with the help of machines will do as much work as 500 without them; and the poor ... scarcely have the heart to earn the little that is obtained by it. For what they used to receive 1s. and 1s. 2d. the pound for spinning, before the application of machinery, they are now allowed only 5d.[6]

In agriculture, too, the introduction of better tools, such as new, stronger, steel scythes instead of sickles for harvesting wheat, led to a reduction in demand for labour during the harvest. This enabled an acre of wheat to be cut in about a third of the time it took by reaping. However, the use of the scythe required great strength and also had the effect of reducing harvest employment for women.[7] Other farm machinery such as the horse hoe, winnowing and threshing machines also eventually reduced the demand for farm labour, although generally after 1830.[8] Keith Snell has argued that Parliamentary enclosure also reduced the need for labour on farms in the late eighteenth and early nineteenth centuries, and Robert Allen has argued in a different way

---

[4] Sara Horrell and Jane Humphries, 'Women's Labour Force Participation and the Transition to the Male-Breadwinner Family, 1790–1865', *Economic History Review*, 48 (1995), pp. 102–3; Sara Horrell and Jane Humphries, 'Old Questions, New Data, and Alternative Perspectives: Families' Living Standards in the Industrial Revolution', *Journal of Economic History*, 52 (1992), pp. 873–4.

[5] Eden, *State of the Poor*, II, pp. 477–8, 644; III, pp. 802, 847–8.

[6] Ibid., III, p. 796.   [7] Overton, *Agricultural Revolution*, pp. 121–3.

[8] Ibid., pp. 123–6.

that increasing farm size led to labour shedding as a result of efficiency gains obtained by farming on a larger scale.[9] Also, as Turner, Becket and Afton have argued, yields of wheat and barley were roughly stable from the mid-eighteenth century until 1820 (although there was some decline from 1780 to 1800 thanks to years of bad weather).[10] So it is possible that opportunity for employment in agriculture was not rising to match the growth of population.

However, the greatest cause of increased poverty in the period after 1780 was undoubtedly the rapid rise in food prices. Prices rose because, as Clark *et al.* have argued, the total available food energy per capita dropped after 1780 as population grew.[11] Looking just at wheat production, Turner, Becket and Afton have calculated that the bushels of wheat grown per capita dropped from 5.9 in 1750, when the population was 5,670,000, to only 4.6 bushels per capita by 1800, when the population had risen to 11,491,000, a reduction of 22 per cent.[12] New foods such as the potato were grown, and imports of sugar from the Caribbean rose to about 25 lb per person per year by 1810, the equivalent of about 150 kcal a day.[13] Ireland also increasingly became a necessary supplier of agricultural produce to England, as Irish peasants survived on potato crops while producing agricultural surpluses to export to England. It has been estimated that by the 1830s Irish exports of agricultural produce were equivalent to 13 per cent of English agricultural output.[14] This, together with continued expansion of the area of land under cultivation and further large increases in yields in the 1820s, caused grain prices to drop by the 1830s. But the relentless rise of population continued to put pressure on food supply. Even by 1850 wheat production had only risen to 5.29 bushels per person, still less than 1750.[15] Certainly the diets of farm labourers surveyed by Eden and Davies show this, and a further Parliamentary survey in 1843 shows continuing lack of sufficient energy and nutrition in farm labourers' diets.[16] The survey of working class household budgets by Sarah Horrell has also indicated that there was little increased demand for new industrial consumer items from these households during the early nineteenth century.[17]

---

[9] Snell, *Labouring Poor*, ch. 4; Allen, *Enclosure and the Yeoman*, pp. 211–36.

[10] Turner *et al.*, *Farm Production*, pp. 224–30.

[11] Clark *et al.*, 'A British Food Puzzle', pp. 215–19.

[12] Turner *et al.*, *Farm Production*, pp. 217–20.

[13] Sidney W. Mintz, *Sweetness and Power: The Place of Sugar in Modern History* (Harmondsworth, 1985), p. 67.

[14] Thomas Brindley, 'Escaping from Constraints: The Industrial Revolution in a Malthusian Context', *Journal of Interdisciplinary History*, 15 (1985), pp. 741–2.

[15] Turner *et al.*, *Farm Production*, pp. 217–20.

[16] Burnett, *Plenty and Want*, pp. 40–7.   [17] Horrell, 'Home Demand', pp. 561–604.

During the period after 1780 there might well have been a return to a more exaggerated division between the standard of living of labourers in employment, who took more of the available food calories to do work, and those who had to make do with less as a result. But as the population grew, a higher percentage of people were increasingly finding work in higher-paid industrial jobs, especially in Lancashire and Yorkshire. In such work, machinery might well have reduced the number of calories needed by the 1830s, but hard work was still required in many areas.[18] I have purposely ended this study around 1780, because after this date it would be necessary to engage with the classic debate about standards of living during industrial revolution.[19] To do this would involve trying to examine the housing and consumption of early nineteenth-century industrial workers as well as agricultural labourers in sources which are outside my scope of expertise. I would also have to examine eighteenth-century cloth workers, metal workers and potters and other industrial occupations for comparison. Certainly a similar study of their standard of living would be extremely valuable, but would require much more space.[20] However, the evidence presented here certainly means that any conceptualisation of the effect of industrialisation on the standard of living of labourers needs to consider how family incomes rose over the long term, in the period from 1660 to 1780, as a result of rising agricultural and textile productivity and low population growth.

The evidence for agricultural labourers presented here shows that England was certainly a high-wage economy with much prosperity, and also a doctrine of 'industriousness' by the eighteenth century. However, the evidence also shows that assessing standards of living in early modern societies is a complex task, where one always has to be attentive to the possibility of non-monetary components, as well as regional food production and customs. On the face of it, the evidence presented here would seem to suggest that English labourers were even better off than those in southern Europe, India and China than already suggested by Allen and others. But we would need to make a similar investigation of the value of the non-money wage component of earnings in these other places.[21] To use an example, a labourer with an inherited advantageous

---

[18] Clark et al., 'A British Food Puzzle', pp. 225–8; Turner et al., Farm Production, pp. 224–30.

[19] For a good summary of this long-running debate between 'optimists', who argue that standards of living rose after 1790, and 'pessimists', who argue that industrialisation brought about insecurity and exploitation, see Daunton, Progress and Poverty, ch. 16.

[20] Work on coal miners by Levine and Wrightson certainly shows increased expenditure in the eighteenth century. Levine and Wrightson, Making of an Industrial Society, pp. 205–73.

[21] Allen, Global Perspective, pp. 33–45.

lease for life or with common rights would be much better off than his potential earnings from wages would suggest, as would a family near Norwich, where high spinning wages could be earned. All these things need to be taken into account. Models of family earning can still be made, and need to be made, but the amount of empirical work is daunting, and certainly more local studies need to be done, especially if we want to be sure that international comparisons are actually measuring like with like.

It seems fitting to end this study with a quotation from Adam Smith on the value of labour, which demonstrates both Smith's unusual sympathy for working men at the time and the importance of their labour in the formation of what he termed public opulence, which was an expression of material wealth through consumption. In contrast to earlier writers like Defoe, who thought that workers were lazy and would remain idle without low wages to drive them forward, Smith thought that workers actually worked too hard and drove themselves into an early grave if offered piece-work and advocated moderate work at a constant rate throughout the year.[22] He was also attuned to the fact that low wages resulting from competition could jeopardise their consumption, but thought that increased production and subsequent lower prices would provide opulence which labourers could afford. It was, in short, workers' productivity and consumption which *was* public opulence:

Is this improvement in the circumstances of the lower ranks of the people to be regarded as an advantage or as an inconveniency to the society? The answer seems at first sight abundantly plain. Servants, labourers and workmen of different kinds, make up the far greater part of every great political society. But what improves the circumstances of the greater part can never be regarded as an inconveniency to the whole. No society can surely be flourishing and happy, of which the far greater part of the members are poor and miserable. It is but equity, besides, that they who feed, cloath and lodge the whole body of the people, should have such a share of the produce of their own labour as to be themselves tolerably well fed, cloathed and lodged.[23]

---

[22] Adam Smith, *An Inquiry into the Nature and Causes of the Wealth of Nations* (Oxford, 1976), Book I, ch. viii, pp. 99–100. The author of *Considerations on Taxes*, however, was willing to concede that there were some industrious workers. *Considerations on Taxes*, p. 43. A. W. Coats, 'Changing Attitudes to Labour in the Mid-Eighteenth Century', *Economic History Review*, 2nd ser., 11:1 (1958–9), pp. 35–51.

[23] Smith, *Wealth of Nations*, Book I, ch. viii, pp. 96–7.

Bibliography

MANUSCRIPT SOURCES

CAMBRIDGESHIRE RECORD OFFICE

Cotton 588A2, E9   Probate Inventories
Vac 1–3, VC 19–46   Probate Inventories

CENTRE FOR KENTISH STUDIES

prc10.1–71   Probate Inventories
prc11.2–80   Probate Inventories
prc21.3–17   Probate Inventories
prc27.2–146   Probate Inventories

CHESHIRE RECORD OFFICE

WC 1618–WC 1800   Probate Inventories
WI 1688–WI 1780   Probate Inventories
WS 1573–WS 1745   Probate Inventories

ESSEX RECORD OFFICE

D/DBa, f.39v, 40r–v. I   John Petre's Account Book, 1576–7
D/DTa/A1   Tabor Family of Bocking Account Book, Nov. 12,
             1690–Sept. 22, 1690; July, 1784; Oct 1, 22, Nov. 5,
             1785

GUILDHALL LIBRARY, LONDON

Bridewell Court Book, IV, fos. 212r–v
Christ's Hospital Treasurer's Accounts, MS 12,819
HB1/2 Ledger 1562–86   St Bartholomew's Hospital Archives
HB1/3 Ledger 1589–1614   St Bartholomew's Hospital Archives

HAMPSHIRE RECORD OFFICE

1575b.66–1757a71.2, zim 65.d.3.799   Probate Inventories

KING'S COLLEGE ARCHIVE CENTRE, CAMBRIDGE

Commons Books   KCAR/4/1/6, 12, 16, 18, 28, 30, 33

LINCOLNSHIRE RECORD OFFICE

INV 8.140–INV 223.69   Probate Inventories

LONDON METROPOLITAN ARCHIVES

Foundling Hospital:
A/FH/B8/6/2–3   Steward's Account Book, Household Expenses 1742–54
A/FH/B8/7/1   Steward's Account Book, Household expenses, 1758
A/FH/K/01/1–3: 11/04/1730; 18/11/1747; 22/01/1755;03/11/1762; 05/06/1776;
    31/12/1777; 09/09/1778   General Court Minutes

NATIONAL ARCHIVES, KEW

E179, 84, 440   Cambridgeshire Hearth Tax Exemptions 1672–3
E190, 440/3, 441   King's Lynn Port Books, 1684–6

NORFOLK RECORD OFFICE

ANF11   Probate Inventories
ANW 23.1–21   Probate Inventories
DCN 73   Probate Inventories
DN/INV/3–44   Probate Inventories
INV 64/10   Probate Inventories
KL/C39/105, 107   King's Lynn Chamberlain's Accounts, 1679–90

NORTHUMBERLAND COLLECTIONS SERVICE

Allgood Family of Nunwick:
ZAL/44/1   Wages and Allowances, 1709–14
ZAL/45/6   Accounts, 1746
ZAL/46/7   Accounts, 1747
ZAL/46/8   Wage Book, 1744
ZAL/57/26   Lists of Days Worked
ZBL/274/1   General Ledgers, 1758–9
ZBL 283/1   Blackett Family of Matfen, Accounts, 1758

SOMERSET RECORD OFFICE

DD/DR 70 Part 1   Day Book of Nathaniel Brewer of Over Stowey, 1713–26
DD/FS/5/9   Bishops Lydeard Farm, Housekeeping Account Book,
    1755
DD/FS/7/4   Bishops Lydeard Farm, Wage Book, 1801–2
DD/FS/7/5   Bishops Lydeard Farm, Farm Produce Account Book,
    1801–2

DD/SAS/1193/4	John Cannon's Memoirs
DD/TB/14/8	Crowcombe Farm, Workmen's Accounts, 1737–8
DD/TB/14/11	Crowcombe Farm, Workmen's Accounts, 1755–60
DD/WO/6	Nettlecomb Estate Accounts, 1752–5

SUFFOLK RECORD OFFICE

| HA 30: 369/249 | Blowfield Family, Bills and Accounts, 1661–96 |

WEST YORKSHIRE ARCHIVE SERVICE, LEEDS

Harewood Estate Records:
WYL 250/3/197	Labourers' Day Work Book, 1789
WYL 250/3/200	Labourers' Day Work Book, 1786–96
WYL/250/3/214	List of Household Servants, 1787–92
WYL/250/3/222	Labourers' Day Work Book, 1779–82
WYL/250/3/263	Weekly Housekeeping Accounts, 1782–7
WYL/250/3/266	Abstracts from Weekly Kitchen Book, 1798–1802

WEST YORKSHIRE ARCHIVE SERVICE, BRADFORD

Tong Family Estate Records:
Tong/4b/7	Accounts of the Profits of the Demesne
Tong/4b/23	Tong Hall Farming Account Book, 1786–91
Tong/5a/5	Household Accounts, 1767–72
Tong/5a/7	Household Accounts, 1771–4
Spencer Stanhope MSS:
Sp St/5/4/1/7	General Accounts, 1633–4
Sp St/6/2/1/2	Household Account Books, 1734–88
Sp St/13/D83/1	Account Book, 1777

WILTSHIRE RECORD OFFICE

WRO 314/1/1	Account Book of George Wansey, Warminster, 1683–92
WRO 415/86	Day Book, 1776
WRO 1178/24	Account Book of Thomas Browne Calley of Burderop House, Jan. 1778–Dec. 1780
WRO 2533/1	Kington Family Accounts, 1701–54, Work Done
WRO 3238/49	Farm and Household Accounts of Edward Fowle of Manningford Abbots and Pewsey, 1784–96

PRINTED PRIMARY AND SECONDARY SOURCES

An Account of Several Workhouses for Employing and Maintaining the Poor (London, 1725).

Adams, Beverly (ed.), *Lifestyle and Culture in Hertford … Wills and Inventories 1660–1725*, Hertfordshire Record Society, 13 (1997).

Albala, Ken, *Eating Right in the Renaissance* (Berkeley, 2002).

Allen, Robert, *The British Industrial Revolution in Global Perspective* (Cambridge, 2009).

Enclosure and the Yeoman: The Agricultural Development of the South Midlands 1450–1850 (Oxford, 1992).

'Progress and Poverty in Early Modern Europe', *Economic History Review*, 56 (2003), pp. 403–43.

Appleby, Andrew, *Famine in Tudor and Stuart England* (Liverpool, 1978).

Appleby, Joyce Oldham, *Economic Thought and Ideology in Seventeenth-Century England* (Princeton, 1978).

Archer, Ian, *The Pursuit of Stability: Social Relations in Elizabethan London* (Cambridge, 1991).

Archer, Ian, Barron, Caroline and Harding, Vanessa (eds.), *Hugh Alley's Caveat: The Markets of London in 1598*, London Topographical Society, 137 (1988).

Archer, John, *Every Man His Own Doctor* (London, 1671).

Arkell, Tom, 'An Examination of the Poll Taxes of the Later Seventeenth Century, the Marriage Duty Act and Gregory King', in Kevin Schurer and Tom Arkell (eds.), *Surveying the People: The Interpretation and Use of Document Sources for the Study of Population in the Later Seventeenth Century* (Oxford, 1992), pp. 142–77.

'The Incidence of Poverty in England in the Later Seventeenth Century', *Social History*, 12 (1987), pp. 23–47.

'Printed Instructions for Administering the Hearth Tax', in Schurer and Arkell, *Surveying the People*, pp. 38–64.

'The Probate Process', in Tom Arkell, Nesta Evans and Nigel Goose (eds.), *When Death Do Us Part: Understanding and Interpreting the Probate Records of Early Modern England* (Oxford, 2000), pp. 3–13.

Armitage, Philip, 'Developments in British Cattle Husbandry from the Romano-British Period to Early Modern Times', *Ark*, 9 (1982), pp. 52–4.

'A Preliminary Description of British Cattle from the Late Twelfth to the Early Sixteenth Century', *Ark*, 7 (1980), pp. 405–13.

Baker, Anne Pimlott, 'Ellis, William (*c.* 1700–1758)', *Oxford Dictionary of National Biography* (Oxford, 2004), www.oxforddnb.com/view/article/8718, accessed 19 March 2009.

Batchelor, Thomas, *General View of the Agriculture of the County of Bedford* (London, 1808).

Beaver, Daniel C., *Hunting and the Politics of Violence before the English Civil War* (Cambridge, 2008).

Beier, A. L., *Masterless Men: the Vagrancy Problem in England 1560–1640* (London, 1985).

Beier, A. L. and Finlay, Roger (eds.), *The Making of the Metropolis: London 1500–1700* (London, 1986).

Bellers, John, *Essays about the Poor, Manufacturers, Trade, Plantations and Immorality and of the Excellency and Divinity of Inward Light* (1699), in George Clarke (ed.), *John Bellers, 1654 to 1725, Quaker Visionary: His Life, Times and Writings* (York, 1993).

Beresford, John (ed.), *The Diary of a Country Parson: The Reverend James Woodforde*, 4 vols. (Oxford, 1968).

Berg, Maxine, *Luxury and Pleasure in Eighteenth-Century Britain* (Oxford, 2005).

Bestall, J. M and Fowkes, D. V. (eds.), *Chesterfield Wills and Inventories 1521–1603*, Derbyshire Record Society, 1 (1977).

Bettie, John, *Crime and the Courts in England 1660–1800* (Oxford, 1986).

Beveridge, William, *Prices and Wages in England* (London, 1939).

Biggs, Norman, 'A Tale Untangled: Measuring the Fineness of Yarn', *Textile History*, 35 (2004), pp. 120–9.

Bird, Ruth (ed.), *The Journal of Giles Moore*, Sussex Record Society, 68 (1971).

Blencowe, Robert Willis (ed.), 'The Journal and Accounts of Timothy Burrell Esq., Barrister-at-Law 1683–1714', *Sussex Archaeological Collections*, 3 (1850), pp. 117–72.

Blith, Walter, *The English Improver Improved or the Survey of Husbandry Surveyed* (London, 1652).

Boorde, Andrew, *A Compendyous Regymnet or a Dyetary of Helth* (London, 1542).

Boulton, Jeremy, 'Wage Labour in Seventeenth Century London', *Economic History Review*, 49 (1996), pp. 268–90.

Bowden, Peter, 'Agricultural Prices, Farm Profits, and Rents', in *AHEW*, IV, pp. 593–695.

'Agricultural Prices, Wages, Farm Profits and Rents', in *AHEW*, V.II, pp. 1–118.

Brassley, Paul Lambert, and Saunders, Philip Anthony (eds.), *Accounts of the Reverend John Crakanthorp of Fowlmere 1682–1710*, Cambridgeshire Records Society, 8 (1988).

Braudel, Fernand, *Civilization and Capitalism*, 3 vols. (New York, 1981).

Brenner, Robert, *Merchants and Revolutionaries: Commercial Change, Political Conflict and London's Overseas Traders 1550–1653* (Cambridge, 1993).

Brindley, Thomas, 'Escaping from Constraints: The Industrial Revolution in a Malthusian Context', *Journal of Interdisciplinary History*, 15 (1985), pp. 729–53.

Britten, James, *Old Country Farming Words* (London, 1880).

Broadberry, Stephen and Gupta, Bishnupriya, 'The Early Modern Great Divergence: Wages, Prices and Economic Development in Europe and Asia, 1500–1800', *Economic History Review*, 59 (2006), pp. 2–31.

Brushfield, T. N., 'The Financial Diary of a Citizen of Exeter 1631–43', *Transactions of the Devonshire Association for the Advancement of Science, Literature, and Art*, 33 (1901).

Burnett, John, *Plenty and Want: A Social History of Diet in England from 1815 to the Present Day* (London, 1979).

Burnette, Joyce, 'An Investigation of the Female–Male Wage Gap during the Industrial Revolution in Britain', *Economic History Review*, 50 (1997), pp. 257–81.

'Labourers at the Oakes: Changes in the Demand for Female Day-Labourers at a Farm near Sheffield during the Agricultural Revolution', *Journal of Economic History*, 59 (1999), pp. 41–67.

'The Wages and Employment of Female Day-Labourers in English Agriculture, 1740–1850', *Economic History Review*, 57 (2004), pp. 664–90.

Burton, Richard, *Anatomy of Melancholy*, 3 vols., ed. Thomas C. Faulkner, Nicolas K. Kiessling and Rhonda L. Blair (Oxford, 1989).

Butcher, E. E. (ed.), *Bristol Corporation of the Poor 1696–1834*, Bristol Record Society, 3 (1932).

Campbell, Andrew, *The Book of Beer* (London, 1956).

Campbell, B. M. S. and Overton, Mark, *Land, Labour and Livestock: Historical Studies in European Agricultural Productivity* (Manchester, 1991).

  'A New Perspective on Medieval and Early Modern Agriculture: Six Centuries of Norfolk Farming c. 1250–c. 1850', *Past and Present*, 141 (1993), pp. 38–105.

Campbell, B. M. S., Galloway, J. A., Keene, D. and Murphy, M., *A Medieval Capital: Agrarian Production and Distribution in the London Region c. 1300*, Historical Geography Research Series, 30 (1991).

Campbell, Mildred, '"Of People Either Too Few or Too Many": The Conflicts of Opinion on Population and Its Relation to Emigration', in William Appleton Aitken and Basil Duke Henning (eds.), *Conflict in Stuart England: Essays in Honour of William Notestein* (London, 1960), pp. 171–201.

Carr, Lois Green, Menard, Russell R. and Walsh, Lorena, *Robert Cole's World: Agriculture and Society in Early Maryland* (Chapel Hill, NC and London, 1994).

Cash, Margaret (ed.), *Devon Inventories of the Sixteenth and Seventeenth Centuries*, Devon and Cornwall Record Society, n.s., 11 (1966).

Choksy, George D., 'The Bifurcated Economics of Sir Dudley North and Roger North: One Holistic Analytical Engine', *History of Political Economy*, 27 (1995), pp. 477–92.

Clark, Alice, *Working Life of Women in the Seventeenth Century* (London, 1992).

Clark, Gregory, 'Farm Wages and Living Standards in the Industrial Revolution: England, 1670–1869', *Economic History Review*, 54 (2001), pp. 477–505.

  'The Long March of History: Farm Wages, Population, and Economic Growth, England 1209–1869', *Economic History Review*, 60 (2007), pp. 97–135.

  'The Price History of English Agriculture, 1209–1914', *Research in Economic History*, 22 (2004), pp. 41–124.

  'Productivity Growth without Technological Change in European Agriculture before 1850', *Journal of Economic History*, 47 (1987), pp. 419–32.

  'Yields per Acre in English Agriculture, 1250–1860: Evidence from Labour Inputs', *Economic History Review*, 44 (1991), pp. 445–60.

Clark, Gregory, Huberman, Michael and Lindert, Peter H., 'A British Food Puzzle, 1770–1850', *Economic History Review*, 48 (1995), pp. 215–37.

Clark, Gregory and van der Werf, Ysbrand, 'Work in Progress? The Industrious Revolution', *Journal of Economic History*, 58 (1998), pp. 830–43.

Clark, Peter, *The English Alehouse: A Social History 1200–1830* (London, 1983).

Clarkson, L. A., 'The Organization of the English Leather Industry in the Late Sixteenth and Seventeenth Centuries', *Economic History Review*, 2nd ser., 14 (1960–1), pp. 245–56.

Clarkson, L. A. and Crawford, Margaret, *Feast and Famine: Food and Nutrition in Ireland 1500–1920* (Oxford, 2001).

Clay, Christopher, *Economic Expansion and Social Change: England 1500–1700*, 2 vols. (Cambridge, 1984).

Clayton, John, *Friendly Advice to the Poor; Written and Published at the Request of the Late and Present Officers of the Town of Manchester* (Manchester, 1755).

Clutton-Brock, Juliet, 'British Cattle in the Eighteenth Century', *Ark*, 9 (1982), pp. 55–7.

Coats, A. W., 'Changing Attitudes to Labour in the Mid-Eighteenth Century', *Economic History Review*, 2nd ser., 11:1 (1958–9), pp. 35–51.

Cock, Thomas, *Kitchin-Physick or, Advice to the Poor by Way of a Dialogue* (London, 1676).

Cockburn, William, *An Account of the Nature, Causes, Symptoms and Cure of the Distempers That Are Incident to Seafaring People with Observations on the Diet of the Sea-Men in His Majesty's Navy* (London, 1696).

Colley, Linda, *Britons: Forging the Nation 1707–1837* (London, 1992).

Collins, E. J. T., 'Harvest Technology and Labour Supply in Britain, 1790–1870', *Economic History Review*, 22 (1969), pp. 453–73.

Collins, John, *Salt and Fishery* (London, 1682).

Considerations on Taxes as They Are Supposed to Affect the Price of Labour in Our Manufactories (London, 1765).

Considerations on the Expediency of Raising at This Time of General Dearth, the Wages of Servants That Are Not Domestic (London, 1767).

Cooper, Sheila McIsaac, 'Service to Servitude? The Decline and Demise of Life-Cycle Service in England', *History of the Family*, 10 (2005), pp. 367–86.

A Copy of the Report of an Essay of Bread … (London, 1758).

Corfield, P. J., *The Impact of English Towns, 1700–1800* (Oxford, 1982).

Cox, J. and Cox, N., 'Valuations in Probate Inventories, Part I', *Local Historian*, 2 (1985), pp. 467–78; Part II, *Local Historian*, 8 (1986), pp. 85–100.

'Probate 1500–1800: A System in Transition', in Tom Arkell, Nesta Evans and Nigel Goose (eds.), *When Death Do Us Part: Understanding and Interpreting the Probate Records of Early Modern England* (Oxford, 2000), pp. 14–37.

Cunningham, William, *The Growth of English Industry and Commerce in Modern Times* (Cambridge, 1929).

Daunton, Martin, *Progress and Poverty: An Economic and Social History of Britain 1700–1850* (Oxford, 1995).

Davies, David, *The Case of the Labourers in Husbandry Stated and Considered* (London, 1795; reprinted 1977).

de Malynes, Gerald, *Consuetudo vel lex Mercatoria* (London, 1622).

de Vries, Jan, 'Between Purchasing Power and the World of Goods: Understanding the Household Economy in Early Modern Europe', in Roy Porter and John Brewer, *Consumption and the World of Goods* (London, 1993), pp. 85–132.

'The Industrial Revolution and the Industrious Revolution', *Journal of Economic History*, 54 (1994), pp. 249–69.

The Industrious Revolution: Consumer Behaviour and the Household Economy, 1650 to the Present (Cambridge, 2008).

Defoe, Daniel, *Giving Alms No Charity and Employing the Poor* (1704), in W. R. Owens and P. N. Furbank, *Political and Economic Writings of Daniel Defoe* (London 2000).

The Great Law of Subordination Considered or, The Insolence and Insuffrable Behaviour of Servants in England Duly Enquired Into (1724), in W. R. Owens and P. N. Furbank, *Religious and Didactic Writings of Daniel Defoe* (London, 2007), vol. VI.

A Tour Thro' the Whole Island of Great Britain (London, 1968).

Drummond, J. C. and Wilbraham, Anne, *The Englishman's Food: Five Centuries of English Diet* (Oxford, 2001).

Dunning, Richard, *Bread for the Poor* (Exeter, 1698).

Durnin, V. G. A. and Passmore, R., *Energy, Work and Leisure* (London, 1967).

Durrant, Peter (ed.), *Berkshire Overseers' Papers, 1654–1834*, Berkshire Record Society, 3 (1997).

Dyer, Alan, *The City of Worcester in the Sixteenth Century* (Leicester, 1973).

Dyer, Christopher, *Standards of Living in the Later Middle Ages: Social Change in England c. 1200–1520* (Cambridge, 1989).

Earle, Peter, 'The Female Labour Market in London in the Late Seventeenth and Early Eighteenth Centuries', *Economic History Review*, 2nd ser., 42 (1989), pp. 328–53.

The Making of the English Middle Class (London, 1989).

Eden, Sir Frederick Morton, *The State of the Poor, or a History of the Labouring Classes in England*, 3 vols. (London, 1797).

Ellis, William, *The London and Country Brewer ... By a Person Formerly Concerned in a Common Brewhouse at London* (London, 1736).

The Country Housewife's Family Companion (London, 1750)

Elyot, Thomas, *The Boke Named the Governour* (London, 1531).

Energy and Protein Requirements: A Report of a Joint FAO/WHO/UNU Expert Consultation, World Health Organization Technical Report Series 724 (1991).

Erickson, Amy Louise, 'An Introduction to Probate Accounts', in G. H. Martin and Peter Spufford (eds.), *The Records of the Nation* (London, 1990), pp. 273–86.

'Married Women's Occupations in Eighteenth-Century London', *Continuity and Change* 23 (2008), pp. 237–66.

Estabrook, Carl, *Urbane and Rustic England: Cultural Ties and Social Spheres in the Provinces, 1660–1780* (Manchester, 1998).

Evans, Nesta and Rose, Susan (eds.), *Cambridgeshire Hearth Tax Returns Michaelmas 1664*, British Record Society Hearth Tax Series, 1 (2000).

Everitt, Alan, 'Farm Labourers', in *AHEW*, IV, pp. 396–465.

Farkas, G., Geldrich, J. and Láng, S, 'Neuere Untersuchungen über den Energieverbrauch beim Ernten', *Arbeits Physiologie*, 5 (1933), pp. 434–62.

Feinstein, Charles, 'Pessimism Perpetuated: Real Wages and the Standard of Living in Britain during the Industrial Revolution', *Economic History Review*, 58 (1998), pp. 625–58.

Fissell, Mary, 'The Marketplace of Print', in Mark Jenner and Patrick Wallis (eds.), *Medicine and the Market in England and Its Colonies, c. 1450–c. 1850* (London, 2007), pp. 108–32.

Floud, Roderick, Wachter, Kenneth and Gregory, Annabel, *Height, Health and History: Nutritional Status in the United Kingdom, 1750–1980* (Cambridge, 1990).

Fogel, Robert, *The Escape from Hunger and Premature Death, 1700–2100: Europe, America, and the Third World* (Cambridge, 2004).

'New Sources and Techniques for the Study of Secular Trends in Nutritional Status, Health, Mortality, and the Process of Aging', *Historical Methods*, 26 (1993), pp. 5–43.

Foster, Charles F., *Cheshire Cheese and Farming in the North West in the Seventeenth and Eighteenth Centuries* (Northwich, 1998).

Four Cheshire Townships in the Eighteenth Century: Arley, Appleton, Stockton Heath and Great Budworth (Northwich, 1992).

Seven Households: Life in Cheshire and Lancashire 1582–1774 (Northwich, 2002).

French, Henry, *The Middle Sort of People in Provincial England 1600–1750* (Oxford, 2007).

Freudenberger, Hermann and Cummins, Gaylord, 'Health, Work and Leisure before the Industrial Revolution', *Explorations in Economic History*, 13 (1976), pp. 1–12.

Furniss, F. S., *The Position of the Laborer in a System of Nationalism: A Study in the Labor Theories of Later English Mercantilism* (New York, 1965).

Fussell, G. E. (ed.), *Robert Loder's Farm Accounts 1610–1620*, Camden Society, 3rd ser., 53 (1936).

Gibson, A. J. S., 'The Size and Weight of Cattle and Sheep in Early Modern Scotland', *Agricultural History Review*, 36 (1988), pp. 162–71.

Gibson, A. J. S. and Smout, T. C., *Prices, Food and Wages in Scotland 1550–1780* (Cambridge, 1995).

Gilboy, E. W., 'Labour at Thornborough: An Eighteenth Century Estate', *Economic History Review*, 1st ser., 3 (1931–2), pp. 388–98.

'Some New Evidence on Wage Assessments in the Eighteenth Century', *English Historical Review*, 43 (1928), pp. 398–40.

'Wages in Eighteenth-Century England', *Journal of Economic & Business History*, 2 (1929–30), pp. 603–29.

Glennie, Paul, 'Measuring Crop Yields in Early Modern England', in B. M. S. Campbell and Mark Overton (eds.), *Land, Labour and Livestock: Historical Studies in European Agricultural Productivity* (Manchester, 1991), pp. 255–83.

Gough, Richard, *History of Myddle*, ed. D. Hey (Harmondsworth, 1981).

Grassby, Richard, *The Business Community of Seventeenth Century England* (Cambridge, 1995).

Griffiths, Paul, *Youth and Authority: Formative Experiences in England 1560–1640* (Oxford, 1996).

Hakluyt, Richard, *Discourse of Western Planting* (1584), in E. G. R. Taylor (ed.), *The Original Writings and Correspondence of the Two Richard Hakluyts*, Hakluyt Society, 2nd ser., 77 (1935).

Hale, Matthew, *A Discourse Touching Provision for the Poor* (London, 1683).

Hallett, Mark and Riding, Christine, *Hogarth* (London, 2006).

Harrington, Duncan, Pearson, Sarah and Rose, Susan (eds.), *Kent Hearth Tax Assessment, Lady Day 1664*, British Record Society Hearth Tax Series, 2 (London, 2000).

Harrison, William, *The Description of England*, ed. George Edelen (New York, 1994).

Hart, James, *The Diet of the Diseased* (London, 1633).

Harte, N. B., 'The Economics of Clothing in the Late Seventeenth Century', *Textile History*, 22 (1991), 277–96.

'The Rise of Protection and the English Linen Trade, 1690–1780', in N. B. Harte and K. G. Ponting (eds.), *Textile History and Economic History* (Manchester, 1973), pp. 74–112.

Hassell Smith, Alan, 'Labourers in Late Sixteenth-Century England: A Case Study from North Norfolk', *Continuity and Change*, [part I] 4:1 (1989), pp. 11–52; [part II] 4:3 (1989), pp. 367–94.

Hatcher, John, *The History of the British Coal Industry, I, Before 1700* (Oxford, 1992).

'Labour, Leisure and Economic Thought', *Past and Present*, 160 (1998), pp. 65–115.

Haynes, John, *Great Britain's Glory: or an Account of the Great Numbers of Poor Employed in the Woollen and Silk Manufactures* (London, 1715).

Hey, David, *An English Rural Community: Myddle under the Tudors and Stuarts* (Leicester, 1974).

'The North-West Midlands: Derbyshire, Staffordshire, Cheshire, and Shropshire', in *AHEW*, V.I, pp. 129–58.

Hill, Christopher, *Society and Puritanism in Pre-Revolutionary England* (Harmondsworth, 1964).

Hindle, Steve, 'Dearth and the English Revolution: The Harvest Crisis of 1647–50', *Economic History Review*, 61 (2008), pp. 64–95.

'Dearth, Fasting and Alms: The Campaign for General Hospitality in Late Elizabethan England', *Past and Present*, 172 (2001), pp. 44–86.

On the Parish: The Micro-Politics of Poor Relief in Rural England c. 1550–1750 (Oxford, 2004).

'Persuasion and Protest in the Caddington Common Enclosure Dispute 1635–1639', *Past and Present*, 158 (1998), pp. 35–78.

'Power, Poor Relief, and Social Relations in Holland Fen, c. 1600–1800', *Historical Journal*, 41 (1998), pp. 67–96.

Hipkin, Stephen, 'Tenant Farming and Short-Term Leasing on Romney Marsh, 1585–1705', *Economic History Review*, 53 (2000), pp. 646–76.

Historical Manuscript Commission Reports, no. 15, *Report on Manuscripts in Various Collections* (London, 1901), I, pp. 160–75.

Hitchcock, Timothy V. (ed.), *Richard Hutton's Complaint Book: The Notebook of the Steward of the Quaker Workhouse at Clerkenwell 1711–1737*, London Record Society, 24 (1987).

Holderness, B. A., 'East Anglia and the Fens: Norfolk, Suffolk, Cambridgeshire, Ely, Huntingdonshire, Essex, and the Lincolnshire Fens', in *AHEW*, V.I, pp. 197–238.

'Prices, Productivity and Output', in *AHEW*, VI, pp. 84–189.

Holmes, Geoffrey, 'Gregory King and the Social Structure of Pre-Industrial England', *Transactions of the Royal Historical Society*, 5th ser., 27 (1977), pp. 41–68.

Horn, Pamela, 'Davies, David (1742–1819)', *Oxford Dictionary of National Biography* (Oxford, 2004), www.oxforddnb.com/view/article/7229, accessed 19 May 2009.

Horrell, Sara, 'Home Demand and British Industrialization', *Journal of Economic History*, 56 (1996), pp. 565–71.

Horrell, Sara and Humphries, Jane, 'Old Questions, New Data, and Alternative Perspectives: Families' Living Standards in the Industrial Revolution', *Journal of Economic History*, 52 (1992), pp. 849–80.

'Women's Labour Force Participation and the Transition to the Male-Breadwinner Family, 1790–1865', *Economic History Review*, 48 (1995), pp. 89–117.

Hoskins, W. G., 'Harvest Fluctuations and English Economic History, 1480–1619', *Agricultural History Review*, 12 (1964), pp. 28–46.

'Harvest Fluctuations and English Economic History, 1620–1759', *Agricultural History Review*, 16 (1968), pp. 15–31.

'The Rebuilding of Rural England 1570–1640', *Past and Present*, 4 (1953), pp. 44–57.

Houghton, John, *England's Great Happiness or, A Dialogue between Content and Complaint* (London, 1677).

Houlbrooke, Ralph, *Death, Religion and the Family in England 1480–1750* (Oxford, 1998).

Houliston, Victor, 'Moffet, Thomas (1553–1604)', *Oxford Dictionary of National Biography* (Oxford, 2004), www.oxforddnb.com/view/article/18877, accessed 19 March 2009.

'Houses of Correction at Maidstone and Westminster', British Museum, MS Lansdowne 5, reprinted in *English Historical Review*, 42 (1927), pp. 251–61.

Hudson, Pat and Sonenscher, Michael (eds.), *Manufacture in Town and Country before the Industrial Revolution* (Cambridge, 1984).

Hughes, Elizabeth and White, Philippa (eds.), *The Hampshire Hearth Tax Assessment 1665*, Hampshire Record Society, 11 (1991).

Humphries, Jane, 'Enclosures, Common Rights, and Women: The Proletarianisation of Families in the Late Eighteenth and Early Nineteenth Centuries', *Journal of Economic History*, 50 (1990), pp. 17–42.

James, John, *History of the Worsted Manufacture in England* (London, 1857).

Jenner, Mark, 'From Conduit Community to Commercial Network? Water in London, 1500–1725', in Paul Griffiths and Mark Jenner (eds.), *Londinopolis: Essays in the Cultural and Social History of Early Modern London* (Manchester, 2000), pp. 250–71.

Jones, Norman, *The Birth of the Elizabethan Age: England in the 1560s* (Oxford, 1993).

Kerridge, Eric, *The Agricultural Revolution* (London, 1967).

Textile Manufactures in Early Modern England (Manchester, 1985).

King, Gregory, 'The Burns Journal' (*c.* 1695–1700), in Peter Laslett (ed.), *The Earliest Classics: John Graunt and Gregory King* (London, 1973).

'Natural and Political Observations and Conclusions upon the State and Condition of England' (1696), in Laslett (ed.), *The Earliest Classics: John Graunt and Gregory King* (London, 1973), pp. 54–5.

King, Peter, 'Pauper Inventories and the Material Lives of the Poor in the Eighteenth and Nineteenth Centuries', in Tim Hitchcock, Peter King and Pamela Sharpe (eds.), *Chronicling Poverty: The Voices and Strategies of the English Poor, 1640–1840*, Basingstoke, 1997), pp. 155–91.

'Social Inequality, Identity and the Labouring Poor in Eighteenth-Century England', in Henry French and Jonathan Barry (eds.), *Identity and Agency in England, 1500–1800* (London, 2004), pp. 60–86.

Kussmaul, Ann, *Servants in Husbandry in Early Modern England* (Cambridge, 1981).

Kussmaul, Ann (ed.), *The Autobiography of Joseph Mayett of Quainton 1783–1839*, Buckingham Record Society, 23 (1986).

Landau, Norma, 'The Eighteenth-Century Context of the Laws of Settlement', *Continuity and Change*, 6 (1991), pp. 417–39.

'The Laws of Settlement and the Surveillance of Immigration in Eighteenth-Century Kent', *Continuity and Change*, 3 (1988), pp. 391–420.

'The Regulation of Immigration, Economic Structures and Definitions of the Poor in Eighteenth-Century England', *Historical Journal*, 33 (1990), pp. 541–71.

Laslett, Peter, *The World We Have Lost Further Explored*, 3rd edn (London, 1983).

Latham, Robert and Mathews, William (eds.), *The Diary of Samuel Pepys*, 10 vols. (London, 1970–83).

Levine, David and Wrightson, Keith, *The Making of an Industrial Society: Wickham 1560–1765* (Oxford, 1991).

Lindert, Peter H. and Williamson, Jeffrey G., 'Revising England's Social Tables 1688–1812', *Explorations in Economic History*, 19 (1982), pp. 385–407.

Littleton, Edward, *The Groans of the Plantations: or a True Account of their Grievous and Extreme Sufferings by the Heavy Impositions upon Sugar* (London, 1689).

Locke, John, *Two Treatises of Government*, ed. Peter Laslett (New York, 1963).

Lodge, Eleanor C. (ed.), *The Account Book of a Kentish Estate 1616–1704* (London, 1927).

Lubbock, Basil (ed.), *Barlow's Journal of His Life at Sea in King's Ships, East and West Indiamen and Other Merchantmen from 1659–1703*, 2 vols. (London, 1934).

Macfarlane, Alan (ed.), *The Diary of Ralph Josselin, 1616–1683* (Oxford, 1976).

Machin, R., 'The Great Rebuilding: A Reassessment', *Past and Present*, 77 (1977), pp. 33–56.

Malcolm, Thick, 'Market Gardening in England and Wales' in *AHEW*, V.II, pp. 503–32.

Malcolmson, Robert W., *Popular Recreations in English Society 1700–1850* (Cambridge, 1973).

Markham, Gervase, *The English Housewife, Containing the Inward and Outward Vertues Which Ought to Be in a Compleat Woman* (London, 1664).

Marshall, William, *The Rural Economy of the Midland Counties*, 2 vols. (London, 1796).

Martins, Susanna and Williamson, Tom (eds.), *The Farming Journal of Randall Burroughes (1794–1799)*, Norfolk Record Society, 58 (1995).

Mathias, Peter, 'Agriculture and the Brewing and Distilling Industries in the Eighteenth Century', *Economic History Review*, n.s., 5 (1952), pp. 249–57.

The Brewing Industry in England 1700–1830 (Cambridge, 1959).

Mayhew, Henry, *London Labour and the London Poor*, 4 vols. (London, 1861).

McClure, Ruth K., *Coram's Children: The London Foundling Hospital in the Eighteenth Century* (New Haven, 1981).

McRae, Andrew, *God Speed the Plough: The Representation of Agrarian England, 1500–1660* (Cambridge, 1996).

Meldrum, Tim, *Domestic Service and Gender 1660–1750: Life and Work in the London Household* (Harlow, 2000).

Memorandum Book of Richard Cholmeley of Brandsby, 1602–1623, North Yorkshire County Record Office Publications, 44 (1988).

Men and Armour for Gloucestershire in 1608 compiled by John Smith (Gloucester, 1980; reprint of 1902 edition).

Mendelson, Sara, and Crawford, Patricia, *Women in Early Modern England* (Oxford, 1998).

Miller, Derek, 'Man's Demand for Energy', in Derek Oddy and Derek Miller (eds.), *Diet and Health in Modern Britain* (London, 1985), pp. 274–95.

Miller, James Arthur (ed.), *The Letters of Stephen Gardiner* (Cambridge, 1933).

Mingay, G. E. (ed.), *The Agrarian History of England and Wales*, VI, *1750–1850* (Cambridge, 1981).

Mintz, Sidney W., *Sweetness and Power: The Place of Sugar in Modern History* (Harmondsworth, 1985).

Misselden, Edward, *The Circle of Commerce* (London, 1623).

Mitchell, B. R. and Deane, Phyllis, *Abstract of British Historical Statistics* (Cambridge, 1971).

Moffet, Thomas, *Health's Improvement: or, Rules Comprizing and Discovering the Nature, Method, and Manner of Preparing All Sorts of Food Used in This Nation* (London, 1655).

Monckton, H. A., *A History of English Ale and Beer* (London, 1966).

Money, John, 'Teaching in the Market-Place, or "Caesar adsum jam forte: Pompey aderat": The Retailing of Knowledge in Provincial England during the Eighteenth Century', in John Brewer and Roy Porter (eds.), *Consumption and the World of Goods* (London, 1993), pp. 355–80.

Moore, Adam, *Bread for the Poor* (London, 1653).

Moore, Sir Norman, *The History of St. Bartholomew's Hospital*, 2 vols. (London, 1918).

Moore-Colyer, R. J., 'Farming Techniques: Cattle', *AHEW*, VI, pp. 313–61.

Mortimer, Ian, 'Why Were Probate Accounts Made? Methodological Issues Surrounding the Historical use of Administrators' and Executors' Accounts', *Archives*, 31 (2006), pp. 2–17.

Muldrew, Craig, '"Th'ancient Distaff and Whirling Spindle": Measuring the Contribution of Spinning to Household Earnings and the National Economy in England 1550–1770', *Economic History Review* (in press).

'Class and Credit: Social Identity, Wealth and the Life Course in Early Modern England', in Henry French and Jonathan Barry (eds.), *Identity and Agency in England, 1500–1800* (London, 2004), pp. 147–77.

'Credit, Market Relations, and Debt Litigation in Late Seventeenth Century England, with Particular Reference to King's Lynn', University of Cambridge Ph.D. thesis, 1991.

'Economic and Urban Development of Seventeenth-Century Britain', in Barry Coward (ed.), *The Blackwell Companion to Stuart Britain* (Oxford, 2003), pp. 148–65.

The Economy of Obligation: The Culture of Credit and Social Relations in Early Modern England (London, 1998).

'"Hard Food for Midas": Cash and Its Social Value in Early Modern England', *Past and Present*, 170 (2001), pp. 78–120.

'Wages and the Problem of Monetary Scarcity in Early Modern England', in Jan Lucassen (ed.), *Wages and Currency: Global Comparisons from Antiquity to the Twentieth Century* (Berne, 2007), pp. 391–410.

Mumby, Lionel M. (ed.), *Early Stuart Household Accounts*, Hertfordshire Record Society, 2 (1986).

Mun, Thomas, *Englands Treasure by Forraign Trade*, in J. P. McCulloch (ed.), *A Select Collection of Early English Tracts on Commerce* (Cambridge, 1954).

Newman-Brown, W., 'The Receipt of Poor Relief and Family Situation, Aldenham, Hertfordshire, 1630–90', in Richard Smith (ed.), *Land, Kinship and Life Cycle* (Cambridge, 1984), pp. 405–22.

North, Dudley, *Discourses upon Trade; Principally Directed to the Cases of the Interest, Coynage, Clipping, Increase of Money* (London, 1691).

North, Roger, *A Discourse of the Poor* (London, 1753).

Oddy, Derek, *From Plain Fare to Fusion Food: British Diet from the 1890s to the 1990s* (Woodbridge, 2003).

Oppenheim, Michael, *A History of the Administration of the Royal Navy and of Merchant Shipping in Relation to the Navy*, I, *1509–1660* (London, 1896).

Ormrod, David, *English Grain Exports and the Structure of Agrarian Capitalism 1700–1760* (Hull, 1985).

Overton, Mark, *Agricultural Revolution in England: The Transformation of the Agrarian Economy 1500–1850* (Cambridge, 1996).

Overton, Mark and Campbell, B. M. S., 'Norfolk Livestock Farming 1250–1740: A Comparative Study of Manorial Accounts and Probate Inventories', *Journal of Historical Geography*, 18 (1992), pp. 377–96.

'Production et productivité dans l'agriculture anglaise, 1086–1871', *Histoire & Mesure*, 11 (1996), pp. 255–97.

Overton, Mark, Whittle, Jane, Dean, Darron and Hann, Andrew, *Production and Consumption in English Households, 1600–1750* (Abingdon, 2004).

Özmucur, Süleyman and Pamuk, Sevket, 'Real Wages and Standards of Living in the Ottoman Empire, 1498–1914', *Journal of Economic History*, 62 (2002), pp. 293–321.

Palliser, D. M., *Tudor York* (Oxford, 1979).

Palmer, John, *How to Brew* (Boulder, 2006).

Paul, A. A. and Southgate, D. T. A., *McCance and Widdowson's The Composition of Foods*, 4th edn (London, 1978).

Peirce, E. H., *Annals of Christ's Hospital* (London, 1908).

Pennell, Sara '"Great Quantities of Gooseberry Pye and Baked Clod of Beef": Victualling and Eating Out in Early Modern London', in Paul Griffiths and Mark Jenner (eds.), *Londinopolis: Essays in the Cultural and Social History of Early Modern London* (Manchester, 2000), pp. 228–49.

'The Material Culture of Food in Early Modern England, circa 1650–1750', University of Oxford D.Phil. thesis, 1997.

Penney, Norman (ed.), *The Household Account Book of Sarah Fell of Swarthmoor Hall* (Cambridge, 1920).

Perkins, J. A., 'Harvest Technology and Labour Supply in Lincolnshire and the East Riding of Yorkshire 1750–1850', *Tools and Tillage*, 3 (1976–7), pp. 46–58, 125–35.

Peterson, Christian, *Bread and the British Economy c. 1770–1870* (Aldershot, 1995).

Petyt, William, *Britannia Languens or a Discourse on Trade* (London, 1680), in J. P. McCulloch (ed.), *A Select Collection of Early English Tracts on Commerce* (Cambridge, 1954).

Phelps Brown, Henry and Hopkins, Sheila V., 'Seven Centuries of Building Wages', in Henry Phelps Brown and Sheila V. Hopkins, *A Perspective of Wages and Prices* (London, 1981), pp. 1–12.

'Seven Centuries of the Prices of Consumables, Compared with Builders' Wage-Rates', in Henry Phelps Brown and Sheila V. Hopkins, *A Perspective of Wages and Prices* (London, 1981), pp. 13–59.

Phillips, Rod, *A Short History of Wine* (New York, 2000).

Platt, Hugh, *Sundrie New and Artificiall Remedies against Famine* (London, 1596).

Pollock, Vivienne, 'Contract and Consumption: Labour Agreements and the Use of Money in Eighteenth-Century Rural Ulster', *Agricultural History Review*, 43 (1995), pp. 19–34.

Porter, Roy, *The Greatest Benefit to Mankind: A Medical History of Humanity from Antiquity to the Present* (London, 1997).

Porter, Roy and Brewer, John (eds.), *Consumption and the World of Goods* (London, 1993).

Pound, John, *Tudor and Stuart Norwich* (Chichester, 1988).

Pounds, N. J. G., 'Barton Farming in Eighteenth Century Cornwall', *Journal of the Royal Institution of Cornwall*, n. s., 7 (1973), pp. 54–75.

Powel, John, *The Assize of Bread* (London, 1636).

Putnam, B. H., 'Northamptonshire Wage Assessments of 1560 and 1667', *Economic History Review*, 1 (1927–8), pp. 124–34.

Rappaport, Steve, *Worlds within Worlds: Structures of Life within Sixteenth-Century London* (Cambridge, 1989).

Reed, Michael, *The Ipswich Probate Inventories, 1583–1631*, Suffolk Records Society, 22 (1981).

Reed, Mick, '"Gnawing It Out": A New Look at Economic Relations in Nineteenth-Century Rural England', *Rural History*, 1 (1990), pp. 83–94.

Reid, Douglas A, 'The Decline of Saint Monday 1766–1876', *Past and Present*, 71 (1976), pp. 76–101.

Richards, Jennifer, *Rhetoric and Courtliness in Early Modern Literature* (Cambridge, 2003).

Richardson, R. C., 'Metropolitan Counties: Bedfordshire, Hertfordshire, and Middlesex', in *AHEW*, V.I, pp. 239–69.

Roche, Daniel, *A History of Everyday Things: The Birth of Consumption in France, 1600–1800* (Cambridge, 2000).

Rodger, N. A. M., *The Wooden World: An Anatomy of the Georgian Navy* (London, 1986).

Rollison, David, *The Local Origins of Modern Society: Gloucestershire 1500–1800* (London, 1993).

Rule, John, *Albion's People: English Society 1714–1815* (London, 1992).

Sambrook, Pamela, *Country House Brewing in England, 1500–1900* (London, 1996).

Sarti, Raffaella, *Europe at Home: Family and Material Culture, 1500–1800* (New Haven, 1999).

Scholliers, Peter and Schwarz, Leonard (eds.), *Experiencing Wages: Social and Cultural Aspects of Wage Forms in Europe since 1500* (New York and Oxford, 2003).

Schurer, Kevin and Arkell, Tom (eds.), *Surveying the People: The Interpretation and Use of Document Sources for the Study of Population in the Later Seventeenth Century* (Oxford, 1992).

Schwartz, Leonard, *London in the Age of Industrialisation: Entrepreneurs, Labour Force and Living Conditions, 1700–1850* (Cambridge, 1993).

Sgroi, Rosemary, 'Piscatorial Politics Revisited: The Language of Economic Debate and the Evolution of Fishing Policy in Elizabethan England', *Albion*, 35 (2003), pp. 1–24.

Shammas, Carole, 'Food Expenditures and Economic Well-Being in Early Modern England', *Journal of Economic History*, 43 (1983), pp. 89–100.

The Pre-Industrial Consumer in England and America (Oxford, 1990).

Sharp, Buchanan, *In Contempt of all Authority: Rural Artisans and Riot in the West of England, 1586–1660* (Berkeley and Los Angeles, 1980).

Sharpe, J. A., *Crime in Seventeenth-Century England: A County Study* (Cambridge, 1983).

Early Modern England: A Social History 1550–1760 (London, 1987).

Shaw-Taylor, Leigh, 'Labourers, Cows, Common Rights and Parliamentary Enclosure: The Evidence of Contemporary Comment c. 1760–1810', *Past and Present*, 171 (2001), pp. 95–126.

'The Nature and Scale of the Cottage Economy', www.geog.cam.ac.uk/research/projects/occupations/abstracts/, accessed 6 July 2010.

'Parliamentary Enclosure and the Emergence of an English Agricultural Proletariat', *Journal of Economic History*, 61:3 (2001), pp. 640–62.

'Proletarianisation, Parliamentary Enclosure and the Household Economy of the Labouring Poor 1750–1850', University of Cambridge Ph.D. thesis, 1999.

Shaw-Taylor, Leigh, and Jones, Amanda, 'The Male Occupational Structure of Northamptonshire 1777–1881: A Case of Partial De-Industrialization?', www.geog.cam.ac.uk/research/projects/occupations/abstracts/, accessed 6 July 2010.

Shepard, Alexandra, 'Poverty, Labour and the Language of Social Description in Early Modern England', *Past and Present*, 201 (2008), pp. 51–95.

Sherman, Sandra, *Imagining Poverty: Quantification and the Decline of Paternalism* (Columbus, OH, 2001).

Short, Brian M., 'The South-East: Kent, Surrey, and Sussex', in *AHEW*, V.I, pp. 270–357.

Slack, Paul, *From Reformation to Improvement: Public Welfare in Early Modern England* (Oxford, 1998).

'Material Progress and the Challenge of Affluence in Seventeenth-Century England', *Economic History Review*, 62 (2009), pp. 576–603.

'Measuring the National Wealth in Seventeenth-Century England', *Economic History Review*, 57 (2004), pp. 607–35.

Slack, Paul (ed.), *Poverty in Early-Stuart Salisbury*, Wiltshire Record Society, 31 (1975).

Smith, Adam, *An Inquiry into the Nature and Causes of the Wealth of Nations*, 2 vols. (Oxford, 1976).

Smith, Charles, *Three Tracts on the Corn-Trade and Corn Laws*, 2nd edn (London, 1766).

Smith, Richard M., 'Ageing and Well-Being in Early Modern England: Pension Trends and Gender Preferences under the Old Poor Law *c*. 1650–1800', in Paul Johnson and Pat Thane (eds.), *Old Age from Antiquity to Post-Modernity* (London, 1998), pp. 64–95.

Smith, Thomas, *Discourse of the Commonweal of This Realm of England* (London, 1581).

Sneath, Ken, 'Consumption, Wealth, Indebtedness and Social Structure in Early Modern England', University of Cambridge Ph.D. thesis, 2009.

Snell, Keith, *Annals of the Labouring Poor: Social Change and Agrarian England 1660–1900* (Cambridge, 1985).

'Pauper Settlement and the Right to Poor Relief in England and Wales', *Continuity and Change*, 6:3 (1991), pp. 375–415.

'Settlement, Poor Law and the Rural Historian: New Approaches and Opportunities', *Rural History*, 3:2 (1992), pp. 145–72.

Sokoll, Thomas, *Household and Family among the Poor: The Case of Two Essex Communities in the Late Eighteenth and Early Nineteenth Centuries* (Bochum, 1993).

Solar, Peter M., 'Poor Relief and English Economic Development before the Industrial Revolution', *Economic History Review*, 2nd ser., 48 (1995), pp. 1–22.

Somerset, H. V. F., 'An Account Book of an Oxford Undergraduate in the Years 1619–1622', *Oxoniensia*, 22 (1957), pp. 85–92.

Sonenscher, Michael, 'Work and Wages in Paris in the Eighteenth Century', in Maxine Berg, Pat Hudson and Michael Sonenscher (eds.), *Manufacture in Town and Country before the Industrial Factory* (Cambridge, 1983), pp. 147–72.

Speechley, Helen, 'Female and Child Agricultural Day Labourers in Somerset, *c*. 1685–1870', University of Exeter Ph.D. thesis, 1999.

Spufford, Margaret, *Contrasting Communities, English Villagers in the Sixteenth and Seventeenth Centuries* (Cambridge, 1974).

'The Limitations of the Probate Inventory', in John Chartres and David Hey (eds.), *English Rural Society, 1500–1800: Essays in Honour of Joan Thirsk* (Cambridge, 1990), pp. 139–74.

Spufford, Margaret and Went, James, *Poverty Portrayed: Gregory King and the Parish of Eccleshall* (Keele, 1995).

Spufford, Peter, Brett, Matthew and Erickson Amy Louise (eds.), *Guide to the Probate Accounts of England and Wales* (London, 1999).

Stanes, Robin, *The Old Farm: A History of Farming Life in the West Country* (Exeter, 1990).

Stedman, Carolyn, *Master and Servant: Love and Labour in the English Industrial Age* (Cambridge, 2007).

Stone, Lawrence, *The Crisis of the Aristocracy, 1558–1641* (Oxford, 1965).

Styles, John, 'Clothing in the North: The Supply of Non-Elite Clothing in the Eighteenth Century North of England', *Textile History*, 25 (1994), pp. 139–66.

'Custom or Consumption? Plebeian Fashion in Eighteenth-Century England', in Maxine Berg and Elizabeth Eger (eds.) *Luxury in the Eighteenth Century: Debates, Desires and Delectable Goods* (Basingstoke, 2003), pp. 103–15.

The Dress of the People: Everyday Fashion in Eighteenth-Century England (New Haven, 2007).

'Embezzlement, Industry and the Law in England, 1500–1800', in Maxine Berg, Pat Hudson and Michael Sonenscher (eds.), *Manufacture in Town and Country before the Factory* (Cambridge, 1983), pp. 173–210.

Svedberg, Peter, *Poverty and Undernutrition: Theory, Measurement, and Policy* (Oxford, 2000).

Swinton, John, *A Proposal for Uniformity of Weights and Measures in Scotland, by Execution of the Laws Now in Force* (Edinburgh, 1779).

Tadmor, Naomi, *Family and Friends in Eighteenth Century England: Household, Kinship, and Patronage* (Cambridge, 2001).

Takahashi, Motoyasu, *Village Inheritance in Early Modern England; Kinship Structure, Inheritance Customs and Generation Continuity* (Matsuyama, Japan, 2003).

Tawney, A. J. and Tawney, R. H., 'An Occupational Census of the Seventeenth Century', *Economic History Review*, 5 (1934–5), pp. 25–64.

Tawney, R. H., *The Agrarian Problem in the Sixteenth Century* (London, 1912; reissued London and New York, 1967).

Thirsk, Joan, *Economic Policy and Projects: The Development of a Consumer Society in Early Modern England* (Oxford, 1978).

English Peasant Farming: The Agrarian History of Lincolnshire from Tudor to Recent Times (London, 1957).

Food in Early Modern England: Phases, Fads, Fashions 1500–1760 (London, 2007).

Thirsk, Joan (ed.), *The Agrarian History of England and Wales*, IV, *1500–1640* (Cambridge, 1967).

The Agrarian History of England and Wales, V, *1640–1750* (Cambridge, 1984).

Thirsk, Joan and Cooper, J. P. (eds.), *Seventeenth-Century Economic Documents* (Oxford, 1972).

Thomas, Keith, *Religion and the Decline of Magic* (Harmondsworth, 1971).

Thompson, E. P., 'The Moral Economy of the English Crowd in the Eighteenth Century', and 'The Moral Economy Reviewed', in *Customs in Common* (London, 1991), pp. 183–305.

Thorold Rogers, J. B., *A History of Agriculture and Prices in England from 1259 to 1793*, 8 vols. (Oxford, 1866–1902).

Tingey, J. C., 'An Assessment of Wages for the County of Norfolk in 1610', *English Historical Review*, 13 (1898), pp. 522–7.

Trinder, Barrie and Cox, Jeff (eds.), *Yeomen and Colliers in Telford: Probate Inventories for Dawley, Lilleshall, Wellington and Wrockwardine, 1660–1750* (Chichester, 1980).

Turner, M. E., Beckett, J. V. and Afton, B., *Farm Production in England 1700–1914* (Oxford, 2001).

Tusser, Thomas, *Five Hundred Points of Good Husbandry* (Oxford, 1984).

Tyrer, Frank and Bagley, J. J. (eds.), *The Great Diurnal of Nicholas Blundell*, 3 vols, Record Society of Lancashire and Cheshire, 110, 112, 114 (1968–72).

Vanderlint, Jacob, *Money Answers All Things: or an Essay to Make Money Sufficiently Plentiful* (London, 1734).

Vaisey, David (ed.), *The Diary of Thomas Turner* (Oxford, 1985).

A Vindication of Strong Beer and Ale (London, 1647).

Voth, Hans-Joachim, *Time and Work in England 1750–1830* (Oxford, 2000).

Walter, John, *Understanding Popular Violence in the English Revolution: The Colchester Plunderers* (Cambridge, 1999).

Walter, John and Wrightson, Keith, 'Dearth and the Social Order in Early Modern England', *Past and Present*, 71 (1976), pp. 22–42.

Warde, Paul, *Energy Consumption in England and Wales, 1560–2000* (Istituto di Studi sulle Società del Mediterraneo, 2007).

Watkins, George, *Compleat English Brewer or, the Whole Art and Mystery of Brewing, in All Its Various Branches* (London, 1767).

Wear, Andrew, *Knowledge and Practice in English Medicine 1550–1680* (Cambridge, 2000).

Weatherill, Lorna, *Consumer Behaviour and Material Culture in Britain 1660–1760* (Cambridge, 1988).

The Pottery Trade and North Staffordshire 1660–1760 (Manchester, 1971).

Weatherill, Lorna (ed.), *The Account Book of Richard Latham 1724–1767* (Oxford, 1990).

Webb, John (ed.), *Poor Relief in Elizabethan Ipswich*, Suffolk Records Society, 9 (1966).

Werner, Lex (ed.), *London Bodies* (London, 1998).

Whitaker, Edward, *Directions for Brewing Malt Liquors* (London, 1700).

Whittle, Jane, *The Development of Agrarian Capitalism: Land and Labour in Norfolk 1440–1580* (Oxford, 2000).

'Housewives and Servants in Rural England, 1440–1650: Evidence of Women's Work from Probate Documents', *Transactions of the Royal Historical Society*, 15 (2005), pp. 51–74.

Willan, T. S., *A Bedfordshire Wage Assessment of 1684*, Bedfordshire Historical Record Society, 25 (1943), pp. 129–37.

Elizabethan Manchester (Manchester, 1980).

Williams, N. J., *The Maritime Trade of the East Anglian Ports 1550–1590* (Oxford, 1988).

Winch, Donald, 'Eden, Sir Frederick Morton, second baronet (1766–1809)', *Oxford Dictionary of National Biography* (Oxford, 2004), www.oxforddnb.com/view/article/8450, accessed 19 May 2009.

Winstanley, R. L., *Parson Woodforde: The Life and Times of a Country Diarist* (Bungay, 1996).

Winstanley, R. L. (ed.), *The Diary of James Woodforde*, X, *1782–1784* (Parson Woodforde Society, 1998).

Winstanley, R. L. and Jameson, Peter (eds.), *The Diary of James Woodforde: 1759–1802*, 17 vols. (Parson Woodforde Society, 1988–2008).

Wood, Andy, 'Fear, Hatred and the Hidden Injuries of Class in Early Modern England', *Journal of Social History*, 39:3 (2006), pp. 803–26.

Riot, Rebellion and Popular Politics in Early Modern England (2002).

Woodward, Donald, 'The Anglo-Irish Livestock Trade of the Seventeenth Century', *Irish Historical Studies*, 18 (1972–3), pp. 489–523.

'The Assessment of Wages by Justices of the Peace, 1563–1813: Some Observations', *Local Historian*, 8:8 (1969), pp. 293–8.

'Cattle Droving in the Seventeenth Century: A Yorkshire Example', in W. H. Chaloner and B. M. Ratcliffe (eds.), *Trade and Transport: Essays in Economic History in Honour of T. S. Willan* (Manchester, 1977), pp. 35–58.

'Early Modern Servants in Husbandry Revisited', *Agricultural History Review*, 48 (2002), pp. 141–50.

'The Means of Payment and Hours of Work in Early Modern England', in Carol S. Leonard and B. N. Mironov (eds.), *Hours of Work and Means of Payment: The Evolution of Conventions in Pre-Industrial Europe*, Proceedings of the Eleventh International Economic History Congress (Milan, 1994).

Men at Work: Labourers and Building Craftsmen in the Towns of Northern England, 1450–1750 (Cambridge, 1995).

Woodward, Donald (ed.), *The Farming and Account Books of Henry Best of Elmswell, 1642* (Oxford, 1984).

Wordie, J. R., 'The Chronology of English Enclosure, 1500–1914', *Economic History Review*, 2nd ser., 36 (1983), pp. 483–505.

'The South: Oxfordshire, Buckinghamshire, Berkshire, Wiltshire, and Hampshire', in *AHEW*, V.I, pp. 317–57.

Worlidge, John, *Systema Horticultra; or The Art of Gardening* (London, 1700).

Wright, Sue, '"Chumaids, Huswyfes and Hucksters": The Employment of Women in Tudor and Stuart Salisbury', in Lindsey Charles and Lorna Duffin (eds.), *Women and Work in Pre-Industrial England* (Beckenham, 1985), pp. 103–21.

Wrightson, Keith, 'Alehouses, Order, and Reformation in Rural England, 1590–1660', in E. Yeo and S. Yeo (eds.), *Popular Culture and Class Conflict 1590–1914* (Brighton, 1981), pp. 167–87.

Earthly Necessities: Economic Lives in Early Modern Britain (New Haven, 2000).

'Mutualities and Obligations: Changing Social Relationships in Early Modern England', *Proceedings of the British Academy*, 139 (2006), pp. 157–94.

'"Sorts of People" in Tudor and Stuart England', in Jonathan Barry and Christopher Brooks (eds.), *The Middling Sort of People: Culture, Society and Politics in England, 1550–1800* (London, 1994), pp. 28–51.

Wrightson, Keith and Levine, David, *Poverty and Piety in an English Village, Terling 1525–1700* (New York, 1979).

Wrigley, E.A., *Continuity, Chance and Change: The Character of the Industrial Revolution in England* (Cambridge, 1988).

'Energy Availability and Agricultural Productivity', in B. M. S. Campbell and Mark Overton (eds.), *Land, Labour and Livestock: Historical Studies in European Agricultural Productivity* (Manchester, 1991), pp. 323–39.

'English County Populations in the Later Eighteenth Century', *Economic History Review*, 60 (2007), pp. 35–69.

'The Quest for the Industrial Revolution', in E. A. Wrigley, *Poverty, Progress and Population* (Cambridge, 2004), pp. 17–43.

'Some Reflections on Corn Yields and Prices in Pre-Industrial Economies', in John Walter and Roger Schofield (eds.), *Famine, Disease and the Social Order in Early Modern Society* (Cambridge, 1989), pp. 235–78.

'The Transition to an Advanced Organic Economy: Half a Millennium of English Agriculture', *Economic History Review*, 59 (2006), pp. 435–80.

'Urban Growth and Agricultural Change: England and the Continent in the Early Modern Period', in E. A. Wrigley, *People, Cities and Wealth* (Oxford, 1987), pp. 157–93.

Wrigley, E. A., Davies, R. S., Oeppen, J. E. and Schofield, R. S., *English Population History from Family Reconstitution 1580–1837* (Cambridge, 1997).

Wrigley, E. A. and Schofield, R. S., *The Population History of England* (Cambridge, 1989).

Young, Arthur, *The Farmer's Guide in Hiring and Stocking Farms*, 2 vols. (London, 1770).

The Farmer's Tour through the East of England, 4 vols. (London, 1771).

A Six Month Tour through the North of England (London, 1771).

A Six Weeks Tour, through the Southern Counties of England and Wales (London, 1768).

Index